The
Sacred Books of the East

translated
by various Oriental scholars
and edited by

F. Max Müller

Vol. I

The Upaniṣads

Translated by F. Max Müller

in two parts

Part I

Chāndogya Upaniṣad

Talavakāra (Kena) Upaniṣad

Aitareya Upaniṣad

Kauṣītaki Upaniṣad

Vājasaneyi (Īśā) Upaniṣad

Dover Publications, Inc.
New York   New York

Published in Canada by General Publishing Company, Ltd., 30 Lesmill Road, Don Mills, Toronto, Ontario.

Published in the United Kingdom by Constable and Company, Ltd.

This new Dover edition, first published in 1962, is an unabridged and unaltered republication of the work first published by the Clarendon Press, Oxford. *The Upanishads,* Part I, first published in 1879, is Volume I of "The Sacred Books of the East" and Part II, first published in 1884, is Volume XV of the same series.

For bibliographic ease and accuracy the modern transliteration of Sanskrit has been adopted for the title page and cover of this book as have the more usual names of several of the upaniṣads. Within the text, however, the older transliteration has been retained.

Standard Book Number: 486-20992-X

Library of Congress Catalog Card Number:62-53180

Manufactured in the United States of America
Dover Publications, Inc.
180 Varick Street
New York, N. Y. 10014

TO

THE RIGHT HONOURABLE THE MARQUIS OF SALISBURY, K.G.

CHANCELLOR OF THE UNIVERSITY OF OXFORD,

LATELY SECRETARY OF STATE FOR INDIA,

SIR HENRY J. S. MAINE, K.C.S.I.

MEMBER OF THE COUNCIL OF INDIA,

AND

THE VERY REV. H. G. LIDDELL, D.D.

DEAN OF CHRIST CHURCH,

TO WHOSE KIND INTEREST AND EXERTIONS

THIS ATTEMPT TO MAKE KNOWN TO THE ENGLISH PEOPLE

THE SACRED BOOKS OF THE EAST

IS SO LARGELY INDEBTED,

I NOW DEDICATE THESE VOLUMES

WITH SINCERE RESPECT AND GRATITUDE,

F. MAX MÜLLER.

'*The general inclinations which are naturally implanted in my soul to some religion, it is impossible for me to shift off: but there being such a multiplicity of religions in the world, I desire now seriously to consider with my self which of them all to restrain these my general inclinations to. And the reason of this my enquiry is not, that I am in the least dissatisfied with that religion I have already embraced; but because 'tis natural for all men to have an overbearing opinion and esteem for that particular religion they are born and bred-up in. That, therefore, I may not seem biassed by the prejudice of education, I am resolved to prove and examine them all; that I may see and hold fast to that which is best. . . . . .*

'*Indeed there was never any religion so barbarous and diabolical, but it was preferred before all other religions whatsoever, by them that did profess it; otherwise they would not have professed it. . . . .*

'*And why, say they, may not you be mistaken as well as we? Especially when there is, at least, six to one against your Christian religion; all of which think they serve God aright; and expect happiness thereby as well as you. . . . . And hence it is that in my looking out for the truest religion, being conscious to my self how great an ascendant Christianity holds over me beyond the rest, as being that religion whereinto I was born and baptized, that which the supreme authority has enjoined and my parents educated me in; that which every one I meet withal highly approves of, and which I my self have, by a long continued profession, made almost natural to me: I am resolved to be more jealous and suspicious of this religion, than of the rest, and be sure not to entertain it any longer without being convinced by solid and substantial arguments, of the truth and certainty of it. That, therefore, I may make diligent and impartial enquiry into all religions and so be sure to find out the best, I shall for a time, look upon my self as one not at all interested in any particular religion whatsoever, much less in the Christian religion; but only as one who desires, in general, to serve and obey Him that made me, in a right manner, and thereby to be made partaker of that happiness my nature is capable of.*'

BISHOP BEVERIDGE (1636–1707).

Private Thoughts on Religion, Part I, Article 2.

CONTENTS.

PREFACE

TO

THE SACRED BOOKS OF THE EAST.

I MUST begin this series of translations of the Sacred Books of the East with three cautions:—the first, referring to the character of the original texts here translated; the second, with regard to the difficulties in making a proper use of translations; the third, showing what is possible and what is impossible in rendering ancient thought into modern speech.

Readers who have been led to believe that the Vedas of the ancient Brahmans, the Avesta of the Zoroastrians, the Tripi*t*aka of the Buddhists, the Kings of Confucius, or the Koran of Mohammed are books full of primeval wisdom and religious enthusiasm, or at least of sound and simple moral teaching, will be disappointed on consulting these volumes. Looking at many of the books that have lately been published on the religions of the ancient world, I do not wonder that such a belief should have been raised; but I have long felt that it was high time to dispel such illusions, and to place the study of the ancient religions of the world on a more real and sound, on a more truly historical basis. It is but natural that those who write on ancient religions, and who have studied them from translations only, not from original documents, should have had eyes for their bright rather than for their dark sides. The former absorb all the attention of the student, the latter, as they teach nothing, seem hardly to deserve any notice. Scholars also who have devoted their life either to the editing of the original texts or to the careful interpretation of some of the sacred books, are more inclined, after they have disinterred from a heap of rubbish some solitary fragments of pure gold, to exhibit these treasures only than to display all the refuse from which they had to extract them. I do not blame them for this, perhaps I should feel that I was open to the same blame myself, for it is but natural that scholars in their joy at finding one or two fragrant fruits or flowers should gladly forget the brambles and thorns that had to be thrown aside in the course of their search.

But whether I am myself one of the guilty or not, I cannot help calling attention to the real mischief that has been done and is still being done by the enthusiasm of those pioneers who have opened the first avenues through the bewildering forest of the sacred literature of the East. They have raised expectations that cannot be fulfilled, fears also that, as will be easily seen, are unfounded. Anyhow they have removed the study of religion from that wholesome and matter-of-fact atmosphere in which alone it can produce valuable and permanent results.

The time has come when the study of the ancient religions of mankind must be approached in a different, in a less enthusiastic, and more discriminating, in fact, in a more scholarlike spirit. Not

that I object to dilettanti, if they only are what by
their name they profess to be, devoted lovers, and not
mere amateurs. The religions of antiquity must
always be approached in a loving spirit, and the dry
and cold-blooded scholar is likely to do here as
much mischief as the enthusiastic sciolist. But true
love does not ignore all faults and failings : on the
contrary, it scans them keenly, though only in order
to be able to understand, to explain, and thus to
excuse them. To watch in the Sacred Books of
the East the dawn of the religious consciousness
of man, must always remain one of the most
inspiring and hallowing sights in the whole history
of the world; and he whose heart cannot quiver
with the first quivering rays of human thought
and human faith, as revealed in those ancient documents, is, in his own way, as unfit for these studies
as, from another side, the man who shrinks from
copying and collating ancient MSS., or toiling
through volumes of tedious commentary. What we
want here, as everywhere else, is the truth, and the
whole truth ; and if the whole truth must be told,
it is that, however radiant the dawn of religious
thought, it is not without its dark clouds, its chilling
colds, its noxious vapours. Whoever does not
know these, or would hide them from his own sight
and from the sight of others, does not know and
can never understand the real toil and travail of the
human heart in its first religious aspirations; and
not knowing its toil and travail, can never know the
intensity of its triumphs and its joys.

In order to have a solid foundation for a com-
parative study of the religions of the East, we must
have before all things complete and thoroughly

faithful translations of their sacred books.   Extracts
will no longer suffice.   We do not know Germany,
if we know the Rhine; nor Rome, when we have
admired St. Peter's.   No one who collects and publishes such extracts can resist, no one at all events,
so far as I know, has ever resisted, the temptation
of giving what is beautiful, or it may be what is
strange and startling, and leaving out what is com-
monplace, tedious, or it may be repulsive, or, lastly,
what is difficult to construe and to understand.   We
must face the problem in its completeness, and I
confess it has been for many years a problem to
me, aye, and to a great extent is so still, how the
Sacred Books of the East should, by the side of so
much that is fresh, natural, simple, beautiful, and
true, contain so much that is not only unmeaning,
artificial, and silly, but even hideous and repellent.
This is a fact, and must be accounted for in some
way or other.

   To some minds this problem may seem to be no
problem at all.   To those (and I do not speak of
Christians only) who look upon the sacred books of
all religions except their own as necessarily the out-
come of human or superhuman ignorance and de-
pravity, the mixed nature of their contents may
seem to be exactly what it ought to be, what they
expected it would be.   But there are other and
more reverent minds who can feel a divine afflatus
in the sacred books, not only of their own, but of
other religions also, and to them the mixed character
of some of the ancient sacred canons must always
be extremely perplexing.

   I can account for it to a certain extent, though
not entirely to my own satisfaction.   Most of the

ancient sacred books have been handed down by oral tradition for many generations before they were consigned to writing. In an age when there was nothing corresponding to what we call literature, every saying, every proverb, every story handed down from father to son, received very soon a kind of hallowed character. They became sacred heirlooms, sacred, because they came from an unknown source, from a distant age. There was a stage in the development of human thought, when the distance that separated the living generation from their grandfathers or great-grandfathers was as yet the nearest approach to a conception of eternity, and when the name of grandfather and great-grandfather seemed the nearest expression of God[1]. Hence, what had been said by these half-human, half-divine ancestors, if it was preserved at all, was soon looked upon as a more than human utterance. It was received with reverence, it was never questioned and criticised.

Some of these ancient sayings were preserved because they were so true and so striking that they could not be forgotten. They contained eternal truths, expressed for the first time in human language. Of such oracles of truth it was said in India that they had been heard, *sruta*, and from it arose the word *sruti*, the recognised term for divine revelation in Sanskrit.

But besides those utterances which had a vitality of their own, strong enough to defy the power of

---

[1] Bishop Callaway, Unkulunkulu, or the Tradition of Creation, as existing among the Amazulu and other tribes of South Africa, p. 7.

time, there were others which might have struck
the minds of the listeners with great force under
the peculiar circumstances that evoked them, but
which, when these circumstances were forgotten, became trivial and almost unintelligible. A few verses
sung by warriors on the eve of a great battle would,
if that battle ended in victory, assume a charm
quite independent of their poetic merit. They
would be repeated in memory of the heroes
who conquered, and of the gods who granted
victory. But when the heroes, and the gods, and
the victory were all forgotten, the song of victory
and thanksgiving would often survive as a relic
of the past, though almost unintelligible to later
generations.

Even a single ceremonial act, performed at the
time of a famine or an inundation, and apparently
attended with a sudden and almost miraculous
success, might often be preserved in the liturgical
code of a family or a tribe with a superstitious awe
entirely beyond our understanding. It might be
repeated for some time on similar emergencies, till
when it had failed again and again it survived only
as a superstitious custom in the memory of priests
and poets.

Further, it should be remembered that in ancient
as in modern times, the utterances of men who had
once gained a certain prestige, would often receive
attention far beyond their merits, so that in many
a family or tribe the sayings and teachings of one
man, who had once in his youth or manhood uttered
words of inspired wisdom, would all be handed
down together, without any attempt to separate
the grain from the chaff.

Nor must we forget that though oral tradition, when once brought under proper discipline, is a most faithful guardian, it is not without its dangers in its incipient stages. Many a word may have been misunderstood, many a sentence confused, as it was told by father to son, before it became fixed in the tradition of a village community, and then resisted by its very sacredness all attempts at emendation.

Lastly, we must remember that those who handed down the ancestral treasures of ancient wisdom, would often feel inclined to add what seemed useful to themselves, and what they knew could be preserved in one way only, namely, if it was allowed to form part of the tradition that had to be handed down, as a sacred trust, from generation to generation. The priestly influence was at work, even before there were priests by profession, and when the priesthood had once become professional, its influence may account for much that would otherwise seem inexplicable in the sacred codes of the ancient world.

These are some of the considerations which may help to explain how, mixed up with real treasures of thought, we meet in the sacred books with so many passages and whole chapters which either never had any life or meaning at all, or if they had, have, in the form in which they have come down to us, completely lost it. We must try to imagine what the Old Testament would have been, if it had not been kept distinct from the Talmud; or the New Testament, if it had been mixed up not only with the spurious gospels, but with the records of the wranglings of the early Councils, if we wish to understand, to some extent at least, the wild confusion of sublime truth with vulgar stupidity that meets us in the pages of the Veda, the Avesta, and the Tripi*t*aka. The idea of keeping the original and genuine tradition separate from apocryphal accretions was an idea of later growth, that could spring up only after the earlier tendency of preserving whatever could be preserved of sacred or half-sacred lore, had done its work, and wrought its own destruction.

In using, what may seem to some of my fellow-workers, this very strong and almost irreverent language with regard to the ancient Sacred Books of the East, I have not neglected to make full allowance for that very important intellectual parallax which, no doubt, renders it most difficult for a Western observer to see things and thoughts under exactly the same angle and in the same light as they would appear to an Eastern eye. There are Western expressions which offend Eastern taste as much as Eastern expressions are apt to offend Western taste. A symphony of Beethoven's would be mere noise to an Indian ear, an Indian Sangîta seems to us without melody, harmony, or rhythm. All this I fully admit, yet after making every allowance for national taste and traditions, I still confidently appeal to the best Oriental scholars, who have not entirely forgotten that there is a world outside the four walls of their study, whether they think that my condemnation is too severe, or that Eastern nations themselves would tolerate, in any of their classical literary compositions, such violations of the simplest rules of taste as they have accustomed themselves to tolerate, if not to admire, in their sacred books.

But then it might no doubt be objected that books of such a character hardly deserve the honour of being translated into English, and that the sooner they are forgotten, the better. Such opinions have of late been freely expressed by some eminent writers, and supported by arguments worthy of the Khalif Omar himself. In these days of anthropological research, when no custom is too disgusting to be recorded, no rules of intermarriage too complicated to be disentangled, it may seem strange that the few genuine relics of ancient religion which, as by a miracle, have been preserved to us, should thus have been judged from a purely æsthetic, and not from an historical point of view. There was some excuse for this in the days of Sir William Jones and Colebrooke. The latter, as is well known, considered ' the Vedas as too voluminous for a complete translation of the whole,' adding that 'what they contain would hardly reward the labour of the reader ; much less that of the translator[1].' The former went still further in the condemnation which he pronounced on Anquetil Duperron's translation of the Zend-avesta. Sir W. Jones, we must remember, was not only a scholar, but also a man of taste, and the man of taste sometimes gained a victory over the scholar. His controversy with Anquetil Duperron, the discoverer of the Zend-avesta, is well known. It was carried on by Sir W. Jones apparently with great success, and yet in the end the victor has proved to be the vanquished. It was easy, no doubt, to pick out from Anquetil Duperron's translation of the sacred writings of Zoroaster hundreds of passages which were or seemed to be utterly unmeaning or absurd. This arose partly, but partly only, from the imperfections

---

[1] Colebrooke's Miscellaneous Essays, 1873, vol. ii, p. 102.

of the translation.   Much, however, of what Sir W.
Jones represented as ridiculous, and therefore unworthy of Zoroaster, and therefore unworthy of being
translated, forms an integral part of the sacred code
of the Zoroastrians.   Sir W. Jones smiles at those who
'think obscurity sublime and venerable, like that of
ancient cloisters and temples, shedding,' as Milton
expresses it, 'a dim religious light[1].'   'On possé-
dait déjà,' he writes in his letter addressed to
Anquetil Duperron, and composed in very good
and sparkling French, 'plusieurs traités attribués à
Zardusht ou Zeratusht, traduits en Persan moderne ;
de prétendues conférences de ce législateur avec
Ormuzd, des prières, des dogmes, des lois religieuses.
Quelques savans, qui ont lu ces traductions, nous ont
assuré que les originaux étaient de la plus haute
antiquité, parce qu'ils renfermaient beaucoup de plati-
tudes, de bévues, et de contradictions : mais nous
avons conclu par les mêmes raisons, qu'ils étaient
très-modernes, ou bien qu'ils n'étaient pas d'un
homme d'esprit, et d'un philosophe, tel que Zoroastre
est peint par nos historiens.   Votre nouvelle traduction, Monsieur, nous confirme dans ce juge-
ment : tout le collège des Guèbres aurait beau
nous l'assurer ; nous ne croirons jamais que le
charlatan le moins habile ait pu écrire les fadaises
dont vos deux derniers volumes sont remplis[2].'
He at last sums up his argument in the following
words : 'Ou Zoroastre n'avait pas le sens commun,
ou il n'écrivit pas le livre que vous lui attribuez :
s'il n'avait pas le sens commun, il fallait le laisser
dans la foule, et dans l'obscurité ; s'il n'écrivit pas

---

[1] Sir W. Jones's Works, vol. iv, p. 113.   [2] Ib., vol. x, p. 408.

ce livre, il était impudent de le publier sous son nom. Ainsi, ou vous avez insulté le goût du public en lui présentant des sottises, ou vous l'avez trompé en lui donnant des faussetés : et de chaque côté vous méritez son mépris [1].'

This alternative holds good no longer. The sacred code of Zoroaster or of any other of the founders of religions may appear to us to be full of absurdities, or may in fact really be so, and it may yet be the duty of the scholar to publish, to translate, and carefully to examine those codes as memorials of the past, as the only trustworthy documents in which to study the growth and decay of religion. It does not answer to say that if Zoroaster was what we believe him to have been, a wise man, in our sense of the word, he could not have written the rubbish which we find in the Avesta. If we are once satisfied that the text of the Avesta, or the Veda, or the Tripiṭaka is old and genuine, and that this text formed the foundation on which, during many centuries, the religious belief of millions of human beings was based, it becomes our duty, both as historians and philosophers, to study these books, to try to understand how they could have arisen, and how they could have exercised for ages an influence over human beings who in all other respects were not inferior to ourselves, nay, whom we are accustomed to look up to on many points as patterns of wisdom, of virtue, and of taste.

The facts, such as they are, must be faced, if the study of the ancient religions of the world is ever to assume a really historical character ; and having

---

[1] Works, vol. x, p. 437.

myself grudged no praise to what to my mind is really
beautiful or sublime in the early revelations of religious truth, I feel the less hesitation in fulfilling the
duty of the true scholar, and placing before historians
and philosophers accurate, complete, and unembel-
lished versions of some of the sacred books of the
East.   Such versions alone will enable them to form
a true and just estimate of the real development of
early religious thought, so far as we can still gain a
sight of it in literary records to which the highest
human or even divine authority has been ascribed
by the followers of the great religions of antiquity.
It often requires an effort to spoil a beautiful sentence by a few words which might so easily be
suppressed, but which are there in the original,
and must be taken into account quite as much
as the pointed ears in the beautiful Faun of the
Capitol.   We want to know the ancient religions
such as they really were, not such as we wish they
should have been.   We want to know, not their
wisdom only, but their folly also; and while we must
learn to look up to their highest points where they
seem to rise nearer to heaven than anything we were
acquainted with before, we must not shrink from
looking down into their stony tracts, their dark
abysses, their muddy moraines, in order to comprehend both the heighth and the depth of the human
mind in its searchings after the Infinite.

I can answer for myself and for those who have
worked with me, that our translations are truthful,
that we have suppressed nothing, that we have
varnished nothing, however hard it seemed sometimes even to write it down.

There is only one exception.   There are in ancient

books, and particularly in religious books, frequent
allusions to the sexual aspects of nature, which,
though perfectly harmless and innocent in themselves, cannot be rendered in modern language without the appearance of coarseness.   We may regret
that it should be so, but tradition is too strong on
this point, and I have therefore felt obliged to leave
certain passages untranslated, and to give the original, when necessary, in a note.   But this has been
done in extreme cases only, and many things which
we should feel inclined to suppress have been left in
all their outspoken simplicity, because those who
want to study ancient man, must learn to study him
as he really was, an animal, with all the strength
and weaknesses of an animal, though an animal that
was to rise above himself, and in the end discover his
true self, after many struggles and many defeats.

After this first caution, which I thought was due
to those who might expect to find in these volumes
nothing but gems, I feel I owe another to those
who may approach these translations under the
impression that they have only to read them in
order to gain an insight into the nature and character
of the religions of mankind.   There are philosophers
who have accustomed themselves to look upon religions as things that can be studied as they study the
manners and customs of savage tribes, by glancing
at the entertaining accounts of travellers or missionaries, and then classing each religion under such
wide categories as fetishism, polytheism, monotheism,
and the rest.   That is not the case.   Translations
can do much, but they can never take the place of the
originals, and if the originals require not only to be

read, but to be read again and again, translations of
sacred books require to be studied with much greater
care, before we can hope to gain a real understanding of the intentions of their authors or venture
on general assertions.

Such general assertions, if once made, are difficult
to extirpate. It has been stated, for instance, that
the religious notion of sin is wanting altogether in
the hymns of the Rig-veda, and some important conclusions have been based on this supposed fact. Yet
the gradual growth of the concept of guilt is one of
the most interesting lessons which certain passages
of these ancient hymns can teach us [1]. It has been
asserted that in the Rig-veda Agni, fire, was adored
essentially as earthly sacrificial fire, and not as an
elemental force. How greatly such an assertion has
to be qualified, may be seen from a more careful
examination of the translations of the Vedic hymns
now accessible [2]. In many parts of the Avesta
fire is no doubt spoken of with great reverence, but those who speak of the Zoroastrians
as fire-worshippers, should know that the true followers of Zoroaster abhor that very name. Again,
there are certainly many passages in the Vedic
writings which prohibit the promiscuous communication of the Veda, but those who maintain that
the Brahmans, like Roman Catholic priests, keep
their sacred books from the people, must have for-

---

[1] M. M., History of Ancient Sanskrit Literature, second edition,
1859, p. 540 seq.

[2] Ludwig, Rig-veda, übersetzt, vol. iii, p. 331 seq. Muir, Sanskrit
Texts, vol. v, p. 199 seq. On the later growth of Agni, see a
very useful essay by Holtzmann, 'Agni, nach den Vorstellungen des
Mahâbhârata,' 1878.

gotten the many passages in the Brâhma*n*as, the
Sûtras, and even in the Laws of Manu, where the
duty of learning the Veda by heart is inculcated for
every Brâhma*n*a, Kshatriya, Vai*s*ya, that is, for every
man except a *S*ûdra.

These are a few specimens only to show how
dangerous it is to generalise even where there exist
complete translations of certain sacred books. It is
far easier to misapprehend, or even totally to misunderstand, a translation than the original; and it
should not be supposed, because a sentence or a
whole chapter seems at first sight unintelligible in
a translation, that therefore they are indeed devoid
of all meaning.

What can be more perplexing than the beginning
of the *Kh*ândogya-upanishad? 'Let a man meditate,' we read, or, as others translate it, 'Let a man
worship the syllable Om.' It may seem impossible
at first sight to elicit any definite meaning from
these words and from much that follows after.
But it would be a mistake, nevertheless, to con-
clude that we have here vox et præterea nihil.
Meditation on the syllable Om consisted in a long-
continued repetition of that syllable with a view
of drawing the thoughts away from all other subjects, and thus concentrating them on some higher
object of thought of which that syllable was made to
be the symbol. This concentration of thought, ekâgratâ or one-pointedness, as the Hindus called it, is
something to us almost unknown. Our minds are
like kaleidoscopes of thoughts in constant motion;
and to shut our mental eyes to everything else, while
dwelling on one thought only, has become to most
of us almost as impossible as to apprehend one

musical note without harmonics. With the life we
are leading now, with telegrams, letters, newspapers,
reviews, pamphlets, and books ever breaking in upon
us, it has become impossible, or almost impossible,
ever to arrive at that intensity of thought which the
Hindus meant by ekâgratâ, and the attainment of
which was to them the indispensable condition of all
philosophical and religious speculation. The loss may
not be altogether on our side, yet a loss it is, and if we
see the Hindus, even in their comparatively mono-
tonous life, adopting all kinds of contrivances in
order to assist them in drawing away their thoughts
from all disturbing impressions and to fix them on
one subject only, we must not be satisfied with
smiling at their simplicity, but try to appreciate the
object they had in view.

When by means of repeating the syllable Om,
which originally seems to have meant 'that,' or 'yes,'
they had arrived at a certain degree of mental tran-
quillity, the question arose what was meant by this
Om, and to this question the most various answers
were given, according as the mind was to be led
up to higher and higher objects. Thus in one
passage we are told at first that Om is the beginning
of the Veda, or, as we have to deal with an Upanishad
of the Sâma-veda, the beginning of the Sâma-veda,
so that he who meditates on Om, may be supposed
to be meditating on the whole of the Sâma-veda.
But that is not enough. Om is said to be the essence
of the Sâma-veda, which, being almost entirely taken
from the Rig-veda, may itself be called the essence
of the Rig-veda. And more than that. The Rig-veda
stands for all speech, the Sâma-veda for all breath
or life, so that Om may be conceived again as the

symbol of all speech and all life. Om thus becomes
the name, not only of all our physical and mental
powers, but especially of the living principle, the
Prâ*n*a or spirit. This is explained by the parable
in the second chapter, while in the third chapter,
that spirit within us is identified with the spirit in
the sun. He therefore who meditates on Om, meditates on the spirit in man as identical with the spirit
in nature, or in the sun; and thus the lesson that
is meant to be taught in the beginning of the
*Kh*ândogya-upanishad is really this, that none of the
Vedas with their sacrifices and ceremonies could
ever secure the salvation of the worshipper, i. e.
that sacred works, performed according to the rules
of the Vedas, are of no avail in the end, but that
meditation on Om alone, or that knowledge of
what is meant by Om alone, can procure true salvation, or true immortality. Thus the pupil is led on
step by step to what is the highest object of the
Upanishads, viz. the recognition of the self in man
as identical with the Highest Self or Brahman.
The lessons which are to lead up to that highest
conception of the universe, both subjective and
objective, are no doubt mixed up with much that
is superstitious and absurd; still the main object is
never lost sight of. Thus, when we come to the
eighth chapter, the discussion, though it begins with
Om or the Udgîtha, ends with the question of the
origin of the world; and though the final answer,
namely, that Om means ether (âkâ*s*a), and that
ether is the origin of all things, may still sound to
us more physical than metaphysical, still the description given of ether or âkâ*s*a, shows that more is
meant by it than the physical ether, and that ether

is in fact one of the earlier and less perfect names
of the Infinite, of Brahman, the universal Self.
This, at least, is the lesson which the Brahmans
themselves read in this chapter[1]; and if we look
at the ancient language of the Upanishads as representing mere attempts at finding expression for
what their language could hardly express as yet,
we shall, I think, be less inclined to disagree with
the interpretation put on those ancient oracles by
the later Vedânta philosophers[2], or, at all events,
we shall hesitate before we reject what is difficult to
interpret, as altogether devoid of meaning.

This is but one instance to show that even behind
the fantastic and whimsical phraseology of the sacred
writings of the Hindus and other Eastern nations,
there may be sometimes aspirations after truth
which deserve careful consideration from the student
of the psychological development and the historical
growth of early religious thought, and that after
careful sifting, treasures may be found in what at
first we may feel inclined to throw away as utterly
worthless.

And now I come to the third caution. Let it
not be supposed that a text, three thousand
years old, or, even if of more modern date, still
widely distant from our own sphere of thought,
can be translated in the same manner as a book

---

[1] The Upanishad itself says: 'The Brahman is the same as the
ether which is around us; and the ether which is around us, is the
same as the ether which is within ·us. And the ether which is
within, that is the ether within the heart. That ether in the heart
is omnipresent and unchanging. He who knows this obtains
omnipresent and unchangeable happiness.' *Kh.* Up. III, 12, 7–9.

[2] Cf. Vedânta-sûtras I, 1, 22.

written a few years ago in French or German. Those who know French and German well enough, know how difficult, nay, how impossible it is, to render justice to certain touches of genius which the true artist knows how to give to a sentence. Many poets have translated Heine into English or Tennyson into German, many painters have copied the Madonna di San Sisto or the so-called portrait of Beatrice Cenci. But the greater the excellence of these translators, the more frank has been their avowal, that the original is beyond their reach. And what is a translation of modern German into modern English compared with a translation of ancient Sanskrit or Zend or Chinese into any modern language? It is an undertaking which, from its very nature, admits of the most partial success only, and a more intimate knowledge of the ancient language, so far from facilitating the task of the translator, renders it only more hopeless. Modern words are round, ancient words are square, and we may as well hope to solve the quadrature of the circle, as to express adequately the ancient thoughts of the Veda in modern English.

We must not expect therefore that a translation of the sacred books of the ancients can ever be more than an approximation of our language to theirs, of our thoughts to theirs. The translator, however, if he has once gained the conviction that it is impossible to translate old thought into modern speech, without doing some violence either to the one or to the other, will hardly hesitate in his choice between two evils. He will prefer to do some violence to language rather than to misrepresent old thoughts by clothing them in words which do

not fit them. If therefore the reader finds some
of these translations rather rugged, if he meets with
expressions which sound foreign, with combinations
of nouns and adjectives such as he has never seen
before, with sentences that seem too long or too
abrupt, let him feel sure that the translator has had
to deal with a choice of evils, and that when the
choice lay between sacrificing idiom or truth, he has
chosen the smaller evil of the two. I do not claim,
of course, either for myself or for my fellow-workers,
that we have always sacrificed as little as was
possible of truth or idiom, and that here and there
a happier rendering of certain passages may not be
suggested by those who come after us. I only wish
to warn the reader once more not to expect too
much from a translation, and to bear in mind that,
easy as it might be to render word by word, it is
difficult, aye, sometimes impossible, to render thought
by thought.

I shall give one instance only from my own
translation of the Upanishads. One of the most
important words in the ancient philosophy of the
Brahmans is Âtman, nom. sing. Âtmâ. It is
rendered in our dictionaries by 'breath, soul, the
principle of life and sensation, the individual soul,
the self, the abstract individual, self, one's self, the
reflexive pronoun, the natural temperament or dis-
position, essence, nature, character, peculiarity, the
person or the whole body, the body, the understanding, intellect, the mind, the faculty of thought and
reason, the thinking faculty, the highest principle
of life, Brahma, the supreme deity or soul of the
universe, care, effort, pains, firmness, the sun, fire,
wind, air, a son.'

This will give classical scholars an idea of the chaotic state from which, thanks to the excellent work done by Boehtlingk, Roth, and others, Sanskrit lexicology is only just emerging. Some of the meanings here mentioned ought certainly not to be ascribed to âtman. It never means, for instance, the understanding, nor could it ever by itself be translated by sun, fire, wind, air, pains or firmness. But after deducting such surplusage, there still remains a large variety of meanings which may, under certain circumstances, be ascribed to âtman.

When âtman occurs in philosophical treatises, such as the Upanishads and the Vedânta system which is based on them, it has generally been translated by soul, mind, or spirit. I tried myself to use one or other of these words, but the oftener I employed them, the more I felt their inadequacy, and was driven at last to adopt self and Self as the least liable to misunderstanding.

No doubt in many passages it sounds strange in English to use self, and in the plural selfs instead of selves; but that very strangeness is useful, for while such words as soul and mind and spirit pass over us unrealised, self and selfs will always ruffle the surface of the mind, and stir up some reflection in the reader. In English to speak even of the I and the Non-I, was till lately considered harsh; it may still be called a foreign philosophical idiom. In German the Ich and Nicht-ich have, since the time of Fichte, become recognised and almost familiar, not only as philosophical terms, but as legitimate expressions in the literary language of the day. But while the Ich with Fichte expressed the highest abstraction of personal existence, the

corresponding word in Sanskrit, the Aham or
Ahaṅkâra, was always looked upon as a secondary
development only, and as by no means free from all
purely phenomenal ingredients. Beyond the Aham
or Ego, with all its accidents and limitations, such
as sex, sense, language, country, and religion, the
ancient sages of India perceived, from a very early
time, the Âtman or the self, independent of all such
accidents.

The individual âtman or self, however, was with
the Brahmans a phase or phenomenal modification
only of the Highest Self, and that Highest Self
was to them the last point which could be reached
by philosophical speculation. It was to them what
in other systems of philosophy has been called by
various names, τὸ ὄν, the Divine, the Absolute. The
highest aim of all thought and study with the
Brahman of the Upanishads was to recognise his
own self as a mere limited reflection of the Highest
Self, to know his self in the Highest Self, and
through that knowledge to return to it, and regain
his identity with it. Here to know was to be, to
know the Âtman was to be the Âtman, and the
reward of that highest knowledge after death was
freedom from new births, or immortality.

That Highest Self which had become to the
ancient Brahmans the goal of all their mental ef-
forts, was looked upon at the same time as the
starting-point of all phenomenal existence, the root
of the world, the only thing that could truly be said
to be, to be real and true. As the root of all that
exists, the Âtman was identified with the Brahman,
which in Sanskrit is both masculine and neuter, and
with the Sat, which is neuter only, that which is,

or Satya, the true, the real. It alone exists in the
beginning and for ever; it has no second. Whatever else is said to exist, derives its real being from
the Sat. How the one Sat became many, how
what we call the creation, what they call emanation
(πρόοδος), constantly proceeds and returns to it, has
been explained in various more or less fanciful ways
by ancient prophets and poets. But what they
all agree in is this, that the whole creation, the
visible and invisible world, all plants, all animals,
all men are due to the one Sat, are upheld by it,
and will return to it.

If we translate Âtman by soul, mind, or spirit,
we commit, first of all, that fundamental mistake
of using words which may be predicated, in place of
a word which is a subject only, and can never become a predicate. We may say in English that
man possesses a soul, that a man is out of his mind,
that man has or even that man is a spirit, but we
could never predicate âtman, or self, of anything
else. Spirit, if it means breath or life; mind, if it
means the organ of perception and conception;
soul, if, like kaitanya, it means intelligence in
general, all these may be predicated of the Âtman,
as manifested in the phenomenal world. But
they are never subjects in the sense in which the
Âtman is; they have no independent being, apart
from Âtman. Thus to translate the beginning of the
Aitareya-upanishad, Âtmâ vâ idam eka evâgra
âsît, by ' This (world) verily was before (the creation
of the world) soul alone' (Röer); or, ' Originally
this (universe) was indeed soul only' (Colebrooke),
would give us a totally false idea. M. Regnaud
in his ' Matériaux pour servir à l'histoire de la philo-

sophie de l'Inde' (vol. ii, p. 24) has evidently felt
this, and has kept the word âtman untranslated,
'Au commencement cet univers n'était que l'âtman.'
But while in French it would seem impossible to
find any equivalent for âtman, I have ventured to
translate in English, as I should have done in
German, 'Verily, in the beginning all this was
Self, one only.'

Thus again when we read in Sanskrit, 'Know the
Self by the self,' âtmânam âtmanâ pasya, tempt-
ing as it may seem, it would be entirely wrong to
render it by the Greek γνῶθι σεαυτόν. The Brahman
called upon his young pupil to know not himself,
but his Self, that is, to know his individual self as
a merely temporary reflex of the Eternal Self.
Were we to translate this so-called âtmavidyâ,
this self-knowledge, by knowledge of the soul, we
should not be altogether wrong, but we should nevertheless lose all that distinguishes Indian from Greek
thought. It may not be good English to say to know
his self, still less to know our selfs, but it would be
bad Sanskrit to say to know himself, to know ourselves; or, at all events, such a rendering would
deprive us of the greatest advantage in the study
of Indian philosophy, the opportunity of seeing in
how many different ways man has tried to solve the
riddles of the world and of his soul.

I have thought it best therefore to keep as close
as possible to the Sanskrit original, and where I
could not find an adequate term in English, I have
often retained the Sanskrit word rather than use a
misleading substitute in English. It is impossible, for
instance, to find an English equivalent for so simple
a word as Sat, τὸ ὄν. We cannot render the Greek τὸ

ὄν and τὸ μὴ ὄν by Being or Not-being, for both are abstract nouns; nor by 'the Being,' for this would almost always convey a wrong impression. In German it is easy to distinguish between das Sein, i. e. being, in the abstract, and das Seiende, τὸ ὄν. In the same way the Sanskrit sat can easily be rendered in Greek by τὸ ὄν, in German by das Sciende, but in English, unless we say 'that which is,' we are driven to retain the original Sat.

From this Sat was derived in Sanskrit Sat-ya, meaning originally 'endowed with being,' then 'true.' This is an adjective; but the same word, as a neuter, is also used in the sense of truth, as an abstract; and in translating it is very necessary always to distinguish between Satyam, the true, frequently the same as Sat, τὸ ὄν, and Satyam, truth, veracity. One example will suffice to show how much the clearness of a translation depends on the right rendering of such words as âtman, sat, and satyam.

In a dialogue between Uddâlaka and his son Svetaketu, in which the father tries to open his son's mind, and to make him see man's true relation to the Highest Self (Khândogya-upanishad VI), the father first explains how the Sat produced what we should call the three elements[1], viz. fire, water, and earth, which he calls heat, water, and food. Having produced them (VI, 2, 4), the Sat entered into them, but not with its real nature, but only with its 'living self' (VI, 3, 3), which is a reflection (âbhâsamâtram) of the real Sat, as the sun in the water is a reflection

---

[1] Devatâs, literally deities, but frequently to be translated by powers or beings. Mahadeva Moreshvar Kunte, the learned editor of the Vedânta-sûtras, ought not (p. 70) to have rendered devâta, in Kh. Up. I, 11, 5, by goddess.

of the real sun.   By this apparent union of the Sat
with the three elements, every form (rûpa) and
every name (nâman) in the world was produced;
and therefore he who knows the three elements is
supposed to know everything in this world, nearly
in the same manner in which the Greeks imagined
that through a knowledge of the elements, everything else became known (VI, 4, 7).   The same
three elements are shown to be also the constituent
elements of man (VI, 5).   Food or the earthy element is supposed to produce not only flesh, but
also mind; water, not only blood, but also breath;
heat, not only bone, but also speech.   This is more
or less fanciful; the important point, however, is
this, that, from the Brahmanic point of view, breath,
speech, and mind are purely elemental, or external
instruments, and require the support of the living
self, the *g*îvâtman, before they can act.

Having explained how the Sat produces pro-
gressively heat, how heat leads to water, water to
earth, and how, by a peculiar mixture of the three,
speech, breath, and mind are produced, the teacher
afterwards shows how in death, speech returns to
mind, mind to breath, breath to heat, and heat to
the Sat (VI, 8, 6).   This Sat, the root of everything, is called parâ devatâ, the highest deity, not
in the ordinary sense of the word deity, but as
expressing the highest abstraction of the human
mind.   We must therefore translate it by the
Highest Being, in the same manner as we translate
devatâ, when applied to heat, water, and earth, not
by deity, but by substance or element.

The same Sat, as the root or highest essence
of all material existence, is called a*n*iman, from

a*n*u, small, subtile, infinitesimal, atom. It is an abstract word, and I have translated it by subtile essence.

The father then goes on explaining in various ways that this Sat is underlying all existence, and that we must learn to recognise it as the root, not only of all the objective, but likewise of our own subjective existence. 'Bring the fruit of a Nyagrodha tree,' he says, 'break it, and what do you find?' 'The seeds,' the son replies, 'almost infinitesimal.' 'Break one of them, and tell me what you see.' 'Nothing,' the son replies. Then the father continues: 'My son, that subtile essence which you do not see there, of that very essence this great Nyagrodha tree exists.'

After that follows this sentence: 'Etadâtmyam ida*m* sarvam, tat satyam, sa âtmâ, tat tvam asi *S*vetaketo.'

This sentence has been rendered by Rajendralal Mitra in the following way: 'All this universe has the (Supreme) Deity for its life. That Deity is Truth. He is the Universal Soul. Thou art He, O *S*vetaketu [1].'

This translation is quite correct, as far as the words go, but I doubt whether we can connect any definite thoughts with these words. In spite of the division adopted in the text, I believe it will be necessary to join this sentence with the last words of the preceding paragraph. This is clear from the commentary, and from later paragraphs, where this sentence is repeated, VI, 9, 4, &c. The division

---

[1] Anquetil Duperron translates: 'Ipso hoc modo (ens) illud est subtile: et hoc omne, unus âtma est: et id verum et rectum est, O Sopatkit, tatoumes, id est, ille âtma tu as.'

in the printed text (VI, 8, 6) is wrong, and VI, 8, 7 should begin with sa ya esho '*n*imâ, i. e. that which is the subtile essence.

The question then is, what is further to be said about this subtile essence. I have ventured to translate the passage in the following way:

'That which is the subtile essence (the Sat, the root of everything), in it all that exists has its self, or more literally, its self-hood. It is the True (not the Truth in the abstract, but that which truly and really exists). It is the Self, i. e. the Sat is what is called the Self of everything[1].' Lastly, he sums up, and tells *S*vetaketu that, not only the whole world, but he too himself is that Self, that Satya, that Sat.

No doubt this translation sounds strange to English ears, but as the thoughts contained in the Upanishads are strange, it would be wrong to smoothe down their strangeness by clothing them in language familiar to us, which, because it is familiar, will fail to startle us, and because it fails to startle us, will fail also to set us thinking.

To know oneself to be the Sat, to know that all that is real and eternal in us is the Sat, that all came from it and will, through knowledge, return to it, requires an independent effort of speculative thought. We must realise, as well as we can, the thoughts of the ancient *R*ishis, before we can hope to translate them. It is not enough simply to read the half-religious, half-philosophical utterances which we find in

---

[1] The change of gender in sa for ta d is idiomatic. One could not say in Sanskrit tad âtmâ, it is the Self, but sa âtmâ. By sa, he, the Sat, that which is, is meant. The commentary explains sa âtmâ by tat sat, and continues tat sat tat tvam asi (p. 443).

the Sacred Books of the East, and to say that they are strange, or obscure, or mystic. Plato is strange, till we know him; Berkeley is mystic, till for a time we have identified ourselves with him. So it is with these ancient sages, who have become the founders of the great religions of antiquity. They can never be judged from without, they must be judged from within. We need not become Brahmans or Buddhists or Taosze altogether, but we must for a time, if we wish to understand, and still more, if we are bold enough to undertake to translate their doctrines. Whoever shrinks from that effort, will see hardly anything in these sacred books or their translations but matter to wonder at or to laugh at; possibly something to make him thankful that he is not as other men. But to the patient reader these same books will, in spite of many drawbacks, open a new view of the history of the human race, of that one race to which we all belong, with all the fibres of our flesh, with all the fears and hopes of our soul. We cannot separate ourselves from those who believed in these sacred books. There is no specific difference between ourselves and the Brahmans, the Buddhists, the Zoroastrians, or the Taosze. Our powers of perceiving, of reasoning, and of believing may be more highly developed, but we cannot claim the possession of any verifying power or of any power of belief which they did not possess as well. Shall we say then that they were forsaken of God, while we are His chosen people? God forbid! There is much, no doubt, in their sacred books which we should tolerate no longer, though we must not forget that there are portions in our own sacred books, too, which many of us would wish to be absent,

which, from the earliest ages of Christianity, have
been regretted by theologians of undoubted piety,
and which often prove a stumblingblock to those
who have been won over by our missionaries to the
simple faith of Christ.   But that is not the question.
The question is, whether there is or whether there is
not, hidden in every one of the sacred books, something that could lift up the human heart from this
earth to a higher world, something that could make
man feel the omnipresence of a higher Power, something that could make him shrink from evil and in-
cline to good, something to sustain him in the short
journey through life, with its bright moments of
happiness, and its long hours of terrible distress.

  If some of those who read and mark these translations learn how to discover some such precious
grains in the sacred books of other nations, though
hidden under heaps of rubbish, our labour 'will not
have been in vain, for there is no lesson which at
the present time seems more important than to learn
that in every religion there are such precious grains ;
that we must draw in every religion a broad distinction
between what is essential and what is not, between
the eternal and the temporary, between the divine
and the human ; and that though the non-essential
may fill many volumes, the essential can often be
comprehended in a few words, but words on which
' hang all the law and the prophets.'

PROGRAM OF A TRANSLATION

OF

THE SACRED BOOKS OF THE EAST.

I here subjoin the program in which I first put forward the idea of a translation of the Sacred Books of the East, and through which I invited the co-operation of Oriental scholars in this undertaking. The difficulty of finding translators, both willing and competent to take a part in it, proved far greater than I had anticipated. Even when I had secured the assistance of a number of excellent scholars, and had received their promises of prompt co-operation, illness, domestic affliction, and even death asserted their control over all human affairs. Professor Childers, who had shown the warmest interest in our work, and on whom I chiefly depended for the Pali literature of the Buddhists, was taken from us, an irreparable loss to Oriental scholarship in general, and to our undertaking in particular. Among native scholars, whose co-operation I had been particularly desired to secure, Rajendralal Mitra, who had promised a translation of the Vâyu-purâna, was prevented by serious illness from fulfilling his engagement. In other cases sorrow and sickness have caused, at all events, serious delay in the translation of the very books which were to have inaugurated this Series. However, new offers of assistance have come, and I hope that more may still come from Oriental scholars both in India and England, so that the limit of time which had been originally

assigned to the publication of twenty-four volumes
may not, I hope, be much exceeded.

THE SACRED BOOKS OF THE EAST, TRANSLATED, WITH INTRODUC-
TIONS AND NOTES, BY VARIOUS ORIENTAL SCHOLARS, AND EDITED
BY F. MAX MÜLLER.

Apart from the interest which the Sacred Books of all religions
possess in the eyes of the theologian, and, more particularly, of the
missionary, to whom an accurate knowledge of them is as indispensable as a knowledge of the enemy's country is to a general, these
works have of late assumed a new importance, as viewed in the
character of ancient historical documents. In every country where
Sacred Books have been preserved, whether by oral tradition or by
writing, they are the oldest records, and mark the beginning of
what may be called documentary, in opposition to purely traditional, history.

There is nothing more ancient in India than the Vedas; and, if
we except the Vedas and the literature connected with them, there
is again no literary work in India which, so far as we know at
present, can with certainty be referred to an earlier date than that
of the Sacred Canon of the Buddhists. Whatever age we may
assign to the various portions of the Avesta and to their final
arrangement, there is no book in the Persian language of greater
antiquity than the Sacred Books of the followers of Zarathustra,
nay, even than their translation in Pehlevi. There may have been
an extensive ancient literature in China long before Khung-fû-ʒze
and Lâo-ʒze, but among all that was rescued and preserved of it,
the five King and the four Shû claim again the highest antiquity.
As to the Koran, it is known to be the fountain-head both of the
religion and of the literature of the Arabs.

This being the case, it was but natural that the attention of the
historian should of late have been more strongly attracted by these
Sacred Books, as likely to afford most valuable information, not
only on the religion, but also on the moral sentiments, the social
institutions, the legal maxims of some of the most important nations
of antiquity. There are not many nations that have preserved
sacred writings, and many of those that have been preserved have
but lately become accessible to us in their original form, through
the rapid advance of Oriental scholarship in Europe. Neither
Greeks, nor Romans, nor Germans, nor Celts, nor Slaves have
left us anything that deserves the name of Sacred Books. The

Homeric Poems are national Epics, like the Râmâya*n*a, and the Nibelunge, and the Homeric Hymns have never received that general recognition or sanction which alone can impart to the poetical effusions of personal piety the sacred or canonical character which is the distinguishing feature of the Vedic Hymns. The sacred literature of the early inhabitants of Italy seems to have been of a liturgical rather than of a purely religious kind, and whatever the Celts, the Germans, the Slaves may have possessed of sacred traditions about their gods and heroes, having been handed down by oral tradition chiefly, has perished beyond all hope of recovery. Some portions of the Eddas alone give us an idea of what the religious and heroic poetry of the Scandinavians may have been. The Egyptians possessed Sacred Books, and some of them, such as the Book of the Dead, have come down to us in various forms. There is a translation of the Book of the Dead by Dr. Birch, published in the fifth volume of Bunsen's Egypt, and a new edition and translation of this important work may be expected from the combined labours of Birch, Chabas, Lepsius, and Naville. In Babylon and Assyria, too, important fragments of what may be called a Sacred Literature have lately come to light. The interpretation, however, of these Hieroglyphic and Cuneiform texts is as yet so difficult that, for the present, they are of interest to the scholar only, and hardly available for historical purposes.

Leaving out of consideration the Jewish and Christian Scriptures, it appears that the only great and original religions which profess to be founded on Sacred Books[1], and have preserved them in manuscript, are:—

1. The religion of the Brahmans.
2. The religion of the followers of Buddha.
3. The religion of the followers of Zarathu*s*tra.
4. The religion of the followers of Khung-fû-*z*ze.
5. The religion of the followers of Lâo-*z*ze.
6. The religion of the followers of Mohammed.

A desire for a trustworthy translation of the Sacred Books of these six Eastern religions has often been expressed. Several have been translated into English, French, German, or Latin, but in some cases these translations are difficult to procure, in others they are loaded with notes and commentaries, which are intended for

---

[1] Introduction to the Science of Religion, by F. Max Müller (Longmans, 1873), p. 104.

students by profession only. Oriental scholars have been blamed for not having as yet supplied a want so generally felt, and so frequently expressed, as a complete, trustworthy, and readable translation of the principal Sacred Books of the Eastern Religions. The reasons, however, why hitherto they have shrunk from such an undertaking are clear enough. The difficulties in many cases of giving complete translations, and not selections only, are very great. There is still much work to be done in a critical restoration of the original texts, in an examination of their grammar and metres, and in determining the exact meaning of many words and passages. That kind of work is naturally far more attractive to scholars than a mere translation, particularly when they cannot but feel that, with the progress of our knowledge, many a passage which now seems clear and easy, may, on being re-examined, assume a new import. Thus while scholars who are most competent to undertake a translation, prefer to devote their time to more special researches, the work of a complete translation is deferred to the future, and historians are left under the impression that Oriental scholarship is still in so unsatisfactory a state as to make any reliance on translations of the Veda, the Avesta, or the Tâo-te King extremely hazardous.

It is clear, therefore, that a translation of the principal Sacred Books of the East can be carried out only at a certain sacrifice. Scholars must leave for a time their own special researches in order to render the general results already obtained accessible to the public at large. And even then, really useful results can be achieved viribus unitis only. If four of the best Egyptologists have to combine in order to produce a satisfactory edition and translation of one of the Sacred Books of ancient Egypt, a much larger number of Oriental scholars will be required for translating the Sacred Books of the Brahmans, the Buddhists, the Zoroastrians, the followers of Khung-fû-ʒze, Lâo-ʒze, and Mohammed.

Lastly, there was the most serious difficulty of all, a difficulty which no scholar could remove, viz. the difficulty of finding the funds necessary for carrying out so large an undertaking. No doubt there exists at present a very keen interest in questions connected with the origin, the growth, and decay of religion. But much of that interest is theoretic rather than historical. How people might or could or should have elaborated religious ideas, is a topic most warmly discussed among psychologists and theologians, but a study of the documents, in which alone the actual growth of religious thought can be traced, is much neglected.

A faithful, unvarnished prose translation of the Sacred Books of India, Persia, China, and Arabia, though it may interest careful students, will never, I fear, excite a widespread interest, or command a circulation large enough to make it a matter of private enterprise and commercial speculation.

No doubt there is much in these old books that is startling by its very simplicity and truth, much that is elevated and elevating, much that is beautiful and sublime; but people who have vague ideas of primeval wisdom and the splendour of Eastern poetry will soon find themselves grievously disappointed. It cannot be too strongly stated, that the chief, and, in many cases, the only interest of the Sacred Books of the East is historical; that much in them is extremely childish, tedious, if not repulsive; and that no one but the historian will be able to understand the important lessons which they teach. It would have been impossible to undertake a translation even of the most important only of the Sacred Books of the East, without the support of an Academy or a University which recognises the necessity of rendering these works more generally accessible, on the same grounds on which it recognises the duty of collecting and exhibiting in Museums the petrifactions of bygone ages, little concerned whether the public admires the beauty of fossilised plants and broken skeletons, as long as hard-working students find there some light for reading once more the darker pages in the history of the earth.

Having been so fortunate as to secure that support, having also received promises of assistance from some of the best Oriental scholars in England and India, I hope I shall be able, after the necessary preparations are completed, to publish about three volumes of translations every year, selecting from the stores of the six so-called 'Book-religions' those works which at present can be translated, and which are most likely to prove useful. All translations will be made from the original texts, and where good translations exist already, they will be carefully revised by competent scholars. Such is the bulk of the religious literature of the Brahmans and the Buddhists, that to attempt a complete translation would be far beyond the powers of one generation of scholars. Still, if the interest in the work itself should continue, there is no reason why this series of translations should not be carried on, even after those who commenced it shall have ceased from their labours.

What I contemplate at present, and I am afraid at my time of life even this may seem too sanguine, is no more than a Series of twenty-four volumes, the publication of which will probably extend over eight years. In this Series I hope to comprehend the following books, though I do not pledge myself to adhere strictly to this outline :—

1. From among the Sacred Books of the Brahmans I hope to give a translation of the Hymns of the Rig-veda. While I shall continue my translation of selected hymns of that Veda, a traduction raisonnée which is intended for Sanskrit scholars only, on the same principles which I have followed in the first volume [1], explaining every word and sentence that seems to require elucidation, and carefully examining the opinions of previous commentators, both native and European, I intend to contribute a freer translation of the hymns to this Series, with a few explanatory notes only, such as are absolutely necessary to enable readers who are unacquainted with Sanskrit to understand the thoughts of the Vedic poets. The translation of perhaps another Samhitâ, one or two of the Brâhmanas, or portions of them, will have to be included in our Series, as well as the principal Upanishads, theosophic treatises of great interest and beauty. There is every prospect of an early appearance of a translation of the Bhagavad-gîtâ, of the most important among the sacred Law-books, and of one at least of the Purânas. I should have wished to include a translation of some of the Gain books, of the Granth of the Sikhs, and of similar works illustrative of the later developments of religion in India, but there is hardly room for them at present.

2. The Sacred Books of the Buddhists will be translated chiefly from the two original collections, the Southern in Pali, the Northern in Sanskrit. Here the selection will, no doubt, be most difficult. Among the first books to be published will be, I hope, Sûtras from the Dîgha Nikâya, a part of the Vinaya-pitaka, the Dhammapada, the Divyâvadâna, the Lalita-vistara, or legendary life of Buddha.

3. The Sacred Books of the Zoroastrians lie within a smaller compass, but they will require fuller notes and commentaries in order to make a translation intelligible and useful.

4. The books which enjoy the highest authority with the followers of Khung-fû-zze are the King and the Shû. Of the former the Shû King or Book of History; the Odes of the Temple and

---

[1] Rig-veda-sanhitâ, The Sacred Hymns of the Brahmans, translated and explained by F. Max Müller. Vol. i. Hymns to the Maruts or the Storm-Gods. London, 1869.

the Altar, and other pieces illustrating the ancient religious views and practices of the Chinese, in the Shih King or Book of Poetry; the Yî King; the Lî *K*î; and the Hsiâo King or Classic of Filial Piety, will all be given, it is hoped, entire. Of the latter, the Series will contain the *K*ung Yung or Doctrine of the Mean; the Tâ Hsio or Great Learning; all Confucius' utterances in the Lun Yü or Confucian Analects, which are of a religious nature, and refer to the principles of his moral system; and Măng-ʓze's Doctrine of the Goodness of Human Nature.

5. For the system of Lâo-ʓze we require only a translation of the Tâo-teh King with some of its commentaries, and, it may be, an authoritative work to illustrate the actual operation of its principles.

6. For Islam, all that is essential is a trustworthy translation of the Koran.

It will be my endeavour to divide the twenty-four volumes which are contemplated in this Series as equally as possible among the six religions. But much must depend on the assistance which I receive from Oriental scholars, and also on the interest and the wishes of the public.

F. MAX MÜLLER.

Oxford, October, 1876.

The following distinguished scholars, all of them occupying the foremost rank in their own special departments of Oriental literature, are at present engaged in preparing translations of some of the Sacred Books of the East: S. Beal, R. G. Bhandarkar, G. Bühler, A. Burnell, E. B. Cowell, J. Darmesteter, T. W. Rhys Davids, J. Eggeling, V. Fausböll, H. Jacobi, J. Jolly, H. Kern, F. Kielhorn, J. Legge, H. Oldenberg, E. H. Palmer, R. Pischel, K. T. Telang, E. W. West.

The works which for the present have been selected for translation are the following:

I. ANCIENT VEDIC RELIGION.

Hymns of the *R*ig-veda.
The *S*atapatha-brâhma*n*a.

The Upanishads.
The Grihya-sûtras of Hiranyakesin and others.

II. LAW-BOOKS IN PROSE.

The Sûtras of Âpastamba, Gautama, Baudhâyana, Vasishtha, Vishnu, &c.

III. LAW-BOOKS IN VERSE.

The Laws of Manu, Yâgñavalkya, &c.

IV. LATER BRAHMANISM.

The Bhagavad-gîtâ.
The Vâyu-purâna.

V. BUDDHISM.

1. Pali Documents.

The Mahâparinibbâna Sutta, the Tevigga Sutta, the Mahasudassana Sutta, the Dhammakakkappa-vattana Sutta; the Suttanipâta; the Mahâvagga, the Kullavagga, and the Pâtimokkha.

2. Sanskrit Documents.

The Divyâvadâna and Saddharmapundarîka.

3. Chinese Documents.

The Phû-yâo King, or life of Buddha.

4. Prakrit Gaina Documents.

The Âkârânga Sûtra, Dasavaikâlika Sûtra, Sûtra-kritânga, and Uttarâdhyayana Sûtra.

VI. PARSI RELIGION.

1. Zend Documents.

The Vendîdâd.

2. Pehlevi and Parsi Documents.

The Bundahi*s*, Bahman Yasht, Shâyast-lâ-shâyast, Dâdistâni Dînî, Mainyôi *K*hard.

VII. MOHAMMEDANISM.

The Koran.

VIII. CHINESE RELIGION.

1. Confucianism.

The Shû King, Shih King, Hsiâo King, Yî King, Lî *K*î, Lun Yü, and Mâng-ʒze.

2. Tâoism.

The Tâo-teh King, *K*wang-ʒze, and Kan Ying Phien.

TRANSLITERATION OF ORIENTAL ALPHABETS.

The system of transcribing Oriental words with Roman types, adopted by the translators of the Sacred Books of the East, is, on the whole, the same which I first laid down in my Proposals for a Missionary Alphabet, 1854, and which afterwards I shortly described in my Lectures on the Science of Language, Second Series, p. 169 (ninth edition). That system allows of great freedom in its application to different languages, and has, therefore, recommended itself to many scholars, even if they had long been accustomed to use their own system of transliteration.

It rests in fact on a few principles only, which may be applied to individual languages according to the views which each student has formed for himself of the character and the pronunciation of the vowels and consonants of any given alphabet.

It does not differ essentially from the Standard Alphabet proposed by Professor Lepsius. It only endeavours to realise, by means of the ordinary types which are found in every printing office, what my learned friend has been enabled to achieve, it may be in a more perfect manner, by means of a number of new types with diacritical marks, cast expressly for him by the Berlin Academy.

The general principles of what, on account of its easy application to all languages, I have called the Missionary Alphabet, are these :

1. No letters are to be used which do not exist in ordinary founts.

2. The same Roman type is always to represent the same foreign letter, and the same foreign letter is always to be represented by the same Roman type.

3. Simple letters are, as a rule, to be represented by simple, compound by compound types.

4. It is not attempted to indicate the pronunciation of foreign languages, but only to represent foreign letters by Roman types, leaving the pronunciation to be learnt, as it is now, from grammars or from conversation with natives.

5. The foundation of every system of transliteration must consist of a classification of the typical sounds of human speech. Such classification may be more or less perfect, more or less minute, according to the objects in view. For ordinary purposes the classification in vowels and consonants, and of consonants again in gutturals, dentals, and labials suffices. In these three classes we distinguish hard (not-voiced) and sonant (voiced) consonants, each being liable to aspiration ; nasals, sibilants, and semivowels, some of these also, being either voiced or not-voiced.

6. After having settled the typical sounds, we assign to them, as much as possible, the ordinary Roman types of the first class.

7. We then arrange in every language which possesses a richer alphabet, all remaining letters, according to their affinities, as modifications of the nearest typical letters, or as letters of the second and third class. Thus linguals in Sanskrit are treated as nearest to dentals, palatals to gutturals.

8. The manner of expressing such modifications is uniform throughout. While all typical letters of

the first class are expressed by Roman types, modified letters of the second class are expressed by
italics, modified letters of the third class by small
capitals. Only in extreme cases, where another class
of modified types is wanted, are we compelled to
have recourse either to diacritical marks, or to a
different fount of types.

9. Which letters in each language are to be
considered as primary, secondary, or tertiary may,
to a certain extent, be left to the discretion of
individual scholars.

10. As it has been found quite impossible to
devise any practical alphabet that should accurately
represent the pronunciation of words, the Missionary
Alphabet, by not attempting to indicate minute
shades of pronunciation, has at all events the
advantage of not misleading readers in their pronunciation of foreign words. An italic *t*, for instance,
or a small capital T, serves simply as a warning that
this is not the ordinary t, though it has some affinity
with it. How it is to be pronounced must be learnt
for each language, as it now is, from a grammar
or otherwise. Thus *t* in Sanskrit is the lingual *t*.
How that is to be pronounced, we must learn from
the Prâtisâkhyas, or from the mouth of a highly
educated *S*rotriya. We shall then learn that its
pronunciation is really that of what we call the
ordinary dental t, as in town, while the ordinary
dental t in Sanskrit has a pronunciation of its own,
extremely difficult to acquire for Europeans.

11. Words or sentences which used to be printed
in italics are spaced.

TRANSLITERATION OF ORIENTAL ALPHABETS ADOPTED FOR THE TRANSLATIONS OF THE SACRED BOOKS OF THE EAST.

CONSONANTS.	MISSIONARY ALPHABET.			Sanskrit.	Zend.	Pehlevi.	Persian.	Arabic.	Hebrew.	Chinese.
	I Class.	II Class.	III Class.							
Gutturales.										
1 Tenuis	k			क	ग	⟩	⟩	⟩	ה	k
2 ,, aspirata	kh			ख	⟩	⟩			ח	kh
3 Media	g			ग	⟩	⟩	⟩		ה	
4 ,, aspirata	gh			घ	⟩	⟩	⟩	⟩	ה	
5 Gutturo-labialis	q			व	⟩		⟩		ב	
6 Nasalis	ṅ (ng)			ङ	{ ⟩ (ng) ⟩ (N) }					h, hs
7 Spiritus asper	h			ह	⟩ (hv)	⟩	»	»	ח	
8 ,, lenis	̓						–	–	צ	
9 ,, asper faucalis	ʼh						ل	ل	ח	
10 ,, lenis faucalis	ʽh						ح	ح	ע	
11 ,, asper fricatus		ʼh					ح	ح		
12 ,, lenis fricatus		ʽh								
Gutturales modificatae (palatales, &c.)										
13 Tenuis		k		च	⟩	د	⟩			k
14 ,, aspirata		kh		छ		د	⟩	⟩		kh
15 Media		g		ज	⟩	د	⟩	⟩		
16 ,, aspirata		gh		झ						
17 ,, Nasalis	ñ			ञ						

CONSONANTS (continued).	MISSIONARY ALPHABET.			Sanskrit.	Zend.	Pehlevi.	Persian.	Arabic.	Hebrew.	Chinese.
	I Class.	II Class.	III Class.							
18 Semivocalis	y			य	३ (init.) २ ५	ゝ	ى	ى	י	y
19 Spiritus asper		(y̆)								
20 ,, lenis		(y̆)		श्र	२ ३	??	٤ ٣	٤ ٣		z
21 ,, asper assibilatus		s				u	٩	٩		t
22 ,, lenis assibilatus		z								th
Dentales.										
23 Tenuis	t			त थ	२ ह	८	ॆ	ॆ	ת	
24 ,, aspirata	th		TH							
25 ,, assibilata							ॎ ॏ	ॎ ॏ		
26 Media	d			ड ध	ह ६	n	॓	॓	ד ד	n
27 ,, aspirata	dh		DH							l
28 ,, assibilata										
29 Nasalis	n			न ३ ४	ॱ	٦, ١, ٠	॑ ढ़	॑ ढ़	נ ן	
30 Semivocalis	l	l								
31 ,, mollis 1			L							
32 ,, mollis 2										
33 Spiritus asper 1	s		s (ʃ)	स	३	ॐ	॒ (ॎ) ॣ	॒	מ ם	s
34 ,, asper 2							॔ ॣ	॔		
35 ,, lenis	z		z (ʒ)		८	५	ज ॱ	ज ॱ	ז	z
36 ,, asperrimus 1			ż (ʒ̇)				ॴ ॲ	ॴ ॲ	צ	ろ, ろh
37 ,, asperrimus 2										

Dentales modificatae (linguales, &c.)

No.		Sanskrit &c.		Zend	Pehlevi	Persian	Arabic	Hebrew	MSS.
38	Tenuis	t	t				ट		2
39	,, aspirata	th	th				ठ		ट
40	Media	d	d				ड		ड
41	,, aspirata	dh	dh				ढ		ढ
42	Nasalis	ɪ	n				ण		ण
43	Semivocalis						र		र
44	,, fricata		r	R					
45	,, diacritica								
46	Spiritus asper	sh			sh		ष		ष
47	,, lenis	zh							

Labiales.

No.		Sanskrit &c.		Zend	Pehlevi	Persian	Arabic	Hebrew	MSS.
48	Tenuis	p			p	p	प	ph	प
49	,, aspirata	ph					फ		फ
50	Media	b					ब		ब
51	,, aspirata	bh					भ		भ
52	Tenuissima		p						
53	Nasalis	m				m	म	m	म
54	Semivocalis	w				w	व		व
55	,, aspirata	hw							
56	Spiritus asper	f				f	फ		फ
57	,, lenis	v							
58	Anusvâra		m						
59	Visarga		h						

VOWELS.	MISSIONARY ALPHABET. I Class	II Class	III Class	Sanskrit.	Zend.	Pehlevi.	Persian.	Arabic.	Hebrew.	Chinese.
1 Neutralis	0								־	ă
2 Laryngo-palatalis	ӗ				ꝝ	fin.				a
3 „ labialis	ŏ				ꜱ	ꝝ init		ا		â
4 Gutturalis brevis	a	(a)		श	ꞁ	ꝝ	ا	ى	‖	ĩ
5 „ longa	â			शा	ꞃ	ꝗ	ى	ی		ĩ̂
6 Palatalis brevis	i	(i)		ᠳᠷᡄᡄᠷ						
7 „ longa	î			ᠼᠼ						
8 Dentalis brevis	t̤			ᠷᠷ						
9 „ longa	t̤̄			ᠷᠷ						
10 Lingualis brevis	ri			ᠷᠷ						
11 „ longa	rî			ᠷᠷ						
12 Labialis brevis	u	(u)		ᠷ						u
13 „ longa	û			ᠷ						ꝛ
14 Gutturo-palatalis brevis	e	(e)		ᠷ ᠷ	ɛ(e) ξ(e) ꝗ				ֵ ֶ	e
15 „ longa	ê (ai)	(ai)			ꝗ	ꝝ			ֳ ׃	ê
16 Diphthongus gutturo-palatalis	âi						ا	ی		âi
17 „	ei (ĕi)									ei, êi
18 „	oi (ŏu)									
19 Gutturo-labialis brevis	o	(o)		ᠷ ᠷ					ֹ ֺ	o
20 „ longa	ô (au)	(au)		ᠷ ᠷ	ꝗ ꝣ (au)	ꝝ				au
21 Diphthongus gutturo-labialis	âu						ا	ی		âu
22 „	eu (ĕu)									
23 „	ou (ŏu)									
24 Gutturalis fracta	ä									
25 Palatalis fracta	ï									
26 Labialis fracta	ü									ü
27 Gutturo-labialis fracta	ö									

Approximate Pronunciation of the Roman Letters as representing the Sanskrit Alphabet.

Vowels.

a	स	as in	sam
â	आ	,,	psalm
i	इ	,,	knit
î	ई	,,	neat
ri	ऋ	,,	fiery
rî	ॠ	,,	—
li	ऌ	,,	friendly
lî	ॡ	,,	—
u	उ	,,	full
û	ऊ	,,	fool
e	ए	,,	date
ai	ऐ	,,	aisle
o	ओ	,,	note
au	औ	,,	proud

Consonants.

Gutturals.

k	क	as in	kite
kh	ख	,,	inkhorn
g	ग	,,	gate
gh	घ	,,	springhead
n (ng)	ङ	,,	sing
h	ह	,,	hear

Palatals.

k	च	as in	church
kh	छ	,,	church-history
g	ज	,,	jolly
gh	झ	,,	bridge-house

ñ	ञ	as in	new
y	य	,,	yet
s	श	,,	sharp

Dentals.

t	त	as in tin (tip of tongue striking the bone of the teeth)
th	थ	,,	lanthorn
d	द	,,	din
dh	ध	,,	landholder
n	न	,,	nay
l	ल	,,	let
l	ऴ	,,	—
s	स	,,	grass

Linguals.

t	ट	as in town (tip of tongue striking alveolar region)
th	ठ	,,	outhouse
d	ड	,,	done
dh	ढ	,,	rodhook
n	ण	,,	no
r	र	,,	red
sh	ष	,,	shun

Labials.

p	प	as in	pan
ph	फ	,,	topheavy
b	ब	,,	bed
bh	भ	,,	clubhouse
m	म	,,	mill
v	व	,,	live
m	ं	,,	Anusvâra (slight nasal)
h	ः	,,	Visarga (slight breathing)

Proper names have frequently been left in their ordinary spelling, e. g. Râjendra, instead of Râgendra. In words which have almost become English, the diacritical marks have often been omitted, e. g. Rig-veda, instead of *Rig*-veda; Brahman, instead of Brâhma*n*a; Confucius, Zoroaster, Koran, &c.

INTRODUCTION

THE UPANISHADS.

First Translation of the Upanishads.

Dârâ Shukoh, Anquetil Duperron, Schopenhauer.

THE ancient Vedic literature, the foundation of the whole literature of India, which has been handed down in that country in an unbroken succession from the earliest times within the recollection of man to the present day, became known for the first time beyond the frontiers of India through the Upanishads. The Upanishads were translated from Sanskrit into Persian by, or, it may be, for Dârâ Shukoh, the eldest son of Shâh Jehân, an enlightened prince, who openly professed the liberal religious tenets of the great Emperor Akbar, and even wrote a book intended to reconcile the religious doctrines of Hindus and Mohammedans. He seems first to have heard of the Upanishads during his stay in Kashmir in 1640. He afterwards invited several Pandits from Benares to Delhi, who were to assist him in the work of translation. The translation was finished in 1657. Three years after the accomplishment of this work, in 1659, the prince was put to death by his brother Aurangzib[1], in reality, no doubt, because he was the eldest son and legitimate successor of Shâh Jehân, but under the pretext that he was an infidel, and dangerous to the established religion of the empire.

When the Upanishads had once been translated from Sanskrit into Persian, at that time the most widely read language of the East and understood likewise by many European scholars, they became generally accessible to

---

[1] Elphinstone, History of India, ed. Cowell, p. 610.

all who took an interest in the religious literature of India. It is true that under Akbar's reign (1556–1586) similar translations had been prepared [1], but neither those nor the translations of Dârâ Shukoh attracted the attention of European scholars till the year 1775. In that year Anquetil Duperron, the famous traveller and discoverer of the Zend-avesta, received one MS. of the Persian translation of the Upanishads, sent to him by M. Gentil, the French resident at the court of Shuja ud daula, and brought to France by M. Bernier. After receiving another MS., Anquetil Duperron collated the two, and translated the Persian translation [2] into French (not published), and into Latin. That Latin translation was published in 1801 and 1802, under the title of 'Oupnek'hat, id est, Secretum tegendum: opus ipsa in India rarissimum, continens antiquam et arcanam, seu theologicam et philosophicam doctrinam, e quatuor sacris Indorum libris Rak baid, Djedjer baid, Sam baid, Athrban baid excerptam; ad verbum, e Persico idiomate, Samkreticis vocabulis intermixto, in Latinum conversum: Dissertationibus et Annotationibus difficiliora explanantibus, illustratum: studio et opera Anquetil Duperron, Indicopleustæ. Argentorati, typis et impensis fratrum Levrault, vol. i, 1801; vol. ii, 1802 [3].'

This translation, though it attracted considerable interest among scholars, was written in so utterly unintelligible a style, that it required the lynxlike perspicacity of an intre-

---

[1] M. M., Introduction to the Science of Religion, p. 79.

[2] Several other MSS. of this translation have since come to light; .one at Oxford, Codices Wilsoniani, 399 and 400. Anquetil Duperron gives the following title of the Persian translation: ' Hanc interpretationem τῶν Oupnekhathai quorumvis quatuor librorum Beid, quod, designatum cum secreto magno (per secretum magnum) est, et integram cognitionem luminis luminum, hic Fakir sine tristitia (Sultan) Mohammed Dara Schakoh ipse, cum significatione recta, cum sinceritate, in tempore sex mensium (postremo die, secundo τοῦ Schonbeh, vigesimo) sexto mensis τοῦ Ramazzan, anno 1067 τοῦ Hedjri (Christi, 1657) in urbe Delhi, in mansione nakhe noudeh, cum absolutione ad finem fecit pervenire.' The MS. was copied by Âtma Ram in the year 1767 A.D. Anquetil Duperron adds: 'Absolutum est hoc Apographum versionis Latinæ τῶν quinquaginta Oupnekhatha, ad verbum, e Persico idiomate, Samskreticis vocabulis intermixto, factæ, die 9 Octobris, 1796, 18 Brumaire, anni 4, Reipublic. Gall. Parisiis.'

[3] M. M., History of Ancient Sanskrit Literature, second edition, p. 325.

pid philosopher, such as Schopenhauer, to discover a thread through such a labyrinth. Schopenhauer, however, not only found and followed such a thread, but he had the courage to proclaim to an incredulous age the vast treasures of thought which were lying buried beneath that fearful jargon.

As Anquetil Duperron's volumes have become scarce, I shall here give a short specimen of his translation, which corresponds to the first sentences of my translation of the *Kh*ândogya-upanishad (p. 1):—'Oum hoc verbum (esse) adkit ut sciveris, sic τò maschghouli fac (de eo meditare), quod ipsum hoc verbum aodkit est; propter illud quod hoc (verbum) oum, in Sam Beid, cum voce altâ, cum harmoniâ pronunciatum fiat.

'Adkiteh porro cremor (optimum, selectissimum) est: quemadmodum ex (præ) omni quieto (non moto), et moto, pulvis (terra) cremor (optimum) est; et e (præ) terra aqua cremor est; et ex aqua, comedendum (victus) cremor est; (et) e comedendo, comedens cremor est; et e comedente, loquela (id quod dicitur) cremor est; et e loquela, aïet τοῦ Beid, et ex aïet, τò siam, id est, cum harmonia (pronunciatum); et e Sam, τò adkit, cremor est; id est, oum, voce alta, cum harmonia pronunciare, aokit, cremor cremorum (optimum optimorum) est. Major, ex (præ) adkit, cremor alter non est.'

Schopenhauer not only read this translation carefully, but he makes no secret of it, that his own philosophy is powerfully impregnated by the fundamental doctrines of the Upanishads. He dwells on it again and again, and it seems both fair to Schopenhauer's memory and highly important for a true appreciation of the philosophical value of the Upanishads, to put together what that vigorous thinker has written on those ancient rhapsodies of truth.

In his 'Welt als Wille und Vorstellung,' he writes, in the preface to the first edition, p. xiii:

' If the reader has also received the benefit of the Vedas, the access to which by means of the Upanishads is in my eyes the greatest privilege which this still young century (1818) may claim before all previous centuries, (for I anticipate that the influence of Sanskrit literature will not be less profound than the revival of Greek in the fourteenth century,)—if then the reader, I say, has received his initiation in primeval Indian wisdom, and received it with an open heart, he will be prepared in the very best way for hearing what I have to tell him. It will not sound to him strange, as to many others, much less disagreeable; for I might, if it did not sound conceited, contend that every one of the detached statements which constitute the Upanishads, may be deduced as a necessary result from the fundamental thoughts which I have to enunciate, though those deductions themselves are by no means to be found there.'

And again [1]:

'If I consider how difficult it is, even with the assistance of the best and carefully educated teachers, and with all the excellent philological appliances collected in the course of this century, to arrive at a really correct, accurate, and living understanding of Greek and Roman authors, whose language was after all the language of our own predecessors in Europe, and the mother of our own, while Sanskrit, on the contrary, was spoken thousands of years ago in distant India, and can be learnt only with appliances which are as yet very imperfect;—if I add to this the impression which the translations of Sanskrit works by European scholars, with very few exceptions, produce on my mind, I cannot resist a certain suspicion that our Sanskrit scholars do not understand their texts much better than the higher class of schoolboys their Greek. Of course, as they are not boys, but men of knowledge and understanding, they put together, out of what they do understand, something like what the general meaning may have been, but much probably creeps in ex ingenio. It is still worse with the Chinese of our European Sinologues.

'If then I consider, on the other hand, that Sultan Mohammed Dârâ Shukoh, the brother of Aurangzib, was born and bred in India, was a learned, thoughtful, and enquiring man, and therefore probably understood his Sanskrit about as well as we our Latin, that moreover

---

[1] Schopenhauer, Parerga, third edition, II, p. 426.

he was assisted by a number of the most learned Pandits, all this together gives me at once a very high opinion of his translation of the Vedic Upanishads into Persian. If, besides this, I see with what profound and quite appropriate reverence Anquetil Duperron has treated that Persian translation, rendering it in Latin word by word, retaining, in spite of Latin grammar, the Persian syntax, and all the Sanskrit words which the Sultan himself had left untranslated, though explaining them in a glossary, I feel the most perfect confidence in reading that translation, and that confidence soon receives its most perfect justification. For how entirely does the Oupnekhat breathe throughout the holy spirit of the Vedas! How is every one who by a diligent study of its Persian Latin has become familiar with that incomparable book, stirred by that spirit to the very depth of his soul! How does every line display its firm, definite, and throughout harmonious meaning! From every sentence deep, original, and sublime thoughts arise, and the whole is pervaded by a high and holy and earnest spirit. Indian air surrounds us, and original thoughts of kindred spirits. And oh, how thoroughly is the mind here washed clean of all early engrafted Jewish superstitions, and of all philosophy that cringes before those superstitions! In the whole world there is no study, except that of the originals, so beneficial and so elevating as that of the Oupnekhat. It has been the solace of my life, it will be the solace of my death!

'Though [1] I feel the highest regard for the religious and philosophical works of Sanskrit literature, I have not been able to derive much pleasure from their poetical compositions. Nay, they seem to me sometimes as tasteless and monstrous as the sculpture of India.

'In [2] most of the pagan philosophical writers of the first Christian centuries we see the Jewish theism, which, as Christianity, was soon to become the faith of the people, shining through, much as at present we may perceive shining through in the writings of the learned, the native

---

[1] Loc. cit. II, pp. 425. [2] Loc. cit. I, p. 59.

pantheism of India, which is destined sooner or later to
become the faith of the people. Ex oriente lux.'

This may seem strong language, and, in some respects,
too strong. But I thought it right to quote it here, because, whatever may be urged against Schopenhauer, he
was a thoroughly honest thinker and honest speaker, and
no one would suspect him of any predilection for what has
been so readily called Indian mysticism. That Schelling
and his school should use rapturous language about the
Upanishads, might carry little weight with that large class
of philosophers by whom everything beyond the clouds
of their own horizon is labelled mysticism. But that
Schopenhauer should have spoken of the Upanishads as
'products of the highest wisdom' (Ausgeburt der höchsten
Weisheit)[1], that he should have placed the pantheism
there taught high above the pantheism of Bruno, Male-
branche, Spinoza, and Scotus Erigena, as brought to light
again at Oxford in 1681[2], may perhaps secure a more considerate reception for these relics of ancient wisdom than
anything that I could say in their favour.

RAMMOHUN ROY.

Greater, however, than the influence exercised on the
philosophical thought of modern Europe, has been the
impulse which these same Upanishads have imparted to
the religious life of modern India. In about the same year
(1774 or 1775) when the first MS. of the Persian translation
of the Upanishads was received by Anquetil Duperron,
Rammohun Roy[3] was born in India, the reformer and
reviver of the ancient religion of the Brahmans. A man
who in his youth could write a book 'Against the Idolatry
of all Religions,' and who afterwards expressed in so many
exact words his 'belief in the divine authority of Christ[4],'
was not likely to retain anything of the sacred literature of
his own religion, unless he had perceived in it the same

---

[1] Loc. cit. II, p. 428.
[2] Loc. cit. I, p. 6. These passages were pointed out to me by Professor Noiré.
[3] Born 1774, died at 2.30 A.M., on Friday, 28th September, 1833.
[4] Last Days of Rammohun Roy, by Mary Carpenter, 1866, p. 135.

divine authority which he recognised in the teaching of Christ. He rejected the Purâ*n*as, he would not have been swayed in his convictions by the authority of the Laws of Manu, or even by the sacredness of the Vedas. He was above all that. But he discovered in the Upanishads and in the so-called Vedânta something different from all the rest, something that ought not to be thrown away, something that, if rightly understood, might supply the right native soil in which alone the seeds of true religion, aye, of true Christianity, might spring up again and prosper in India, as they had once sprung up and prospered from out the philosophies of Origen or Synesius. European scholars have often wondered that Rammohun Roy, in his defence of the Veda, should have put aside the Sa*m*hitâs and the Brâhma*n*as, and laid his finger on the Upanishads only, as the true kernel of the whole Veda. Historically, no doubt, he was wrong, for the Upanishads presuppose both the hymns and the liturgical books of the Veda. But as the ancient philosophers distinguished in the Veda between the Karma-kâ*nd*a and the Gñâna-kâ*nd*a, between works and knowledge; as they themselves pointed to the learning of the sacred hymns and the performance of sacrifices as a preparation only for that enlightenment which was reserved as the highest reward for the faithful performance of all previous duties[1], Rammohun Roy, like Buddha and other enlightened men before him, perceived that the time for insisting on all that previous discipline with its minute prescriptions and superstitious observances was gone, while the knowledge conveyed in the Upanishads or the Vedânta, enveloped though it may be in strange coverings, should henceforth form the foundation of a new religious life[2]. He would tolerate nothing idolatrous, not even in his mother, poor woman, who after joining his most bitter opponents, confessed to her son, before she set out on her

---

[1] M. M., History of Ancient Sanskrit Literature, p. 319.

[2] 'The adoration of the invisible Supreme Being is exclusively prescribed by the Upanishads or the principal parts of the Vedas and also by the Vedant.' Rammohun Roy, Translation of the Kena-upanishad, Calcutta, 1816, p. 6. M. M., History of Ancient Sanskrit Literature, p. 320.

last pilgrimage to Juggernaut, where she died, that 'he was right, but that she was a weak woman, and grown too old to give up the observances which were a comfort to her.' It was not therefore from any regard of their antiquity or their sacred character that Rammohun Roy clung to the Upanishads, that he translated them into Bengali, Hindi, and English, and published them at his own expense. It was because he recognised in them seeds of eternal truth, and was bold enough to distinguish between what was essential in them and what was not,—a distinction, as he often remarked with great perplexity, which Christian teachers seemed either unable or unwilling to make[1].

The death of that really great and good man during his stay in England in 1833, was one of the severest blows that have fallen on the prospects of India. But his work has not been in vain. Like a tree whose first shoot has been killed by one winter frost, it has broken out again in a number of new and more vigorous shoots, for whatever the outward differences may be between the Âdi Brahmo Samâj of Debendranath Tagore, or the Brahmo Samâj of India of Keshub Chunder Sen, or the Sadharan Brahmo Samâj, the common root of them all is the work done, once for all, by Rammohun Roy. That work may have disappeared from sight for a time, and its present manifestations may seem to many observers who are too near, not very promising. But in one form or another, under one name or another, I feel convinced that work will live. 'In India,' Schopenhauer writes, ' our religion will now and never strike root : the primitive wisdom of the human race will never be pushed aside there by the events of Galilee. On the contrary, Indian wisdom will flow back upon Europe, and produce a thorough change in our knowing and thinking.' Here, again, the great philosopher seems to me to have allowed himself to be carried away too far by his enthusiasm for the less known. He is blind for the dark sides of the Upanishads, and he wilfully shuts his eyes against the bright rays of eternal truth in the Gospels, which even

---

[1] Last Days, p. 11.

Rammohun Roy was quick enough to perceive behind the mists and clouds of tradition that gather so quickly round the sunrise of every religion.

POSITION OF THE UPANISHADS IN VEDIC LITERATURE.

If now we ask what has been thought of the Upanishads by Sanskrit scholars or by Oriental scholars in general, it must be confessed that hitherto they have not received at their hands that treatment which in the eyes of philosophers and theologians they seem so fully to deserve. When the first enthusiasm for such works as Sakuntalâ and Gîta-Govinda had somewhat subsided, and Sanskrit scholars had recognised that a truly scholarlike study of Indian literature must begin with the beginning, the exclusively historical interest prevailed to so large an extent that the hymns of the Veda, the Brâhmanas, and the Sûtras absorbed all interest, while the Upanishads were put aside for a time as of doubtful antiquity, and therefore of minor importance.

My real love for Sanskrit literature was first kindled by the Upanishads. It was in the year 1844, when attending Schelling's lectures at Berlin, that my attention was drawn to those ancient theosophic treatises, and I still possess my collations of the Sanskrit MSS. which had then just arrived at Berlin, the Chambers collection, and my copies of commentaries, and commentaries on commentaries, which I made at that time. Some of my translations which I left with Schelling, I have never been able to recover, though to judge from others which I still possess, the loss of them is of small consequence. Soon after leaving Berlin, when continuing my Sanskrit studies at Paris under Burnouf, I put aside the Upanishads, convinced that for a true appreciation of them it was necessary to study, first of all, the earlier periods of Vedic literature, as represented by the hymns and the Brâhmanas of the Vedas.

In returning, after more than thirty years, to these favourite studies, I find that my interest in them, though it has changed in character, has by no means diminished.

It is true, no doubt, that the stratum of literature
which contains the Upanishads is later than the Samhitâs, and later than the Brâhma*n*as, but the first germs
of Upanishad doctrines go back at least as far as the
Mantra period, which provisionally has been fixed between
1000 and 800 B. C. Conceptions corresponding to the
general teaching of the Upanishads occur in certain hymns
of the Rig-veda-sa*m*hitâ, they must have existed therefore before that collection was finally closed. One hymn
in the Sa*m*hitâ of the Rig-veda (I, 191) was designated
by Kâtyâyana, the author of the Sarvânukrama*n*ikâ, as
an Upanishad. Here, however, upanishad means rather
a secret charm than a philosophical doctrine. Verses
of the hymns have often been incorporated in the Upanishads, and among the Oupnekhats translated into Persian
by Dârâ Shukoh we actually find the Purusha-sûkta,
the 90th hymn of the tenth book of the Rig-veda [1],
forming the greater portion of the Bark'heh Soukt. In the
Sa*m*hitâ of the Ya*g*ur-veda, however, in the Vâ*g*asaneyi-
*s*âkhâ, we meet with a real Upanishad, the famous Îsâ or
Îsâvâsya-upanishad, while the *S*ivasa*m*kalpa, too, forms part
of its thirty-fourth book [2]. In the Brâhma*n*as several Upanishads occur, even in portions which are not classed as
Âra*n*yakas, as, for instance, the well-known Kena or Talavakâra upanishad. The recognised place, however, for the
ancient Upanishads is in the Âra*n*yakas, or forest-books,
which, as a rule, form an appendix to the Brâhma*n*as, but
are sometimes included also under the general name of
Brâhma*n*a. Brâhma*n*a, in fact, meaning originally the
sayings of Brahmans, whether in the general sense of
priests, or in the more special of Brahman-priest, is a name
applicable not only to the books, properly so called,
but to all old prose traditions, whether contained in the
Sa*m*hitâs, such as the Taittirîya-sa*m*hitâ, the Brâhma*n*as,
the Âra*n*yakas, the Upanishads, and even, in certain cases,
in the Sûtras. We shall see in the introduction to the
Aitareya-âra*n*yaka, that that Âra*n*yaka is in the beginning

---

[1] See Weber, Indische Studien, IX, p. 1 seq.
[2] See M. M., History of Ancient Sanskrit Literature, p. 317.

a Brâhma*n*a, a mere continuation of the Aitareya-brâhma*n*a, explaining the Mahâvrata ceremony, while its last
book contains the Sûtras or short technical rules explaining the same ceremony which in the first book had been
treated in the style peculiar to the Brâhma*n*as. In the same
Aitareya-âra*n*yaka, III, 2, 6, 6, a passage of the Upanishad
is spoken of as a Brâhma*n*a, possibly as something like a
Brâhma*n*a, while something very like an Upanishad occurs
in the Âpastamba-sûtras, and might be quoted therefore
as a Sûtra[1]. At all events the Upanishads, like the
Âra*n*yakas, belong to what Hindu theologians call *S*ruti,
or revealed literature, in opposition to Sm*ri*ti, or traditional
literature, which is supposed to be founded on the former,
and allowed to claim a secondary authority only ; and the
earliest of these philosophical treatises will always, I believe, maintain a place in the literature of the world, among
the most astounding productions of the human mind in any
age and in any country.

DIFFERENT CLASSES OF UPANISHADS.

The ancient Upanishads, i. e. those which occupy a
place in the Sa*m*hitâs, Brâhma*n*as, and Âra*n*yakas, must
be, if we follow the chronology which at present is commonly, though, it may be, provisionally only, received
by Sanskrit scholars, older than 600 B. C., i.e. anterior
to the rise of Buddhism. As to other Upanishads, and
their number is very large, which either stand by themselves, or which are ascribed to the Atharva-veda, it is
extremely difficult to fix their age. Some of them are,
no doubt, quite modern, for mention is made even of
an Allah-upanishad ; but others may claim a far higher
antiquity than is generally assigned to them on internal
evidence. I shall only mention that the name of Atharva-
*s*iras, an Upanishad generally assigned to a very modern
date, is quoted in the Sûtras of Gautama and Baudhâyana[2];

---

[1] Âpastamba, translated by Bühler, Sacred Books of the East, vol. ii, p. 75.
[2] Gautama, translated by Bühler, Sacred Books of the East, vol. ii, p. 272,
and Introduction, p. lvi.

that the *Svetâsvatara-upanishad*, or the *Svetâsvatarânâm*
Mantropanishad, though bearing many notes of later periods
of thought, is quoted by *Sankara* in his commentary on
the Vedânta-sûtras [1]; while the N*ri*si*m*hottaratâpanîya-
upanishad forms part of the twelve Upanishads explained
by Vidyâra*n*ya in his Sarvopanishad-arthânubhûti-prakâ*s*a.
The Upanishads comprehended in that work are:

1. Aitareya-upanishad.
2. Taittirîya-upanishad.
3. *Kh*ândogya-upanishad.
4. Mu*nd*aka-upanishad.
5. Pra*s*na-upanishad.
6. Kaushîtaki-upanishad.
7. Maitrâya*n*îya-upanishad.
8. Ka*th*avallî-upanishad.
9. *Svetâsvatara-upanishad.
10. B*ri*had-âra*n*yaka-upanishad.
11. Talavakâra (Kena)-upanishad.
12. N*ri*si*m*hottaratâpanîya-upanishad [2].

The number of Upanishads translated by Dârâ Shukoh
amounts to 50; their number, as given in the Mahâvâkya-
muktâvalî and in the Muktikâ-upanishad, is 108 [3]. Professor Weber thinks that their number, so far as we know
at present, may be reckoned at 235 [4]. In order, however,
to arrive at so high a number, every title of an Upanishad
would have to be counted separately, while in several cases
it is clearly the same Upanishad which is quoted under different names. In an alphabetical list which I published in
1865 (Zeitschrift der Deutschen Morgenländischen Gesellschaft XIX, 137–158), the number of real Upanishads
reached 149. To that number Dr. Burnell [5] in his Catalogue

---

[1] Vedânta-sûtras I, 1, 11.

[2] One misses the Îsâ or Îsâvâsya-upanishad in this list. The Upanishads
chiefly studied in Bengal are the B*ri*had-âra*n*yaka, Aitareya, *Kh*ândogya, Taittirîya, Îsâ, Kena, Ka*th*a, Pra*s*na, Mu*nd*aka, and Mâ*nd*ûkya, to which should be
added the *Svetâsvatara. M. M., History of Ancient Sanskrit Literature, p. 325.

[3] Dr. Burnell thinks that this is an artificial computation, 108 being a sacred
number in Southern India. See Kielhorn in Gough's Papers on Ancient Sanskrit
Literature, p. 193.

[4] Weber, History of Sanskrit Literature, p. 155 note.

[5] Indian Antiquary, II, 267.

(p. 59) added 5, Professor Haug (Brahma und die Brah-manen) 16, making a sum total of 170. New names, however, are constantly being added in the catalogues of MSS. published by Bühler, Kielhorn, Burnell, Rajendralal Mitra, and others, and I shall reserve therefore a more complete list of Upanishads for a later volume.

Though it is easy to see that these Upanishads belong to very different periods of Indian thought, any attempt to fix their relative age seems to me for the present almost hopeless. No one can doubt that the Upanishads which have had a place assigned to them in the Samhitâs, Brâhmanas, and Âranyakas are the oldest. Next to these we can draw a line to include the Upanishads clearly referred to in the Vedânta-sûtras, or explained and quoted by Sankara, by Sâyana, and other more modern commentators. We can distinguish Upanishads in prose from Upanishads in mixed prose and verse, and again Upanishads in archaic verse from Upanishads in regular and continuous Anushtubh Slokas. We can also class them according to their subjects, and, at last, according to the sects to which they belong. But beyond this it is hardly safe to venture at present. Attempts have been made by Professor Weber and M. Regnaud to fix in each class the relative age of certain Upanishads, and I do not deny to their arguments, even where they conflict with each other, considerable weight in forming a preliminary judgment. But I know of hardly any argument which is really convincing, or which could not be met by counter arguments equally strong. Simplicity may be a sign of antiquity, but it is not so always, for what seems simple, may be the result of abbreviation. One Upanishad may give the correct, another an evidently corrupt reading, yet it does not follow that the correct reading may not be the result of an emendation. It is quite clear that a large mass of traditional Upanishads must have existed before they assumed their present form. Where two or three or four Upanishads contain the same story, told almost in the same words, they are not always copied from one another, but they have been settled independently, in different localities, by different teachers, it may be, for different purposes.

Lastly, the influence of Sâkhâs or schools may have told more or less on certain Upanishads. Thus the Maitrâyanîya-upanishad, as we now possess it, shows a number of irregular forms which even the commentator can account for only as peculiarities of the Maitrâyanîya-sâkhâ[1]. That Upanishad, as it has come down to us, is full of what we should call clear indications of a modern and corrupt age. It contains in VI, 37, a sloka from the Mânava-dharma-sâstra, which startled even the commentator, but is explained away by him as possibly found in another Sâkhâ, and borrowed from there by Manu. It contains corruptions of easy words which one would have thought must have been familiar to every student. Thus instead of the passage as found in the Khân-dogya-upanishad VIII, 7, 1, ya âtmâpahatapâpmâ vigaro vimrityur visoko 'vigighatso 'pipâsah, &c., the text of the Maitrâyanîya-upanishad (VII, 7) reads, âtmâpahatapâpmâ vigaro vimrityur visoko 'vikikitso 'vipâsah. But here again the commentator explains that another Sâkhâ reads 'vigi-ghatsa, and that avipâsa is to be explained by means of a change of letters as apipâsa. Corruptions, therefore, or modern elements which are found in one Upanishad, as handed down in one Sâkhâ, do not prove that the same existed in other Sâkhâs, or that they were found in the original text.

All these questions have to be taken into account before we can venture to give a final judgment on the relative age of Upanishads which belong to one and the same class. I know of no problem which offers so many similarities with the one before us as that of the relative age of the four Gospels. All the difficulties which occur in the Upanishads occur here, and no critical student who knows the difficulties that have to be encountered in determining the relative age of the four Gospels, will feel inclined, in the present state of Vedic scholarship, to speak with confidence on the relative age of the ancient Upanishads.

---

[1] They are generally explained as khândasa, but in one place (Maitr. Up. II, 4) the commentator treats such irregularities as etakkhâkhâsanketapâthah, a reading peculiar to the Maitrâyanîya school. Some learned remarks on this point may be seen in an article by Dr. L. Schroeder, Über die Maitrâyanî Samhitâ.

CRITICAL TREATMENT OF THE TEXT OF THE UPANISHADS.

With regard to a critical restoration of the text of the Upanishads, I have but seldom relied on the authority of new
MSS., but have endeavoured throughout to follow that text
which is presupposed by the commentaries, whether they are
the work of the old Sankarâkârya, or of the more modern
Sankarânanda, or Sâyana, or others. Though there still
prevails some uncertainty as to the date of Sankarâkârya,
commonly assigned to the eighth century A.D., yet I doubt
whether any MSS. of the Upanishads could now be found
prior to 1000 A.D. The text, therefore, which Sankara
had before his eyes, or, it may be, his ears, commands, I
think, a higher authority than that of any MSS. likely to
be recovered at present.

It may be objected that Sankara's text belonged to one
locality only, and that different readings and different
recensions may have existed in other parts of India.
That is perfectly true. We possess various recensions of
several Upanishads, as handed down in different Sâkhâs of
different Vedas, and we know of various readings recorded
by the commentators. These, where they are of importance for our purposes, have been carefully taken into
account.

It has also been supposed that Sankara, who, in writing
his commentaries on the Upanishad, was chiefly guided by
philosophical considerations, his chief object being to use
the Upanishads as a sacred foundation for the Vedânta
philosophy, may now and then have taken liberties with
the text. That may be so, but no stringent proof of
it has as yet been brought forward, and I therefore
hold that when we succeed in establishing throughout
that text which served as the basis of Sankara's commentaries, we have done enough for the present, and have
fulfilled at all events the first and indispensable task in a
critical treatment of the text of the Upanishads.

But in the same manner as it is easy to see that the text

of the Rig-veda, which is presupposed by Sâya*n*a's commentary and even by earlier works, is in many places palpably corrupt, we cannot resist the same conviction with regard to the text of the Upanishads. In some cases the metre, in others grammar, in others again the collation of analogous passages enable us to detect errors, and probably very ancient errors, that had crept into the text long before *S*ankara composed his commentaries.

Some questions connected with the metres of the Upanishads have been very learnedly treated by Professor Gildemeister in his essay, 'Zur Theorie des *S*loka.' The lesson to be derived from that essay, and from a study of the Upanishads, is certainly to abstain for the present from conjectural emendations. In the old Upanishads the same metrical freedom prevails as in the hymns; in the later Upanishads, much may be tolerated as the result of conscious or unconscious imitation. The metrical emendations that suggest themselves are generally so easy and so obvious that, for that very reason, we should hesitate before correcting what native scholars would have corrected long ago, if they had thought that there was any real necessity for correction.

It is easy to suggest, for instance, that in the Vâ*g*asaneyi-sa*m*hitâ-upanishad, verse 5, instead of tad antar asya sarvasya tadu sarvasyâsya bâhyata*h*, the original text may have been tad antar asya sarvasya tadu sarvasya bâhyata*h*; yet *S*ankara evidently read sarvasyâsya, and as the same reading is found in the text of the Vâ*g*asaneyi-sa*m*hitâ, who would venture to correct so old a mistake?

Again, if in verse 8, we left out yâthâtathyata*h*, we should get a much more regular metre,

> Kavir manîshî paribhû*h* svyambhû*h*
> arthân vya̯dădhā*k* *kh*ā̄svăti̯bhya*h* sămăbhya*h*.

Here vya̯dă forms one syllable by what I have proposed to call synizesis [1], which is allowed in the Upanishads as well as in the hymns. All would then seem right, except

---

that it is difficult to explain how so rare a word as yâthâ-tathyata*h* could have been introduced into the text.

In verse 10 one feels tempted to propose the omission of eva in anyad âhur avidyayâ, while in verse 11, an eva inserted after vidyâ*m* *k*a would certainly improve the metre.

In verse 15 the expression satyadharmâya d*r*ish*t*aye is archaic, but perfectly legitimate in the sense of 'that we may see the nature of the True,' or 'that we see him whose nature is true.' When this verse is repeated in the Maitr. Up. VI, 35, we find instead, satyadharmâya vish*n*ave, 'for the true Vish*n*u.' But here, again, no sound critic would venture to correct a mistake, intentional or unintentional, which is sanctioned both by the MSS. of the text and by the commentary.

Such instances, where every reader feels tempted at once to correct the textus receptus, occur again and again, and when they seem of any interest they have been mentioned in the notes. It may happen, however, that the correction, though at first sight plausible, has to be surrendered on more mature consideration. Thus in the Vâ*g*asaneyi-sa*m*hitâ-upanishad, verse 2, one feels certainly inclined to write eva*m* tve nânyatheto 'sti, instead of eva*m* tvayi nânyatheto 'sti. But tve, if it were used here, would probably itself have to be pronounced dissyllabically, while tvayi, though it never occurs in the Rig-veda, may well keep its place here, in the last book of the Vâ*g*asaneyi-sa*m*hitâ, provided we pronounce it by synizesis, i. e. as one syllable.

Attempts have been made sometimes to go beyond *S*ankara, and to restore the text, as it ought to have been originally, but as it was no longer in *S*ankara's time. It is one thing to decline to follow *S*ankara in every one of his interpretations, it is quite another to decline to accept the text which he interprets. The former is inevitable, the latter is always very precarious.

Thus I see, for instance, that M. Regnaud, in the Errata to the second volume of his excellent work on the Upanishads (Matériaux pour servir à l'histoire de la philosophie de l'Inde, 1878) proposes to read in the B*r*ihad-âra*n*yaka-upanishad IV, 3, 1–8, sam anena vadishya iti, instead of sa mene na vadishya iti. *S*ankara adopted the latter reading, and explained accordingly, that Yâ*g*ñavalkya went to king *G*anaka, but made up his mind not to speak. M. Regnaud, reading sam anena vadishya iti, takes the very opposite view, namely, that Yâ*g*ñavalkya went to king *G*anaka, having made up his mind to have a conversation with him. As M. Regnaud does not rest this emendation on the authority of any new MSS., we may examine it as an ingenious conjecture; but in that case it seems to me clear that, if we adopted it, we should have at the same time to omit the whole sentence which follows. *S*ankara saw clearly that what had to be accounted or explained was why the king should address the Brahman first, samrâ*d* eva pûrva*m* papra*kkh*a; whereas if Yâ*g*ñavalkya had come with the intention of having a conversation with the king, he, the Brahman, should have spoken first. This irregularity is explained by the intervening sentence, in which we are reminded that on a former occasion, when *G*anaka and Yâ*g*ñavalkya had a disputation on the Agnihotra, Yâ*g*ñavalkya granted *G*anaka a boon to choose, and he chose as his boon the right of asking questions according to his pleasure. Having received that boon, *G*anaka was at liberty to question Yâ*g*ñavalkya, even though he did not like it, and hence *G*anaka is introduced here as the first to ask a question.

All this hangs well together, while if we assume that Yâ*g*ñavalkya came for the purpose of having a conversation with *G*anaka, the whole sentence from 'atha ha ya*g* *g*anaka*s* *k*a' to 'pûrvam papra*kkh*a' would be useless, nor would there be any excuse for *G*anaka beginning the conversation, when Yâ*g*ñavalkya came himself on purpose to question him.

It is necessary, even when we feel obliged to reject an interpretation of *S*ankara's, without at the same time altering the text, to remember that *S*ankara, where he is not blinded by philosophical predilections, commands the highest respect as an interpreter. I cannot help thinking therefore that M. Regnaud (vol. i, p. 59) was right in translating the passage in the *Kh*ând. Up. V, 3, 7, tasmâd u sarveshu lokeshu kshattrasyaiva pra*s*âsanam abhût, by 'que le kshatriya seul l'a enseignée dans tous les mondes.' For when he proposes in the 'Errata' to translate instead, 'c'est pourquoi l'empire dans tous les mondes fut attribué au kshatriya seulement,' he forgets that such an idea is foreign to the ordinary atmosphere in which the Upanishads move. It is not on account of the philosophical knowledge possessed by a few Kshatriyas, such as *G*anaka or Pravâha*n*a, that the privilege of government belongs everywhere to the second class. That rests on a totally different basis. Such exceptional knowledge, as is displayed by a few kings, might be an excuse for their claiming the privileges belonging to the Brahmans, but it would never, in the eyes of the ancient Indian Âryas, be considered as an argument for their claiming kingly power. Therefore, although I am well aware that pra*s*âs is most frequently used in the sense of ruling, I have no doubt that *S*ankara likewise was fully aware of that, and that if he nevertheless explained pra*s*âsana here in the sense of pra*s*âst*ri*tva*m* *s*ishyâ*n*âm, he did so because this meaning too was admissible, particularly here, where we may actually translate it by proclaiming, while the other meaning, that of ruling, would simply be impossible in the concatenation of ideas, which is placed before us in the Upanishad.

It seems, no doubt, extremely strange that neither the last redactors of the text of the Upanishads, nor the commentators, who probably knew the principal Upanishads by heart, should have perceived how certain passages in one Upanishad represented the same or nearly the same text which is found in another Upanishad, only occasionally with the most palpable corruptions.

Thus when the ceremony of offering a mantha or mash is described, we read in the *Kh*ândogya-upanishad V, 2, 6, that it is to be accompanied by certain words which on the whole are intelligible. But when the same passage occurs again in the Br*i*had-âra*n*yaka, those words have been changed to such a degree, and in two different ways in the two *S*âkhâs of the Mâdhyandinas and Kâ*n*vas, that, though the commentator explains them, they are almost unintelligible. I shall place the three passages together in three parallel lines:

   I. _Kh_ândogya-upanishad V, 2, 6   :
  II. B_ri_had-âra_ny_aka, Mâdhyandina-_s_âkhâ, XIV, 9, 3, 10:
 III. B_ri_had-âra_ny_aka-upanishad, Kâ_n_va-_s_âkhâ, VI, 3, 5 :

   I. Amo nâmâsy amâ hi te sarvam ida_m_ sa hi _g_yesh_tha_h
  II. âmo 'sy   âma_m_ hi te mayi   sa hi
 III. âma_m_sy   âma_m_hi te mahi   sa hi

   I. _s_resh_th_o râ_g_âdhipati_h_   sa mâ _g_yaish_th_ya_m_ _s_rai-
  II.   râ_g_e_s_âno 'dhipati_h_ sa mâ râ_g_e_s_âno
 III.   ra_g_e_s_âno

   I. sh_th_ya_m_ râ_g_yam âdhipatya_m_ gamayatv aham eveda_m_
  II.   'dhipati_m_   karotv iti.
 III.   'dhipati_m_   karotv iti.

   I. sarvam asânîti.
  II.
 III.

The text in the _Kh_ândogya-upanishad yields a certain sense, viz. 'Thou art Ama by name, for all this together exists in thee. He is the oldest and best, the king, the sovereign. May he make me the oldest, the best, the king, the sovereign. May I be all this.' This, according to the commentator, is addressed to Prâ_n_a, and Ama, though a purely artificial word, is used in the sense of Prâ_n_a, or breath, in another passage also, viz. B_ri_had-âra_ny_aka-up. I, 3, 22. If therefore we accept this meaning of Ama, the rest is easy and intelligible.

But if we proceed to the B_ri_had-âra_ny_aka, in the Mâdhyandina-_s_âkhâ, we find the commentator proposing the following interpretation : 'O Mantha, thou art a full knower, complete knowledge of me belongs to thee.' This meaning is obtained by deriving âma_h_ from â + man, in the sense of knower, and then taking âmam, as a neuter, in the sense of knowledge, derivations which are simply impossible.

Lastly, if we come to the text of the Kâ_n_va-_s_âkhâ, the grammatical interpretation becomes bolder still. _S_ankara does not explain the passage at all, which is strange, but Ânandagiri interprets âma_m_si tvam by 'Thou knowest (all),' and âma*m*hi te mahi, by 'we know thy great (shape),' which are again impossible forms.

But although there can be little doubt here that the reading of the *Kh*ândogya-upanishad gives us the original text, or a text nearest to the original, no sound critic would venture to correct the readings of the B*ri*had-âra*n*yaka. They are corruptions, but even as corruptions they possess authority, at all events up to a certain point, and it is the fixing of those certain points or chronological limits, which alone can impart a scientific character to our criticism of ancient texts.

In the Kaushîtaki-brâhma*n*a-upanishad Professor Cowell has pointed out a passage to me, where we must go beyond the text as it stood when commented on by the *S*ankarânanda. In the beginning of the fourth adhyâya all MSS. of the text read savasan, and this is the reading which the commentator seems anxious to explain, though not very successfully. I thought that possibly the commentator might have had before him the reading sa vasan, or so 'vasan, but both would be very unusual. Professor Cowell in his Various Readings, p. xii, conjectured sa*m*vasan, which would be liable to the same objection. He now, however, informs me that, as B. has sa*m*tvan, and C. satvan, he believes the original text to have been Satvan-Matsyeshu. This seems to me quite convincing, and is borne out by the reading of the Berlin MS., so far as it can be made out from Professor Weber's essay on the Upanishads, Indische Studien I, p. 419. I see that Boehtlingk and Roth in their Sanskrit Dictionary, s. v. satvat, suggest the same emendation.

The more we study the nature of Sanskrit MSS., the more, I believe, we shall feel convinced that their proper arrangement is one by locality rather than by time. I have frequently dwelt on this subject in the introductions to the successive volumes of my edition of the Rig-veda and its commentary by Sâya*n*â*k*ârya, and my convictions on this point have become stronger ever since. A MS., however modern, from the south of India or from the north, is more important as a check on the textus receptus of any Sanskrit work, as prevalent in Bengal or Bombay, than ever so many MSS., even if of greater antiquity, from the same locality. When therefore I was informed by my friend Dr. Bühler that he had discovered in Kashmir a MS. of the Aitareya-upanishad, I certainly expected some real help from such a treasure. The MS. is described by its discoverer in the last number of the Journal of the Bombay Asiatic Society, p. 34 [1], and has since been sent to me by the Indian Government. It is written on birch bark (bhûrga), and in the alphabet commonly called Sâradâ. The leaves are very much injured on the margin, and it is almost impossible to handle them without some injury. In many places the bark has shrunk, probably on being moistened, and the letters have become illegible. Apart from these drawbacks, there remain the difficulties inherent in the Sâradâ alphabet which, owing to its numerous combinations, is extremely difficult to read, and very trying to eyes which are growing weak. However, I collated the Upanishad from the Aitareya-âranyaka, which turned out to be the last portion only, viz. the Samhitâ-upanishad (Ait. Âr. III, 1–2), or, as it is called here, Samhitâranya, and I am sorry to say my expectations have been disappointed. The MS. shows certain graphic peculiarities which Dr. Bühler has pointed out. It is particularly careful in the use of the sibilants, replacing the Visarga by sibilants, writing s + s and s + s instead of h + s and h + s; distinguishing also the Gihvâmûlîya and Upadhmanîya. If therefore the MS. writes antastha, we may be sure that it really meant to write so, and not antahstha, or, as it would have written, antasstha. It shows equal care in the use of the nasals, and generally carries on the sandhi between different paragraphs. Here and there I met with better readings than those given in Rajendralal Mitra's edition, but in most cases the commentary would have been sufficient to restore the right reading. A few various readings, which seemed to deserve being mentioned, will be found

---

[1] Journal of the Bombay Branch of the Royal Asiatic Society, 1877. Extra Number, containing the Detailed Report of a Tour in search of Sanskrit MSS., made in Kásmír, Rajputana, and Central India, by G. Bühler.

in the notes. The MS., though carefully written, is not free from the ordinary blunders. At first one feels inclined to attribute some importance to every peculiarity of a new MS., but very soon one finds out that what seems peculiar, is in reality carelessness. Thus Ait. Âr. III, 1, 5, 2, the Kashmir MS. has pûrvam aksharam rûpam, instead of what alone can be right, pûrvarûpam. Instead of pragayâ pasubhih it writes repeatedly pragaya pasubhih, which is impossible. In III, 2, 2, it leaves out again and again manomaya between khandomaya and vânmaya; but that this is a mere accident we learn later on, where in the same sentence manomayo is found in its right place. Such cases reduce this MS. to its proper level, and make us look with suspicion on any accidental variations, such as I have noticed in my translation.

The additional paragraph, noticed by Dr. Bühler, is very indistinct, and contains, so far as I am able to find out, sânti verses only.

I have no doubt that the discovery of new MSS. of the Upanishads and their commentaries will throw new light on the very numerous difficulties with which a translator of the Upanishads, particularly in attempting a complete and faithful translation, has at present to grapple. Some of the difficulties, which existed thirty years ago, have been removed since by the general progress of Vedic scholar-ship, and by the editions of texts and commentaries and translations of Upanishads, many of which were known at that time in manuscript only. But I fully agree with M. Regnaud as to the difficultés considérables que les meilleures traductions laissent subsister, and which can be solved only by a continued study of the Upanishads, the Âranyakas, the Brâhmanas, and the Vedânta-sûtras.

MEANING OF THE WORD UPANISHAD.

How Upanishad became the recognised name of the philosophical treatises contained in the Veda is difficult to explain. Most European scholars are agreed in deriving upa-ni-shad from the root sad, to sit down, preceded by the two prepositions ni, down, and upa, near, so that it would express the idea of session, or assembly of pupils sitting down near their teacher to listen to his instruction. In the Trikâ*nd*a*s*esha, upanishad is explained by samîpasa-dana, sitting down near a person [1].

Such a word, however, would have been applicable, it would seem, to any other portion of the Veda as well as to the chapters called Upanishad, and it has never been explained how its meaning came thus to be restricted. It is still more strange that upanishad, in the sense of session or assembly, has never, so far as I am aware, been met with. Whenever the word occurs, it has the meaning of doctrine, secret doctrine, or is simply used as the title of the philosophic treatises which constitute the *g*ñânakâ*nd*a, the knowledge portion, as opposed to the karmakâ*nd*a, the work or ceremonial portion, of the Veda.

Native philosophers seem never to have thought of deriving upanishad from sad, to sit down. They derive it either from the root sad, in the sense of destruction, supposing these ancient treatises to have received their name because they were intended to destroy passion and ignorance by means of divine revelation [2], or from the root sad, in the sense of approaching, because a knowledge of Brahman comes near to us by means of the Upanishads, or because we approach Brahman by their help. Another explanation proposed by *S*ankara in his commentary on the Taittirîya-upanishad II, 9, is that the highest bliss is contained in the Upanishad (para*m s*reyo 'syâ*m* nisha*nn*am).

These explanations seem so wilfully perverse that it is difficult to understand the unanimity of native scholars. We ought to take into account, however, that very general tendency among half-educated people, to acquiesce in any etymology which accounts for the most prevalent meaning of a word. The Âra*n*yakas abound in

---

[1] Pâ*n*ini I, 4, 79, has upanishatkr*i*tya.

[2] M. M., History of Ancient Sanskrit Literature, p. 318; Colebrooke, Essays, I, 92; Regnaud, Matériaux, p. 7.

such etymologies, which probably were never intended as real etymologies, in our sense of the word, but simply as plays on words, helping to account somehow for their meaning. The Upanishads, no doubt, were meant to destroy ignorance and passion, and nothing seemed more natural therefore than that their etymological meaning should be that of destroyers[1].

The history and the genius of the Sanskrit language leave little doubt that upanishad meant originally session, particularly a session consisting of pupils, assembled at a respectful distance round their teacher.

With upa alone, sad occurs as early as the hymns of the Rig-veda, in the sense of approaching respectfully[2] :—

Rig-veda IX, 11, 6. Námasâ ít úpa sîdata, 'approach him with praise.' See also Rig-veda X, 73, 11 ; I, 65, 1.

In the *Kh*ândogya-upanishad VI, 13, 1, a teacher says to his pupil, atha mâ prâtar upasîdathâ*h*, 'come to me (for advice) to-morrow morning.'

In the same Upanishad VII, 8, 1, a distinction is made between those who serve their teachers (pari*k*aritâ), and those who are admitted to their more intimate society (upasattâ, comm. samîpaga*h*, antaraṅga*h*, priya*h*).

Again, in the *Kh*ândogya-upanishad VII, 1, we read of a pupil approaching his teacher (upâsasâda or upasasâda), and of the teacher telling him to approach with what he knows, i. e. to tell him first what he has learnt already (yad vettha tena mopasîda[3]).

In the Sûtras (Gobhilîya G*ri*hya-sûtra II, 10, 38) upasad is the recognised term for the position assumed by a pupil with his hands folded and his eyes looking up to the teacher who is to instruct him.

It should be stated, however, that no passage has yet been met with in which upa-ni-sad is used in the sense of pupils approaching and listening to their teacher. In the

---

[1] The distinction between possible and real etymologies is as modern as that between legend and history.

[2] See M. M.'s History of Ancient Sanskrit Literature, p. 318.

[3] See also *Kh*and. Up. VI, 7, 2.

only passage in which upanishasâda occurs (Ait. Âr. II, 2, 1), it is used of Indra sitting down by the side of Visvâmitra, and it is curious to observe that both MSS. and commentaries give here upanishasasâda, an entirely irregular form.

The same is the case with two other roots which are used almost synonymously with sad, viz. âs and vis. We find upa + âs used to express the position which the pupil occupies when listening to his teacher, e.g. Pân. III, 4, 72, upâsito gurum bhavân, 'thou hast approached the Guru,' or upâsito gurur bhavatâ, 'the Guru has been approached by thee.' We find pari + upa + âs used with regard to relations assembled round the bed of a dying friend, Khând. Up. VI, 15; or of hungry children sitting round their mother, and likened to people performing the Agnihotra sacrifice (Khând. Up. V, 24, 5). But I have never met with upa-ni-as in that sense.

We likewise find upa-vis used in the sense of sitting down to a discussion (Khând. Up. I, 8, 2), but I have never found upa + ni + vis as applied to a pupil listening to his teacher.

The two prepositions upa and ni occur, however, with pat, to fly, in the sense of flying down and settling near a person, Khând. Up. IV, 7, 2; IV, 8, 2. And the same prepositions joined to the verb sri, impart to it the meaning of sitting down beneath a person, so as to show him respect: Brih. Âr. I, 4, 11. 'Although a king is exalted, he sits down at the end of the sacrifice below the Brahman,' brahmaivântata upanisrayati.

Sad, with upa and ni, occurs in upanishâdin only, and has there the meaning of subject, e.g. Satap. Brâhm. IX, 4, 3, 3, kshatrâya tad visam adhastâd upanishâdinîm karoti, 'he thus makes the Vis (citizen) below, subject to the Kshatriya.'

Sometimes nishad is used by the side of upanishad, and so far as we can judge, without any difference of meaning [1].

All we can say therefore, for the present, is that upani-

---

[1] Mahâbhârata, Sântiparva, 1613.

shad, besides being the recognised title of certain philosophical treatises, occurs also in the sense of doctrine and
of secret doctrine, and that it seems to have assumed this
meaning from having been used originally in the sense of
session or assembly in which one or more pupils receive
instruction from a teacher.

Thus we find the word upanishad used in the Upanishads
themselves in the following meanings :

1. Secret or esoteric explanation, whether true or false.

2. Knowledge derived from such explanation.

3. Special rules or observances incumbent on those who
have received such knowledge.

4. Title of the books containing such knowledge.

I. Ait. Âr. III, 1, 6, 3. 'For this Upanishad, i.e. in order
to obtain the information about the true meaning of Samhitâ, Târukshya served as a cowherd for a whole year.'

Taitt. Up. I, 3. 'We shall now explain the Upanishad of
the Samhitâ.'

Ait. Âr. III, 2, 5, 1. 'Next follows this Upanishad of the
whole speech. True, all these are Upanishads of the whole
speech, but this they declare especially.'

Talav. Up. IV, 7. 'As you have asked me to tell you the
Upanishad, the Upanishad has now been told you. We
have told you the Brâhmî Upanishad,' i.e. the true meaning
of Brahman.

In the *Kh*ând. Up. III, 11, 3, after the meaning of
Brahman has been explained, the text says : 'To him who
thus knows this Brahma upanishad (the secret doctrine of
Brahman) the sun does not rise and does not set.' In the
next paragraph brahma itself is used, meaning either
Brahman as the object taught in the Upanishad, or, by a
slight change of meaning, the Upanishad itself.

*Kh*ând. Up. I, 13, 4. 'Speech yields its milk to him who
knows this Upanishad (secret doctrine) of the Sâmans in
this wise.'

*Kh*ând. Up. VIII, 8, 4. When Indra and Viro*k*ana had
both misunderstood the teaching of Pra*g*âpati, he says :
'They both go away without having perceived and without
having known the Self, and whoever of these two, whether

Devas or Asuras, will follow this doctrine (upanishad), will perish.'

II. In the *Kh*ând. Up. I, 1, after the deeper meaning of the Udgîtha or Om has been described, the advantage of knowing that deeper meaning is put forward, and it is said that the sacrifice which a man performs with knowledge, with faith, and with the Upanishad, i. e. with an understanding of its deeper meaning, is more powerful.

III. In the Taittirîya-upanishad, at the end of the second chapter, called the Brahmânandavallî, and again at the end of the tenth chapter, the text itself says : Ity upanishad, 'this is the Upanishad, the true doctrine.'

IV. In the Kaushîtaki-upanishad II, 1 ; 2, we read: 'Let him not beg, this is the Upanishad for him who knows this.' Here upanishad stands for vrata or rahasya-vrata, ruie.

Works on the Upanishads.

Anquetil Duperron, Oupnek'hat, 1801, 1802. See page clii.

Rammohun Roy, Translation of Several Principal Books, Passages, and Texts of the Veds. Second edition. London, 1832.

> Translation of the Moonduk-Oopunishud of the Uthurvu Ved, p. 23.
> Translation of the Céna Upanishad, one of the Chapters of the Sáma Véda, p. 41.
> Translation of the Kut'h-Oopunishud of the Ujoor-Ved, p. 55.
> Translation of the Ishopanishad, one of the Chapters of the Yajur Véda, p. 81.

H. T. Colebrooke, Miscellaneous Essays, in three volumes, 1873.

K. J. H. Windischmann, Die Philosophie im Fortgange der Weltgeschichte, 1827–34.

F. W. Windischmann, Sancara, seu de theologumenis Vedanticorum, 1833.

E. Röer, The Taittirîya, Aitareya, *S*vetâ*s*vatara, Kena Îs*â, Ka*th*a, Pra*s*na, Mu*nd*aka, and Mân*d*ûkya Upanishads translated ; Bibliotheca Indica. Calcutta, 1853.

Rajendralal Mitra, The *Kh*ândogya Upanishad, with extracts from the commentary of *S*ankara ; Bibliotheca Indica. Calcutta, 1862.

E. B. Cowell, The Kaushîtaki - brâhma*n*a - upanishad, edited with an English translation; Bibliotheca Indica. Calcutta, 1861.

E. B. Cowell, The Maitri Upanishad, edited with an English translation ; Bibliotheca Indica. Calcutta, 1870.

A. Weber, Die Va*g*rasû*k*î des A*s*vaghosha. Berlin, 1860.

A. Weber, Die Râma-tâpanîya Upanishad. Berlin, 1864.

A. Weber, Analyse der in Anquetil du Perron's Übersetzung enthalten Upanishad ; Indische Studien, vol. i, p. 247 et seq.

A. E. Gough, The Philosophy of the Upanishads ; Calcutta Review, CXXXI.

P. Regnaud, Matériaux pour servir à l'histoire de la Philosophie de l'Inde. Paris, 1876.

Editions of the Upanishads, their commentaries and glosses have been published in the Tattvabodhinî patrikâ, and by Poley (who has also translated several Upanishads into French), by Röer, Cowell, Rajendralal Mitra, Hara*k*andra Vidyâbhûsha*n*a, Vi*s*vanâtha *S*âstrî, Râmamaya Tarkaratna, and others. For fuller titles see Gildemeister, Bibliotheca Sanscrita, and E. Haas, Catalogue of Sanskrit and Pali Books in the British Museum, s. v. Upanishads.

I.

THE *KH*ÂNDOGYA-UPANISHAD.

THE *Kh*ândogya-upanishad belongs to the Sâma-veda. Together with the B*ri*had-âra*n*yaka, which belongs to the Ya*g*ur-veda, it has contributed the most important materials to what may be called the orthodox philosophy of India, the Vedânta [1], i. e. the end, the purpose, the highest object of the Veda. It consists of eight adhyâyas or lectures, and formed part of a *Kh*ândogya-brâhma*n*a, in which it was preceded by two other adhyâyas. While MSS. of the *Kh*ândogya-upanishad and its commentary are frequent, no MSS. of the whole Brâhma*n*a has been met with in Europe. Several scholars had actually doubted its existence, but Rajendralal Mitra [2], in the Introduction to his translation of the *Kh*ândogya-upanishad, states that in India 'MSS. of the work are easily available, though as yet he has seen no commentary attached to the Brâhma*n*a portion of any one of them.' 'According to general accep-

---

[1] Vedânta, as a technical term, did not mean originally the last portions of the Veda, or chapters placed, as it were, at the end of a volume of Vedic literature, but the end, i. e. the object, the highest purpose of the Veda. There are, of course, passages, like the one in the Taittirîya-âra*n*yaka (ed. Rajendralal Mitra, p. 820), which have been misunderstood both by native and European scholars, and where vedânta means simply the end of the Veda :—yo vedâdau svara*h* prokto vedânte *k*a pratish*th*ita*h*, 'the Om which is pronounced at the beginning of the Veda, and has its place also at the end of the Veda.' Here vedânta stands simply in opposition to vedâdau, and it is impossible to translate it, as Sâya*n*a does, by Vedânta or Upanishad. Vedânta, in the sense of philosophy, occurs in the Taittirîya-âra*n*yaka (p. 817), in a verse of the Nârâya*n*îya-upanishad, repeated in the Mu*nd*aka-upanishad III, 2, 6, and elsewhere, vedântavi*g*ñânasunis*k*itârthâ*h*, 'those who have well understood the object of the knowledge arising from the Vedânta,' not 'from the last books of the Veda ;' and *S*vetâsvatara-up. VI, 22, vedânte parama*m* guhyam, 'the highest mystery in the Vedânta.' Afterwards it is used in the plural also, e. g. Kshurikopanishad, 10 (Bibl. Ind. p. 210), pu*nd*arîketi vedânteshu nigadyate, 'it is called pu*nd*arîka in the Vedântas,' i. e. in the *Kh*ândogya and other Upanishads, as the commentator says, but not in the last books of each Veda. A curious passage is found in the Gautama-sûtras XIX, 12, where a distinction seems to be made between Upanishad and Vedânta. Sacred Books, vol. ii, p. 272.

[2] *Kh*ândogya-upanishad, translated by Rajendralal Mitra, Calcutta, 1862, Introduction, p. 17.

tation,' he adds, 'the work embraces ten chapters, of which
the first two are reckoned to be the Brâhmaṇa, and the rest
is known under the name of Khândogya-upanishad. In
their arrangement and style the two portions differ greatly,
and judged by them they appear to be productions of very
different ages, though both are evidently relics of pretty
remote antiquity. Of the two chapters of the Khândogya-
brâhmaṇa [1], the first includes eight sûktas (hymns) on the
ceremony of marriage, and the rites necessary to be observed at the birth of a child. The first sûkta is intended
to be recited when offering an oblation to Agni on the
occasion of a marriage, and its object is to pray for prosperity in behalf of the married couple. The second prays
for long life, kind relatives, and a numerous progeny. The
third is the marriage pledge by which the contracting
parties bind themselves to each other. Its spirit may be
guessed from a single verse. In talking of the unanimity
with which they will dwell, the bridegroom addresses his
bride, " That heart of thine shall be mine, and this heart of
mine shall be thine [2]." The fourth and the fifth invoke
Agni, Vâyu, Kandramas, and Sûrya to bless the couple and
ensure healthful progeny. The sixth is a mantra for
offering an oblation on the birth of a child; and the seventh
and the eighth are prayers for its being healthy, wealthy,
and powerful, not weak, poor, or mute, and to ensure a
profusion of wealth and milch-cows. The first sûkta of the
second chapter is addressed to the Earth, Agni, and Indra,
with a prayer for wealth, health, and prosperity ; the
second, third, fourth, fifth, and sixth are mantras for offering oblations to cattle, the manes, Sûrya, and divers minor
deities. The seventh is a curse upon worms, insects, flies,
and other nuisances, and the last, the concluding mantra of
the marriage ceremony, in which a general blessing is
invoked for all concerned.'

After this statement there can be but little doubt that

---

[1] It begins, Om, deva savitaḥ, pra suva yagñam pra suva yagñapatim
bhagâya. The second begins, yaḥ prâkyâm disi sarparâga esha te baliḥ.

[2] Yad etad dhridayam tava tad astu hridayam mama, Yad idam hridayam
mama tad astu hridayam tava.

this Upanishad originally formed part of a Brâhma*n*a. This may have been called either by a general name, the Brâhma*n*a of the *Kh*andogas, the followers of the Sâma-veda, or, on account of the prominent place occupied in it by the Upanishad, the Upanishad-brâhma*n*a[1]. In that case it would be one of the eight Brâhma*n*as of the Sâma-veda, enumerated by Kumârila Bha*tt*a and others[2], and called simply Upanishad, scil. Brâhma*n*a.

The text of the Upanishad with the commentary of *S*ankara and the gloss of Ânandagiri has been published in the Bibliotheca Indica. The edition can only claim the character of a manuscript, and of a manuscript not always very correctly read.

A translation of the Upanishad was published, likewise in the Bibliotheca Indica, by Rajendralal Mitra.

It is one of the Upanishads that was translated into Persian under the auspices of Dârâ Shukoh[3], and from Persian into French by Anquetil Duperron, in his Oupnekhat, i. e. Secretum Tegendum. Portions of it were translated into English by Colebrooke in his Miscellaneous Essays, into Latin and German by F. W. Windischmann, in his Sankara, seu de theologumenis Vedanticorum (Bonn, 1833), and in a work published by his father, K. J. H. Windischmann, Die Philosophie im Fortgang der Weltgeschichte (Bonn, 1827–34). Professor A. Weber has treated of this Upanishad in his Indische Studien I, 254; likewise M. P. Regnaud in his Matériaux pour servir à l'histoire de la philosophie de l'Inde (Paris, 1876) and Mr. Gough in several articles on 'the Philosophy of the Upanishads,' in the Calcutta Review, No. CXXXI.

I have consulted my predecessors whenever there was a serious difficulty to solve in the translation of these ancient texts. These difficulties are very numerous, as those know

---

[1] The same name seems, however, to be given to the adhyâya of the Talavakâra-brâhma*n*a, which contains the Kena-upanishad.

[2] M. M., History of Ancient Sanskrit Literature, p. 348. Most valuable information on the literature of the Sâma-veda may be found in Dr. Burnell's editions of the smaller Brâhma*n*as of that Veda.

[3] M. M., History of Ancient Sanskrit Literature, p. 325.

best who have attempted to give complete translations of these ancient texts. It will be seen that my translation differs sometimes very considerably from those of my predecessors. Though I have but seldom entered into any controversy with them, they may rest assured that I have not deviated from them without careful reflection.

II.

THE TALAVAKÂRA-UPANISHAD.

THIS Upanishad is best known by the name of Kena-upanishad, from its first word. The name of brâhmî-upanishad (IV, 7) can hardly be considered as a title. It means 'the teaching of Brahman,' and is used with reference to other Upanishads also[1]. Sankara, in his commentary, tells us that this Upanishad forms the ninth adhyâya of a Brâhmana, or, if we take his words quite literally, he says, 'the beginning of the ninth adhyâya is "the Upanishad beginning with the words Keneshitam, and treating of the Highest Brahman has to be taught."' In the eight preceeding adhyâyas, he tells us, all the sacred rites or sacrifices had been fully explained, and likewise the meditations (upâsana) on the prâna (vital breath) which belongs to all these sacrifices, and those meditations also which have reference to the fivefold and sevenfold Sâmans. After that followed Gâyatra-sâman and the Vamsa, the genealogical list. All this would naturally form the subject of a Sâma-veda-brâhmana, and we find portions corresponding to the description given by Sankara in the Khândogya-upanishad, e. g. the fivefold Sâman, II, 2 ; the sevenfold Sâman, II, 8 ; the Gâyatra-sâman, III, 12, 1.

Ânandagñâna tells us that our Upanishad belonged to the Sâkhâ of the Talavakâras.

All this had formerly to be taken on trust, because no Brâhmana was known containing the Upanishad. Dr. Burnell, however, has lately discovered a Brâhmana of the Sâma-veda which comes very near the description given by Sankara. In a letter dated Tanjore, 8th Dec. 1878, he

---

[1] See before, p. lxxxiii.

writes: 'It appears to me that you would be glad to know
the following about the Kena-upanishad, as it occurs in my
MS. of the Talavakâra-brâhma*n*a.

'The last book but one of this Brâhma*n*a is termed
Upanishad-brâhma*n*a. It consists of 145 kha*nd*as treating
of the Gâyatra-sâman, and the 134th is a Va*m*sa. The
Kena-upanishad comprises the 135–145 kha*nd*as, or the
tenth anuvâka of a chapter. The 139th section begins: âsâ
vâ idam agra âsît, &c.

'My MS. of the Talavakâra-brâhma*n*a agrees, as regards
the contents, exactly with what *S*ankara says, but not in
the divisions. He says that the Kena-upanishad begins the
ninth adhyâya, but that is not so in my MS. Neither
the beginning nor the end of this Upanishad is noticed
particularly.

'The last book of this Brâhma*n*a is the Ârsheya-brâh-
ma*n*a, which I printed last February.

'Among the teachers quoted in the Brâhma*n*a I have
noticed both Tâ*nd*ya and *S*â*t*yâyani. I should not be
surprised to find in it the difficult quotations which are
incorrectly given in the MSS. of Sâya*n*a's commentary on
the Rig-veda. The story of Apâlâ, quoted by Sâya*n*a in
his commentary on the Rig-veda, VIII, 80, as from the
*S*â*t*yâyanaka, is found word for word, except some trivial
var. lectiones, in sections 220–221 of the Agnish*t*oma book
of the Talavakâra-brâhma*n*a. The *S*â*t*yâyanins seem to
be closely connected with the Talavakâra-*s*âkhâ.'

From a communication made by Dr. Burnell to the
Academy (1 Feb. 79), I gather that this Talavakâra-brâhma*n*a is called by those who study it '*G*aiminîya-brâhma*n*a,'
after the *S*âkhâ of the Sâma-veda which they follow. The
account given in the Academy differs on some particulars
slightly from that given in Dr. Burnell's letter to me. He
writes: 'The largest part of the Brâhma*n*a treats of the
sacrifices and the Sâmans used at them. The first chapter
is on the Agnihotra, and the Agnish*t*oma and other rites
follow at great length. Then comes a book termed
Upanishad-brâhma*n*a. This contains 145 sections in four
chapters. It begins with speculations on the Gâyatra-

sâman, followed by a Va*ms*a ; next, some similar matter and another Va*ms*a. Then (§§ 135–138) comes the Kena-upanishad (Talavakâra). The last book is the Ârsheya. The Upanishad forms the tenth anuvâka of the fourth chapter, not the beginning of a ninth chapter, as *S*ankara remarks.'

The Kena-upanishad has been frequently published and translated. It forms part of Dârâ Shukoh's Persian, and Anquetil Duperron's Latin translations. It was several times published in English by Rammohun Roy (Translations of Several Principal Books, Passages, and Texts of the Veda, London, 1832, p. 41), in German by Windischmann, Poley, and others. It has been more or less fully discussed by Colebrooke, Windischmann, Poley, Weber, Röer, Gough, and Regnaud in the books mentioned before.

Besides the text of this Upanishad contained in the Brâhma*n*a of the Sâma-veda, there is another text, slightly differing, belonging to the Atharva-veda, and there are commentaries on both texts (Colebrooke, Misc. Essays, 1873, II, p. 80).

III.

THE AITAREYA-ÂRA*N*YAKA.

IN giving a translation of the Aitareya-upanishad, I found it necessary to give at the same time a translation of that portion of the Aitareya-âra*n*yaka which precedes the Upanishad. The Âra*n*yakas seem to have been from the beginning the proper repositories of the ancient Upanishads, though it is difficult at first sight to find out in what relation the Upanishads stood to the Âra*n*yakas. The Âra*n*yakas are to be read and studied, not in the village (grâme), but in the forest, and so are the Upanishads. But the subjects treated in the Upanishads belong to a very different order from those treated in the other portions of the Âra*n*yakas, the former being philosophical, the latter liturgical.

The liturgical chapters of the Âra*n*yakas might quite as well have formed part of the Brâhma*n*as, and but for the restriction that they are to be read in the forest, it is difficult to distinguish between them and the Brâhma*n*as. The first chapter of the Aitareya-âraṇyaka is a mere continuation of the Aitareya-brâhmaṇa, and gives the description of the Mahâvrata, the last day but one of the Gavâmayana, a sattra or sacrifice which is supposed to last a whole year. The duties which are to be performed by the Hotri priests are described in the Aitareya-âraṇyaka; not all, however, but those only which are peculiar to the Mahâvrata day. The general rules for the performance of the Mahâvrata are to be taken over from other sacrifices, such as the Viṣvagit, Katurviṃsa, &c., which form the type (prakriti) of the Mahâvrata. Thus the two ṣastras or recitations, called âgya-praüga, are taken over from the Viṣvagit, the ṣastras of the Hotrakas from the Katurviṃsa. The Mahâvrata is treated here as belonging to the Gavâmayana sattra, which is described in a different Ṣâkhâ, see Taittirîya Saṃhitâ VII, 5, 8, and partly in other Vedas. It is the day preceding the udayanîya, the last day of the sattra. It can be celebrated, however, by itself also, as an ekâha or ahîna sacrifice, and in the latter case it is the tenth day of the Ekadaṣarâtra (eleven nights sacrifice) called Puṇḍarîka.

Sâyaṇa does not hesitate to speak of the Aitareya-âraṇyaka as a part of the Brâhmaṇa[1]; and a still earlier authority, Ṣankara, by calling the Aitareya-upanishad by the name of Bahvrika-brâhmaṇa-upanishad[2], seems to imply that both the Upanishad and the Âraṇyaka may be classed as Brâhmaṇa.

The Aitareya-âraṇyaka appears at first sight a miscellaneous work, consisting of liturgical treatises in the first, fourth, and fifth Âraṇyakas, and of three Upanishads, in the second and third Âraṇyakas. This, however, is not the case. The first Âraṇyaka is purely liturgical, giving a description of the Mahâvrata, so far as it concerns the Hotri priest. It is written in the ordinary Brâhmaṇa style. Then follows the first Upanishad, Âraṇyaka II, 1–3, showing

---

[1] Aitareyabrâhmaṇe 'sti kâṇḍam âraṇyakâbhidham (introduction), a remark which he repeats in the fifth Âraṇyaka. He also speaks of the Âraṇyaka-vratarûpam brâhmaṇam; see p. cxiv, l. 24.

[2] In the same manner the Kaushîtaki-upanishad is properly called Kaushîtaki-brâhmaṇa-upanishad, though occurring in the Âraṇyaka; see Kaushîtaki-brâhmaṇa-upanishad, ed. Cowell, p. 30.

how certain portions of the Mahâvrata, as described in the first Âra*n*yaka, can be made to suggest a deeper meaning, and ought to lead the mind of the sacrificer away from the purely outward ceremonial to meditation on higher subjects. Without a knowledge of the first Âra*n*yaka therefore the first Upanishad would be almost unintelligible, and though its translation was extremely tedious, it could not well have been omitted.

The second and third Upanishads are not connected with the ceremonial of the Mahâvrata, but in the fourth and fifth Âra*n*yakas the Mahâvrata forms again the principal subject, treated, however, not as before in the style of the Brâhma*n*as, but in the style of Sûtras. The fourth Âra*n*yaka contains nothing but a list of the Mahânâmnî hymns [1], but the fifth describes the Mahâvrata again, so that if the first Âra*n*yaka may be looked upon as a portion of the Aitareya-brâhma*n*as, the fifth could best be classed with the Sûtras of Â*s*valâyana.

To a certain extent this fact, the composite character of the Aitareya-âra*n*yaka, is recognised even by native scholars, who generally do not trouble themselves much on such questions. They look both on the Aitareya-brâhma*n*a and on the greater portion of Aitareya-âra*n*yaka as the works of an inspired *R*ishi, Mahidâsa Aitareya [2], but they consider the fourth and fifth books of the Âra*n*yaka as contributed by purely human authors, such as Â*s*valâyana and *S*aunaka, who, like other Sûtrakâras, took in verses belonging to other *S*âkhâs, and did not confine their rules to their own *S*âkhâ only.

There are many legends about Mahidâsa, the reputed author of the Aitareya-brâhma*n*a and Âra*n*yaka. He is

---

[1] See Boehtlingk and Roth, s.v. 'Neun Vedische Verse die in ihrem vollständigen Wortlaut aber noch nicht nachgewiesen sind.' Weber, Indische Studien VIII, 68. How these hymns are to be employed we learn from the Â*s*valâyana-sûtras VII, 12, 10, where we are told that if the Udgâtr*i*s sing the *S*âkvara Sâman as the Pr*i*sh*th*astotra, the nine verses beginning with Vidâ maghavan, and known by the name of Mahânâmnî, are to be joined in a peculiar manner. The only excuse given, why these Mahânâmnîs are mentioned here, and not in the Brâhma*n*a, is that they are to be studied in the forest.

[2] M. M., History of Ancient Sanskrit Literature, pp. 177, 335.

quoted several times as Mahidâsa Aitareya in the Âra*n*yaka itself, though not in the Brâhma*n*a. We also meet his name in the *Kh*ândogya-upanishad (III, 16, 7), where we are told that he lived to an age of 116 years[1]. All this, however, would only prove that, at the time of the composition or collection of these Âra*n*yakas and Upanishads, a sage was known of the name of Mahidâsa Aitareya, descended possibly from Itara or Itarâ, and that one text of the Brâhma*n*as and the Âra*n*yakas of the Bahv*ri*ƙas was handed down in the family of the Aitareyins.

Not content with this apparently very obvious explanation, later theologians tried to discover their own reasons for the name of Aitareya. Thus Sâya*n*a, in his introduction to the Aitareya-brâhma*n*a[2], tells us that there was once a *Ri*shi who had many wives. One of them was called Itarâ, and she had a son called Mahidâsa. His father preferred the sons of his other wives to Mahidâsa, and once he insulted him in the sacrificial hall, by placing his other sons on his lap, but not Mahidâsa. Mahidâsa's mother, seeing her son with tears in his eyes, prayed to her tutelary goddess, the Earth (svîyakuladevatâ Bhûmi*h*), and the goddess in her heavenly form appeared in the midst of the assembly, placed Mahidâsa on a throne, and on account of his learning, gave him the gift of knowing the Brâhma*n*a, consisting of forty adhyâyas, and, as Sâya*n*a calls it, another Brâhma*n*a, 'treating of the Âra*n*yaka duties' (âra*n*yakavratarûpam brâhma*n*am).

Without attaching much value to the legend of Itarâ, we see at all events that Sâya*n*a considered what we call the Aitareyâra*n*yaka as a kind of Brâhma*n*a, not however the whole of it, but only the first, second, and third Âra*n*yakas (atha mahâvratam îtyâdikam a*k*âryâ a*k*âryâ ityantam). How easy it was for Hindu theologians to invent such legends we see from another account of Mahidâsa, given by Ânandatîrtha in his notes on the Aitareya-upani-

---

[1] Not 1600 years, as I printed by mistake; for 24 + 44 + 48 make 116 years. Rajendralal Mitra should not have corrected his right rendering 116 into 1600. Ait. Âr. Introduction, p. 3.

[2] M. M., History of Ancient Sanskrit Literature, p. 336.

shad. He, as Colebrooke was the first to point out, takes Mahidâsa 'to be an incarnation of Nârâya*n*a, proceeding from Vi*s*âla, son of Ab*g*a,' and he adds, that on the sudden appearance of this deity at a solemn celebration, the whole assembly of gods and priests (suraviprasaṅgha) fainted, but at the intercession of Brahmâ, they were revived, and after making their obeisance, they were instructed in holy science. This avatâra was called Mahidâsa, because those venerable personages (mahin) declared themselves to be his slaves (dâsa) [1].

In order properly to understand this legend, we must remember that Ânandatîrtha, or rather Vi*s*ve*s*varatîrtha, whose commentary he explains, treated the whole of the Mahaitareya-upanishad from a Vaish*n*ava point of view, and that his object was to identify Mahidâsa with Nârâya*n*a. He therefore represents Nârâya*n*a or Hari as the avatâra of Vi*s*âla, the son of Brahman (ab*g*asuta), who appeared at a sacrifice, as described before, who received then and there the name of Mahidâsa (or Mahîdâsa), and who taught this Upanishad. Any other person besides Mahidâsa would have been identified with the same ease by Vi*s*ve*s*vara-tîrtha with Vish*n*u or Bhagavat.

A third legend has been made up out of these two by European scholars who represent Mahidâsa as the son of Vi*s*âla and Itarâ, two persons who probably never met before, for even the Vaish*n*ava commentator does not attempt to take liberties with the name of Aitareya, but simply states that the Upanishad was called Aitareyî, from Aitareya.

Leaving these legends for what they are worth, we may at all events retain the fact that, whoever was the author of the Aitareya-brâhma*n*a and the first three books of the Aitareya-âra*n*yaka, was not the author of the two concluding Âra*n*yakas. And this is confirmed in different ways. Sâya*n*a, when quoting in his commentary on the Rig-veda from the last books, constantly calls it a Sûtra of *S*aunaka, while the fourth Âra*n*yaka is specially ascribed

---

[1] Colebrooke, Miscellaneous Essays, 1873, II, p. 42.

to Âsvalâyana, the pupil and successor of Saunaka[1]. These two names of Saunaka and Âsvalâyana are frequently intermixed. If, however, in certain MSS. the whole of the Aitareya-âranyaka is sometimes ascribed either to Âsvalâyana or Saunaka, this is more probably due to the colophon of the fourth and fifth Âranyakas having been mistaken for the title of the whole work than to the fact that such MSS. represent the text of the Âranyaka, as adopted by the school of Âsvalâyana.

The Aitareya-âranyaka consists of the following five Âranyakas:

The first Âranyaka has five Adhyâyas:

1. First Adhyâya, Atha mahâvratam, has four Khandas, 1–4.
2. Second Adhyâya, Â tvâ ratham, has four Khandas, 5–8.
3. Third Adhyâya, Hiṅkârena, has eight[2] Khandas, 9–16.
4. Fourth Adhyâya, Atha sûdadohâh, has three Khandas, 17–19.
5. Fifth Adhyâya, Vasam samsati, has three Khandas, 20–22.

The second Âranyaka has seven Adhyâyas:

6. First Adhyâya, Eshâ panthâh, has eight Khandas, 1–8.
7. Second Adhyâya, Esha imam lokam, has four Khandas, 9–12.
8. Third Adhyâya, Yo ha vâ âtmânam, has eight (not three) Khandas, 13–20.
9. Fourth Adhyâya, Âtmâ vâ idam, has three Khandas, 21–23.
10. Fifth Adhyâya, Purushe ha vâ, has one Khanda, 24.
11. Sixth Adhyâya, Ko 'yam âtmeti, has one Khanda, 25.
12. Seventh Adhyâya, Vâṅ me manasi, has one Khanda, 26.

The third Âranyaka has two Adhyâyas:

13. First Adhyâya, Athâtah samhitâyâ upanishat, has six Khandas, 1–6.
14. Second Adhyâya, Prâno vamsa iti sthavirah Sâkalyah, has six Khandas, 7–12.

The fourth Âranyaka has one Adhyâya:

15. First Adhyâya, Vidâ maghavan, has one Khanda (the Mahânâmnî's).

The fifth Âranyaka has three Adhyâyas:

16. First Adhyâya, Mahâvratasya paṅkavimsatim, has six Khandas, 1–6.
17. Second Adhyâya, (Grîvâh) Yasyedam, has five Khandas, 7–11.
18. Third Adhyâya, (Ûrû) Indrâgnî, has four Khandas, 11–14.

Bahvrika-upanishad — *Aitareya-upanishad* (items 9–11)

---

[1] M. M., History of Ancient Sanskrit Literature, p. 235.
[2] Not six, as in Rajendralal Mitra's edition.

With regard to the Upanishad, we must distinguish between the Aitareya-upanishad, properly so-called, which fills the fourth, fifth, and sixth adhyâyas of the second Âra*n*yaka, and the Mahaitareya-upanishad [1], also called by a more general name Bahv*ri*ka-upanishad, which comprises the whole of the second and third Âra*n*yakas.

The Persian translator seems to have confined himself to the second Âra*n*yaka [2], to which he gives various titles, Sarbsar, Asarbeh, Antrteheh. That Antrteheh انترتہ is a misreading of ايترتہ was pointed out long ago by Burnouf, and the same explanation applies probably to اسربہ, asarbeh, and if to that, then to Sarbsar also. No explanation has ever been given why the Aitareya-upanishad should have been called Sarvasâra, which Professor Weber thinks was corrupted into Sarbsar. At all events the Aitareya-upanishad is not the Sarvasâra-upanishad, the Oupnek'hat Sarb, more correctly called Sarvopanishatsâra, and ascribed either to the Taittirîyaka or to the Atharva-veda [3].

The Aitareya-upanishad, properly so called, has been edited and translated in the Bibliotheca Indica by Dr. Röer. The whole of the Aitareya-âra*n*yaka with Sâya*n*a's commentary was published in the same series by Rajendralal Mitra.

Though I have had several MSS. of the text and commentary at my disposal, I have derived little aid from them, but have throughout endeavoured to restore that text which *S*ankara (the pupil of Govinda) and Sâya*n*a had before them. Sâya*n*a, for the Upanishad portion, follows *S*ankara's commentary, of which we have a gloss by Ânanda*g*ñâna.

Colebrooke in his Essays (vol. ii, p. 42) says that he

---

[1] This may have been the origin of a *Ri*shi Mahaitareya, by the side of the *Ri*shi Aitareya, mentioned in the Â*s*valâyana G*ri*hya-sûtras III, 4 (ed. Stenzler). Professor Weber takes Aitareya and Mahaitareya here as names of works, but he admits that in the *S*ânkhâyana G*ri*hya-sûtras they are clearly names of *Ri*shis (Ind. Stud. I, p. 389).

[2] He translates II, 1–II, 3, 4, leaving out the rest of the third adhyâya; afterwards II, 4–II, 7.

[3] Bibliotheca Indica, the Atharva*n*a-upanishads, p. 394.

possessed one gloss by Nârâya*n*endra on *S*ankara's commentary, and another by Ânandatîrtha on a different gloss
for the entire Upanishad. The gloss by Nârâya*n*endra[1],
however, is, so Dr. Rost informs me, the same as that of
Ânanda*g*ñâna, while, so far as I can see, the gloss contained
in MS. E. I. H. 2386 (also MS. Wilson 401), to which Colebrooke refers, is not a gloss by Ânandatîrtha at all, but a
gloss by Vi*s*ve*s*varatîrtha on a commentary by Ânandatîr-
thabhagavatpâdâ*k*ârya, also called Pûr*n*apra*g*ñâ*k*ârya, who
explained the whole of the Mahaitareya-upanishad from a
Vaish*n*ava point of view.

IV.

THE KAUSHÎTAKI-BRÂHMA*N*A-UPANISHAD.

THE Kaushîtaki-upanishad, or, as it is more properly
called, the Kaushîtaki-brâhma*n*a-upanishad, belongs, like
the Aitareya-upanishad, to the followers of the Rig-veda. It
was translated into Persian under the title of Kokhenk, and
has been published in the Bibliotheca Indica with *S*ankarânanda's commentary and an excellent translation by
Professor Cowell.

Though it is called the Kaushîtaki-brâhma*n*a-upanishad,
it does not form part of the Kaushîtaki-brâhma*n*a in 30
adhyâyas which we possess, and we must therefore account
for its name by admitting that the Âra*n*yaka, of which it
formed a portion, could be reckoned as part of the Brâhma*n*a literature of the Rig-veda (see Aitareya-âra*n*yaka,
Introduction, p. xcii), and that hence the Upanishad might
be called the Upanishad of the Brâhma*n*a of the Kaushîtakins[2].

From a commentary discovered by Professor Cowell
it appears that the four adhyâyas of this Upanishad

---

[1] A MS. in the Notices of Sanskrit MSS., vol. ii, p. 133, ascribed to Abhi-
navanârâya*n*endra, called Âtmasha*t*kabhâshya*t*îkâ, begins like the gloss edited
by Dr. Röer, and ends like Sâya*n*a's commentary on the seventh adhyâya, as
edited by Rajendralal Mitra. The same name is given in MS. Wilson 94,
*S*rîmatkaivaly*e*ndrasarasvatîpû*g*yapâda*s*ishya-*s*rîmadabhinavanârâya*n*endrasara-
svatî.

[2] A Mahâ-kaush*î*taki-brâhma*n*a is quoted, but has not yet been met with.

were followed by five other adhyâyas, answering, so far as
we can judge from a few extracts, to some of the adhyâyas
of the Aitareya-âra*n*yaka, while an imperfect MS. of an
Âra*n*yaka in the Royal Library at Berlin (Weber, Catalogue,
p. 20) begins, like the Aitareya-âra*n*yaka, with a description of the Mahâvrata, followed by discussions on the uktha
in the second adhyâya; and then proceeds in the third
adhyâya to give the story of *K*itra Gâṅgyâyani in the same
words as the Kaushîtaki-upanishad in the first adhyâya.
Other MSS. again adopt different divisions. In one MS.
of the commentary (MS. A), the four adhyâyas of the
Upanishad are counted as sixth, seventh, eighth, and ninth
(ending with ityârâ*n*yake navamo 'dhyâya*h*); in another
(MS. P) the third and fourth adhyâyas of the Upanishad
are quoted as the fifth and sixth of the Kaushîtakyâra*n*yaka,
possibly agreeing therefore, to a certain extent, with the
Berlin MS. In a MS. of the *S*âṅkhâyana Âra*n*yaka in
the Royal Library at Berlin, there are 15 adhyâyas, 1 and 2
corresponding to Ait. Âr. 1 and 5; 3–6 containing the Kaushîtaki-upanishad; 7 and 8 corresponding to Ait. Âr. 3 [1].
Poley seems to have known a MS. in which the four
adhyâyas of the Upanishad formed the first, seventh,
eighth, and ninth adhyâyas of a Kaushîtaki-brâhma*n*a.

As there were various recensions of the Kaushîtaki-brâhma*n*a (the *S*âṅkhâyana, Kauthuma, &c.), the Upanishad
also exists in at least two texts. The commentator, in
some of its MSS., refers to the various readings of the
*S*âkhâs, explaining them, whenever there seems to be
occasion for it. I have generally followed the text which is
presupposed by *S*aṅkarânanda's Dîpikâ, and contained in
MSS. F, G (Cowell, Preface, p. v), so far as regards the
third and fourth adhyâyas. According to Professor Cowell,
Vidyâra*n*ya in his Sarvopanishadarthânubhûtiprakâ*s*a followed the text of the commentary, while *S*aṅkarâ*k*ârya,
if we may trust to extracts in his commentary on the
Vedânta-sûtras, followed the other text, contained in MS.
A (Cowell, Preface, p. v).

---

[1] See Weber, History of Sanskrit Literature, p. 50.

The style of the commentator differs in so marked a manner from that of *Sankarâkârya*, that even without the fact that the author of the commentary on the Kaushîtaki-upanishad is called *Sankarânanda*, it would have been difficult to ascribe it, as has been done by some scholars, to the famous *Sankarâkârya*. *Sankarânanda* is called the teacher of Mâdhavâkârya (Hall, Index, p. 98), and the disciple of Ânandâtma Muni (Hall, Index, p. 116).

I have had the great advantage of being able to consult for the Kaushîtaki-upanishad, not only the text and commentary as edited by Professor Cowell, but also his excellent translation. If I differ from him in some points, this is but natural, considering the character of the text and the many difficulties that have still to be solved, before we can hope to arrive at a full understanding of these ancient philosophical treatises.

V.

THE VÂGASANEYI-SAMHITÂ-UPANISHAD.

THE Vâgasaneyi-samhitâ-upanishad, commonly called from its beginning, Îsâ or Îsâvâsya, forms the fortieth and concluding chapter of the Samhitâ of the White Yagur-veda. If the Samhitâs are presupposed by the Brâhmanas, at least in that form in which we possess them, then this Upanishad, being the only one that forms part of a Samhitâ, might claim a very early age. The Samhitâ of the White Yagur-veda, however, is acknowledged to be of modern origin, as compared with the Samhitâ of the Black Yagur-veda, and it would not be safe therefore to ascribe to this Upanishad a much higher antiquity than to those which have found a place in the older Brâhmanas and Âranyakas.

There are differences between the text, as contained in the Yagur-veda-samhitâ, and the text of the Upanishad by itself. Those which are of some interest have been mentioned in the notes.

In some notes appended to the translation of this Upanishad I have called attention to what seems to me its peculiar character, namely, the recognition of the necessity of works as a preparation for the reception of the highest knowledge. This agrees well with the position occupied by this Upanishad at the end of the Samhitâ, in which the sacrificial works and the hymns that are to accompany them are contained. The doctrine that the moment a man is enlightened, he becomes free, as taught in other Upanishads, led to a rejection of all discipline and a condemnation of all sacrifices, which could hardly have been tolerated in the last chapter of the Yagur-veda-samhitâ, the liturgical Veda par excellence.

Other peculiarities of this Upanishad are the name Îs, lord, a far more personal name for the highest Being than Brahman; the asurya (demoniacal) or asûrya (sunless) worlds to which all go who have lost their self; Mâtarisvan, used in the sense of prâna or spirit; asnâviram, without muscles, in the sense of incorporeal; and the distinction between sambhûti and asambhûti in verses 12–14.

The editions of the text, commentaries, and glosses, and the earlier translations may be seen in the works quoted before, p. lxxxiv.

*KH*ÂNDOGYA-UPANISHAD.

*KH*ÂNDOGYA-UPANISHAD.

FIRST PRAPÂ*TH*AKA.

First Kha*nd*a [1].

1. Let a man meditate on the syllable [2] Om, called the udgîtha; for the udgîtha (a portion of the Sâma-veda) is sung, beginning with Om.

The full account, however, of Om is this:—

2. The essence [3] of all beings is the earth, the essence of the earth is water, the essence of water

---

[1] The *KH*ândogya-upanishad begins with recommending meditation on the syllable Om, a sacred syllable that had to be pronounced at the beginning of each Veda and of every recitation of Vedic hymns. As connected with the Sâma-veda, that syllable Om is called udgîtha. Its more usual name is pra*n*ava. The object of the Upanishad is to explain the various meanings which the syllable Om may assume in the mind of a devotee, some of them being extremely artificial and senseless, till at last the highest meaning of Om is reached, viz. Brahman, the intelligent cause of the universe.

[2] Akshara means both syllable and the imperishable, i.e. Brahman.

[3] Essence, rasa, is explained in different ways, as origin, support, end, cause, and effect. Rasa means originally the sap of trees. That sap may be conceived either as the essence extracted from the tree, or as what gives vigour and life to a tree. In the former case it might be transferred to the conception of effect, in the latter to that of cause. In our sentence it has sometimes the one, sometimes the other meaning. Earth is the support of all beings, water pervades the earth, plants arise from water, man lives by plants, speech is the best part of man, the Rig-veda the best part of speech, the Sâma-veda the best extract from the *Ri*k, udgîtha, or the syllable Om, the crown of the Sâma-veda.

the plants, the essence of plants man, the essence of man speech, the essence of speech the Rig-veda, the essence of the Rig-veda the Sâma-veda [1], the essence of the Sâma-veda the udgîtha (which is Om).

3. That udgîtha (Om) is the best of all essences, the highest, deserving the highest place [2], the eighth.

4. What then is the *Rik?* What is the Sâman? What is the udgîtha? This is the question.

5. The *Rik* indeed is speech, Sâman is breath, the udgîtha is the syllable Om. Now speech and breath, or *Rik* and Sâman, form one couple.

6. And that couple is joined together in the syllable Om. When two people come together, they fulfil each other's desire.

7. Thus he who knowing this, meditates on the syllable (Om), the udgîtha, becomes indeed a fulfiller of desires.

8. That syllable is a syllable of permission, for whenever we permit anything, we say Om, yes. Now permission is gratification. He who knowing this meditates on the syllable (Om), the udgîtha, becomes indeed a gratifier of desires.

9. By that syllable does the threefold knowledge (the sacrifice, more particularly the Soma-sacrifice, as founded on the three Vedas) proceed. When the Adhvaryu priest gives an order, he says Om. When the Hot*ri* priest recites, he says Om. When the Udgât*ri* priest sings, he says Om,

---

[1] Because most of the hymns of the Sâma-veda are taken from the Rig-veda.

[2] Parârdhya is here derived from para, highest, and ardha, place. The eighth means the eighth or last in the series of essences.

—all for the glory of that syllable. The threefold knowledge (the sacrifice) proceeds by the greatness of that syllable (the vital breaths), and by its essence (the oblations) [1].

10. Now therefore it would seem to follow, that both he who knows this (the true meaning of the syllable Om), and he who does not, perform the same sacrifice [2]. But this is not so, for knowledge and ignorance are different. The sacrifice which a man performs with knowledge, faith, and the Upanishad [3] is more powerful. This is the full account of the syllable Om.

---

[1] These are allusions to sacrificial technicalities, all intended to show the importance of the syllable Om, partly as a mere word, used at the sacrifices, partly as the mysterious name of the Highest Self. As every priest at the Soma-sacrifices, in which three classes of priests are always engaged, has to begin his part of the ceremonial with Om, therefore the whole sacrifice is said to be dependent on the syllable Om, and to be for the glory of that syllable, as an emblem of the Highest Self, a knowledge of whom is the indirect result of all sacrifices. The greatness of the syllable Om is explained by the vital breaths of the priest, the sacrificer, and his wife; its essence by rice, corn, &c., which constitute the oblations. Why breath and food are due to the syllable Om is explained by the sacrifice, which is dependent on that syllable, ascending to the sun, the sun sending rain, rain producing food, and food producing breath and life.

[2] He who simply pronounces the syllable Om as part of his recitation at a sacrifice, and he who knows the hidden meaning of that syllable, both may perform the same sacrifice. But that performed by the latter is more powerful, because knowledge is better than ignorance. This is, as usual, explained by some comparisons. It is true that both he who knows the quality of the harîtakî and he who does not, are purged alike if they take it. But on the other hand, if a jeweller and a mere clod sell a precious stone, the knowledge of the former bears better fruit than the ignorance of the latter.

[3] Upanishad is here explained by yoga, and yoga by devatâdi-vishayam upâsanam, meditation directed to certain deities. More

SECOND KHA*ND*A [1].

1. Whent he Devas and Asuras [2] struggled together, both of the race of Pra*g*âpati, the Devas took
the udgîtha [3] (Om), thinking they would vanquish
the Asuras with it.

2. They meditated on the udgîtha [3] (Om) as
the breath (scent) in the nose [4], but the Asuras
pierced it (the breath) with evil. Therefore we smell
by the breath in the nose both what is good-
smelling and what is bad-smelling. For the breath
was pierced by evil.

3. Then they meditated on the udgîtha (Om) as
speech, but the Asuras pierced it with evil. Therefore we speak both truth and falsehood. For
speech is pierced by evil.

4. Then they meditated on the udgîtha (Om) as
the eye, but the Asuras pierced it with evil. There-

---

likely, however, it refers to this very upanishad, i.e. to the udgîtha-
vidyâ, the doctrine of the secret meaning of Om, as here explained.

[1] A very similar story is told in the B*ri*had-âra*ny*aka I, 1, 3, 1.
But though the coincidences between the two are considerable,
amounting sometimes to verbal identity, the purport of the two
seems to be different. See Vedânta-sûtra III, 3, 6.

[2] Devas and Asuras, gods and demons, are here explained by
the commentator as the good and evil inclinations of man ; Pra-
*g*âpati as man in general.

[3] Udgîtha stands, according to the commentator, for the sacrificial act to be performed by the Udgât*ri*, the Sâma-veda priest,
with the udgîtha hymns ; and as these sacrificial acts always form
part of the *G*yotish*i*oma &c., these great Soma-sacrifices are really
intended. In the second place, however, the commentator takes
udgîtha in the sense of Udgât*ri*, the performer of the udgîtha,
which is or was by the Devas thought to be the breath in the
nose. I have preferred to take udgîtha in the sense of Om, and
all that is implied by it.

[4] They asked that breath should recite the udgîtha. Comm.

fore we see both what is sightly and unsightly. For
the eye is pierced by evil.

5. Then they meditated on the udgîtha (Om) as
the ear, but the Asuras pierced it with evil. Therefore we hear both what should be heard and what
should not be heard. For the ear is pierced by
evil.

6. Then they meditated on the udgîtha (Om) as
the mind, but the Asuras pierced it with evil.
Therefore we conceive both what should be conceived and what should not be conceived. For
the mind is pierced by evil.

7. Then comes this breath (of life) in the mouth[1].
They meditated on the udgîtha (Om) as that breath.
When the Asuras came to it, they were scattered,
as (a ball of earth) would be scattered when hitting
a solid stone.

8. Thus, as a ball of earth is scattered when hitting on a solid stone, will he be scattered who wishes
evil to one who knows this, or who persecutes him ;
for he is a solid stone.

9. By it (the breath in the mouth) he distinguishes
neither what is good nor what is bad-smelling, for
that breath is free from evil. What we eat and
drink with it supports the other vital breaths (i. e.
the senses, such as smell, &c.) When at the time
of death he[2] does not find that breath (in the

---

[1] Mukhya prâ*n*a is used in two senses, the principal or vital
breath, also called *s*resh*th*a, and the breath in the mouth, also called
âsanya.

[2] According to the commentator, the assemblage of the other
vital breaths or senses is here meant. They depart when the
breath of the mouth, sometimes called sarvambhari, all-supporting,
does no longer, by eating and drinking, support them.

mouth, through which he eats and drinks and lives), then he departs. He opens the mouth at the time of death (as if wishing to eat).

10. Angiras [1] meditated on the udgîtha (Om) as that breath, and people hold it to be Angiras, i. e. the essence of the members (angânâm rasa*h*);

11. Therefore B*ri*haspati meditated on udgîtha (Om) as that breath, and people hold it to be B*ri*-haspati, for speech is b*ri*hatî, and he (that breath) is the lord (pati) of speech;

12. Therefore Ayâsya meditated on the udgîtha (Om) as that breath, and people hold it to be Ayâsya, because it comes (ayati) from the mouth (âsya);

13. Therefore Vaka Dâlbhya knew it. He was the Udgât*ri* (singer) of the Naimishîya-sacrificers, and by singing he obtained for them their wishes.

14. He who knows this, and meditates on the syllable Om (the imperishable udgîtha) as the breath of life in the mouth, he obtains all wishes by singing. So much for the udgîtha (Om) as meditated on with reference to the body [2].

---

[1] The paragraphs from 10 to 14 are differently explained by Indian commentators. By treating the nominatives angirâs, b*ri*haspatis, and ayâsyas (here the printed text reads ayâsyam) as accusatives, or by admitting the omission of an iti after them, they connect paragraphs 9, 10, and 11 with paragraph 12, and thus gain the meaning that Vaka Dâlbhya meditated on the breath in the mouth as Angiras, B*ri*haspati, and Ayâsya, instead of those saints having themselves thus meditated; and that he, knowing the secret names and qualities of the breath, obtained, when acting as Udgât*ri* priest, the wishes of those for whom he sacrificed. Tena is diffi- cult to explain, unless we take it in the sense of tenânu*s*ish*ta*h, taught by him.

[2] Adhyâtma means with reference to the body, not with refer- ence to the self or the soul. Having explained the symbolical

THIRD KHA*N*DA.

1. Now follows the meditation on the udgîtha with reference to the gods. Let a man meditate on the udgîtha (Om) as he who sends warmth (the sun in the sky). When the sun rises it sings as Udgât*ri* for the sake of all creatures. When it rises it destroys the fear of darkness. He who knows this, is able to destroy the fear of darkness (ignorance).

2. This (the breath in the mouth) and that (the sun) are the same. This is hot and that is hot. This they call svara (sound), and that they call pra-tyâsvara[1] (reflected sound). Therefore let a man meditate on the udgîtha (Om) as this and that (as breath and as sun).

3. Then let a man meditate on the udgîtha (Om) as vyâna indeed. If we breathe up, that is prâ*n*a, the up-breathing. If we breathe down, that is apâna, the down-breathing. The combination of prâ*n*a and apâna is vyâna, back-breathing or holding in of the breath. This vyâna is speech. Therefore when we utter speech, we neither breathe up nor down.

4. Speech is *Rik*, and therefore when a man utters a *Rik* verse he neither breathes up nor down.

---

meaning of Om as applied to the body and its organs of sense, he now explains its symbolical meaning adhidaivatam, i.e. as applied to divine beings.

[1] As applied to breath, svara is explained by the commentator in the sense of moving, going out; pratyâsvara, as applied to the sun, is explained as returning every day. More likely, however, svara as applied to breath means sound, Om itself being called svara (*Kh*. Up. I, 4, 3), and prasvâra in the Rig-veda-prâti*s*âkhya, 882. As applied to the sun, svara and pratyâsvara were probably taken in the sense of light and reflected light.

Rik is Sâman, and therefore when a man utters a Sâman verse he neither breathes up nor down.

Sâman is udgîtha, and therefore when a man sings (the udgîtha, Om) he neither breathes up nor down.

5. And other works also which require strength, such as the production of fire by rubbing, running a race, stringing a strong bow, are performed without breathing up or down. Therefore let a man meditate on the udgîtha (Om) as vyâna.

6. Let a man meditate on the syllables of the udgîtha, i. e. of the word udgîtha. Ut is breath (prâ*n*a), for by means of breath a man rises (ut-tish*th*ati). Gî is speech, for speeches are called gira*h*. Tha is food, for by means of food all subsists (sthita).

7. Ut is heaven, gî the sky, tha the earth. Ut is the sun, gî the air, tha the fire. Ut is the Sâma-veda, gî the Ya*g*ur-veda, tha the Rig-veda[1].

---

[1] The commentator supplies explanations to all these fanciful etymologies. The heaven is ut, because it is high; the sky is gî, because it gives out all the worlds (gira*n*ât); earth is tha, because it is the place (sthâna) of living beings. The sun is ut, because it is high. The wind is gî, because it gives out fire, &c. (gira*n*ât); fire is tha, because it is the place (sthâna) of the sacrifice. The Sâma-veda is ut, because it is praised as svarga; the Ya*g*ur-veda is gî, because the gods take the oblation offered with a Ya*g*us; the Rig-veda is tha, because the Sâma verses stand in it. All this is very childish, and worse than childish, but it is interesting as a phase of human folly which is not restricted to the Brahmans of India. I take the following passage from an interesting article, 'On the Ogam Beithluisnin and on Scythian Letters,' by Dr. Charles Graves, Bishop of Limerick. 'An Irish antiquary,' he says, 'writing several hundred years ago, proposes to give an account of the origin of the names of the notes in the musical scale.

'"It is asked here, according to Saint Augustine, What is chanting, or why is it so called? Answer. From this word *cantalena;*

Speech yields the milk, which is the milk of speech itself [1], to him who thus knowing meditates on those

and *cantalena* is the same thing as *lenis cantus*, i. e. a soft, sweet chant to God, and to the Virgin Mary, and to all the Saints. And the reason why the word *puincc* (*puncta*) is so called is because the points (or musical notes) *ut, re, mi, fa, sol, la,* hurt the devil and puncture him. And it is thus that these points are to be understood: viz. When Moses the son of Amram with his people in their Exodus was crossing the Red Sea, and Pharaoh and his host were following him, this was the chant which Moses had to protect him from Pharaoh and his host—these six points in praise of the Lord :—

' "The first point of these, i. e. *ut:* and *ut* in the Greek is the same as *liberat* in the Latin; and that is the same as *saer* in the Gaelic; i. e. O God, said Moses, deliver us from the harm of the devil.

' "The second point of them, i.e. *re:* and *re* is the same as *saer;* i. e. O God, deliver us from everything hurtful and malignant.

' "The third point, i. e. *mi:* and *mi* in the Greek is the same as *militum* in the Latin; and that is the same as *ridere* (a knight) in the Gaelic; i. e. O God, said Moses, deliver us from those knights who are pursuing us.

' "The fourth point, i. e. *fa:* and *fa* in the Greek is the same as *famulus* in the Latin; and that is the same as *mug* (slave) in the Gaelic; i. e. O God, said Moses, deliver us from those slaves who are pursuing us.

' "The fifth point, i. e. *sol:* and *sol* is the same as *grian* (sun); and that is the same as righteousness; because righteousness and Christ are not different; i. e. O Christ, said Moses, deliver us.

' "The sixth point, i. e. *la,* is the same as *lav;* and that is the same as *indail* (wash); i.e. O God, said Moses, wash away our sins from us.

' "And on the singing of that laud Pharaoh and his host were drowned.

' "Understand, O man, that in whatever place this laud, i. e. this chant, is sung, the devil is bound by it, and his power is extirpated thence, and the power of God is called in."

' We have been taught that the names of the first six notes

---

[1] The milk of speech consists in rewards to be obtained by the Rig-veda, &c. Or we may translate, Speech yields its milk to him who is able to milk speech.

syllables of the name of udgîtha, he becomes rich in food and able to eat food.

8. Next follows the fulfilment of prayers. Let a man thus meditate on the Upasaraṇas, i. e. the objects which have to be approached by meditation: Let him (the Udgâtṛi) quickly reflect on the Sâman with which he is going to praise;

9. Let him quickly reflect on the Rik in which that Sâman occurs; on the Ṛishi (poet) by whom it was seen or composed; on the Devatâ (object) which he is going to praise;

10. On the metre in which he is going to praise; on the tune with which he is going to sing for himself;

11. On the quarter of the world which he is going to praise. Lastly, having approached himself (his name, family, &c.) by meditation, let him sing the hymn of praise, reflecting on his desire, and avoiding all mistakes in pronunciation, &c. Quickly [1] will the desire be then fulfilled to him, for the sake of which he may have offered his hymn of praise, yea, for which he may have offered his hymn of praise [2].

---

in the gamut were suggested by the initial syllables of the first six hemistichs in one of the stanzas of a hymn to St. John:

> Ut queant laxis
> Resonare fibris
> Mira gestorum
> Famuli tuorum,
> Solve polluti
> Labii reatum,
>   Sancte Ioannes.'

[1] Abhyâso ha yat, lit. depend on it that it will be fulfilled, but always explained by quickly. See Kh. Up. II, 1, 4; III, 19, 4; V, 10, 7. Frequently, but wrongly, written with a dental s.

[2] The repetition of the last sentence is always an indication that a chapter is finished. This old division into chapters is of great importance for a proper study of the Upanishads.

FOURTH KHANDA.

1. Let a man meditate on the syllable Om, for the udgîtha is sung beginning with Om. And this is the full account of the syllable Om :—

2. The Devas, being afraid of death, entered upon (the performance of the sacrifice prescribed in) the threefold knowledge (the three Vedas). They covered themselves with the metrical hymns. Because they covered (*kh*ad) themselves with the hymns, therefore the hymns are called *kh*andas.

3. Then, as a fisherman might observe a fish in the water, Death observed the Devas in the *Rik*, Ya*g*us, and Sâman-(sacrifices). And the Devas seeing this, rose from the *Rik*, Ya*g*us, and Sâman-sacrifices, and entered the Svara [1], i. e. the Om (they meditated on the Om).

4. When a man has mastered the Rig-veda, he says quite loud Om; the same, when he has mastered the Sâman and the Ya*g*us. This Svara is the imperishable (syllable), the immortal, free from fear. Because the Devas entered it, therefore they became immortal, and free from fear.

5. He who knowing this loudly pronounces (pra*n*auti) [2] that syllable, enters the same (imperishable) syllable, the Svara, the immortal, free from fear, and having entered it, becomes immortal, as the Devas are immortal.

---

[1] Cf. I, 3, 2.
[2] Pra*n*auti, he lauds, i. e. he meditates on.   Comm.

FIFTH KHANDA.

1. The udgîtha is the pranava[1], the pranava is the udgîtha. And as the udgîtha is the sun[2], so is the pranava, for he (the sun) goes sounding Om.

2. 'Him I sang praises to, therefore art thou my only one,' thus said Kaushîtaki to his son. 'Do thou revolve his rays, then thou wilt have many sons.' So much in reference to the Devas.

3. Now with reference to the body. Let a man meditate on the udgîtha as the breath (in the mouth), for he goes sounding Om[3].

4. 'Him I sang praises to, therefore art thou my only son,' thus said Kaushîtaki to his son. 'Do thou therefore sing praises to the breath as manifold, if thou wishest to have many sons.'

5. He who knows that the udgîtha is the pranava, and the pranava the udgîtha, rectifies from the seat of the Hotri priest any mistake committed by the Udgâtri priest in performing the udgîtha, yea, in performing the udgîtha.

SIXTH KHANDA.

1. The Rik (veda) is this earth, the Sâman (veda) is fire. This Sâman (fire) rests on that Rik (earth)[4]. Therefore the Sâman is sung as resting on the Rik.

---

[1] Pranava is the name used chiefly by the followers of the Rig-veda, udgîtha the name used by the followers of the Sâma-veda. Both words are intended for the syllable Om.

[2] Cf. Kh. Up. I, 3, 1.

[3] The breath in the mouth, or the chief breath, says Om, i. e. gives permission to the five senses to act, just as the sun, by saying Om, gives permission to all living beings to move about.

[4] The Sâma verses are mostly taken from the Rig-veda.

Sâ is this earth, ama is fire, and that makes Sâma.

2. The *Rik* is the sky, the Sâmân air. This Sâman (air) rests on that *Rik* (sky). Therefore the Sâman is sung as resting on the *Rik*. Sâ is the sky, ama the air, and that makes Sâma.

3. *Rik* is heaven, Sâman the sun. This Sâman (sun) rests on that *Rik* (heaven). Therefore the Sâman is sung as resting on the *Rik*. Sâ is heaven, ama the sun, and that makes Sâma.

4. *Rik* is the stars, Sâman the moon. This Sâman (moon) rests on that *Rik* (stars). Therefore the Sâman is sung as resting on the *Rik*. Sâ is the stars, ama the moon, and that makes Sâma.

5. *Rik* is the white light of the sun, Sâman the blue exceeding darkness[1] (in the sun). This Sâman (darkness) rests on that *Rik* (brightness). Therefore the Sâman is sung as resting on the *Rik*.

6. Sâ is the white light of the sun, ama the blue exceeding darkness, and that makes Sâma.

Now that golden[2] person, who is seen within the sun, with golden beard and golden hair, golden altogether to the very tips of his nails,

7. Whose eyes are like blue lotus's[3], his name is ut, for he has risen (udita) above all evil. He also who knows this, rises above all evil.

8. *Rik* and Sâman are his joints, and therefore he is udgîtha. And therefore he who praises him

---

[1] The darkness which is seen by those who can concentrate their sight on the sun.

[2] Bright as gold.

[3] The colour of the lotus is described by a comparison with the Kapyâsa, the seat of the monkey (kapi*prish*th*h*ânto yena upavi*s*ati), It was probably a botanical name.

(the ut) is called the Ud-gât*ri*[1] (the out-singer). He (the golden person, called ut) is lord of the worlds beyond that (sun), and of all the wishes of the Devas (inhabiting those worlds). So much with reference to the Devas.

SEVENTH KHAN*D*A.

1. Now with reference to the body. *Rik* is speech, Sâman breath[2]. This Sâman (breath) rests on that *Rik* (speech). Therefore the Sâman is sung as resting on the *Rik*. Sâ is speech, ama is breath, and that makes Sâma.

2. *Rik* is the eye, Sâman the self[3]. This Sâman (shadow) rests on that *Rik* (eye). Therefore the Sâman is sung as resting on the *Rik*. Sâ is the eye, ama the self, and that makes Sâma.

3. *Rik* is the ear, Sâman the mind. This Sâman (mind) rests on that *Rik* (ear). Therefore the Sâman is sung as resting on the *Rik*. Sâ is the ear, ama the mind, and that makes Sâma.

4. *Rik* is the white light of the eye, Sâman- the blue exceeding darkness. This Sâman (darkness) rests on the *Rik* (brightness). Therefore the Sâman is sung as resting on the *Rik*. Sâ is the white light of the eye, ama the blue exceeding darkness, and that makes Sâma.

5. Now the person who is seen in the eye, he is *Rik*, he is Sâman, Uktha[4], Ya*g*us, Brahman. The form of that person (in the eye) is the same[5] as the

---

[1] Name of the principal priest of the Sâma-veda.

[2] Breath in the nose, sense of smelling. Comm.

[3] The shadow-self, the likeness or image thrown upon the eye; see *Kh.* Up. VIII, 9, 1.

[4] A set of hymns to be recited, whereas the Sâman is sung, and the Ya*g*us muttered.

[5] Cf. *Kh.* Up. I, 6, 6.

form of the other person (in the sun), the joints of the one (*Rik* and Sâman) are the joints of the other, the name of the one (ut) is the name of the other.

6. He is lord of the worlds beneath that (the self in the eye), and of all the wishes of men. Therefore all who sing to the vî*n*â (lyre), sing him, and from him also they obtain wealth.

7. He who knowing this sings a Sâman, sings to both (the adhidaivata and adhyâtma self, the person in the sun and the person in the eye, as one and the same person). He obtains through the one, yea, he obtains the worlds beyond that, and the wishes of the Devas;

8. And he obtains through the other the worlds beneath that, and the wishes of men.

Therefore an Udgât*ri* priest who knows this, may say (to the sacrificer for whom he officiates);

9. 'What wish shall I obtain for you by my songs?' For he who knowing this sings a Sâman is able to obtain wishes through his song, yea, through his song.

EIGHTH KHA*N*DA.

1. There were once three men, well-versed in udgîtha [1], *S*ilaka *S*âlâvatya, *K*aikitâyana Dâlbhya, and Pravâha*n*a *G*aivali. They said: 'We are well-versed in udgîtha. Let us have a discussion on udgîtha.'

2. They all agreed and sat down. Then Pravâha*n*a *G*aivali [2] said: 'Sirs, do you both speak first,

---

[1] Cognisant of the deeper meanings of udgîtha, i. e. Om.

[2] He, though not being a Brâhma*n*a, turns out to be the only one who knows the true meaning of udgîtha, i. e. the Highest Brahman.

for I wish to hear what two Brâhma*n*as[1] have to say.'

3. Then *S*ilaka *S*âlâvatya said to *K*aikitâyana Dâlbhya : 'Let me ask you.'

'Ask,' he replied.

4. 'What is the origin of the Sâman ?' 'Tone (svara),' he replied.

'What is the origin of tone ?' 'Breath,' he replied.

'What is the origin of breath ?' 'Food,' he replied.

'What is the origin of food ?' 'Water,' he replied.

5. 'What is the origin of water ?' 'That world (heaven),' he replied.

'And what is the origin of that world ?'—

He replied : 'Let no man carry the Sâman beyond the world of svarga (heaven). We place (recognise) the Sâman in the world of svarga, for the Sâman is extolled as svarga (heaven).'

6. Then said *S*ilaka *S*âlâvatya to *K*aikitâyana Dâlbhya : 'O Dâlbhya, thy Sâman is not firmly established. And if any one were to say, Your head shall fall off (if you be wrong), surely your head would now fall.'

7. 'Well then, let me know this from you, Sir,' said Dâlbhya.

'Know it,' replied *S*ilaka *S*âlâvatya.

'What is the origin of that world (heaven) ?' 'This world,' he replied.

'And what is the origin of this world ?'—

He replied : 'Let no man carry the Sâman beyond this world as its rest. We place the Sâman

---

[1] In V, 3, 5, Pravâha*n*a *G*aivali is distinctly called a râ*g*anyabandhu.

in this world as its rest, for the Sâman is extolled as rest.'

8. Then said Pravâhana Gaivali to Silaka Sâlâvatya : 'Your Sâman (the earth), O Sâlâvatya, has an end. And if any one were to say, Your head shall fall off (if you be wrong), surely your head would now fall.'

'Well then, let me know this from you, Sir,' said Sâlâvatya.

'Know it,' replied Gaivali.

NINTH KHANDA.

1. 'What is the origin of this world?' 'Ether[1],' he replied. For all these beings take their rise from the ether, and return into the ether. Ether is older than these, ether is their rest.

2. He is indeed the udgîtha (Om = Brahman), greater than great (parovarîyas), he is without end.

He who knowing this meditates on the udgîtha, the greater than great, obtains what is greater than great, he conquers the worlds which are greater than great.

3. Atidhanvan Saunaka, having taught this udgîtha to Udara-sândilya, said : 'As long as they will know in your family this udgîtha, their life in this world will be greater than great.

4. 'And thus also will be their state in the other world.' He who thus knows the udgîtha, and meditates on it thus, his life in this world will be greater than great, and also his state in the other world, yea, in the other world.

---

[1] Ether, or we might translate it by space, both being intended, however, as names or symbols of the Highest Brahman. See Vedânta-sûtra I, 1, 22.

TENTH KHANDA.

1. When the Kurus had been destroyed by (hail) stones [1], Ushasti Kâkrâyana lived as a beggar with his virgin [2] wife at Ibhyagrâma.

2. Seeing a chief eating beans, he begged of him. The chief said: 'I have no more, except those which are put away for me here.'

3. Ushasti said: 'Give me to eat of them.' He gave him the beans, and said: 'There is something to drink also.' Then said Ushasti: 'If I drank of it, I should have drunk what was left by another, and is therefore unclean.'

4. The chief said: 'Were not those beans also left over and therefore unclean?'

'No,' he replied; 'for I should not have lived, if I had not eaten them, but the drinking of water would be mere pleasure [3].'

5. Having eaten himself, Ushasti gave the remaining beans to his wife. But she, having eaten before, took them and put them away.

6. Rising the next morning, Ushasti said to her: 'Alas, if we could only get some food, we might gain a little wealth. The king here is going to offer a sacrifice, he should choose me for all the priestly offices.'

---

[1] When they had been killed either by stone weapons, or by a shower of stones, which produced a famine in the land. Comm.

[2] Âñkî is not the name of the wife of Ushasti, nor does it mean strong enough to travel. Sankara explains it as anupagâtapayodharâdistrîvyañganâ, and Ânandagiri adds, Svairasamkâre 'pi na vyabhikârasañketi darsayitum âñkyeti viseshanam. She was so young that she was allowed to run about freely, without exciting any suspicion. Another commentator says, Grihâd bahirgantumarhâ anupagâtapayodharâ.

[3] Or, according to the commentator, 'water I can get whenever I like.'

7. His wife said to him : ' Look, here are those beans of yours.' Having eaten them, he went to the sacrifice which was being performed.

8. He went and sat down on the orchestra near the Udgât*ri*s, who were going to sing their hymns of praise. And he said to the Prastot*ri* (the leader):

9. ' Prastot*ri*, if you, without knowing[1] the deity which belongs to the prastâva (the hymns &c. of the Prastot*ri*), are going to sing it, your head will fall off.'

10. In the same manner he addressed the Udgât*ri*: ' Udgât*ri*, if you, without knowing the deity which belongs to the udgîtha (the hymns of the Udgât*ri*), are going to sing it, your head will fall off.'

11. In the same manner he addressed the Pratihart*ri*: ' Pratihart*ri*, if you, without knowing the deity which belongs to the pratihâra (the hymns of the Pratihart*ri*), are going to sing it, your head will fall off.'

They stopped, and sat down in silence.

ELEVENTH KHA*ND*A.

1. Then the sacrificer said to him: ' I should like to know who you are, Sir.' He replied: ' I am Ushasti *K*âkrâya*n*a.'

2. He said : ' I looked for you, Sir, for all these sacrificial offices, but not finding you[2], I chose others.'

---

[1] The commentator is at great pains to show that a priest may officiate without knowing the secret meanings here assigned to certain parts of the sacrifice, and without running any risk of punishment. Only, if another priest is present, who is initiated, then the uninitiated, taking his place, is in danger of losing his head.

[2] Should it be avittvâ, as in I, 2, 9?

3. 'But now, Sir, take all the sacrificial offices.'

Ushasti said: 'Very well; but let those, with my permission, perform the hymns of praise. Only as much wealth as you give to them, so much give to me also.'

The sacrificer assented.

4. Then the Prastot*ri* approached him, saying: 'Sir, you said to me, "Prastot*ri*, if you, without knowing the deity which belongs to the prastâva, are going to sing it, your head will fall off,"—which then is that deity?'

5. He said: 'Breath (prâ*n*a). For all these beings merge into breath alone, and from breath they arise. This is the deity belonging to the prastâva. If, without knowing that deity, you had sung forth your hymns, your head would have fallen off, after you had been warned by me.'

6. Then the Udgât*ri* approached him, saying: 'Sir, you said to me, "Udgât*ri*, if you, without knowing the deity which belongs to the udgîtha, are going to sing it, your head will fall off,"— which then is that deity?'

7. He said: 'The sun (âditya). For all these beings praise the sun when it stands on high. This is the deity belonging to the udgîtha. If, without knowing that deity, you had sung out your hymns, your head would have fallen off, after you had been warned by me.'

8. Then the Pratihart*ri* approached him, saying: 'Sir, you said to me, "Pratihart*ri*, if you, without knowing the deity belonging to the pratihâra, are going to sing it, your head will fall off,"—which then is that deity?'

9. He said: 'Food (anna). For all these beings

live when they partake of food. This is the deity belonging to the pratihâra. If, without knowing that deity, you had sung your hymns, your head would have fallen off, after you had been warned by me[1].'

TWELFTH KHANDA.

1. Now follows the udgîtha of the dogs. Vaka Dâlbhya, or, as he was also called, Glâva Maitreya, went out to repeat the Veda (in a quiet place).

2. A white (dog) appeared before him, and other dogs gathering round him, said to him : 'Sir, sing and get us food, we are hungry.'

3. The white dog said to them : 'Come to me to-morrow morning.' Vaka Dâlbhya, or, as he was also called, Glâva Maitreya, watched.

4. The dogs came on, holding together, each dog keeping the tail of the preceding dog in his mouth, as the priests do when they are going to sing praises with the Vahishpavamâna hymn[2]. After they had settled down, they began to say Hiṅ.

5. 'Om, let us eat! Om, let us drink! Om, may the divine Varuna, Pragâpati, Savitri[3] bring us food! Lord of food, bring hither food, bring it, Om !'

---

[1] There are certain etymological fancies for assigning each deity to a certain portion of the Sâma-veda ceremonial. Thus prâna is assigned to the prastâva, because both words begin with pra. Âditya is assigned to the udgîtha, because the sun is ut. Anna, food, is assigned to the pratihâra, because food is taken, pratihriyate, &c.

[2] This alludes to a ceremony where the priests have to walk in procession, each priest holding the gown of the preceding priest.

[3] The commentator explains Varuna and Pragâpati as epithets of Savitri, or the sun, meaning rain-giver and man-protector.

THIRTEENTH KHA*N*DA [1].

1. The syllable Hâu [2] is this world (the earth), the syllable Hâi [3] the air, the syllable Atha the moon, the syllable Iha the self, the syllable Î [4] is Agni, fire.

2. The syllable Û is the sun, the syllable E is the Nihava or invocation, the syllable Auhoi [5] is the Vi*s*ve Devas, the syllable Hi*n* is Pra*g*âpati, Svara [6] (tone) is breath (prâ*n*a), the syllable Yâ is food, the syllable Vâg [7] is Virâ*g*.

3. The thirteenth stobha syllable, viz. the indistinct syllable Hu*n*, is the Undefinable (the Highest Brahman).

4. Speech yields the milk, which is the milk of speech itself to him who knows this Upanishad (secret doctrine) of the Sâmans in this wise. He becomes rich in food, and able to eat food [8],—yea, able to eat food.

---

[1] The syllables here mentioned are the so-called stobhâksharas, sounds used in the musical recitation of the Sâman hymns, probably to fill out the intervals in the music for which there were no words in the hymns. These syllables are marked in the MSS. of the Sâma-veda, but their exact character and purpose are not quite clear.

[2] A stobha syllable used in the Rathantara Sâman.

[3] Used in the Vâmadevya Sâman.

[4] The Sâman addressed to Agni takes the syllable î as nidhana.

[5] The stobha syllables used in the Sâman addressed to the Vi*s*ve Devas.

[6] See *Kh.* Up. I, 4, 4.

[7] The commentator takes vâg as a stobha, as a syllable occurring in hymns addressed to Virâ*g*, and as implying either the deity Virâ*g* or food.

[8] I. e. wealthy and healthy.

SECOND PRAPÂTHAKA.

FIRST KHANDA.

1. Meditation on the whole [1] of the Sâman is good, and people, when anything is good, say it is Sâman ; when it is not good, it is not Sâman.

2. Thus they also say, he approached him with Sâman, i. e. becomingly; and he approached him without Sâman, i. e. unbecomingly.

3. And they also say, truly this is Sâman for us, i. e. it is good for us, when it is good; and truly that is not Sâman for us, i. e. it is not good for us, when it is not good.

4. If any one knowing this meditates on the Sâman as good, depend upon it all good qualities will approach quickly, aye, they will become his own [2].

SECOND KHANDA.

1. Let a man meditate on the fivefold Sâman [3] as the five worlds. The hiṅkâra is the earth, the prastâva the fire, the udgîtha the sky, the pratihâra the sun, the nidhana heaven; so in an ascending line.

2. In a descending line, the hiṅkâra is heaven,

---

[1] Hitherto meditation on certain portions only of the Sâmaveda and the Sâma-sacrifice had been enjoined, and their deeper meaning explained. Now the same is done for the whole of the Sâman.

[2] Cf. *Kh*. Up. III, 19, 4.

[3] The five forms in which the Sâman is used for sacrificial purposes. The Sâman is always to be understood as the Good, as Dharma, and as Brahman.

the prastâva the sun, the udgîtha the sky, the pratihâra the fire, the nidhana the earth.

3. The worlds in an ascending and in a descending line belong to him who knowing this meditates on the fivefold Sâman as the worlds [1].

THIRD KHANDA.

1. Let a man meditate on the fivefold Sâman as rain. The hinkâra is wind (that brings the rain); the prastâva is, 'the cloud is come;' the udgîtha is, 'it rains;' the pratihâra, 'it flashes, it thunders;'

2. The nidhana is, 'it stops.' There is rain for him, and he brings rain for others who thus knowing meditates on the fivefold Sâman as rain.

FOURTH KHANDA.

1. Let a man meditate on the fivefold Sâman in all waters. When the clouds gather, that is the hinkâra; when it rains, that is the prastâva; that which flows in the east [2], that is the udgîtha; that which flows in the west [3], that is the pratihâra; the sea is the nidhana.

2. He does not die in water [4], nay, he is rich in

---

[1] The commentator supplies some fanciful reasons why each of the five Sâmans is identified with certain objects. Earth is said to be the hinkâra, because both always come first. Agni is prastâva, because sacrifices are praised in the fire (prastûyante). The sky is udgîtha, because it is also called gagana, and both words have the letter g in common. The sun is pratihâra, because everybody wishes the sun to come towards him (prati). Heaven is nidhana, because those who depart from here are placed there (nidhî-yante), &c.

[2] The Ganges, &c. Comm.

[3] The Narmadâ, &c. Comm.

[4] The commentator adds, 'unless he wishes to die in the Ganges.'

water who knowing this meditates on the fivefold
Sâman as all waters.

FIFTH KHANDA.

1. Let a man meditate on the fivefold Sâman as
the seasons. The hiṅkâra is spring, the prastâva
summer (harvest of yava, &c.), the udgîtha the
rainy season, the pratihâra autumn, the nidhana
winter.

2. The seasons belong to him, nay, he is always
in season (successful) who knowing this meditates
on the fivefold Sâman as the seasons.

SIXTH KHANDA.

1. Let a man meditate on the fivefold Sâman in
animals. The hiṅkâra is goats, the prastâva sheep,
the udgîtha cows, the pratihâra horses, the nidhana
man.

2. Animals belong to him, nay, he is rich in
animals who knowing this meditates on the fivefold
Sâman as animals.

SEVENTH KHANDA.

1. Let a man meditate on the fivefold Sâman,
which is greater than great, as the prânas (senses).
The hiṅkâra is smell[1] (nose), the prastâva speech
(tongue), the udgîtha sight (eye), the pratihâra
hearing (ear), the nidhana mind. These are one
greater than the other.

2. What is greater than great belongs to him,
nay, he conquers the worlds which are greater than

---

[1] Prâna is explained by ghrâna, smell; possibly ghrâna may
have been the original reading. Anyhow, it cannot be the mukhya
prâna here, because it is distinctly represented as the lowest sense.

great, who knowing this meditates on the fivefold Sâman, which is greater than great, as the prâ*n*as (senses).

EIGHTH KHA*N*DA.

1. Next for the sevenfold Sâman. Let a man meditate on the sevenfold Sâman in speech. Whenever there is in speech the syllable hu*n* [1], that is hi*n*kâra, pra is the prastâva, â is the âdi, the first, i. e. Om,

2. Ud is the udgîtha, pra the pratihâra, upa the upadrava, ni the nidhana.

3. Speech yields the milk, which is the milk of speech itself, to him who knowing this meditates on the sevenfold Sâman in speech. He becomes rich in food, and able to eat food.

NINTH KHA*N*DA.

1. Let a man meditate on the sevenfold Sâman as the sun. The sun is Sâman, because he is always the same (sama); he is Sâman because he is the same, everybody thinking he looks towards me, he looks towards me [2].

2. Let him know that all beings are dependent on him (the sun). What he is before his rising, that is the hi*n*kâra. On it animals are dependent. Therefore animals say hi*n* (before sunrise), for they share the hi*n*kâra of that Sâman (the sun).

3. What he is when first risen, that is the prastâva. On it men are dependent. Therefore men love praise (prastuti) and celebrity, for they share the prastâva of that Sâman.

---

[1] These are again the stobhâksharas, or musical syllables used in the performance of the Sâman hymns ; see p. 22.

[2] Cf. *Kh*. Up. II, 2, 2. Comm.

4. What he is at the time of the sangava [1], that is the âdi, the first, the Om. On it birds are dependent. Therefore birds fly about in the sky without support, holding themselves, for they share the âdi [2] (the Om) of that Sâman.

5. What he is just at noon, that is the udgîtha. On it the Devas are dependent (because they are brilliant). Therefore they are the best of all the descendants of Pra*g*âpati, for they share the udgîtha of that Sâman.

6. What he is after midday and before afternoon, that is the pratihâra. On it all germs are dependent. Therefore these, having been conceived (pratih*ri*ta), do not fall, for they share the pratihâra of that Sâman.

7. What he is after the afternoon and before sunset, that is the upadrava. On it the animals of the forest are dependent. Therefore, when they see a man, they run (upadravanti) to the forest as a safe hiding-place, for they share the upadrava of that Sâman.

8. What he is when he first sets, that is the nidhana. On it the fathers are dependent. Therefore they put them [3] down (nidadhati), for they share the nidhana of that Sâman. Thus a man meditates on the sevenfold Sâman as the sun.

---

[1] When the sun puts forth his rays, and when the cows are together with their calves, i.e. as Rajendralal Mitra says, after the cows have been milked and are allowed by the cowherds to suckle their young.

[2] The tertium comparationis is here the â of âdi and the â of âdâya, i.e. holding. The d might have been added.

[3] The cakes for the ancestral spirits, or the spirits themselves.

TENTH KHANDA.

1. Next let a man meditate on the sevenfold Sâman which is uniform in itself[1] and leads beyond death. The word hiṅkâra has three syllables, the word prastâva has three syllables : that is equal (sama).

2. The word âdi (first, Om) has two syllables, the word pratihâra has four syllables. Taking one syllable from that over, that is equal (sama).

3. The word udgîtha has three syllables, the word upadrava has four syllables. With three and three syllables it should be equal. One syllable being left over, it becomes trisyllabic. Hence it is equal.

4. The word nidhana has three syllables, therefore it is equal. These make twenty-two syllables.

5. With twenty-one syllables a man reaches the sun (and death), for the sun is the twenty-first[2] from here; with the twenty-second he conquers what is beyond the sun: that is blessedness, that is freedom from grief.

6. He obtains here the victory over the sun (death), and there is a higher victory than the victory over the sun for him, who knowing this meditates on the sevenfold Sâman as uniform in itself, which leads beyond death, yea, which leads beyond death.

ELEVENTH KHANDA[3].

1. The hiṅkâra is mind, the prastâva speech, the udgîtha sight, the pratihâra hearing, the nidhana

---

[1] Âtmasammita is explained by the commentator either as having the same number of syllables in the names of the different Sâmans, or as equal to the Highest Self.

[2] There are twelve months, five seasons, three worlds, then follows the sun as the twenty-first. Comm.

[3] After having explained the secret meaning of the whole Sâma-

breath. That is the Gâyatra Sâman, as interwoven in the (five) prâ*n*as [1].

2. He who thus knows this Gâyatra interwoven in the prâ*n*as, keeps his senses, reaches the full life, he lives long [2], becomes great with children and cattle, great by fame. The rule of him who thus meditates on the Gâyatra is, ' Be not high-minded.'

TWELFTH KHA*ND*A.

1. The hiṅkâra is, he rubs (the fire-stick); the prastâva, smoke rises; the udgîtha, it burns; the pratihâra, there are glowing coals; the nidhana, it goes down; the nidhana, it is gone out. This is the Rathantara Sâman as interwoven in fire [3].

2. He who thus knows this Rathantara interwoven in fire, becomes radiant [4] and strong. He reaches the full life, he lives long, becomes great with children and cattle, great by fame. The rule is, 'Do not rinse the mouth or spit before the fire.'

THIRTEENTH KHA*ND*A.

1, 2. Next follows the Vâmadevya as interwoven in generation [5].

---

veda ceremonial, as it is to be understood by meditation only (dhyâna), he proceeds to explain the secret meaning of the same ceremonial, giving to each its proper name in proper succession (gâyatra, rathantara, &c.), and showing the hidden purport of those names.

[1] Cf. *Kh.* Up. II, 7, 1, where prâ*n*a is explained differently. The Gâyatrî itself is sometimes called prâ*n*a.

[2] The commentator generally takes *g*yok in the sense of bright.

[3] The Rathantara is used for the ceremony of producing fire.

[4] Brahmavar*k*asa is the 'glory of countenance' produced by higher knowledge, an inspired look. Annâda, lit. able to eat, healthy, strong.

[5] Upamantrayate sa hiṅkâro, *g*ñapayate sa prastâva*h*, striyâ saha

FOURTEENTH KHA*N*DA.

1. Rising, the sun is the hiṅkâra, risen, he is the prastâva, at noon he is the udgîtha, in the afternoon he is the pratihâra, setting, he is the nidhana. That is the B*ri*hat Sâman as interwoven in the sun [1].

2. He who thus knows the B*ri*hat as interwoven in the sun, becomes refulgent [2] and strong, he reaches the full life, he lives long, becomes great with children and cattle, great by fame. His rule is, ' Never complain of the heat of the sun.'

FIFTEENTH KHA*N*DA.

1. The mists gather, that is the hiṅkâra; the cloud has risen, that is the prastâva; it rains, that is the udgîtha; it flashes and thunders, that is the pratihâra; it stops, that is the nidhana. That is the Vair*g*upa Sâman, as interwoven in Par*g*anya, the god of rain.

2. He who thus knows the Vairûpa as interwoven in Par*g*anya, obtains all kinds of cattle (virûpa), he reaches the full life, he lives long, becomes great with children and cattle, great by fame. His rule is, ' Never complain of the rain.'

SIXTEENTH KHA*N*DA.

1. The hiṅkâra is spring, the prastâva summer, the udgîtha the rainy season, the pratihâra autumn,

---

*s*ete sa udgîtha*h*, pratistrî saha sete sa pratihâra*h*, kâlam ga*kkh*ati tan nidhanam, pâra*m* ga*kkh*ati tan nidhanam. Etad vâmadevyam mithune protam. 2. Sa ya evam etad vâmadevyam mithune pro-ta*m* veda, mithunî bhavati, mithunân mithunât pra*g*âyate, sarvam âyur eti, *gy*og *g*îvati, mahân pra*g*ayâ pa*s*ubhir bhavati, mahân kîrttyâ. Na kâm*k*ana pariharet tad vratam.

[1] The sun is b*ri*hat. The B*ri*hat Sâman is to be looked upon as the sun, or the B*ri*hat has Âditya for its deity.

[2] The *s*ame as brahmavar*k*asin.

the nidhana winter.   That is the Vairâ*g*a Sâman, as interwoven in the seasons.

2.   He who thus knows the Vairâ*g*a, as interwoven in the seasons, shines (virâ*g*ati) through children, cattle, and glory of countenance.   He reaches the full life, he lives long, becomes great with children and cattle, great by fame.   His rule is, ' Never complain of the seasons.'

SEVENTEENTH KHANDA.

1.   The hiṅkâra is the earth, the prastâva the sky, the udgîtha heaven, the pratihâra the regions, the nidhana the sea.   These are the *S*akvarî Sâmans, as interwoven in the worlds[1].

2.   He who thus knows the *S*akvarîs, as interwoven in the worlds, becomes possessed of the worlds, he reaches the full life, he lives long, becomes great with children and cattle, great by fame. His rule is, ' Never complain of the worlds.'

EIGHTEENTH KHANDA.

1.   The hiṅkâra is goats, the prastâva sheep, the udgîtha cows, the pratihâra horses, the nidhana man.   These are the Revatî Sâmans, as interwoven in animals.

2.   He who thus knows these Revatîs, as interwoven in animals, becomes rich in animals[2], he reaches the full life, he lives long, becomes great with children and cattle, great by fame.   His rule is, ' Never complain of animals.'

---

[1] The *S*akvarîs are sung with the Mahânâmnîs.   These are said to be water, and the worlds are said to rest on water.

[2] Revat means rich.

NINETEENTH KHANDA.

1. The hiṅkâra is hair, the prastâva skin, the udgîtha flesh, the pratihâra bone, the nidhana marrow. That is the Yagñâyagñîya Sâman, as interwoven in the members of the body.

2. He who thus knows the Yagñâyagñîya, as interwoven in the members of the body, becomes possessed of strong limbs, he is not crippled in any limb, he reaches the full life, he lives long, becomes great with children and cattle, great by fame. His rule is, 'Do not eat marrow for a year,' or 'Do not eat marrow at all.'

TWENTIETH KHANDA.

1. The hiṅkâra is fire, the prastâva air, the udgîtha the sun, the pratihâra the stars, the nidhana the moon. That is the Râgana Sâman, as interwoven in the deities.

2. He who thus knows the Râgana, as interwoven in the deities, obtains the same world, the same happiness, the same company as the gods, he reaches the full life, he lives long, becomes great with children and cattle, great by fame. His rule is, 'Do not speak evil of the Brâhmanas.'

TWENTY-FIRST KHANDA.

1. The hiṅkâra is the threefold knowledge, the prastâva these three worlds, the udgîtha Agni (fire), Vâyu (air), and Âditya (sun), the pratihâra the stars, the birds, and the rays, the nidhana the serpents, Gandharvas, and fathers. That is the Sâman, as interwoven in everything.

2. He who thus knows this Sâman, as interwoven in everything, he becomes everything.

3. And thus it is said in the following verse: 'There are the fivefold three (the three kinds of sacrificial knowledge, the three worlds &c. in their fivefold form, i. e. as identified with the hiṅkâra, the prastâva, &c.), and the other forms of the Sâman. Greater than these there is nothing else besides.'

4. He who knows this, knows everything. All regions offer him gifts. His rule is, 'Let him meditate (on the Sâman), knowing that he is everything, yea, that he is everything[1].'

TWENTY-SECOND KHANDA[2].

1. The udgîtha, of which a poet said, I choose the deep sounding note of the Sâman as good for cattle, belongs to Agni; the indefinite note belongs to Pragâpati, the definite note to Soma, the soft and smooth note to Vâyu, the smooth and strong note to Indra, the heron-like note to Brihaspati, the dull note to Varuna. Let a man cultivate all of these, avoiding, however, that of Varuna.

2. Let a man sing[3], wishing to obtain by his song immortality for the Devas. 'May I obtain by my song oblations (svadhâ) for the fathers, hope for men, fodder and water for animals, heaven for the sacrificer, food for myself,' thus reflecting on these in his mind, let a man (Udgâtri priest) sing praises, without making mistakes in pronunciation, &c.

---

[1] Here ends the Sâmopâsana.

[2] These are lucubrations on the different tones employed in singing the Sâman hymns, and their names, such as vinardi, anirukta, nirukta, mridu slakshna, slakshna balavad, krauñka, apadhvânta.

[3] It would be better if the first ity âgâyet could be left out. The commentator ignores these words.

3. All vowels (svara) belong to Indra, all sibilants (ûshman) to Pragâpati, all consonants (sparsa) to Mrityu (death). If somebody should reprove him for his vowels, let him say, 'I went to Indra as my refuge (when pronouncing my vowels) : he will answer thee.'

4. And if somebody should reprove him for his sibilants, let him say, 'I went to Pragâpati as my refuge : he will smash thee.' And if somebody should reprove him for his consonants, let him say, 'I went to Mrityu as my refuge : he will reduce thee to ashes.'

5. All vowels are to be pronounced with voice (ghosha) and strength (bala), so that the Udgâtri may give strength to Indra. All sibilants are to be pronounced, neither as if swallowed (agrasta)[1], nor as if thrown out (nirasta)[2], but well opened[3] (vivrita), so that the Udgâtri may give himself to Pragâpati. All consonants are to be pronounced slowly, and without crowding them together[4], so that the Udgâtri may withdraw himself from Mrityu.

---

[1] Grâsa, according to the Rig-veda-prâtisâkhya 766, is the stiffening of the root of the tongue in pronunciation.

[2] Nirâsa, according to the Rig-veda-prâtisâkhya 760, is the withdrawing of the active from the passive organ in pronunciation.

[3] The opening, vivrita, may mean two things, either the opening of the vocal chords (kha), which imparts to the ûshmans their surd character (Rig. Prât. 709), or the opening of the organs of pronunciation (karana), which for the ûshmans is asprishtam sthitam (Rig. Prât. 719), or vivrita (Ath. Prât. I, 31 ; Taitt. Prât. II, 5).

[4] Anabhinihita, for thus the commentaries give the reading, is explained by anabhinikshipta. On the real abhinidhâna, see Rig. Prât. 393. The translation does not follow the commentary. The genitive pragâpateh is governed by paridadâni.

Twenty-third Kha*n*da.

1. There are three branches of the law. Sacrifice, study, and charity are the first [1],

2. Austerity the second, and to dwell as a Brahma*k*ârin in the house of a tutor, always mortifying the body in the house of a tutor, is the third. All these obtain the worlds of the blessed; but the Brahmasa*m*stha alone (he who is firmly grounded in Brahman) obtains immortality.

3. Pra*g*âpati brooded on the worlds. From them, thus brooded on, the threefold knowledge (sacrifice) issued forth. He brooded on it, and from it, thus brooded on, issued the three syllables, Bhû*h*, Bhuva*h*, Sva*h*.

4. He brooded on them, and from them, thus brooded on, issued the Om. As all leaves are attached to a stalk, so is all speech (all words) attached to the Om (Brahman). Om is all this, yea, Om is all this.

Twenty-fourth Kha*n*da.

1. The teachers of Brahman (Veda) declare, as the Prâta*h*-savana (morning-oblation) belongs to the Vasus, the Mâdhyandina-savana (noon-libation) to

---

[1] Not the first in rank or succession, but only in enumerating the three branches of the law. This first branch corresponds to the second stage, the â*s*rama of the householder. Austerity is meant for the Vânaprastha, the third â*s*rama, while the third is intended for the Brahma*k*ârin, the student, only that the naish*th*ika or perpetual Brahma*k*ârin here takes the place of the ordinary student. The Brahmasa*m*stha would represent the fourth â*s*rama, that of the Sannyâsin or parivrâ*g*, who has ceased to perform any works, even the tapas or austerities of the Vânaprastha.

the Rudras, the third Savana (evening-libation) to
the Âdityas and the Vi*s*ve Devas,

2. Where then is the world of the sacrificer? He
who does not know this, how can he perform the
sacrifice? He only who knows, should perform it [1].

3. Before the beginning of the Prâtaranuvâka
(matin-chant), the sacrificer, sitting down behind the
household altar (gârhapatya), and looking towards
the north, sings the Sâman, addressed to the
Vasus :

4. 'Open the door of the world (the earth), let
us see thee, that we may rule (on earth).'

5. Then he sacrifices, saying : 'Adoration to
Agni, who dwells on the earth, who dwells in the
world! Obtain that world for me, the sacrificer!
That is the world for the sacrificer!'

6. 'I (the sacrificer) shall go thither, when this life
is over. Take this! (he says, in offering the libation.) Cast back the bolt!' Having said this,
he rises. For him the Vasus fulfil the morning-
oblation.

7. Before the beginning of the Mâdhyandina-
savana, the noon-oblation, the sacrificer, sitting down
behind the Âgnidhrîya altar, and looking towards
the north, sings the Sâman, addressed to the
Rudras :

8. 'Open the door of the world (the sky), let us
see thee, that we may rule wide (in the sky).'

9. Then he sacrifices, saying : 'Adoration to

---

[1] The commentator is always very anxious to explain that
though it is better that a priest should know the hidden meaning
of the sacrificial acts which he has to perform, yet there is nothing
to prevent a priest, who has not yet arrived at this stage of knowledge, from performing his duties.

Vâyu (air), who dwells in the sky, who dwells in the world. Obtain that world for me, the sacrificer! That is the world for the sacrificer!'

10. 'I (the sacrificer) shall go thither, when this life is over. Take this! Cast back the bolt!' Having said this, he rises. For him the Rudras fulfil the noon-oblation.

11. Before the beginning of the third oblation, the sacrificer, sitting down behind the Âhavanîya altar, and looking towards the north, sings the Sâman, addressed to the Âdityas and Vi*s*ve Devas:

12. 'Open the door of the world (the heaven), let us see thee, that we may rule supreme (in heaven).' This is addressed to the Âdityas.

13. Next the Sâman addressed to the Vi*s*ve Devas: 'Open the door of the world (heaven), let us see thee, that we may rule supreme (in heaven).'

14. Then he sacrifices, saying: 'Adoration to the Âdityas and to the Vi*s*ve Devas, who dwell in heaven, who dwell in the world. Obtain that world for me, the sacrificer!'

15. 'That is the world for the sacrificer! I (the sacrificer) shall go thither, when this life is over. Take this! Cast back the bolt!' Having said this, he rises.

16. For him the Âdityas and the Vi*s*ve Devas fulfil the third oblation. He who knows this, knows the full measure of the sacrifice, yea, he knows it.

THIRD PRAPÂ*TH*AKA.

FIRST KHA*N*DA [1].

1. The sun is indeed the honey [2] of the Devas. The heaven is the cross-beam (from which) the sky (hangs as) a hive, and the bright vapours are the eggs of the bees [3].

2. The eastern rays of the sun are the honey-cells in front. The *Rik* verses are the bees, the Rig-veda (sacrifice) is the flower, the water (of the sacrificial libations) is the nectar (of the flower).

3. Those very *Rik* verses then (as bees) brooded over the Rig-veda sacrifice (the flower); and from it, thus brooded on, sprang as its (nectar) essence, fame, glory of countenance, vigour, strength, and health [4].

4. That (essence) flowed forth and went towards the sun [5]. And that forms what we call the red (rohita) light of the rising sun.

---

[1] After the various meditations on the Sâma-veda sacrifice, the sun is next to be meditated on, as essential t othe performance of all sacrifices.

[2] Everybody delights in the sun, as the highest reward of all sacrifices.

[3] I am not certain whether this passage is rightly translated. Rajendralal Mitra speaks of an arched bamboo, whence the atmosphere hangs pendant like a hive, in which the vapours are the eggs. Apûpa means a cake, and may mean a hive. In order to understand the simile, we ought to have a clearer idea of the construction of the ancient bee-hive.

[4] Annâdya, explained as food, but more likely meaning power to eat, appetite, health. See III, 13, 1.

[5] The commentator explains: The *Rik* verses, on becoming part of the ceremonial, perform the sacrifice. The sacrifice (the flower), when surrounded by the *Rik* verses (bees), yields its essence, the nectar. That essence consists in all the rewards to be obtained through sacrifice, and as these rewards are to be enjoyed in the

SECOND KHA*ND*A.

1. The southern rays of the sun are the honey-cells on the right. The Ya*g*us verses are the bees, the Ya*g*ur-veda sacrifice is the flower, the water (of the sacrificial libations) is the nectar (of the flower).

2. Those very Ya*g*us verses (as bees) brooded over the Ya*g*ur-veda sacrifice (the flower); and from it, thus brooded on, sprang as its (nectar) essence, fame, glory of countenance, vigour, strength, and health.

3. That flowed forth and went towards the sun. And that forms what we call the white (*s*ukla) light of the sun.

THIRD KHA*ND*A.

1. The western rays of the sun are the honey-cells behind. The Sâman verses are the bees, the Sâma-veda sacrifice is the flower, the water is the nectar.

2. Those very Sâman verses (as bees) brooded over the Sâma-veda sacrifice; and from it, thus brooded on, sprang as its (nectar) essence, fame, glory of countenance, vigour, strength, and health.

3. That flowed forth and went towards the sun. And that forms what we call the dark (k*ri*sh*n*a) light of the sun.

FOURTH KHA*ND*A.

1. The northern rays of the sun are the honey-cells on the left. The (hymns of the) Atharvâṅgiras are the bees, the Itihâsa-purâ*n*a [1] (the reading of the old stories) is the flower, the water is the nectar.

next world and in the sun, therefore that essence or nectar is said to ascend to the sun.

[1] As there is no Atharva-veda sacrifice, properly so called, we have corresponding to the Atharva-veda hymns the so-called fifth

2. Those very hymns of the Atharvângiras (as bees) brooded over the Itihâsa-pur*a*na; and from it, thus brooded on, sprang as its (nectar) essence, fame, glory of countenance, vigour, strength, and health.

3. That flowed forth, and went towards the sun. And that forms what we call the extreme dark (para*h* k*ri*sh*n*am) light of the sun.

FIFTH KHA*N*DA.

1. The upward rays of the sun are the honey-cells above. The secret doctrines are the bees, Brahman (the Om) is the flower, the water is the nectar.

2. Those secret doctrines (as bees) brooded over Brahman (the Om); and from it, thus brooded on, sprang as its (nectar) essence, fame, glory of countenance, brightness, vigour, strength, and health.

3. That flowed forth, and went towards the sun. And that forms what seems to stir in the centre of the sun.

4. These (the different colours in the sun) are the essences of the essences. For the Vedas are essences (the best things in the world); and of them (after they have assumed the form of sacrifice) these (the colours rising to the sun) are again the essences. They are the nectar of the nectar. For the Vedas are nectar (immortal), and of them these are the nectar.

Veda, the Itihâsa-pur*a*na. This may mean the collection of legends and traditions, or the old book of traditions. At all events it is taken as one Purâ*n*a, not as many. These ancient stories were repeated at the A*s*vamedha sacrifice during the so-called Pariplava nights. Many of them have been preserved in the Brâhma*n*as; others, in a more modern form, in the Mahâbhârata. See Weber, Indische Studien, I, p. 258, note.

Sixth Kha*nd*a.

1. On the first of these nectars (the red light, which represents fame, glory of countenance, vigour, strength, health) the Vasus live, with Agni at their head. True, the Devas do not eat or drink, but they enjoy by seeing the nectar.

2. They enter into that (red) colour, and they rise from that colour [1].

3. He who thus knows this nectar, becomes one of the Vasus, with Agni at their head, he sees the nectar and rejoices. And he, too, having entered that colour, rises again from that colour.

4. So long as the sun rises in the east and sets in the west [2], so long does he follow the sovereign supremacy of the Vasus.

Seventh Kha*nd*a.

1. On the second of these nectars the Rudras live, with Indra at their head. True, the Devas do not eat or drink, but they enjoy by seeing the nectar.

2. They enter into that white colour, and they rise from that colour.

3. He who thus knows this nectar, becomes one of the Rudras, with Indra at their head, he sees the

---

[1] This is differently explained by the commentator. He takes it to mean that, when the Vasus have gone to the sun, and see that there is no opportunity for enjoying that colour, they rest; but when they see that there is an opportunity for enjoying it, they exert themselves for it. I think the colour is here taken for the colour of the morning, which the Vasus enter, and from which they go forth again.

[2] 1. East: Vasus: red: Agni.   2. South: Rudras: white: Indra.   3. West: Âditya: dark: Varu*n*a.   4. North: Marut: very dark: Soma.   5. Upward: Sâdhya: centre: Brahman.

nectar and rejoices. And he, having entered that colour, rises again from that colour.

4. So long as the sun rises in the east and sets in the west, twice as long does it rise in the south and set in the north ; and so long does he follow the sovereign supremacy of the Rudras.

EIGHTH KHA*N*DA.

1. On the third of these nectars the Âdityas live, with Varu*n*a at their head. True, the Devas do not eat or drink, but they enjoy by seeing the nectar.

2. They enter into that (dark) colour, and they rise from that colour.

3. He who thus knows this nectar, becomes one of the Âdityas, with Varu*n*a at their head, he sees the nectar and rejoices. And he, having entered that colour, rises again from that colour.

4. So long as the sun rises in the south and sets in the north, twice as long does it rise in the west and set in the east; and so long does he follow the sovereign supremacy of the Âdityas.

NINTH KHA*N*DA.

1. On the fourth of these nectars the Maruts live, with Soma at their head. True, the Devas do not eat or drink, but they enjoy by seeing the nectar.

2. They enter in that (very dark) colour, and they rise from that colour.

3. He who thus knows this nectar, becomes one of the Maruts, with Soma at their head, he sees the nectar and rejoices. And he, having entered that colour, rises again from that colour.

4. So long as the sun rises in the west and sets

in the east, twice as long does it rise in the north and set in the south; and so long does he follow the sovereign supremacy of the Maruts.

TENTH KHANDA.

1. On the fifth of these nectars the Sâdhyas live, with Brahman at their head. True, the Devas do not eat or drink, but they enjoy by seeing the nectar.

2. They enter into that colour, and they rise from that colour.

3. He who thus knows this nectar, becomes one of the Sâdhyas, with Brahman at their head; he sees the nectar and rejoices. And he, having entered that colour, rises again from that colour.

4. So long as the sun rises in the north and sets in the south, twice as long does it rise above, and set below; and so long does he follow the sovereign power of the Sâdhyas[1].

---

[1] The meaning of the five Khandas from 6 to 10 is clear, in so far as they are intended to show that he who knows or meditates on the sacrifices as described before, enjoys his reward in different worlds with the Vasus, Rudras, &c. for certain periods of time, till at last he reaches the true Brahman. Of these periods each succeeding one is supposed to be double the length of the preceding one. This is expressed by imagining a migration of the sun from east to south, west, north, and zenith. Each change of the sun marks a new world, and the duration of each successive world is computed as double the durâtion of the preceding world. Similar ideas have been more fully developed in the Purânas, and the commentator is at great pains to remove apparent contradictions between the Paurânik and Vaidik accounts, following, as Ânandagñânagiri remarks, the Dravidâkârya (p. 173, l. 13).

ELEVENTH KHANDA.

1. When from thence he has risen upwards, he neither rises nor sets. He is alone, standing in the centre. And on this there is this verse:

2. 'Yonder he neither rises nor sets at any time. If this is not true, ye gods, may I lose Brahman.'

3. And indeed to him who thus knows this Brahma-upanishad (the secret doctrine of the Veda) the sun does not rise and does not set. For him there is day, once and for all [1].

4. This doctrine (beginning with III, 1, 1) Brahman (m. Hiranyagarbha) told to Pragâpati (Virâg), Pragâpati to Manu, Manu to his offspring (Ikshvâku, &c.) And the father told that (doctrine of) Brahman (n.) to Uddâlaka Âruni.

5. A father may therefore tell that doctrine of Brahman to his eldest son [2], or to a worthy pupil.

But no one should tell it to anybody else, even if he gave him the whole sea-girt earth, full of treasure, for this doctrine is worth more than that, yea, it is worth more.

TWELFTH KHANDA.

1. The Gâyatrî [3] (verse) is everything whatsoever here exists. Gâyatrî indeed is speech, for speech

---

[1] Cf. Kh. Up. VIII, 4, 2.

[2] This was the old, not the present custom, says Ânandagiri. Not the father, but an âkârya, has now to teach his pupils.

[3] The Gâyatrî is one of the sacred metres, and is here to be meditated on as Brahman. It is used in the sense of verse, and as the name of a famous hymn. The Gâyatrî is often praised as the most powerful metre, and whatever can be obtained by means of the recitation of Gâyatrî verses is described as the achievement of the Gâyatrî. The etymology of gâyatrî from gai and trâ is, of course, fanciful.

sings forth (gâya-ti) and protects (trâya-te) everything that here exists.

2. That Gâyatrî is also the earth, for everything that here exists rests on the earth, and does not go beyond.

3. That earth again is the body in man, for in it the vital airs (prâ*n*as [1], which are everything) rest, and do not go beyond.

4. That body again in man is the heart within man, for in it the prâ*n*as (which are everything) rest, and do not go beyond.

5. That Gâyatrî has four feet [2] and is sixfold [3]. And this is also declared by a *Rik* verse (Rig-veda X, 90, 3) :—

6. 'Such is the greatness of it (of Brahman, under the disguise of Gâyatrî [4]); greater than it is the Person [5] (purusha). His feet are all things. The immortal with three feet is in heaven (i. e. in himself).'

---

[1] The prâ*n*as may be meant for the five senses, as explained in *Kh.* I, 2, 1; II, 7, 1; or for the five breathings, as explained immediately afterwards in III, 13, 1. The commentator sees in them everything that here exists (*Kh.* Up. III, 15, 4), and thus establishes the likeness between the body and the Gâyatrî. As Gâyatrî is the earth, and the earth the body, and the body the heart, Gâyatrî is in the end to be considered as the heart.

[2] The four feet are explained as the four quarters of the Gâyatrî metre, of six syllables each. The Gâyatrî really consists of three feet of eight syllables each.

[3] The Gâyatrî has been identified with all beings, with speech, earth, body, heart, and the vital airs, and is therefore called sixfold. This, at least, is the way in which the commentator accounts for the epithet ' sixfold.'

[4] Of Brahman modified as Gâyatrî, having four feet, and being sixfold.

[5] The real Brahman, unmodified by form and name.

7. The Brahman which has been thus described (as immortal with three feet in heaven, and as Gâyatrî) is the same as the ether which is around us;

8. And the ether which is around us, is the same as the ether which is within us. And the ether which is within us,

9. That is the ether within the heart. That ether in the heart (as Brahman) is omnipresent and unchanging. He who knows this obtains omnipresent and unchangeable happiness.

THIRTEENTH KHA*ND*A[1].

1. For that heart there are five gates belonging to the Devas (the senses). The eastern gate is the Prâ*n*a (up-breathing), that is the eye, that is Âditya (the sun). Let a man meditate on that as brightness (glory of countenance) and health. He who knows this, becomes bright and healthy.

2. The southern gate is the Vyâna (back-breathing), that is the ear, that is the moon. Let a man meditate on that as happiness and fame. He who knows this, becomes happy and famous.

3. The western gate is the Apâna (down-breathing), that is speech, that is Agni (fire). Let a man meditate on that as glory of countenance and health. He who knows this, becomes glorious and healthy.

4. The northern gate is the Samâna (on-breathing), that is mind, that is Par*g*anya (rain). Let a man meditate on that as celebrity and beauty.

---

[1] The meditation on the five gates and the five gate-keepers of the heart is meant to be subservient to the meditation on Brahman, as the ether in the heart, which, as it is said at the end, is actually seen and heard by the senses as being within the heart.

He who knows this, becomes celebrated and beautiful.

5. The upper gate is the Udâna (out-breathing), that is air, that is ether. Let a man meditate on that as strength and greatness. He who knows this, becomes strong and great.

6. These are the five men of Brahman, the door-keepers of the Svarga (heaven) world. He who knows these five men of Brahman, the door-keepers of the Svarga world, in his family a strong son is born. He who thus knows these five men of Brahman, as the door-keepers of the Svarga world, enters himself the Svarga world.

7. Now that light which shines above this heaven, higher than all, higher than everything, in the highest world, beyond which there are no other worlds, that is the same light which is within man. And of this we have this visible proof[1]:

8. Namely, when we thus perceive by touch the warmth here in the body[2]. And of it we have this audible proof: Namely, when we thus, after stopping our ears, listen to what is like the rolling of a carriage, or the bellowing of an ox, or the sound of a burning fire[3] (within the ears). Let a man meditate on this as the (Brahman) which is seen and heard.

---

[1] The presence of Brahman in the heart of man is not to rest on the testimony of revelation only, but is here to be established by the evidence of the senses. Childish as the argument may seem to us, it shows at all events how intently the old Brahmans thought on the problem of the evidence of the invisible.

[2] That warmth must come from something, just as smoke comes from fire, and this something is supposed to be Brahman in the heart.

[3] Cf. Ait. Âr. III, 2, 4, 11–13.

He who knows this, becomes conspicuous and celebrated, yea, he becomes celebrated.

FOURTEENTH KHANDA.

1. All this is Brahman (n.) Let a man meditate on that (visible world) as beginning, ending, and breathing [1] in it (the Brahman).

Now man is a creature of will. According to what his will is in this world, so will he be when he has departed this life. Let him therefore have this will and belief:

2. The intelligent, whose body is spirit, whose form is light, whose thoughts are true, whose nature is like ether (omnipresent and invisible), from whom all works, all desires, all sweet odours and tastes proceed; he who embraces all this, who never speaks, and is never surprised,

3. He is my self within the heart, smaller than a corn of rice, smaller than a corn of barley, smaller than a mustard seed, smaller than a canary seed or the kernel of a canary seed. He also is my self within the heart, greater than the earth, greater than the sky, greater than heaven, greater than all these worlds.

4. He from whom all works, all desires, all sweet odours and tastes proceed, who embraces all this, who never speaks and who is never surprised, he, my self within the heart, is that Brahman (n.) When I shall have departed from hence, I shall obtain him (that Self). He who has this faith [2] has no doubt; thus said Sândilya [3], yea, thus he said.

---

[1] Galân is explained by ga, born, la, absorbed, and an, breathing. It is an artificial term, but fully recognised by the Vedânta school, and always explained in this manner.

[2] Or he who has faith and no doubt, will obtain this.

[3] This chapter is frequently quoted as the Sândilya-vidyâ, Vedântasâra, init; Vedânta-sûtra III, 3, 31.

FIFTEENTH KHANDA [1].

1. The chest which has the sky for its circumference and the earth for its bottom, does not decay, for the quarters are its sides, and heaven its lid above. That chest is a treasury, and all things are within it.

2. Its eastern quarter is called Guhû, its southern Sahamânâ, its western Râgñî, its northern Subhûtâ [2]. The child of those quarters is Vâyu, the air, and he who knows that the air is indeed the child of the quarters, never weeps for his sons. 'I know the wind to be the child of the quarters, may I never weep for my sons.'

3. 'I turn to the imperishable chest with such and such and such [3].' 'I turn to the Prâna (life) with such and such and such.' 'I turn to Bhûh with such and such and such.' 'I turn to Bhuvah with such and such and such.' 'I turn to Svah with such and such and such.'

4. 'When I said, I turn to Prâna, then Prâna means all whatever exists here—to that I turn.'

5. 'When I said, I turn to Bhûh, what I said is, I turn to the earth, the sky, and heaven.'

---

[1] The object of this section, the Kosavignâna, is to show how the promise made in III, 13, 6, 'that a strong son should be born in a man's family,' is to be fulfilled.

[2] These names are explained by the commentator as follows: Because people offer libations (guhvati), turning to the east, therefore it is called Guhû. Because evil doers suffer (sahante) in the town of Yama, which is in the south, therefore it is called Sahamânâ. The western quarter is called Râgñî, either because it is sacred to king Varuna (râgan), or on account of the red colour (râga) of the twilight. The north is called Subhûtâ, because wealthy beings (bhûtimat), like Kuvera &c., reside there.

[3] Here the names of the sons are to be pronounced.

6. 'When I said, I turn to Bhuva*h*, what I said is, I turn to Agni (fire), Vâyu (air), Âditya (sun).'

7. 'When I said, I turn to Sva*h*, what I said is, I turn to the *R*ig-veda, Ya*g*ur-veda, and Sâma-veda. That is what I said, yea, that is what I said.'

Sixteenth Kha*n*da [1].

1. Man is sacrifice. His (first) twenty-four years are the morning-libation. The Gâyatrî has twenty-four syllables, the morning-libation is offered with Gâyatrî hymns. The Vasus are connected with that part of the sacrifice. The Prâ*n*as (the five senses) are the Vasus, for they make all this to abide (vâsayanti).

2. If anything ails him in that (early) age, let him say: 'Ye Prâ*n*as, ye Vasus, extend this my morning-libation unto the midday-libation, that I, the sacrificer, may not perish in the midst of the Prâ*n*as or Vasus.' Thus he recovers from his illness, and becomes whole.

3. The next forty-four years are the midday-libation. The Trish*t*ubh has forty-four syllables, the midday-libation is offered with Trish*t*ubh hymns. The Rudras are connected with that part of it. The Prâ*n*as are the Rudras, for they make all this to cry (rodayanti).

4. If anything ails him in that (second) age, let him say: 'Ye Prâ*n*as, ye Rudras, extend this my midday-libation unto the third libation, that I, the sacrificer, may not perish in the midst of the Prâ*n*as or Rudras.' Thus he recovers from his illness, and becomes whole.

5. The next forty-eight years are the third

---

[1] The object of this Kha*n*da is to show how to obtain long life, as promised before.

libation. The *G*agatî has forty-eight syllables, the
third libation is offered with *G*agatî hymns. The
Âdityas are connected with that part of it. The
Prâ*n*as are the Âdityas, for they take up all this
(âdadate).

6. If anything ails him in that (third) age, let him
say: 'Ye Prâ*n*as, ye Âdityas, extend this my third
libation unto the full age, that I, the sacrificer, may
not perish in the midst of the Prâ*n*as or Âdityas.'
Thus he recovers from his illness, and becomes whole.

7. Mahidâsa Aitareya (the son of Itarâ), who
knew this, said (addressing a disease): 'Why dost
thou afflict me, as I shall not die by it?' He lived
a hundred and sixteen years (i.e. 24 + 44 + 48). He,
too, who knows this lives on to a hundred and sixteen years.

SEVENTEENTH KHA*ND*A [1].

1. When a man (who is the sacrificer) hungers,
thirsts, and abstains from pleasures, that is the
Dîkshâ (initiatory rite).

2. When a man eats, drinks, and enjoys pleasures,
he does it with the Upasadas (the sacrificial days on
which the sacrificer is allowed to partake of food).

3. When a man laughs, eats, and delights himself, he does it with the Stuta-*s*astras (hymns sung
and recited at the sacrifices).

4. Penance, liberality, righteousness, kindness,
truthfulness, these form his Dakshi*n*âs (gifts be-
stowed on priests, &c.)

5. Therefore when they say, 'There will be a

---

[1] Here we have a representation of the sacrifice as performed
without any ceremonial, and as it is often represented when
performed in thought only by a man living in the forest.

birth,' and 'there has been a birth' (words used at
the Soma-sacrifice, and really meaning, 'He will
pour out the Soma-juice,' and 'he has poured out
the Soma-juice'), that is his new birth. His death
is the Avabhr*i*tha ceremony (when the sacrificial
vessels are carried away to be cleansed).

6. Ghora Âṅgirasa, after having communicated
this (view of the sacrifice) to Kr*i*sh*n*a, the son of
Devăkî [1]—and he never thirsted again (after other
knowledge)—said: 'Let a man, when his end ap-

---

[1] The curious coincidence between Kr*i*sh*n*a Devakîputra, here
mentioned as a pupil of Ghora Âṅgirasa, and the famous Kr*i*sh*n*a,
the son of Devakî, was first pointed out by Colebrooke, Miscell.
Essays, II, 177. Whether it is more than a coincidence, is difficult
to say. Certainly we can build no other conclusions on it than
those indicated by Colebrooke, that new fables may have been
constructed elevating this personage to the rank of a god. We
know absolutely nothing of the old Kr*i*sh*n*a Devakîputra except
his having been a pupil of Ghora Âṅgirasa, nor does there seem
to have been any attempt made by later Brahmans to connect
their divine Kr*i*sh*n*a, the son of Vasudeva, with the Kr*i*sh*n*a
Devakîputra of our Upanishad. This is all the more remarkable
because the author of the Sân*d*ilya-sûtras, for instance, who is
very anxious to find a *s*rauta authority for the worship of Kr*i*sh*n*a
Vâsudeva as the supreme deity, had to be satisfied with quoting
such modern compilations as the Nârâya*n*opanishad, Atharva*s*iras,
VI, 9, brahma*n*yo devakîputro brahma*n*yo madhusûdana*h* (see
Sân*d*ilya-sûtras, ed. Ballantyne, p. 36, translated by Cowell, p. 51),
without venturing to refer to the Kr*i*sh*n*a Devakîputra of the
*Kh*ândogya-upanishad. The occurrence of such names as Kr*i*sh*n*a,
Vâsudeva, Madhusûdana stamps Upanishads, like the Âtmabodha-
upanishad, as modern (Colebrooke, Essays, I, 101), and the same
remark applies, as Weber has shown, to the Gopâlatâpanî-upani-
shad (Bibliotheca Indica, No. 183), where we actually find such
names as *S*rîkr*i*sh*n*a Govinda, Gop*i*ganavallabha, Devakyâm *g*âta*h*
(p. 38), &c. Professor Weber has treated these questions very
fully, but it is not quite clear to me whether he wishes to go
beyond Colebrooke and to admit more than a similarity of name
between the pupil of Ghora Âṅgirasa and the friend of the Gopîs.

proaches, take refuge with this Triad [1] : " Thou art
the imperishable," " Thou art the unchangeable,"
" Thou art the edge of Prâ*n*a." ' On this subject
there are two *Rik* verses (Rig-veda VIII, 6, 30) :—

7. ' Then they see (within themselves) the ever-
present light of the old seed (of the world, the Sat),
the highest, which is lighted in the brilliant (Brahman).' Rig-veda I, 50, 10 :—

' Perceiving above the darkness (of ignorance)
the higher light (in the sun), as the higher light
within the heart, the bright source (of light and
life) among the gods, we have reached the highest
light, yea, the highest light [2].'

EIGHTEENTH KHA*N*DA [3].

1. Let a man meditate on mind as Brahman (n.),
this is said with reference to the body. Let a
man meditate on the ether as Brahman (n.), this is
said with reference to the Devas. Thus both the
meditation which has reference to the body, and the
meditation which has reference to the Devas, has
been taught.

2. That Brahman (mind) has four feet (quarters).

---

[1] Let him recite these three verses.

[2] Both these verses had to be translated here according to their
scholastic interpretation, but they had originally a totally different
meaning. Even the text was altered, divâ being changed to divi,
sva*h* to sve. The first is taken from a hymn addressed to Indra,
who after conquering the dark clouds brings back the light of
the sun. When he does that, then the people see again, as
the poet says, the daily light of the old seed (from which the sun
rises) which is lighted in heaven. The other verse belongs to
a hymn addressed to the sun. Its simple meaning is : ' Seeing
above the darkness (of the night) the rising light, the Sun, bright
among the bright, we came towards the highest light.'

[3] This is a further elucidation of *Kh*. Up. III, 14, 2.

Speech is one foot, breath is one foot, the eye is one foot, the ear is one foot—so much with reference to the body. Then with reference to the gods, Agni (fire) is one foot, Vâyu (air) is one foot, Âditya (sun) is one foot, the quarters are one foot. Thus both the worship which has reference to the body, and the worship which has reference to the Devas, has been taught.

3. Speech is indeed the fourth foot of Brahman. That foot shines with Agni (fire) as its light, and warms. He who knows this, shines and warms through his celebrity, fame, and glory of countenance.

4. Breath is indeed the fourth foot of Brahman. That foot shines with Vâyu (air) as its light, and warms. He who knows this, shines and warms through his celebrity, fame, and glory of countenance.

5. The eye is indeed the fourth foot of Brahman. That foot shines with Âditya (sun) as its light, and warms. He who knows this, shines and warms through his celebrity, fame, and glory of countenance.

6. The ear is indeed the fourth foot of Brahman. That foot shines with the quarters as its light, and warms. He who knows this, shines and warms through his celebrity, fame, and glory of countenance.

NINETEENTH KHA*N*DA.

1. Âditya (the sun [1]) is Brahman, this is the doctrine, and this is the fuller account of it :—

In the beginning this was non-existent [2]. It be-

---

[1] Âditya, or the sun, had before been represented as one of the four feet of Brahman. He is now represented as Brahman, or as to be meditated on as such.

[2] Not yet existing, not yet developed in form and name, and therefore as if not existing.

came existent, it grew. It turned into an egg [1].
The egg lay for the time of a year. The egg
broke open. The two halves were one of silver,
the other of gold.

2. The silver one became this earth, the golden
one the sky, the thick membrane (of the white) the
mountains, the thin membrane (of the yoke) the
mist with the clouds, the small veins the rivers, the
fluid the sea.

3. And what was born from it that was Âditya,
the sun. When he was born shouts of hurrah arose,
and all beings arose, and all things which they desired. Therefore whenever the sun rises and sets,
shouts of hurrah arise, and all beings arise, and all
things which they desire.

4. If any one knowing this meditates on the sun
as Brahman, pleasant shouts will approach him and
will continue, yea, they will continue.

FOURTH PRAPÂ*TH*AKA.

FIRST KHA*ND*A [2].

1. There lived once upon a time *G*âna*s*ruti Pautrâya*n*a (the great-grandson of *G*ana*s*ruta), who was
a pious giver, bestowing much wealth upon the

---

[1] Â*nd*a instead of a*nd*a is explained as a Vedic irregularity.
A similar cosmogony is given in Manu's Law Book, I, 12 seq.
See Kellgren, Mythus de ovo mundano, Helsingfors, 1849.

[2] Vâyu (air) and Prâ*n*a (breath) had before been represented
as feet of Brahman, as the second pair. Now they are represented as Brahman, and as to be meditated on as such. This
is the teaching of Raikva. The language of this chapter is very
obscure, and I am not satisfied with the translation.

people, and always keeping open house. He built places of refuge everywhere, wishing that people should everywhere eat of his food.

2. Once in the night some Ha*m*sas (flamingoes) flew over his house, and one flamingo said to another: 'Hey, Bhallâksha, Bhallâksha (short-sighted friend). The light (glory) of *G*âna*s*ruti Pautrâya*n*a has spread like the sky. Do not go near, that it may not burn thee.'

3. The other answered him: 'How can you speak of him, being what he is (a râ*g*anya, noble), as if he were like Raikva with the car [1]?'

4. The first replied: 'How is it with this Raikva with the car of whom thou speakest?'

The other answered: 'As (in a game of dice) all the lower casts [2] belong to him who has conquered with the K*r*ita cast, so whatever good deeds other people perform, belong to that Raikva. He who knows what he knows, he is thus spoken of by me.'

5. *G*âna*s*ruti Pautrâya*n*a overheard this conversation, and as soon as he had risen in the morning, he said to his door-keeper (kshatt*ri*): 'Friend, dost thou speak of (me, as if I were) Raikva with the car?'

He replied: 'How is it with this Raikva with the car?'

6. The king said: 'As (in a game of dice), all the lower casts belong to him who has conquered with the K*r*ita cast, so whatever good deeds other people perform, belong to that Raikva. He who knows what he knows, he is thus spoken of by me.'

---

[1] Sayugvan is explained as possessed of a car with yoked horses or oxen. Could it have meant originally, 'yoke-fellow, equal,' as in Rig-veda X, 130, 4? Anquetil renders it by 'semper cum se ipso camelum solutum habens.'

[2] Instead of adhareyâ*h*, we must read adhare 'yâ*h*.

7. The door-keeper went to look for Raikva, but returned saying, ' I found him not.'   Then the king said : 'Alas! where a Brâhma*n*a should be searched for (in the solitude of the forest), there go for him.'

8. The door-keeper came to a man who was lying beneath a car and scratching his sores [1].   He addressed him, and said : ' Sir, are you Raikva with the car ? '

He answered : ' Here I am.'

Then the door-keeper returned, and said: 'I have found him.'

SECOND KHA*ND*A.

1.   Then *G*âna*s*ruti Pautrâya*n*a took six hundred cows, a necklace, and a carriage with mules, went to Raikva and said :

2. ' Raikva, here are six hundred cows, a necklace, and a carriage with mules ; teach me the deity which you worship.'

3.   The other replied : 'Fie, necklace and carriage be thine, O *S*ûdra, together with the cows.'

Then *G*âna*s*ruti Pautrâya*n*a took again a thousand cows, a necklace, a carriage with mules, and his own daughter, and went to him.

4.   He said to him : ' Raikva, there are a thousand cows, a necklace, a carriage with mules, this wife, and this village in which thou dwellest.   Sir, teach me ! '

5.   He, opening her mouth [2], said : ' You have

---

[1] It is curious that in a hymn of the Atharva-veda (V, 22, 5, 8) takman, apparently a disease of the skin, is relegated to the Mahâ-vr*i*shas, where Raikva dwelt.   Roth, Zur Literatur des Veda, p. 36.

[2] To find out her age.   The commentator translates, ' Raikva, knowing her mouth to be the door of knowledge, i. e. knowing that for her he might impart his knowledge to *G*âna*s*ruti, and that

brought these (cows and other presents), O Sûdra, but only by that mouth did you make me speak.'

These are the Raikva-parna villages in the country of the Mahâvrishas (mahâpunyas) where Raikva dwelt under him [1]. And he said to him :

THIRD KHANDA.

1. 'Air (vâyu) is indeed the end of all [2]. For when fire goes out, it goes into air. When the sun goes down, it goes into air. When the moon goes down, it goes into air.

2. 'When water dries up, it goes into air. Air indeed consumes them all. So much with reference to the Devas.

3. ' Now with reference to the body. Breath (prâna) is indeed the end of all. When a man sleeps, speech goes into breath, so do sight, hearing, and mind. Breath indeed consumes them all.

4. ' These are the two ends, air among the Devas, breath among the senses (prânâh).'

5. Once while Saunaka Kâpeya and Abhipratârin Kâkshaseni were being waited on at their meal, a religious student begged of them. They gave him nothing.

6. He said: ' One god—who is he ?—swallowed the four great ones [3], he, the guardian of the world.

Gânasruti by bringing such rich gifts had become a proper receiver of knowledge, consented to do what he had before refused.'

[1] The commentator supplies adât, the king gave the villages to him.

[2] Samvarga, absorption, whence samvargavidyâ, not samsarga. It is explained by samvargana, samgrahana, and samgrasana, in the text itself by adana, eating.

[3] This must refer to Vâyu and Prâna swallowing the four, as explained in IV, 3, 2, and IV, 3, 3. The commentator explains

O Kâpeya, mortals see him not, O Abhipratârin, though he dwells in many places. He to whom this food belongs, to him it has not been given [1].'

7. *S*aunaka Kâpeya, pondering on that speech, went to the student and said : 'He is the self of the Devas, the creator of all beings, with golden tusks, the eater, not without intelligence. His greatness is said to be great indeed, because, without being eaten, he eats even what is not food [2]. Thus do we, O Brahma*k*ârin, meditate on that Being.' Then he said : 'Give him food.'

8. They gave him food. Now these five (the eater Vâyu (air), and his food, Agni (fire), Âditya (sun), *K*andramas (moon), Ap (water)) and the other five (the eater Prâ*n*a (breath), and his food, speech, sight, hearing, mind) make ten, and that is the K*ri*ta (the highest [3]) cast (representing the ten, the eaters and the food). Therefore in all quarters those ten are food (and) K*ri*ta (the highest cast). These are again the Virâ*g* [4] (of ten syllables)

---

it by Pra*g*âpati, who is sometimes called Ka. In one sense it would be Brahman, as represented by Vâyu and Prâ*n*a.

[1] The food which you have refused to me, you have really refused to Brahman.

[2] *S*aunaka wishes the student to understand that though 'mortals see him not,' he sees and knows him, viz. the god who, as Vâyu, swallows all the gods, but produces them again, and who, as prâ*n*a, swallows during sleep all senses, but produces them again at the time of waking.

[3] The words are obscure, and the commentator does not throw much light on them. He explains, however, the four casts of the dice, the K*ri*ta=4, the Tretâ=3, the Dvâpara=2, the Kali=1, making together 10, the K*ri*ta cast absorbing the other casts, and thus counting ten.

[4] Virâ*g*, name of a metre of ten syllables, and also a name of food. One expects, 'which is the food and eats the food.'

which eats the food. Through this all this becomes
seen. He who knows this sees all this and becomes an
eater of food, yea, he becomes an eater of food.

FOURTH KHA*ND*A[1].

1. Satyakâma, the son of *G*abâlâ, addressed his
mother and said: 'I wish to become a Brahma*k*ârin
(religious student), mother. Of what family am I?'

2. She said to him: 'I do not know, my child,
of what family thou art. In my youth when I had
to move about much as a servant (waiting on the
guests in my father's house), I conceived thee. I do
not know of what family thou art. I am *G*abâlâ by
name, thou art Satyakâma (Philalethes). Say that
thou art Satyakâma *G*âbâla.'

3. He going to Gautama Hâridrumata said to
him, 'I wish to become a Brahma*k*ârin with you,
Sir. May I come to you, Sir?'

4. He said to him: 'Of what family are you, my
friend?' He replied: 'I do not know, Sir, of what
family I am. I asked my mother, and she answered:
"In my youth when I had to move about much as
a servant, I conceived thee. I do not know of what
family thou art. I am *G*abâlâ by name, thou art
Satyakâma," I am therefore Satyakâma *G*âbâla, Sir.'

5. He said to him: 'No one but a true Brâhma*n*a would thus speak out. Go and fetch fuel,
friend, I shall initiate you. You have not swerved
from the truth.'

Having initiated him, he chose four hundred
lean and weak cows, and said: 'Tend these, friend.'

---

[1] This carries on the explanation of the four feet of Brahman,
as first mentioned in III, 18, 1. Each foot or quarter of Brahman
is represented as fourfold, and the knowledge of these sixteen parts
is called the Sho*d*a*s*akalâvidyâ.

He drove them out and said to himself, 'I shall not return unless I bring back a thousand.' He dwelt a number of years (in the forest), and when the cows had become a thousand,

FIFTH KHA*ND*A.

1. The bull of the herd (meant for Vâyu) said to him: 'Satyakâma!' He replied: 'Sir!' The bull said: 'We have become a thousand, lead us to the house of the teacher;

2. 'And I will declare to you one foot of Brahman.' 'Declare it, Sir,' he replied.

He said to him: 'The eastern region is one quarter, the western region is one quarter, the southern region is one quarter, the northern region is one quarter. This is a foot of Brahman, consisting of the four quarters, and called Prakâ*s*avat (endowed with splendour).

3. 'He who knows this and meditates on the foot of Brahman, consisting of four quarters, by the name of Prakâ*s*avat, becomes endowed with splendour in this world. He conquers the resplendent worlds, whoever knows this and meditates on the foot of Brahman, consisting of the four quarters, by the name of Prakâ*s*avat.

SIXTH KHA*ND*A.

1. 'Agni will declare to you another foot of Brahman.'

(After these words of the bull), Satyakâma, on the morrow, drove the cows (toward the house of the teacher). And when they came towards the evening, he lighted a fire, penned the cows, laid wood on the fire, and sat down behind the fire, looking to the east.

2. Then Agni (the fire) said to him: 'Satyakâma!'
He replied: 'Sir.'

3. Agni said: 'Friend, I will declare unto you
one foot of Brahman.'

'Declare it, Sir,' he replied.

He said to him: 'The earth is one quarter, the
sky is one quarter, the heaven is one quarter, the
ocean is one quarter. This is a foot of Brahman,
consisting of four quarters, and called Anantavat
(endless).'

4. 'He who knows this and meditates on the foot
of Brahman, consisting of four quarters, by the name
of Anantavat, becomes endless in this world. He
conquers the endless worlds, whoever knows this
and meditates on the foot of Brahman, consisting of
four quarters, by the name of Anantavat.

Seventh Khan*d*a.

1. 'A Ha*m*sa (flamingo, meant for the sun) will
declare to you another foot of Brahman.'

(After these words of Agni), Satyakâma, on the
morrow, drove the cows onward. And when they
came towards the evening, he lighted a fire, penned
the cows, laid wood on the fire, and sat down behind
the fire, looking toward the east.

2. Then a Ha*m*sa flew near and said to him:
'Satyakâma.' He replied: 'Sir.'

3. The Ha*m*sa said: 'Friend, I will declare unto
you one foot of Brahman.'

'Declare it, Sir,' he replied.

He said to him: 'Fire is one quarter, the sun
is one quarter, the moon is one quarter, lightning is
one quarter. This is a foot of Brahman, consisting
of four quarters, and called *G*yotishmat (full of light).

4. 'He who knows this and meditates on the foot of Brahman, consisting of four quarters, by the name of Gyotishmat, becomes full of light in this world. He conquers the worlds which are full of light, whoever knows this and meditates on the foot of Brahman, consisting of four quarters, by the name of Gyotishmat.

EIGHTH KHANDA.

1. 'A diver-bird (Madgu, meant for Prâna) will declare to you another foot of Brahman.'

(After these words of the Hamsa), Satyakâma, on the morrow, drove the cows onward. And when they came towards the evening, he lighted a fire, penned the cows, laid wood on the fire, and sat down behind the fire, looking toward the east.

2. Then a diver flew near and said to him: 'Satyakâma.' He replied: 'Sir.'

3. The diver said: 'Friend, I will declare unto you one foot of Brahman.'

'Declare it, Sir,' he replied.

He said to him: 'Breath is one quarter, the eye is one quarter, the ear is one quarter, the mind is one quarter. This is a foot of Brahman, consisting of four quarters, and called Âyatanavat (having a home).

'He who knows this and meditates on the foot of Brahman, consisting of four quarters, by the name of Âyatanavat, becomes possessed of a home in this world. He conquers the worlds which offer a home, whoever knows this and meditates on the foot of Brahman, consisting of four quarters, by the name of Âyatanavat.'

NINTH KHANDA.

1. Thus he reached the house of his teacher. The teacher said to him : 'Satyakâma.' He replied : 'Sir.'

2. The teacher said: 'Friend, you shine like one who knows Brahman. Who then has taught you[1]?' He replied : 'Not men. But you only, Sir, I wish, should teach me[2];

3. 'For I have heard from men like you, Sir, that only knowledge which is learnt from a teacher (Âkârya), leads to real good.' Then he taught him the same knowledge. Nothing was left out, yea, nothing was left out.

TENTH KHANDA[3].

1. Upakosala Kâmalâyana dwelt as a Brahmakârin (religious student) in the house of Satyakâma Gâbâla. He tended his fires for twelve years. But the teacher, though he allowed other pupils (after they had learnt the sacred books) to depart to their own homes, did not allow Upakosala to depart.

2. Then his wife said to him : 'This student, who is quite exhausted (with austerities), has carefully tended your fires. Let not the fires themselves blame you, but teach him.' The teacher, however, went away on a journey without having taught him.

3. The student from sorrow was not able to eat.

---

[1] It would have been a great offence if Satyakâma had accepted instruction from any man, except his recognised teacher.

[2] The text should be, bhagavâms tv eva me kâme brûyât (me kâme = mamekkhâyâm).

[3] The Upakosala-vidyâ teaches first Brahman as the cause, and then in its various forms, and is therefore called âtmavidyâ and agnividyâ.

Then the wife of the teacher said to him : 'Student,
eat! Why do you not eat ?' He said : 'There are
many desires in this man here, which lose themselves
in different directions. I am full of sorrows, and
shall take no food.'

4. Thereupon the fires said among themselves :
'This student, who is quite exhausted, has carefully
tended us. Well, let us teach him.' They said to
him :

5. 'Breath is Brahman, Ka (pleasure) is Brahman,
Kha (ether) is Brahman.'

He said : 'I understand that breath is Brahman,
but I do not understand Ka or Kha [1].'

They said : 'What is Ka is Kha, what is Kha is
Ka [2].' They therefore taught him Brahman as
breath, and as the ether (in the heart) [3].

ELEVENTH KHA*ND*A.

1. After that the Gârhapatya fire [4] taught him :
'Earth, fire, food, and the sun (these are my forms, or

---

[1] I do not understand, he means, how Ka, which means pleasure,
and is non-eternal, and how Kha, which means ether, and is not
intelligent, can be Brahman.

[2] The commentator explains as follows :—Ka is pleasure, and
Kha is ether, but these two words are to determine each other
mutually, and thus to form one idea. Ka therefore does not
mean ordinary pleasures, but pleasures such as belong to Kha,
the ether. And Kha does not signify the ordinary outward ether,
but the ether in the heart, which alone is capable of pleasure.
What is meant by Ka and Kha is therefore the sentient ether
in the heart, and that is Brahman, while Prâ*na*, breath, is Brahman,
in so far as it is united with the ether in the heart.

[3] And as its ether, i. e. as the ether in the heart, the Brahman,
with which prâ*na* is connected. Comm.

[4] The household altar.

forms of Brahman). The person that is seen in the sun, I am he, I am he indeed [1].

2. 'He who knowing this meditates on him, destroys sin, obtains the world (of Agni Gârhapatya), reaches his full age, and lives long ; his descendants do not perish. We guard him in this world and in the other, whosoever knowing this meditates on him.'

TWELFTH KHA*N*DA.

1. Then the Anvâhârya fire [2] taught him : 'Water, the quarters, the stars, the moon (these are my forms). The person that is seen in the moon, I am he, I am he indeed.

2. 'He who knowing this meditates on him, destroys sin, obtains the world (of Agni Anvâhârya), reaches his full age, and lives long; his descendants do not perish. We guard him in this world and in the other, whosoever knowing this meditates on him.'

THIRTEENTH KHA*N*DA.

1. Then the Âhavanîya [3] fire taught him : 'Breath, ether, heaven, and lightning (these are my forms). The person that is seen in the lightning, I am he, I am he indeed.

---

[1] Fanciful similarities and relations between the fires of the three altars and their various forms and manifestations are pointed out by the commentator. Thus earth and food are represented as warmed and boiled by the fire. The sun is said to give warmth and light like the fire of the altar. The chief point, however, is that in all of them Brahman is manifested.

[2] The altar on the right. Anvâhârya is a sacrificial oblation, chiefly one intended for the manes.

[3] The Âhavanîya altar is the altar on the eastern side of the sacrificial ground.

2. 'He who knowing this meditates on him, destroys sin, obtains the world (of Agni Âhava-nîya), reaches his full age, and lives long; his descendants do not perish. We guard him in this world and in the other, whosoever knowing this meditates on him.'

FOURTEENTH KHANDA.

1. Then they all said : 'Upakosala, this is our knowledge, our friend, and the knowledge of the Self, but the teacher will tell you the way (to another life).'

2. In time his teacher came back, and said to him : 'Upakosala.' He answered : 'Sir.' The teacher said : 'Friend, your face shines like that of one who knows Brahman. Who has taught you ?'

'Who should teach me, Sir ?' he said. He denies, as it were. And he said (pointing) to the fires : 'Are these fires other than fires ?'

The teacher said : 'What, my friend, have these fires told you ?'

3. He answered : 'This' (repeating some of what they had told him).

The teacher said : 'My friend, they have taught you about the worlds, but I shall tell you this; and as water does not cling to a lotus leaf, so no evil deed clings to one who knows it.' He said : 'Sir, tell it me.'

FIFTEENTH KHANDA.

1. He said : 'The person that is seen in the eye, that is the Self. This is the immortal, the fearless, this is Brahman [1]. Even though they drop melted

---

[1] This is also the teaching of Pragâpati in VIII, 7, 4.

butter or water on him, it runs away on both
sides [1].

2. 'They call him Sa*m*yadvâma, for all blessings
(vâma) go towards him (sa*m*yanti). All blessings
go towards him who knows this.

3. 'He is also Vâmanî, for he leads (nayati) all
blessings (vâma). He leads all blessings who
knows this.

4. 'He is also Bhâmanî, for he shines (bhâti)
in all worlds. He who knows this, shines in all
worlds.

5. 'Now (if one who knows this, dies), whether
people perform obsequies for him or no, he goes
to light (ar*k*is) [2], from light to day, from day to
the light half of the moon, from the light half of
the moon to the six months during which the sun
goes to the north, from the months to the year,
from the year to the sun, from the sun to the moon,
from the moon to the lightning. There is a person
not human,

6. 'He leads them to Brahman. This is the path
of the Devas, the path that leads to Brahman.
Those who proceed on that path, do not return
to the life of man, yea, they do not return.'

SIXTEENTH KHA*N*DA [3].

1. Verily, he who purifies (Vâyu) is the sacrifice,
for he (the air) moving along, purifies everything.

---

[1] It does so in the eye, and likewise with the person in the eye,
who is not affected by anything. Cf. *Kh*. Up. IV, 14, 3.

[2] The commentator takes light, day, &c. as persons, or devatâs.
Cf. *Kh*. Up. V, 10, 1.

[3] If any mistakes happen during the performance of a sacrifice, as described before, they are remedied by certain interjectional

Because moving along he purifies everything, therefore he is the sacrifice. Of that sacrifice there are two ways, by mind and by speech.

2. The Brahman priest performs one of them in his mind [1], the Hot*ri*, Adhvaryu, and Udgât*ri* priests perform the other by words. When the Brahman priest, after the Prâtaranuvâka ceremony has begun, but before the recitation of the Paridhâniyâ hymn, has (to break his silence and) to speak,

3. He performs perfectly the one way only (that by words), but the other is injured. As a man walking on one foot, or a carriage going on one wheel, is injured, his sacrifice is injured, and with the injured sacrifice the sacrificer is injured; yes, having sacrificed, he becomes worse.

4. But when after the Prâtaranuvâka ceremony has begun, and before the recitation of the Paridhâniyâ hymn, the Brahman priest has not (to break his silence and) to speak, they perform both ways perfectly, and neither of them is injured.

5. As a man walking on two legs and a carriage going on two wheels gets on, so his sacrifice gets on, and with the successful sacrifice the sacrificer gets on; yes, having sacrificed, he becomes better.

---

syllables (vyâh*ri*ti), the nature of which is next described. All this is supposed to take place in the forest.

[1] While the other priests perform the sacrifice, the Brahman priest has to remain silent, following the whole sacrifice in his mind, and watching that no mistake be committed. If a mistake is committed, he has to correct it, and for that purpose certain corrective penances (prâya*sk*itta) are enjoined. The performance of the Brahman priest resembles the meditations of the sages in the forest, and therefore this chapter is here inserted.

SEVENTEENTH KHANDA.

1. Pragâpati brooded: over the worlds, and from them thus brooded on he squeezed out the essences, Agni (fire) from the earth, Vâyu (air) from the sky, Âditya (the sun) from heaven.

2. He brooded over these three deities, and from them thus brooded on he squeezed out the essences, the Rik verses from Agni, the Yagus verses from Vâyu, the Sâman verses from Âditya.

3. He brooded over the threefold knowledge (the three Vedas), and from it thus brooded on he squeezed out the essences, the sacred interjection Bhûs from the Rik verses, the sacred interjection Bhuvas from the Yagus verses, the sacred interjection Svar from the Sâman verses.

4. If the sacrifice is injured from the Rig-veda side, let him offer a libation in the Gârhapatya fire, saying, Bhûh, Svâha! Thus does he bind together and heal, by means of the essence and the power of the Rik verses themselves, whatever break the Rik sacrifice may have suffered.

5. If the sacrifice is injured from the Yagur-veda side, let him offer a libation in the Dakshina fire, saying, Bhuvah, Svâhâ! Thus does he bind together and heal, by means of the essence and the power of the Yagus verses themselves, whatever break the Yagus sacrifice may have suffered.

6. If the sacrifice is injured by the Sâma-veda side, let him offer a libation in the Âhavanîya fire, saying, Svah, Svâhâ! Thus does he bind together and heal, by means of the essence and the power of the Sâman verses themselves, whatever break the Sâman sacrifice may have suffered.

7. As one binds (softens) gold by means of lava*n*a[1] (borax), and silver by means of gold, and tin by means of silver, and lead by means of tin, and iron (loha) by means of lead, and wood by means of iron, or also by means of leather,

8. Thus does one bind together and heal any break in the sacrifice by means of (the Vyâh*r*itis or sacrificial interjections which are) the essence and strength of the three worlds, of the deities, and of the threefold knowledge. That sacrifice is healed[2] in which there is a Brahman priest who knows this.

9. That sacrifice is inclined towards the north (in the right way) in which there is a Brahman priest who knows this. And with regard to such a Brahman priest there is the following Gâthâ[3]: 'Wherever it falls back, thither the man[4] goes,'—viz. the Brahman only, as one of the *R*itvig priests. 'He saves the Kurus as a mare' (viz. a Brahman priest who

---

[1] Lava*n*a, a kind of salt, explained by kshâra and *t*a*n*ka or *t*a*n*kana. It is evidently borax, which is still imported from the East Indies under the name of tincal, and used as a flux in chemical processes.

[2] Bhesha*g*ak*r*ita, explained by bhesha*g*ena 'iva k*r*ita*h* sa*m*sk*r*ita*h*, and also by *k*ikitsakena su*s*ikshitena 'esha ya*g*ño bhavati,' which looks as if the commentator had taken it as a genitive of bhesha*g*ak*r*it.

[3] This Gâthâ (or, according to *S*ankara, Anugâthâ) is probably a Gâyatrî, though Ânandagiri says that it is not in the Gâyatrî or any other definite metre. It may have been originally 'yato yata âvartate, tattad ga*kkh*ati mânava*h*, kurûn a*s*vâbhirakshati.' This might be taken from an old epic ballad, 'Wherever the army fell back, thither the man went; the mare (mares being preferred to stallions in war) saves the Kurus.' That verse was applied to the Brahman priest succouring the sacrifice, whenever it seemed to waver, and protecting the Kurus, i. e. the performers of the sacrifice.

[4] Mânava, explained from mauna, or manana, but possibly originally, a descendant of Manu.

knows this, saves the sacrifice, the sacrificer, and all
the other priests). Therefore let a man make him
who knows this his Brahman priest, not one who
does not know it, who does not know it.

FIFTH PRAPÂ*THA*KA [1].

FIRST KHA*ND*A.

1. He who knows the oldest and the best becomes himself the oldest and the best. Breath
indeed is the oldest and the best.

2. He who knows the richest, becomes himself
the richest. Speech indeed is the richest.

3. He who knows the firm rest, becomes himself
firm in this world and in the next. The eye indeed
is the firm rest.

4. He who knows success, his wishes succeed,
both his divine and human wishes. The ear indeed
is success.

5. He who knows the home, becomes a home
of his people. The mind indeed is the home.

6. The five senses quarrelled together [2], who was
the best, saying, I am better, I am better.

---

[1] The chief object is to show the different ways on which people
proceed after death. One of these ways, the Devapatha that leads
to Brahman and from which there is no return, has been described,
IV, 15. The other ways for those who on earth know the
conditioned Brahman only, have to be discussed now.

[2] The same fable, the prâ*n*asa*m*vâda or prâ*n*avidyâ, is told in
the B*ri*hadâra*n*yaka VI, 1, 1–14, the Aitareya Âr. II, 4, the Kaush.
Up. III, 3, and the Pra*s*na Up. II, 3. The last is the simplest
version of all, but it does not follow therefore that it is the oldest.
It would be difficult to find two fables apparently more alike, yet
in reality differing from each other more characteristically than this
fable and the fable told to the plebeians by Menenius Agrippa.

7. They went to their father Pra*g*âpati and said : 'Sir, who is the best of us?' He replied : 'He by whose departure the body seems worse than worst, he is the best of you.'

8. The tongue (speech) departed, and having been absent for a year, it came round and said : 'How have you been able to live without me?' They replied: 'Like mute people, not speaking, but breathing with the breath, seeing with the eye, hearing with the ear, thinking with the mind. Thus we lived.' Then speech went back.

9. The eye (sight) departed, and having been absent for a year, it came round and said : 'How have you been able to live without me?' They replied : 'Like blind people, not seeing, but breathing with the breath, speaking with the tongue, hearing with the ear, thinking with the mind. Thus we lived.' Then the eye went back.

10. The ear (hearing) departed, and having been absent for a year, it came round and said : 'How have you been able to live without me?' They replied : 'Like deaf people, not hearing, but breathing with the breath, speaking with the tongue, thinking with the mind. Thus we lived.' Then the ear went back.

11. The mind departed, and having been absent for a year, it came round and said : 'How have you been able to live without me?' They replied: 'Like children whose mind is not yet formed, but breathing with the breath, speaking with the tongue, seeing with the eye, hearing with the ear. Thus we lived.' Then the mind went back.

12. The breath, when on the point of departing, tore up the other senses, as a horse, going to start,

might tear up the pegs to which he is tethered[1]. They came to him and said: 'Sir, be thou (our lord); thou art the best among us. Do not depart from us!'

13. Then the tongue said to him: 'If I am the richest, thou art the richest.' The eye said to him: 'If I am the firm rest, thou art the firm rest[2].'

14. The ear said to him: 'If I am success, thou art success.' The mind said to him: 'If I am the home, thou art the home.'

15. And people do not call them, the tongues, the eyes, the ears, the minds, but the breaths (prâna, the senses). For breath are all these.

SECOND KHANDA.

1. Breath said: 'What shall be my food?' They answered: 'Whatever there is, even unto dogs and birds.' Therefore this is food for Ana (the breather). His name is clearly Ana[3]. To him who knows this there is nothing that is not (proper) food.

2. He said: 'What shall be my dress?' They answered: 'Water.' Therefore wise people, when they are going to eat food, surround their food before and after with water[4].' He (prâna) thus gains a dress, and is no longer naked[5].

---

[1] Padvîsa, fetter, πέδη, pedica, a word now well known, but which Burnouf (Commentaire sur le Yaçna, Notes, CLXXIV) tried in vain to decipher.

[2] Burnouf rightly preferred pratishthâsi to pratishtho 'si, though the commentary on the corresponding passage of the Brihadâranyaka seems to favour tatpratishtho 'si.

[3] Ana, breather, more general than pra-ana=prâna, forth-breather, and the other more specified names of breath.

[4] They rinse the mouth before and after every meal.

[5] We expect, 'He who knows this' instead of prâna, but as

3. Satyakâma Gâbâla, after he had communicated this to Gosruti Vaiyâghrapadya, said to him : 'If you were to tell this to a dry stick, branches would grow, and leaves spring from it.'

4. If[1] a man wishes to reach greatness, let him perform the Dîkshâ[2] (preparatory rite) on the day of the new moon, and then, on the night of the full moon, let him stir a mash of all kinds of herbs with curds and honey, and let him pour ghee on the fire (âvasathya laukika), saying, 'Svâhâ to the oldest and the best.' After that let him throw all that remains (of the ghee)[3] into the mash.

5. In the same manner let him pour ghee on the fire, saying, ' Svâhâ to the richest.' After that let him throw all that remains together into the mash.

In the same manner let him pour ghee on the fire, saying, ' Svâhâ to the firm rest.' After that let him throw all that remains together into the mash.

In the same manner let him pour ghee on the fire, saying, ' Svâhâ to success.' After that let him throw all that remains together into the mash.

6. Then going forward and placing the mash

prâna may apply to every individual prâna, the usual finishing sentence was possibly dropt on purpose.

[1] The oblation here described is called mantha, a mortar, or what is pounded in a mortar, i. e. barley stirred in some kind of gravy. See Gaim. N. M. V. p. 406.

[2] Not the real dîkshâ, which is a preparatory rite for great sacrifices, but penance, truthfulness, abstinence, which take the place of dîkshâ with those who live in the forest and devote themselves to upâsana, meditative worship.

[3] What is here called sampâtam avanayati is the same as samsravam avanayati in the Brih. Âr. VI, 3, 2. The commentator says : Sruvâvalepanam âgyam mantham samsrâvayati.

in his hands, he recites : ' Thou (Prâ*n*a) art Ama [1]
by name, for all this together exists in thee.   He
is the oldest and best, the king, the sovereign.
May he make me the oldest, the best, the king,
the sovereign.   May I be all this.'

7. Then he eats with the following *Rik* verse at
every foot : ' We choose that food '—here he swallows—' Of the divine Savit*ri* (prâ*n*a) '—here he
swallows—' The best and all-supporting food '—here
he swallows—' We meditate on the speed of Bhaga
(Savit*ri*, prâ*n*a)'—here he drinks all.

8. Having cleansed the vessel, whether it be a
ka*m*sa or a *k*amasa, he sits down behind the fire on
a skin or on the bare ground, without speaking or
making any other effort.   If in his dream he sees a
woman, let him know this to be a sign that his
sacrifice has succeeded.

9. On this there is a *S*loka : ' If during sacrifices which are to fulfil certain wishes he sees in
his dreams a woman, let him know success from
this vision in a dream, yea, from this vision in
a dream.'

THIRD KHA*N*DA [2].

1. *S*vetaketu Âru*n*eya went to an assembly [3] of
the Pañ*k*âlas.   Pravâha*n*a *G*aivali [4] said to him :
' Boy, has your father instructed you ? '   ' Yes, Sir,'
he replied.

2. ' Do you know to what place men go from
here ? '   ' No, Sir,' he replied.

---

[1] Cf. Br*i*h. Âr. I, 1, 3, 22.

[2] This story is more fully told in the Br*i*hadâra*n*yaka VI, 2,
*S*atapatha-brâhma*n*a XIV, 8, 16.

[3] Samiti, or parishad, as in the Br*i*h. Âr.

[4] He is the same Kshatriya sage who appeared in I, 8, 1, silencing
the Brâhmans.

'Do you know how they return again?' 'No Sir,' he replied.

'Do you know where the path of Devas and the path of the fathers diverge?' 'No, Sir,' he replied.

3. 'Do you know why that world[1] never becomes full?' 'No, Sir,' he replied.

'Do you know why in the fifth libation water is called Man[2]?' 'No, Sir,' he replied.

4. 'Then why did you say (you had been) instructed? How could anybody who did not know these things say that he had been instructed?' Then the boy went back sorrowful to the place of his father, and said: 'Though you had not instructed me, Sir, you said you had instructed me.

5. 'That fellow of a Râ*g*anya asked me five questions, and I could not answer one of them.' The father said: 'As you have told me these questions of his, I do not know any one of them[3]. If I knew these questions, how should I not have told you[4]?'

6. Then Gautama went to the king's place, and when he had come to him, the king offered him proper respect. In the morning the king went out on his way to the assembly[5]. The king said to him:

---

[1] That of the fathers. Comm.

[2] Or, according to others, why the water has a human voice; purushavâ*kah* in B*ri*h. Âr. XIV, 9, 3.

[3] I doubt whether the elliptical construction of these sentences is properly filled out by the commentator. In the B*ri*hadâra*n*yaka the construction is much easier. 'You know me well enough to know that whatever I know, I told you.'

[4] I read avedishyam, though both the text and commentary give avadishyam. Still viditavân asmi points to an original avedishyam, and a parallel passage, VI, 1, 7, confirms this emendation.

[5] Cf. *Kh*. U*p*. V, 11, 5.

'Sir, Gautama, ask a boon of such things as men possess.' He replied: 'Such things as men possess may remain with you. Tell me the speech which you addressed to the boy.'

7. The king was perplexed, and commanded him, saying: 'Stay with me some time.' Then he said: 'As (to what) you have said to me, Gautama, this knowledge did not go to any Brâhma*n*a before you, and therefore this teaching belonged in all the worlds to the Kshatra class alone. Then he began:

FOURTH KHA*N*DA [1].

1. 'The altar (on which the sacrifice is supposed to be offered) is that world (heaven), O Gautama; its fuel is the sun itself, the smoke his rays, the light the day, the coals the moon, the sparks the stars.

2. 'On that altar the Devas (or prâ*n*as, represented by Agni, &c.) offer the *s*raddhâ libation (consisting of water). From that oblation rises Soma, the king [2] (the moon).

FIFTH KHA*N*DA.

1. 'The altar is Par*g*anya (the god of rain), O Gautama; its fuel is the air itself, the smoke the cloud, the light the lightning, the coals the thunderbolt, the sparks the thunderings [3].

---

[1] He answers the last question, why water in the fifth libation is called Man, first.

[2] The sacrificers themselves rise through their oblations to heaven, and attain as their reward a Soma-like nature.

[3] Hrâduni, generally explained by hail, but here by stanayitnu-*s*abdâ*h*, rumblings.

2. 'On that altar the Devas offer Soma, the king (the moon).   From that oblation rises rain [1].

SIXTH KHA*ND*A.

1. 'The altar is the earth, O Gautama; its fuel is the year itself, the smoke the ether, the light the night, the coals the quarters, the sparks the intermediate quarters.

2. 'On that altar the Devas (prâ*n*as) offer rain. From that oblation rises food (corn, &c.)

SEVENTH KHA*ND*A.

1. 'The altar is man, O Gautama; its fuel speech itself, the smoke the breath, the light the tongue, the coals the eye, the sparks the ear.

2. 'On that altar the Devas (prâ*n*as) offer food. From that oblation rises seed.

EIGHTH KHA*ND*A.

1. 'The altar is woman, O Gautama [2].

2. 'On that altar the Devas (prâ*n*as) offer seed. From that oblation rises the germ.

NINTH KHA*ND*A.

1. 'For this reason is water in the fifth oblation called Man. This germ, covered in the womb, having dwelt there ten months, or more or less, is born.

2. 'When born, he lives whatever the length of his life may be.   When he has departed, his friends carry him, as appointed, to the fire (of the funeral pile) from whence he came, from whence he sprang.

---

[1] The water, which had assumed the nature of Soma, now becomes rain.

[2] Tasyâ upastha eva samid, yad upamantrayate sa dhûmo, yonir ar*k*ir, yad anta*h* karoti te 'ngârâ abhinandâ vishphulingâ*h*.

TENTH KHANDA.

1. 'Those who know this [1] (even though they still be grihasthas, householders) and those who in the forest follow faith and austerities (the vânaprasthas, and of the parivrâgakas those who do not yet know the Highest Brahman) go [2] to light (arkis), from light to day, from day to the light half of the moon, from the light half of the moon to the six months when the sun goes to the north, from the six months when the sun goes to the north to the year, from the year to the sun, from the sun to the moon, from the moon to the lightning. There is a person not human [3],—

2. 'He leads them to Brahman (the conditioned Brahman). This is the path of the Devas.

3. 'But they who living in a village practise (a life of) sacrifices, works of public utility, and alms, they go to the smoke, from smoke to night, from night to the dark half of the moon, from the dark half of the moon to the six months when the sun goes to the south. But they do not reach the year.

4. 'From the months they go to the world of the fathers, from the world of the fathers to the ether, from the ether to the moon. That is Soma, the king. Here they are loved (eaten) by the Devas, yes, the Devas love (eat) them [4].

---

[1] The doctrine of the five fires, and our being born in them, i. e. in heaven, rain, earth, man, and woman.

[2] Cf. Kh. Up. IV, 15, 5.

[3] Instead of mânava, human, or amânava, not human, the Brih. Âr. reads mânasa, mental, or created by manas, mind.

[4] This passage has been translated, 'They are the food of the gods. The gods do eat it.' And this is indeed the literal meaning of the words. But bhag (to enjoy) and bhaksh (to eat) are often

5. 'Having dwelt there, till their (good) works are consumed, they return again that way as they came[1], to the ether, from the ether to the air. Then the sacrificer, having become air, becomes smoke, having become smoke, he becomes mist,

6. 'Having become mist, he becomes a cloud, having become a cloud, he rains down. Then he is born as rice and corn, herbs and trees, sesamum and beans. From thence the escape is beset with most difficulties. For whoever the persons may be that eat the food, and beget offspring, he henceforth becomes like unto them.

---

used by theosophical writers in India, in the more general sense of cherishing or loving, and anna in the sense of an object of desire, love, and protection. The commentators, however, as the use of bhaksh in this sense is exceptional, or as it has no support in the use of the ancients, warn us here against a possible misunderstanding. If those, they say, who have performed sacrifices enter at last into the essence of Soma, the moon, and are eaten by the Devas, by Indra, &c., what is the use of their good works? No, they reply, they are not really eaten. Food (anna) means only what is helpful and delightful; it is not meant that they are eaten by morsels, but that they form the delight of the Devas. Thus we hear it said that men, women, and cattle are food for kings. And if it is said that women are loved by men, they are, in being loved, themselves loving. Thus these men also, being loved by the Devas, are happy and rejoice with the Devas. Their body, in order to be able to rejoice in the moon, becomes of a watery substance, as it was said before, that the water, called the *S*raddhâ libation, when offered in heaven, as in the fire of the altar, becomes Soma, the king (*Kh.* Up. V, 4, 1). That water becomes, after various changes, the body of those who have performed good works, and when a man is dead and his body burnt (*Kh.* Up. V, 9, 2), the water rises from the body upwards with the smoke, and carries him to the moon, where, in that body, he enjoys the fruits of his good works, as long as they last. When they are consumed, like the oil in a lamp, he has to return to a new round of existences.

[1] But only to a certain point.

7. 'Those whose conduct has been good, will quickly attain some good birth, the birth of a Brâhmana, or a Kshatriya, or a Vaisya. But those whose conduct has been evil, will quickly attain an evil birth, the birth of a dog, or a hog, or a Kandâla.

8. 'On neither of these two ways those small creatures (flies, worms, &c.) are continually returning of whom it may be said, Live and die. Theirs is a third place.

'Therefore that world never becomes full[1] (cf. V, 3, 2).

---

[1] In this manner all the five questions have been answered. First, why in the fifth oblation water is called man; secondly, to what place men go after death, some by the path of the Devas, others by the path of the fathers, others again by neither of these paths; thirdly, how they return, some returning to Brahman, others returning to the earth; fourthly, where the paths of the Devas and the fathers diverge, viz. when from the half-year the path of the Devas goes on to the year, while that of the fathers branches off to the world of the fathers; fifthly, why that world, the other world, does never become full, viz. because men either go on to Brahman or return again to this world.

Many questions are raised among Indian philosophers on the exact meaning of certain passages occurring in the preceding paragraphs. First, as to who is admitted to the path of the Devas? Householders, who know the secret doctrine of the five fires or the five libations of the Agnihotra, as described above, while other householders, who only perform the ordinary sacrifices, without a knowledge of their secret meaning, go by the path of the fathers. Secondly, those who have retired to the forest, and whose worship there consists in faith and austerities, i. e. Vânaprasthas and Parivrâgakas, before they arrive at a knowledge of the true Brahman. The question then arises, whether religious students also enter the path of the Devas? This is affirmed, because Purânas and Smritis assert it, or because our text, if properly understood, does not exclude it. Those, on the contrary, who know not only a conditioned, but the highest unconditioned Brahman, do not proceed on the path of the Devas, but obtain Brahman immediately.

Again, there is much difference of opinion whether, after a man

'Hence let a man take care to himself[1]! And thus it is said in the following *S*loka[2] :—

9. 'A man who steals gold, who drinks spirits,

---

has been in the moon, consuming his works, he can be born again. Birth is the result of former works, and if former works are altogether consumed, there can be no new birth. This, however, is shown to be an erroneous view, because, besides the good sacrificial works, the fruits of which are consumed in the moon, there are other works which have to be enjoyed or expiated, as the case may be, in a new existence.

The great difficulty or danger in the round of transmigration arises when the rain has fructified the earth, and passes into herbs and trees, rice, corn, and beans. For, first of all, some of the rain does not fructify at once, but falls into rivers and into the sea, to be swallowed up by fishes and sea monsters. Then, only after these have been dissolved in the sea, and after the sea water has been attracted by the clouds, the rain falls down again, it may be on desert or stony land. Here it may be swallowed by snakes or deer, and these may be swallowed by other animals, so that the round of existence seems endless. Nor is this all. Some rain may dry up, or be absorbed by bodies that cannot be eaten. Then, if the rain is absorbed by rice, corn, &c., and this be eaten, it may be eaten by children or by men who have renounced marriage, and thus again lose the chance of a new birth. Lastly, there is the danger arising from the nature of the being in whom the food, such as rice and corn, becomes a new seed, and likewise from the nature of the mother. All these chances have to be met before a new birth as a Brâhma*n*a, Kshatriya, or Vai*s*ya can be secured.

Another curious distinction is here made by *S*ankara in his commentary. There are some, he says, who assume the form of rice, corn, &c., not in their descent from a higher world, as described in the Upanishad, but as a definite punishment for certain evil deeds they have committed. These remain in that state till the results of their evil deeds are over, and assume then a new body, according to their work, like caterpillars. With them there is also a consciousness of these states, and the acts which caused them to

---

[1] Let him despise it. Comm.

[2] Evidently an old Trish*t*ubh verse, but irregular in the third line. See Manu XI, 54.

who dishonours his Guru's bed, who kills a Brahman, these four fall, and as a fifth he who associates with them.

10. 'But he who thus knows the five fires is not defiled by sin even though he associates with them. He who knows this, is pure, clean, and obtains the world of the blessed, yea, he obtains the world of the blessed.'

ELEVENTH KHAṆḌA[1].

1. Prâ*k*înas*â*la Aupamanyava, Satyaya*g*ña Paulushi, Indradyumna Bhâllaveya, *G*ana *S*ârkarâkshya, and Bu*d*ila Â*s*vatara*s*vi, these five great householders and great theologians came once together and held a discussion as to What is our Self, and what is Brahman[2].

2. They reflected and said: 'Sirs, there is that Uddâlaka Âru*n*i, who knows at present that Self,

---

assume this or that body, leave impressions behind, like dreams. This is not the case with those who in their descent from the moon, pass, as we saw, through an existence as rice, corn, &c. They have no consciousness of such existences, at least not in their descent. In their ascent to the moon, they have consciousness, as a man who climbs up a tree knows what he is about. But in their descent, that consciousness is gone, as it is when a man falls down from a tree. Otherwise a man, who by his good works had deserved rewards in the moon, would, while corn is being ground, suffer tortures, as if he were in hell, and the very object of good works, as taught by the Veda, would be defeated. As we see that a man struck by a hammer can be carried away unconscious, so it is in the descent of souls, till they are born again as men, and gain a new start for the attainment of the Highest Brahman.

---

[1] The same story is found in the *S*atapatha-brâhma*n*a X, 6, 1, 1.

[2] Âtman and Brâhman are to be taken as predicate and subject.

called Vaisvânara. Well, let us go to him.' They
went to him.

3. But he reflected: 'Those great householders
and great theologians will examine me, and I shall
not be able to tell them all; therefore I shall
recommend another teacher to them.'

4. He said to them: 'Sirs, Asvapati Kaikeya
knows at present that Self, called Vaisvânara. Well,
let us go to him.' They went to him.

5. When they arrived (the king) ordered proper
presents to be made separately to each of them.
And rising the next morning[1] he said: 'In my
kingdom there is no thief, no miser, no drunkard,
no man without an altar in his house, no ignorant
person, no adulterer, much less an adulteress. I[2]
am going to perform a sacrifice, Sirs, and as much
wealth as I give to each *R*itvig priest, I shall give
to you, Sirs. Please to stay here.'

6. They replied: 'Every man ought to say for
what purpose he comes. You know at present that
Vaisvânara Self, tell us that.'

7. He said: 'To-morrow I shall give you an
answer.' Therefore on the next morning they approached him, carrying fuel in their hands (like
students), and he, without first demanding any preparatory rites[3], said to them:

---

[1] The commentator explains that the king, seeing that they would
not accept his presents, and thinking that they did not consider him
worthy of bestowing presents on them, made these remarks.

[2] When they still refused his presents, he thought the presents
he had offered were too small, and therefore invited them to a
sacrifice.

[3] He was satisfied with the humility of the Brahmans, who, being
Brahmans, came to him, who was not a Brahman, as pupils. Gene-

TWELFTH KHANDA.

1. 'Aupamanyava, whom do you meditate on as the Self?' He replied: 'Heaven only, venerable king.' He said: 'The Self which you meditate on is the Vai*s*vânara Self, called Sute*g*as (having good light). Therefore every kind of Soma libation is seen in your house [1].

2. 'You eat food, and see your desire (a son, &c.), and whoever thus meditates on that Vai*s*vânara Self, eats food, sees his desire, and has Vedic glory (arising from study and sacrifice) in his house. That, however, is but the head of the Self, and thus your head would have fallen (in a discussion), if you had not come to me.'

THIRTEENTH KHANDA.

1. Then he said to Satyaya*g*ña Paulushi: 'O Prâ*k*înayogya, whom do you meditate on as the Self?' He replied: 'The sun only, venerable king.' He said: 'The Self which you meditate on is the Vai*s*vânara Self, called Vi*s*varûpa (multiform). Therefore much and manifold wealth is seen in your house.

2. 'There is a car with mules, full of slaves and jewels. You eat food and see your desire, and whoever thus meditates on that Vai*s*vânara Self, eats food and sees his desire, and has Vedic glory in his house.

'That, however, is but the eye of the Self, and you would have become blind, if you had not come to me.'

---

rally a pupil has first to pass through several initiatory rites before he is admitted to the benefit of his master's teaching.

[1] Soma is said to be suta in the Ekâha, prasuta in the Ahîna, âsuta in the Sattra-sacrifices.

FOURTEENTH KHANDA.

1. Then he said to Indradyumna Bhâllaveya : 'O Vaiyâghrapadya, whom do you meditate on as the Self?' He replied: 'Air only, venerable king.' He said: 'The Self which you meditate on is the Vaisvânara Self, called Prithagvartman (having various courses). Therefore offerings come to you in various ways, and rows of cars follow you in various ways.

2. 'You eat food and see your desire, and whoever thus meditates on that Vaisvânara Self, eats food and sees his desire, and has Vedic glory in his house.

'That, however, is but the breath of the Self, and your breath would have left you, if you had not come to me.'

FIFTEENTH KHANDA.

1. Then he said to Gana Sârkarâkshya: 'Whom do you meditate on as the Self?' He replied: 'Ether only, venerable king.' He said : 'The Self which you meditate on is the Vaisvânara Self, called Bahula (full). Therefore you are full of offspring and wealth.

2. 'You eat food and see your desire, and whoever thus meditates on that Vaisvânara Self, eats food and sees his desire, and has Vedic glory in his house.

'That, however, is but the trunk of the Self, and your trunk would have perished, if you had not come to me.'

SIXTEENTH KHANDA.

1. Then he said to Budila Âsvatarâsvi, 'O Vaiyâghrapadya, whom do you meditate on as the Self?' He replied : 'Water only, venerable king.' He said ;

' The Self which you meditate on is the Vai*s*vânara Self, called Rayi (wealth).   Therefore are you wealthy and flourishing.

2. 'You eat food and see your desire, and who-ever thus meditates on that Vai*s*vânara Self, eats food and sees his desire, and has Vedic glory in his house.

' That, however, is but the bladder of the Self, and your bladder would have burst, if you had not come to me.'

Seventeenth Kha*n*da.

1. Then he said to Auddâlaka Âruni : ' O Gau-tama, whom do you meditate on as the Self?'   He replied: 'The earth only, venerable king.'   He said : ' The Self which you meditate on is the Vai*s*vânara Self, called Pratish*th*â (firm rest).   Therefore you stand firm with offspring and cattle.

2. 'You eat food and see your desire, and who-ever thus meditates on that Vai*s*vânara Self, eats food and sees his desire, and has Vedic glory in his house.

' That, however, are but the feet of the Self, and your feet would have given way, if you had not come to me.'

Eighteenth Kha*n*da.

1. Then he said to them all : 'You eat your food, knowing that Vai*s*vânara Self as if it were many.   But he who worships the Vai*s*vânara Self as a span long, and as[1] identical with himself, he eats food in all worlds, in all beings, in all Selfs.

---

[1] The two words prâde*s*amâtra and abhivimâna are doubtful. The commentator explains the first in different ways, which are all more or less fanciful.   He is measured or known (mâtra) as Self,

2. 'Of that Vai*s*vânara Self the head is Sute*g*as (having good light), the eye Vi*s*varûpa (multiform), the breath P*ri*thagvartman (having various courses), the trunk Bahula (full), the bladder Rayi (wealth), the feet the earth, the chest the altar, the hairs the grass on the altar, the heart the Gârhapatya fire, the mind the Anvâhârya fire, the mouth the Âhavanîya fire.

NINETEENTH KHA*ND*A.

1. 'Therefore [1] the first food which a man may take, is in the place of Homa. And he who offers that first oblation, should offer it to Prâ*n*a (up-breathing), saying Svâhâ. Then Prâ*n*a (up-breathing) is satisfied,

2. 'If Prâ*n*a is satisfied, the eye is satisfied, if the eye is satisfied, the sun is satisfied, if the sun is satisfied, heaven is satisfied, if heaven is satisfied, whatever is under heaven and under the sun is satisfied. And through their satisfaction he (the sacrificer or eater) himself is satisfied with offspring, cattle, health, brightness, and Vedic splendour.

---

by means of heaven as his head and the earth as his feet, these being the prâde*s*as; or, in the mouth and the rest, which are instruments, he is known as without action himself; or, he has the length from heaven to earth, heaven and earth being called prâde*s*a, because they are taught. The interpretation, supported by the *G*âbâla-*s*ruti, that prâde*s*a is the measure from the forehead to the chin, he rejects. Abhivimâna is taken in the same meaning as abhimâna in the Vedânta, seeing everything in oneself. Vai*s*vânara is taken as the real Self of all beings, and, in the end, of all Selfs, and as thus to be known and worshipped.

[1] The object now is to show that to him who knows the Vai*s*vânara Self, the act of feeding himself is like feeding Vai*s*vânara, and that feeding Vai*s*vânara is the true Agnihotra.

TWENTIETH KHA*N*DA.

1. 'And he who offers the second oblation, should offer it to Vyâna (back-breathing), saying Svâhâ. Then Vyâna is satisfied,

2. 'If Vyâna is satisfied, the ear is satisfied, if the ear is satisfied, the moon is satisfied, if the moon is satisfied, the quarters are satisfied, if the quarters are satisfied, whatever is under the quarters and under the moon is satisfied. And through their .satisfaction he (the sacrificer or eater) himself is satisfied with offspring, cattle, health, brightness, and Vedic splendour.

TWENTY-FIRST KHA*N*DA.

1. 'And he who offers the third oblation, should offer it to Apâna (down-breathing), saying Svâhâ. Then Apâna is satisfied. If Apâna is satisfied, the tongue is satisfied, if the tongue is satisfied, Agni (fire) is satisfied, if Agni is satisfied, the earth is satisfied, if the earth is satisfied, whatever is under the earth and under fire is satisfied.

2. 'And through their satisfaction he (the sacrificer or eater) himself is satisfied with offspring, cattle, health, brightness, and Vedic splendour.

TWENTY-SECOND KHA*N*DA.

1. 'And he who offers the fourth oblation, should offer it to Samâna (on-breathing), saying Svâhâ. Then Samâna is satisfied,

2. 'If Samâna is satisfied, the mind is satisfied, if the mind is satisfied, Par*g*anya (god of rain) is satisfied, if Par*g*anya is satisfied, lightning is satisfied, if lightning is satisfied, whatever is under Par*g*anya and under lightning is satisfied. And through their

satisfaction he (the sacrificer or eater) himself is satisfied with offspring, cattle, health, brightness, and Vedic splendour.

TWENTY-THIRD KHANDA.

1. 'And he who offers the fifth oblation, should offer it to Udâna (out-breathing), saying Svâhâ. Then Udâna is satisfied,

2. 'If Udâna is satisfied, Vâyu (air) is satisfied, if Vâyu is satisfied, ether is satisfied, if ether is satisfied, whatever is under Vâyu and under the ether is satisfied. And through their satisfaction he (the sacrificer or eater) himself is satisfied with offspring, cattle, health, brightness, and Vedic splendour.

TWENTY-FOURTH KHANDA.

1. 'If, without knowing this, one offers an Agnihotra, it would be as if a man were to remove the live coals and pour his libation on dead ashes.

2. 'But he who offers this Agnihotra with a full knowledge of its true purport, he offers it (i. e. he eats food)[1] in all worlds, in all beings, in all Selfs.

3. 'As the soft fibres of the Ishîkâ reed, when thrown into the fire, are burnt, thus all his sins are burnt whoever offers this Agnihotra with a full knowledge of its true purport.

4. 'Even if he gives what is left of his food to a Kandâla, it would be offered in his (the Kandâla's) Vaisvânara Self. And so it is said in this Sloka :—

'As hungry children here on earth sit (expectantly) round their mother, so do all beings sit round the Agnihotra, yea, round the Agnihotra.'

---

[1] Cf. V, 18, 1.

SIXTH PRAPÂ*TH*AKA.

FIRST KHA*ND*A.

1. Hari*h*, Om. There lived once *S*vetaketu Âru*n*eya (the grandson of Aru*n*a). To him his father (Uddâlaka, the son of Aru*n*a) said: '*S*vetaketu, go to school; for there is none belonging to our race, darling, who, not having studied (the Veda), is, as it were, a Brâhma*n*a by birth only.'

2. Having begun his apprenticeship (with a teacher) when he was twelve years of age [1], *S*vetaketu returned to his father, when he was twenty-four, having then studied all the Vedas,—conceited, considering himself well-read, and stern.

3. His father said to him: '*S*vetaketu, as you are so conceited, considering yourself so well-read, and so stern, my dear, have you ever asked for that instruction by which we hear what cannot be heard, by which we perceive what cannot be perceived, by which we know what cannot be known?'

4. 'What is that instruction, Sir?' he asked.

The father replied: 'My dear, as by one clod of clay all that is made of clay is known, the difference [2] being only a name, arising from speech, but the truth being that all is clay;

5. 'And as, my dear, by one nugget of gold [3]

---

[1] This was rather late, for the son of a Brahman might have begun his studies when he was seven years old. Âpastamba-sûtras I, 1, 18. Twelve years was considered the right time for mastering one of the Vedas.

[2] Vikâra, difference, variety, change, by form and name, development, cf. VI, 3, 3.

[3] The commentator takes lohama*n*i here as suvar*n*api*nd*a.

all that is made of gold is known, the difference being only a name, arising from speech, but the truth being that all is gold?

6. 'And as, my dear, by one pair of nail-scissors all that is made of iron (kârsh*n*âyasam) is known, the difference being only a name, arising from speech, but the truth being that all is iron,—thus, my dear, is that instruction.'

7. The son said : 'Surely those venerable men (my teachers) did not know that. For if they had known it, why should they not have told it me? Do you, Sir, therefore tell me that.' 'Be it so,' said the father.

SECOND KHA*ND*A [1].

1. 'In the beginning,' my dear, 'there was that only which is (τὸ ὄν), one only, without a second. Others say, in the beginning there was that only which is not (τὸ μὴ ὄν), one only, without a second; and from that which is not, that which is was born.

2. 'But how could it be thus, my dear?' the father continued. 'How could that which is, be born of that which is not? No, my dear, only that which is, was in the beginning, one only, without a second.

3. 'It thought [2], may I be many, may I grow forth. It sent forth fire [3].

---

[1] Cf. Taitt. Up. II, 6.

[2] Literally, it saw. This verb is explained as showing that the Sat is conscious, not unconscious (bewusst, nicht unbewusst).

[3] In other Upanishads the Sat produces first âkâ*s*a, ether, then vâyu, air, and then only te*g*as, fire. Fire is a better rendering for te*g*as than light or heat. See Jacobi, Zeitschrift der Deutschen Morgenl. Gesellschaft, XXIX, p. 242. The difficulties, however, of

'That fire [1] thought, may I be many, may I grow forth. It sent forth water [2].

'And therefore whenever anybody anywhere is hot and perspires, water is produced on him from fire alone.

4. 'Water thought, may I be many, may I grow forth. It sent forth earth [3] (food).

'Therefore whenever it rains anywhere, most food is then produced. From water alone is eatable food produced.

THIRD KHANDA.

1. 'Of all living things there are indeed three origins only [4], that which springs from an egg (oviparous), that which springs from a living being (viviparous), and that which springs from a germ.

2. 'That Being [5] (i. e. that which had produced fire, water, and earth) thought, let me now enter those three beings [5] (fire, water, earth) with this living

---

accurately translating tegas are not removed by rendering it by fire, as may be seen immediately afterward in VI, 4, 1, where tegas is said to supply the red colour of agni, the burning fire, not the god of fire. See also VI, 8, 6. In later philosophical treatises the meaning of tegas is more carefully determined than in the Upanishads.

[1] Really the Sat, in the form of fire. Fire is whatever burns, cooks, shines, and is red.

[2] By water is meant all that is fluid, and bright in colour.

[3] By anna, food, is here meant the earth, and all that is heavy, firm, dark in colour.

[4] In the Ait. Up. four are mentioned, andaga, here ândaga, gâruga (i.e. garâyuga), here gîvaga, svedaga, and udbhigga, svedaga, born from heat, being additional. Cf. Atharva-veda I, 12, 1.

[5] The text has devatâ, deity; here used in a very general sense. The Sat, though it has produced fire, water, and earth, has not yet obtained its wish of becoming many.

Self (*gî*va âtmâ)[1], and let me then reveal (develop) names and forms.

3. 'Then that Being having said, Let me make each of these three tripartite (so that fire, water, and earth should each have itself for its principal ingredient, besides an admixture of the other two) entered into those three beings (devatâ) with this living self only, and revealed names and forms.

4. 'He made each of these tripartite; and how these three beings become each of them tripartite, that learn from me now, my friend!

Fourth Kha*nd*a.

1. 'The red colour of burning fire (agni) is the colour of fire, the white colour of fire is the colour of water, the black colour of fire the colour of earth. Thus vanishes what we call fire, as a mere variety, being a name, arising from speech. What is true (satya) are the three colours (or forms).

2. 'The red colour of the sun (âditya) is the colour of fire, the white of water, the black of earth. Thus vanishes what we call the sun, as a mere variety, being a name, arising from speech. What is true are the three colours.

3. 'The red colour of the moon is the colour of fire, the white of water, the black of earth. Thus vanishes what we call the moon, as a mere variety, being a name, arising from speech. What is true are the three colours.

4. 'The red colour of the lightning is the colour of fire, the white of water, the black of earth. Thus

---

[1] This living self is only a shadow, as it were, of the Highest Self; and as the sun, reflected in the water, does not suffer from the movement of the water, the real Self does not suffer pleasure or pain on earth, but the living self only.

vanishes what we call the lightning, as a mere variety, being a name, arising from speech. What is true are the three colours.

5. 'Great householders and great theologians of olden times who knew this, have declared the same, saying, " No one can henceforth mention to us anything which we have not heard, perceived, or known[1]." Out of these (three colours or forms) they knew all.

6. 'Whatever they thought looked red, they knew was the colour of fire. Whatever they thought looked white, they knew was the colour of water. Whatever they thought looked black, they knew was the colour of earth.

7. 'Whatever they thought was altogether unknown, they knew was some combination of those three beings (devatâ).

'Now learn from me, my friend, how those three beings, when they reach man, become each of them tripartite.

FIFTH KHA*N*DA.

1. 'The earth (food) when eaten becomes threefold; its grossest portion becomes feces, its middle portion flesh, its subtilest ˙portion mind.

2. 'Water when drunk becomes threefold; its grossest portion becomes water, its middle portion blood, its subtilest portion breath.

3. 'Fire (i. e. in oil, butter, &c.) when eaten becomes threefold; its grossest portion becomes bone, its middle portion marrow, its subtilest portion speech [2].

---

[1] This reminds one of the Aristotelian διὰ γὰρ ταῦτα καὶ ἐκ τούτων τἄλλα γνωρίζεται, ἀλλ᾽ οὐ ταῦτα διὰ τῶν ὑποκειμένων.

[2] Food, water, and fire are each to be taken as tripartite; hence animals which live on one of the three elements only, still share in some measure the qualities of the other elements also.

4. 'For truly, my child, mind comes of earth, breath of water, speech of fire.'

'Please, Sir, inform me still more,' said the son.

'Be it so, my child,' the father replied.

SIXTH KHA*N*DA.

1. 'That which is the subtile portion of curds, when churned, rises upwards, and becomes butter.

2. 'In the same manner, my child, the subtile portion of earth (food), when eaten, rises upwards, and becomes mind.

3. 'That which is the subtile portion of water, when drunk, rises upwards, and becomes breath.

4. 'That which is the subtile portion of fire, when consumed, rises upwards, and becomes speech.

5. 'For mind, my child, comes of earth, breath of water, speech of fire.'

'Please, Sir, inform me still more,' said the son.

'Be it so, my child,' the father replied.

SEVENTH KHA*N*DA.

1. 'Man (purusha), my son, consists of sixteen parts. Abstain from food for fifteen days, but drink as much water as you like, for breath comes from water, and will not be cut off, if you drink water.'

2. *S*vetaketu abstained from food for fifteen days. Then he came to his father and said: 'What shall I say?' The father said: 'Repeat the *Ri*k, Ya*g*us, and Sâman verses.' He replied: 'They do not occur to me, Sir.'

3. The father said to him: 'As of a great lighted fire one coal only of the size of a firefly may be left, which would not burn much more than this (i. e. very

little), thus, my dear son, one part only of the sixteen parts (of you) is left, and therefore with that one part you do not remember the Vedas. Go and eat!

4. 'Then wilt thou understand me.' Then Svetaketu ate, and afterwards approached his father. And whatever his father asked him, he knew it all by heart. Then his father said to him:

5. 'As of a great lighted fire one coal of the size of a firefly, if left, may be made to blaze up again by putting grass upon it, and will thus burn more than this,

6. 'Thus, my dear son, there was one part of the sixteen parts left to you, and that, lighted up with food, burnt up, and by it you remember now the Vedas.' After that, he understood what his father meant when he said: 'Mind, my son, comes from food, breath from water, speech from fire.' He understood what he said, yea, he understood it[1].

EIGHTH KHANDA.

1. Uddâlaka Âruni said to his son Svetaketu: 'Learn from me the true nature of sleep (svapna). When a man sleeps here, then, my dear son, he becomes united with the True[2], he is gone to his

---

[1] The repetition shows that the teaching of the Trivritkarana, the tripartite nature of things, is ended.

[2] The deep sushupta sleep is meant, in which personal consciousness is lost, and the self for a time absorbed in the Highest Self. Sleep is produced by fatigue. Speech, mind, and the senses rest, breath only remains awake, and the gîva, the living soul, in order to recover from his fatigue, returns for a while to his true Self (âtmâ). The Sat must be taken as a substance, nay, as the highest substance or subject, the Brahman. The whole purpose of the Upanishad is obscured if we translate sat or satyam by truth, instead of the True, the true one, τὸ ὄντως ὄν.

own (Self). Therefore they say, svapiti, he sleeps, because he is gone (apîta) to his own (sva)[1].

2. 'As a bird when tied by a string flies first in every direction, and finding no rest anywhere, settles down at last on the very place where it is fastened, exactly in the same manner, my son, that mind (the *gî*va, or living Self in the mind, see VI, 3, 2), after flying in every direction, and finding no rest anywhere, settles down on breath[2]; for indeed, my son, mind is fastened to breath.

3. 'Learn from me, my son, what are hunger and thirst. When a man is thus said to be hungry, water is carrying away (digests) what has been eaten by him. Therefore as they speak of a cow-leader (go-nâya), a horse-leader (a*s*va-nâya), a man-leader (purusha-nâya), so they call water (which digests food and causes hunger) food-leader (a*s*a-nâya). Thus (by food digested &c.), my son, know this offshoot (the body) to be brought forth, for this (body) could not be without a root (cause).

4. 'And where could its root be except in food (earth)[3]? And in the same manner, my son, as

---

[1] This is one of the many recognised plays on words in the Upanishads and the Vedânta philosophy. Svapiti, he sleeps, stands for sva (his own), i.e. the self, and apîta, gone to.

[2] The commentator takes prâ*n*a here in the sense of Sat, which it often has elsewhere. If so, this illustration would have the same object as the preceding one. If we took prâ*n*a in the sense of breath, breath being the result of water, this paragraph might be taken to explain the resignation of the living Self to its bondage to breath, while on earth.

[3] That food is the root of the body is shown by the commentator in the following way : Food when softened by water and digested becomes a fluid, blood (*s*onita). From it comes flesh, from flesh fat, from fat bones, from bones marrow, from marrow seed. Food eaten by a woman becomes equally blood (lohita),

food (earth) too is an offshoot, seek after its root, viz. water. And as water too is an offshoot, seek after its root, viz. fire. And as fire too is an offshoot, seek after its root, viz. the True. Yes, all these creatures, my son, have their root in the True, they dwell in the True, they rest in the True.

5. 'When a man is thus said to be thirsty, fire carries away what has been drunk by him. Therefore as they speak of a cow-leader (go-nâya), of a horse-leader (a*s*va-nâya), of a man-leader (purusha-nâya), so they call fire udanyâ, thirst, i. e. water-leader. Thus (by water digested &c.), my son, know this offshoot (the body) to be brought forth : this (body) could not be without a root (cause).

6. 'And where could its root be except in water ? As water is an offshoot, seek after its root, viz. fire. As fire is an offshoot, seek after its root, viz. the True. Yes, all these creatures, O son, have their root in the True, they dwell in the True, they rest in the True.

'And how these three beings (devatâ), fire, water, earth, O son, when they reach man, become each of them tripartite, has been said before (VI, 4, 7). When a man departs from hence, his speech [1] is merged

---

and from seed and blood combined the new body is produced. We must always have before us the genealogical table :—

$$\text{Sat, } τὸ ὄν.$$
$$|$$
$$\text{Te}g\text{as (fire)} = \text{Vâ}k \text{ (speech).}$$
$$|$$
$$\text{Ap (water)} = \text{Prâ}n\text{a (breath).}$$
$$|$$
$$\text{Anna (earth)} = \text{Manas (mind).}$$

[1] If a man dies, the first thing which his friends say is, He speaks no more. Then, he understands no more. Then, he moves no more. Then, he is cold.

in his mind, his mind in his breath, his breath in
heat (fire), heat in the Highest Being.

7. 'Now that which is that subtile essence (the
root of all), in it all that exists has its self. It is the
True. It is the Self, and thou, O *S*vetaketu, art it.'

' Please, Sir, inform me still more,' said the son.

' Be it so, my child,' the father replied.

NINTH KHA*N*DA.

1. 'As the bees [1], my son, make honey by collecting the juices of distant trees, and reduce the
juice into one form,

2. 'And as these juices have no discrimination,
so that they might say, I am the juice of this tree
or that, in the same manner, my son, all these creatures, when they have become merged in the True
(either in deep sleep or in death), know not that
they are merged in the True.

3. 'Whatever these creatures are here, whether
a lion, or a wolf, or a boar, or a worm, or a midge,
or a gnat, or a musquito, that they become again
and again.

4. ' Now that which is that subtile essence, in it
all that exists has its self. It is the True. It is
the Self, and thou, O *S*vetaketu, art it.'

' Please, Sir, inform me still more,' said the son.

' Be it so, my child,' the father replied.

---

[1] At the beginning of each chapter the commentator supplies
the question which the son is supposed to have asked his father.
The first is: All creatures falling every day into deep sleep (sushupti) obtain thereby the Sat, the true being. How is it then
that they do not know that they obtain the Sat every day?

TENTH KHANDA [1].

1. 'These rivers, my son, run, the eastern (like the Gangâ) toward the east, the western (like the Sindhu) toward the west. They go from sea to sea (i. e. the clouds lift up the water from the sea to the sky, and send it back as rain to the sea). They become indeed sea. And as those rivers, when they are in the sea, do not know, I am this or that river,

2. 'In the same manner, my son, all these creatures, when they have come back from the True, know not that they have come back from the True. Whatever these creatures are here, whether a lion, or a wolf, or a boar, or a worm, or a midge, or a gnat, or a musquito, that they become again and again.

3. 'That which is that subtile essence, in it all that exists has its self. It is the True. It is the Self, and thou, O Svetaketu, art it.'·

'Please, Sir, inform me still more,' said the son.

'Be it so, my child,' the father replied.

ELEVENTH KHANDA [2].

1. 'If some one were to strike at the root of this large tree here, it would bleed, but live. If he were to strike at its stem, it would bleed, but live. If he were to strike at its top, it would bleed, but live.

---

[1] The next question which the son is supposed to have asked is: If a man who has slept in his own house, rises and goes to another village, he knows that he has come from his own house. Why then do people not know that they have come from the Sat?

[2] The next question is: Waves, foam, and bubbles arise from the water, and when they merge again in the water, they are gone. How is it that living beings, when in sleep or death they are merged again in the Sat, are not destroyed?

Pervaded by the living Self that tree stands firm, drinking in its nourishment and rejoicing ;

2. 'But if the life (the living Self) leaves one of its branches, that branch withers; if it leaves a second, that branch withers ; if it leaves a third, that branch withers. If it leaves the whole tree, the whole tree withers [1]. In exactly the same manner, my son, know this.' Thus he spoke :

3. 'This (body) indeed withers and dies when the living Self has left it ; the living Self dies not.

'That which is that subtile essence, in it all that exists has its self. It is the True. It is the Self, and thou, *S*vetaketu, art it.'

'Please, Sir, inform me still more,' said the son.

'Be it so, my child,' the father replied.

---

[1] The commentator remarks that according to the Veda, trees are conscious, while Buddhists and followers of Ka*n*âda hold them to be unconscious. They live, because one sees how their sap runs and how it dries up, just as one sees the sap in a living body, which, as we saw, was produced by food and water. Therefore the simile holds good. The life, or, more correctly, the liver, the living Self, pervades the tree, as it pervades man, when it has entered the organism which produces breath, mind, and speech. If any accident happens to a branch, the living Self draws himself away from that branch, and then the branch withers. The sap which caused the living Self to remain, goes, and the living Self goes away with it. The same applies to the whole tree. The tree dies when the living Self leaves it, but the living Self does not die ; it only leaves an abode which it had before occupied. Some other illustrations, to show that the living Self remains, are added by the commentator : First, with regard to the living Self being the same when it awakes from deep sleep (sushupti), he remarks that we remember quite well that we have left something unfinished before we fell asleep. And then with regard to the living Self being the same when it awakes from death to a new life, he shows that creatures, as soon as they are born take the breast, and exhibit terror, which can only be explained, as he supposes, by their possessing a recollection of a former state of existence.

Twelfth Khanda [1].

1. 'Fetch me from thence a fruit of the Nyagrodha tree.'

'Here is one, Sir.'

'Break it.'

'It is broken, Sir.'

'What do you see there?'

'These seeds, almost infinitesimal.'

'Break one of them.'

'It is broken, Sir.'

'What do you see there?'

'Not anything, Sir.'

2. The father said: 'My son, that subtile essence which you do not perceive there, of that very essence this great Nyagrodha tree exists.

3. 'Believe it, my son. That which is the subtile essence, in it all that exists has its self. It is the True. It is the Self, and thou, O *S*vetaketu, art it.'

'Please, Sir, inform me still more,' said the son.

'Be it so, my child,' the father replied.

Thirteenth Khanda [2].

1. 'Place this salt in water, and then wait on me in the morning.'

The son did as he was commanded.

The father said to him: 'Bring me the salt, which you placed in the water last night.'

---

[1] The question which the son is supposed to have asked is: How can this universe which has the form and name of earth &c. be produced from the Sat which is subtile, and has neither form nor name?

[2] The question here is supposed to have been: If the Sat is the root of all that exists, why is it not perceived?

The son having looked for it, found it not, for, of course, it was melted.

2. The father said: 'Taste it from the surface of the water. How is it?'

The son replied: 'It is salt.'

'Taste it from the middle. How is it?'

The son replied: 'It is salt.'

'Taste it from the bottom. How is it?'

The son replied: 'It is salt.'

The father said: 'Throw it away[1] and then wait on me.'

He did so; but salt exists for ever.

Then the father said: 'Here also, in this body, forsooth, you do not perceive the True (Sat), my son; but there indeed it is.

3. 'That which is the subtile essence, in it all that exists has its self. It is the True. It is the Self, and thou, O *S*vetaketu, art it.'

'Please, Sir, inform me still more,' said the son.

'Be it so, my child,' the father replied.

FOURTEENTH KHA*ND*A[2].

1. 'As one might lead a person with his eyes covered away from the Gandhâras[3], and leave him

---

[1] Read abhiprâsya, which is evidently intended by the commentary: abhiprâyasya parityag*y*a. See B. R. Sanskrit Dictionary, s. v.

[2] The question here asked is: The salt, though no longer perceptible by means of sight or touch, could be discovered by taste. Then how can the Sat be discovered, although it is imperceptible by all the senses?

[3] The Gandhâras, but rarely mentioned in the Rig-veda and the Ait. Brâhma*n*a, have left their name in Κάνδαροι and Candahar. The fact of their name being evidently quite familiar to the author of the Upanishad might be used to prove either its antiquity or its Northern origin.

then in a place where there are no human beings;
and as that person would turn towards the east, or
the north, or the west, and shout, "I have been
brought here with my eyes covered, I have been
left here with my eyes covered,"

2. 'And as thereupon some one might loose his
bandage and say to him, "Go in that direction, it
is Gandhâra, go in that direction;" and as thereupon, having been informed and being able to judge
for himself, he would by asking his way from village
to village arrive at last at Gandhâra,—in exactly the
same manner does a man, who meets with a teacher
to inform him, obtain the true knowledge [1]. For him

---

[1] Tedious as the commentator is in general, he is sometimes almost
eloquent in bringing out all that is implied or supposed to be implied
in the sacred text. He explains the last simile as follows: A man
was carried away by robbers from his own country. After his eyes
had been covered, he was taken to a forest full of terrors and dangers
arising from tigers, robbers, &c. Not knowing where he was, and
suffering from hunger and thirst, he began to cry, wishing to be delivered from his bonds. Then a man took pity on him and removed
his bonds, and when he had returned to his home, he was happy.
Next follows the application. Our real home is the True (Sat), the
Self of the world. The forest into which we are driven is the
body, made of the three elements, fire, water, earth, consisting of
blood, flesh, bones, &c., and liable to cold, heat, and many other
evils. The bands with which our eyes are covered are our desires
for many things, real or unreal, such as wife, children, cattle, &c.,
while the robbers by whom we are driven into the forest are our
good and evil deeds. Then we cry and say: 'I am the son of so
and so, these are my relatives, I am happy, I am miserable, I am
foolish, I am wise, I am just, I am born, I am dead, I am old,
I am wretched, my son is dead, my fortune is gone, I am undone,
how shall I live, where shall I go, who will save me?' These and
hundreds and thousands of other evils are the bands which blind
us. Then, owing to some supererogatory good works we may
have done, we suddenly meet a man who knows the Self of
Brahman, whose own bonds have been broken, who takes pity
on us and shows us the way to see the evil which attaches to all

there is only delay so long as he is not delivered
(from the body); then he will be perfect[1].

3. 'That which is the subtile essence, in it all
that exists has its self. It is the True. It is the
Self, and thou, O *S*vetaketu, art it.'

'Please, Sir, inform me still more,' said the son.

'Be it so, my child,' the father replied.

FIFTEENTH KHA*N*DA[2].

1. 'If a man is ill, his relatives assemble round
him and ask: "Dost thou know me? Dost thou
know me?" Now as long as his speech is not

---

that we love in this world. We then withdraw ourselves from all
worldly pleasures. We learn that we are not mere creatures of
the world, the son of so and so, &c., but that we are that which is
the True (Sat). The bands of our ignorance and blindness are
removed, and, like the man of Gandhâra, we arrive at our own
home, the Self, or the True. Then we are happy and blessed.

[1] The last words are really—'for him there is only delay so long
as I shall not be delivered; then I shall be perfect.' This requires
some explanation. First of all, the change from the third to the
first person, is best explained by assuming that at the point where
all individuality vanishes, the father, as teacher, identifies himself
with the person of whom he is speaking.

The delay (the *k*ira or kshepa) of which he speaks is the time
which passes between the attainment of true knowledge and death,
or freedom from the effects of actions performed before the attainment of knowledge. The actions which led to our present
embodiment must be altogether consumed, before the body can
perish, and then only are we free. As to any actions performed
after the attainment of knowledge, they do not count; otherwise
there would be a new embodiment, and the attainment of even true
knowledge would never lead to final deliverance.

[2] The question supposed to be asked is: By what degrees a man,
who has been properly instructed in the knowledge of Brahman,
obtains the Sat, or returns to the True. To judge from the text
both he who knows the True and he who does not, reach, when they
die, the Sat, passing from speech to mind and breath and heat (fire).
But whereas he who knows, remains in the Sat, they who do not

merged in his mind, his mind in breath, breath in heat (fire), heat in the Highest Being (devatâ), he knows them.

2. 'But when his speech is merged in his mind, his mind in breath, breath in heat (fire), heat in the Highest Being, then he knows them not.

'That which is the subtile essence, in it all that exists has its self. It is the True. It is the Self, and thou, O Svetaketu, art it.'

'Please, Sir, inform me still more,' said the son.

'Be it so, my child,' the father replied.

SIXTEENTH KHANDA[1].

1. 'My child, they bring a man hither whom they have taken by the hand, and they say: "He has taken something, he has committed a theft." (When

---

know, return again to a new form of existence. It is important to observe that the commentator denies that he who knows, passes at his death through the artery of the head to the sun, and then to the Sat. He holds that with him who knows there is no further cause for delay, and that as soon as he dies, he returns to the Sat.

[1] The next question is: Why does he who knows, on obtaining the Sat, not return, while he who does not know, though obtaining the Sat in death, returns? An illustration is chosen which is intended to show how knowledge produces a material effect. The belief in the efficacy of ordeals must have existed at the time, and appealing to that belief, the teacher says that the man who knows himself guilty, is really burnt by the heated iron, while the man who knows himself innocent, is not. In the same manner the man who knows his Self to be the true Self, on approaching after death the true Self, is not repelled and sent back into a new existence, while he who does not know, is sent back into a new round of births and deaths. The man who tells a falsehood about himself, loses his true Self and is burnt; the man who has a false conception about his Self, loses likewise his true Self, and not knowing the true Self, even though approaching it in death, he has to suffer till he acquires some day the true knowledge.

he denies, they say), "Heat the hatchet for him."
If he committed the theft, then he makes himself to
be what he is not. Then the false-minded, having
covered his true Self by a falsehood, grasps the
heated hatchet—he is burnt, and he is killed.

2. 'But if he did not commit the theft, then he
makes himself to be what he is. Then the true-
minded, having covered his true Self by truth,
grasps the heated hatchet—he is not burnt, and he
is delivered.

'As that (truthful) man is not burnt, thus has all
that exists its self in That. It is the True. It is
the Self, and thou, O *S*vetaketu, art it.' He understood what he said, yea, he understood it.

SEVENTH PRAPÂ*TH*AKA.

FIRST KHA*N*DA.

1. Nârada approached Sanatkumâra and said,
'Teach me, Sir!' Sanatkumâra said to him: 'Please
to tell me what you know; afterward I shall tell you
what is beyond.'

2. Nârada said: 'I know the *Ri*g-veda, Sir, the
Ya*g*ur-veda, the Sâma-veda, as the fourth the Âtharva*n*a, as the fifth the Itihâsa-purâ*n*a (the Bhârata);
the Veda of the Vedas (grammar); the Pitrya (the
rules for the sacrifices for the ancestors); the Râ*s*i
(the science of numbers); the Daiva (the science of
portents); the Nidhi (the science of time); the
Vâkovâkya (logic); the Ekâyana (ethics); the Deva-
vidyâ (etymology); the Brahma-vidyâ (pronunciation,
*s*ikshâ, ceremonial, kalpa, prosody, *kh*andas); the
Bhûta-vidyâ (the science of demons); the Kshatra-

vidyâ (the science of weapons); the Nakshatra-vidyâ (astronomy); the Sarpa and Devagana-vidyâ (the science of serpents or poisons, and the sciences of the genii, such as the making of perfumes, dancing, singing, playing, and other fine arts)[1]. All this I know, Sir.

3: 'But, Sir, with all this I know the Mantras only, the sacred books, I do not know the Self. I have heard from men like you, that he who knows the Self overcomes grief. I am in grief. Do, Sir, help me over this grief of mine.'

Sanatkumâra said to him: 'Whatever you have read, is only a name.

4. 'A name is the _Rig_-veda, Yagur-veda, Sâma-veda, and as the fourth the Âtharvana, as the fifth the Itihâsa-purâna, the Veda of the Vedas, the Pitrya, the Râsi, the Daiva, the Nidhi, the Vâko-vâkya, the Ekâyana, the Deva-vidyâ, the Brahma-vidyâ, the Bhûta-vidyâ, the Kshatra-vidyâ, the Nakshatra-vidyâ, the Sarpa and Devagana-vidyâ. All these are a name only. Meditate on the name.

5. 'He who meditates on the name as Brahman [2],

---

[1] This passage, exhibiting the sacred literature as known at the time, should be compared with the Br_i_hadâran_y_aka, II, 4, 10. The explanation of the old titles rests on the authority of _S_ankara, and he is not always consistent. See Colebrooke, Miscellaneous Essays, 1873, II, p. 10.

[2] Why a man who knows the Veda should not know the Self, while in other places it is said that the Veda teaches the Self, is well illustrated by the commentary. If a royal procession approaches, he says, then, though we do not see the king, because he is hidden by flags, parasols, &c., yet we say, there is the king. And if we ask who is the king, then again, though we cannot see him and point him out, we can say, at least, that he is different from all that is seen. The Self is hidden in the Veda as a king is hidden in a royal procession.

is, as it were, lord and master as far as the name
reaches—he who meditates on the name as Brahman.'

'Sir, is there something better than a name?'

'Yes, there is something better than a name.'

'Sir, tell it me.'

SECOND KHA*ND*A.

1. 'Speech is better than a name. Speech makes
us understand the *Ri*g-veda, Ya*g*ur-veda, Sâma-veda,
and as the fourth the Âtharva*n*a, as the fifth the
Itihâsa-purâ*n*a, the Veda of the Vedas, the Pitrya,
the Râ*s*i, the Daiva, the Nidhi, the Vâkovâkya, the
Ekâyana, the Deva-vidyâ, the Brahma-vidyâ, the
Kshatra-vidyâ, the Nakshatra-vidyâ, the Sarpa and
Deva*g*ana-vidyâ; heaven, earth, air, ether, water,
fire, gods, men, cattle, birds, herbs, trees, all
beasts down to worms, midges, and ants; what is
right and what is wrong; what is true and what
is false; what is good and what is bad; what is
pleasing and what is not pleasing. For if there
were no speech, neither right nor wrong would be
known [1], neither the true nor the false, neither the
good nor the bad, neither the pleasant nor the
unpleasant. Speech makes us understand all this.
Meditate on speech.

2. 'He who meditates on speech as Brahman, is,
as it were, lord and master as far as speech reaches—
he who meditates on speech as Brahman.'

'Sir, is there something better than speech?'

'Yes, there is something better than speech.'

'Sir, tell it me.'

---

[1] The commentator explains vya*gñ*âpayishyat by avi*gñ*âtam
abhavishyat. Possibly h*ri*dayag*ñ*o stands for h*ri*dayag*ñ*am.

THIRD KHAN*D*A.

1. 'Mind (manas) is better than speech. For as the closed fist holds two amalaka or two kola or two aksha fruits, thus does mind hold speech and name. For if a man is minded in his mind to read the sacred hymns, he reads them; if he is minded in his mind to perform any actions, he performs them; if he is minded to wish for sons and cattle, he wishes for them; if he is minded to wish for this world and the other, he wishes for them. For mind is indeed the self[1], mind is the world, mind is Brahman. Meditate on the mind.

2. 'He who meditates on the mind as Brahman, is, as it were, lord and master as far as the mind reaches—he who meditates on the mind as Brahman.'

'Sir, is there something better than mind?'

'Yes, there is something better than mind.'

'Sir, tell it me.'

FOURTH KHAN*D*A.

1. 'Will[2] (sankalpa) is better than mind. For when a man wills, then he thinks in his mind, then he sends forth speech, and he sends it forth in a name. In a name the sacred hymns are contained, in the sacred hymns all sacrifices.

2. 'All these therefore (beginning with mind and

---

[1] The commentator explains this by saying that, without the instrument of the mind, the Self cannot act or enjoy.

[2] Sankalpa is elsewhere defined as a modification of manas. The commentator says that, like thinking, it is an activity of the inner organ. It is difficult to find any English term exactly corresponding to sankalpa. Rajendralal Mitra translates it by will, but it implies not only will, but at the same time conception, determination, and desire.

ending in sacrifice) centre in will, consist of will,
abide in will. Heaven and earth willed, air and
ether willed, water and fire willed. Through the
will ,of heaven and earth &c. rain wills; through
the will of rain food wills; through the will of food
the vital airs will; through the will of the vital airs
the sacred hymns will; through the will of the sacred
hymns the sacrifices will; through the will of the
sacrifices the world (as their reward) wills; through
the will of the world everything wills [1]. This is will.
Meditate on will.

3. 'He who meditates on will as Brahman, he,
being himself safe, firm, and undistressed, obtains
the safe, firm, and undistressed worlds which he has
willed; he is, as it were, lord and master as far as
will reaches—he who meditates on will as Brahman.'
'Sir, is there something better than will?'
'Yes, there is something better than will.'
'Sir, tell it me.'

FIFTH KHA*ND*A.

1. 'Consideration (*k*itta)[2] is better than will. For
when a man considers, then he wills, then he thinks
in his mind, then he sends forth speech, and he

---

[1] This paragraph is obscure. The text seems doubtful, for
instance, in samak*l*ipatâm, samakalpetâm, and samakalpatâm.
Then the question is the exact meaning of sa*m*k*l*iptyai, which
must be taken as an instrumental case. What is intended is that,
without rain, food is impossible &c. or inconceivable ; but the text
says, 'By the will of rain food wills,' &c. Will seems almost to be
taken here in the sense in which modern philosophers use it, as a
kind of creative will. By the will of rain food wills, would mean,
that first rain wills and exists, and afterwards the vital airs will
and exist, &c.

[2] *K*itta, thought, implies here consideration and reflection.

sends it forth in a name. In a name the sacred hymns are contained, in the sacred hymns all sacrifices.

2. 'All these (beginning with mind and ending in sacrifice) centre in consideration, consist of consideration, abide in consideration. Therefore if a man is inconsiderate, even if he possesses much learning, people say of him, he is nothing, whatever he may know; for, if he were learned, he would not be so inconsiderate. But if a man is considerate, even though he knows but little, to him indeed do people listen gladly. Consideration is the centre, consideration is the self, consideration is the support of all these. Meditate on consideration.

3. 'He who meditates on consideration as Brahman, he, being himself safe, firm, and undistressed, obtains the safe, firm, and undistressed worlds which he has considered; he is, as it were, lord and master as far as consideration reaches—he who meditates on consideration as Brahman.'

'Sir, is there something better than consideration?'

'Yes, there is something better than consideration.'

'Sir, tell it me.'

Sixth Khanda.

1. 'Reflection (dhyâna) [1] is better than consideration. The earth reflects, as it were, and thus does the sky, the heaven, the water, the mountains, gods and men. Therefore those who among men obtain

---

[1] Reflection is concentration of all our thoughts on one object, ekâgratâ. And as a man who reflects and meditates on the highest objects acquires thereby repose, becomes firm and immovable, so the earth is supposed to be in repose and immovable, as it were, by reflection and meditation.

greatness here on earth, seem to have obtained a part of the object of reflection (because they show a certain repose of manner). Thus while small and vulgar people are always quarrelling, abusive, and slandering, great men seem to have obtained a part of the reward of reflection. Meditate on reflection.

2. 'He who meditates on reflection as Brahman, is lord and master, as it were, as far as reflection reaches—he who meditates on reflection as Brahman.'

'Sir, is there something better than reflection?'

'Yes, there is something better than reflection.'

'Sir, tell it me.'

SEVENTH KHA*ND*A.

1. 'Understanding (vig*ñ*âna) is better than reflection. Through understanding we understand the *R*ig-veda, the Ya*g*ur-veda, the Sâma-veda, and as the fourth the Âtharva*n*a, as the fifth the Itihâsa-purâ*n*a [1], the Veda of the Vedas, the Pitrya, the Râ*s*i, the Daiva, the Nidhi, the Vâkovâkya, the Ekâyana, the Deva-vidyâ, the Brahma-vidyâ, the Bhûta-vidyâ, the Kshatra-vidyâ, the Nakshatra-vidyâ, the Sarpa and Deva*g*ana-vidyâ, heaven, earth, air, ether, water, fire, gods, men, cattle, birds, herbs, trees, all beasts down to worms, midges, and ants; what is right and what is wrong; what is true and what is false; what is good and what is bad; what is pleasing and what is not pleasing; food and savour, this world and that, all this we understand through understanding. Meditate on understanding.

2. 'He who meditates on understanding as Brahman, reaches the worlds where there is understanding

---

[1] See before, p. 109.

and knowledge [1]; he is, as it were, lord and master as far as understanding reaches—he who meditates on understanding as Brahman.'

'Sir, is there something better than understanding?'

'Yes, there is something better than understanding.'

'Sir, tell it me.'

EIGHTH KHA*ND*A.

1. 'Power (bala) is better than understanding. One powerful man shakes a hundred men of understanding. If a man is powerful, he becomes a rising man. If he rises, he becomes a man who visits wise people. If he visits, he becomes a follower of wise people. If he follows them, he becomes a seeing, a hearing, a perceiving, a knowing, a doing, an understanding man. By power the earth stands firm, and the sky, and the heaven, and the mountains, gods and men, cattle, birds, herbs, trees, all beasts down to worms, midges, and ants; by power the world stands firm. Meditate on power.

2. 'He who meditates on power as Brahman, is, as it were, lord and master as far as power reaches—he who meditates on power as Brahman.'

'Sir, is there something better than power?'

'Yes, there is something better than power.'

'Sir, tell it me.'

NINTH KHA*ND*A.

1. 'Food (anna) is better than power. Therefore if a man abstain from food for ten days, though he live, he would be unable to see, hear, perceive, think, act, and understand. But when he obtains

---

[1] The commentator takes vig*ñâ*na here as understanding of sacred books, *gñâ*na as cleverness with regard to other subjects.

food, he is able to see, hear, perceive, think, act, and understand. Meditate on food.

2. 'He who meditates on food as Brahman, obtains the worlds rich in food and drink; he is, as it were, lord and master as far as food reaches— he who meditates on food as Brahman.'

'Sir, is there something better than food?'

'Yes, there is something better than food.'

'Sir, tell it me.'

TENTH KHA*N*DA.

1. 'Water (ap) is better than food. Therefore if there is not sufficient rain, the vital spirits fail from fear that there will be less food. But if there is sufficient rain, the vital spirits rejoice, because there will be much food. This water, on assuming different forms, becomes this earth, this sky, this heaven, the mountains, gods and men, cattle, birds, herbs and trees, all beasts down to worms, midges, and ants. Water indeed assumes all these forms. Meditate on water.

2. 'He who meditates on water as Brahman, obtains all wishes, he becomes satisfied; he is, as it were, lord and master as far as water reaches— he who meditates on water as Brahman.'

'Sir, is there something better than water?'

'Yes, there is something better than water.'

'Sir, tell it me.'

ELEVENTH KHA*N*DA.

1. 'Fire (te*g*as) is better than water. For fire united with air, warms the ether. Then people say, It is hot, it burns, it will rain. Thus does fire, after showing this sign (itself) first, create water. And

thus again thunderclaps come with lightnings, flashing upwards and across the sky. Then people say, There is lightning and thunder, it will rain. Then also does fire, after showing this sign first, create water. Meditate on fire.

2. 'He who meditates on fire as Brahman, obtains, resplendent himself, resplendent worlds, full of light and free of darkness; he is, as it were, lord and master as far as fire reaches—he who meditates on fire as Brahman.'

'Sir, is there something better than fire?'

'Yes, there is something better than fire.'

'Sir, tell it me.'

TWELFTH KHAN*D*A.

1. 'Ether (or space) is better than fire. For in the ether exist both sun and moon, the lightning, stars, and fire (agni). Through the ether we call, through the ether we hear, through the ether we answer[1]. In the ether or space we rejoice (when we are together), and rejoice not (when we are separated). In the ether everything is born, and towards the ether everything tends when it is born[2]. Meditate on ether.

2. 'He who meditates on ether as Brahman, obtains the worlds of ether and of light, which are free from pressure and pain, wide and spacious[3]; he is, as it were, lord and master as far as ether reaches—he who meditates on ether as Brahman.'

'Sir, is there something better than ether?'

---

[1] Cf. *Kh.* Up. IV, 5, 1.

[2] The seed grows upwards towards the ether; not downwards.

[3] Cf. Kâ*th.* Up. II, 11.

'Yes, there is something better than ether.'
'Sir, tell it me.'

THIRTEENTH KHA*ND*A.

1. 'Memory[1] (smara) is better than ether. Therefore where many are assembled together, if they have no memory, they would hear no one, they would not perceive, they would not understand. Through memory we know our sons, through memory our cattle. Meditate on memory.

2. 'He who meditates on memory as Brahman, is, as it were, lord and master as far as memory reaches—he who meditates on memory as Brahman.'
'Sir, is there something better than memory?'
'Yes, there is something better than memory.'
'Sir, tell it me.'

FOURTEENTH KHA*ND*A.

1. 'Hope (âsâ) is better than memory. Fired by hope does memory read the sacred hymns, perform sacrifices, desire sons and cattle, desire this world and the other. Meditate on hope.

2. 'He who meditates on hope as Brahman, all his desires are fulfilled by hope, his prayers are not in vain; he is, as it were, lord and master as far as hope reaches—he who meditates on hope as Brahman.'
'Sir, is there something better than hope?'
'Yes, there is something better than hope.'
'Sir, tell it me.'

---

[1] The apparent distance between ether and memory is bridged over by the commentator pointing out that without memory everything would be as if it were not, so far as we are concerned.

FIFTEENTH KHA*N*DA.

1. 'Spirit [1] (prâ*n*a) is better than hope. As the spokes of a wheel hold to the nave [2], so does all this (beginning with names and ending in hope) hold to spirit. That spirit moves by the spirit, it gives spirit to the spirit. Father means spirit, mother is spirit, brother is spirit, sister is spirit, tutor is spirit, Brâhma*n*a is spirit.

2. 'For if one says anything unbecoming to a father, mother, brother, sister, tutor or Brâhma*n*a, then people say, Shame on thee! thou hast offended thy father, mother, brother, sister, tutor, or a Brâhma*n*a.

3. 'But, if after the spirit has departed from them, one shoves them together with a poker, and burns them to pieces, no one would say, Thou offendest thy father, mother, brother, sister, tutor or a Brâhma*n*a.

4. 'Spirit then is all this. He who sees this, perceives this, and understands this, becomes an ativâdin [3]. If people say to such a man, Thou

---

[1] Prâ*n*a is used here in a technical sense. It does not mean simply breath, but the spirit, the conscious self (prag*ñ*âtman) which, as we saw, enters the body in order to reveal the whole variety of forms and names. It is in one sense the mukhya prâ*n*a.

[2] The commentary carries the simile still further. The felloe, he says, holds to the spokes, the spokes to the nave. So do the bhûtamâtrâs hold to the prag*ñ*âmâtrâs, and these to the prâ*n*a.

[3] One who declares something that goes beyond all the declarations made before, beginning with the declaration that names are Brahman, and ending with the declaration that hope is Brahman;—one who knows that prâ*n*a, spirit, the conscious self, is Brahman. This declaration represents the highest point reached by ordinary people, but Nârada wishes to go beyond. In the Mu*nd*aka, III, 1, 4, an ativâdin is contrasted with one who really knows the highest truth.

art an ativâdin, he may say, I am an ativâdin ; he
need not deny it.'

SIXTEENTH KHA*ND*A [1].

I. ' But in reality he is an ativâdin who declares
the Highest Being to be the True (Satya, τὸ ὄντως
ὄν).'

'Sir, may I become an ativâdin by the True ?'
' But we must desire to know the True.'
' Sir, I desire to know the True.'

SEVENTEENTH KHA*ND*A.

I. ' When one understands the True, then one
declares the True. One who does not understand
it, does not declare the True [2]. Only he who understands it, declares the True. This understanding,
however, we must desire to understand.'

' Sir, I desire to understand it.'

EIGHTEENTH KHA*ND*A.

I. ' When one perceives, then one understands.
One who does not perceive, does not understand.
Only he who perceives, understands. This percep-
tion, however, we must desire to understand.'

' Sir, I desire to understand it.'

---

[1] As Nârada asks no further, whether there is anything better,
higher, truer than prâ*n*a, he is supposed to be satisfied with his
belief that prâ*n*a is the Highest Being. Sanatkumâra, however,
wishes to lead him on to a still higher view; hence the paragraphs
which follow from 16 to 26.

[2] He would, for instance, call fire real, not knowing that fire is
only a mixture of the three elements (cf. VI, 4), the rûpatraya, a
mere variety (vikâra), and name (nâman).

NINETEENTH KHANDA.

1. 'When one believes, then one perceives. One who does not believe, does not perceive. Only he who believes, perceives. This belief, however, we must desire to understand.'

'Sir, I desire to understand it.'

TWENTIETH KHANDA.

1. 'When one attends on a tutor (spiritual guide), then one believes. One who does not attend on a tutor, does not believe. Only he who attends, believes. This attention on a tutor, however, we must desire to understand.'

'Sir, I desire to understand it.'

TWENTY-FIRST KHANDA.

1. 'When one performs all sacred duties[1], then one attends really on a tutor. One who does not perform his duties, does not really attend on a tutor. Only he who performs his duties, attends on his tutor. This performance of duties, however, we must desire to understand.'

'Sir, I desire to understand it.'

TWENTY-SECOND KHANDA.

1. 'When one obtains bliss (in oneself), then one performs duties. One who does not obtain bliss, does not perform duties. Only he who obtains bliss, performs duties. This bliss, however, we must desire to understand.'

'Sir, I desire to understand it.'

---

[1] The duties of a student, such as restraint of the senses, concentration of the mind, &c.

Twenty-third Kha*n*da.

1. 'The Infinite (bhûman) [1] is bliss. There is no bliss in anything finite. Infinity only is bliss. This Infinity, however, we must desire to understand.'

'Sir, I desire to understand it.'

Twenty-fourth Kha*n*da.

1. 'Where one sees nothing else, hears nothing else, understands nothing else, that is the Infinite. Where one sees something·else, hears something else, understands something else, that is the finite. The Infinite is immortal, the finite is mortal.'

'Sir, in what does the Infinite rest?'

'In its own greatness—or not even in greatness [2].'

2. 'In the world they call cows and horses, elephants and gold, slaves, wives, fields and houses greatness. I do not mean this,' thus he spoke; 'for in that case one being (the possessor) rests in something else, (but the Infinite cannot rest in something different from itself.)

Twenty-fifth Kha*n*da.

1. 'The Infinite indeed is below, above, behind, before, right and left—it is indeed all this.

'Now follows the explanation of the Infinite as

---

[1] Bhûman is sometimes translated by grandeur, the superlative, the akme. It is the highest point that can be reached, the infinite and the true.

[2] This phrase reminds one of the last verse in the No sad âsîd hymn, where, likewise, the expression of the highest certainty is followed by a misgiving that after all it may be otherwise. The commentator takes yadi vâ in the sense of, If you ask in the highest sense, then I say no; for the Infinite cannot rest in anything, not even in greatness.

the I : I am below, I am above, I am behind, before, right and left—I am all this.

2. ' Next follows the explanation of the Infinite as the Self : Self is below, above, behind, before, right and left—Self is all this.

' He who sees, perceives, and understands this, loves the Self, delights in the Self, revels in the Self, rejoices in the Self—he becomes a Svarâg, (an autocrat or self-ruler); he is lord and master in all the worlds.

' But those who think differently from this, live in perishable worlds, and have other beings for their rulers.

TWENTY-SIXTH KHA*N*DA.

1. ' To him who sees, perceives, and understands this [1], the spirit (prâ*n*a) springs from the Self, hope springs from the Self, memory springs from the Self; so do ether, fire, water, appearance and dis-appearance [2], food, power, understanding, reflection, consideration, will, mind, speech, names, sacred hymns, and sacrifices—aye, all this springs from the Self.

2. ' There is this verse, " He who sees this, does not see death, nor illness, nor pain; he who sees this, sees everything, and obtains everything everywhere.

' " He is one (before creation), he becomes three

---

[1] Before the acquirement of true knowledge, all that has been mentioned before, spirit, hope, memory, &c., on to names, was supposed to spring from the Sat, as something different from one-self. Now he is to know that the Sat is the Self.

[2] In the preceding paragraphs appearance and disappearance (birth and death) are not mentioned. This shows how easy it was in these treatises either to omit or to add anything that seemed important.

(fire, water, earth), he becomes five, he becomes seven, he becomes nine; then again he is called the eleventh, and hundred and ten and one thousand and twenty[1]."

'When the intellectual aliment has been purified, the whole nature becomes purified. When the whole nature has been purified, the memory becomes firm. And when the memory (of the Highest Self) remains firm, then all the ties (which bind us to a belief in anything but the Self) are loosened.

'The venerable Sanatkumâra showed to Nârada, after his faults had been rubbed out, the other side of darkness. They call Sanatkumâra Skanda, yea, Skanda they call him.'

EIGHTH PRAPÂ*TH*AKA.

FIRST KHA*N*DA[2].

1. Hari*h*, Om. There is this city of Brahman (the body), and in it the palace, the small lotus (of

---

[1] This too is meant as a verse. The commentary says that the various numbers are intended to show the endless variety of form on the Self after creation. Cf. Mait. Up. V, 2.

[2] The eighth Prapâ*th*aka seems to form a kind of appendix to the Upanishad. The highest point that can be reached by specu-lation had been reached in the seventh Prapâ*th*aka, the identity of our self and of everything else with the Highest Self. This speculative effort, however, is too much for ordinary people. They cannot conceive the Sat or Brahman as out of space and time, as free from all qualities, and in order to help them, they are taught to adore the Brahman, as it appears in space and time, an object endowed with certain qualities, living in nature and in the human heart. The Highest Brahman, besides which there is nothing, and which can neither be reached as an object, nor be considered as

the heart), and in it that small ether. Now what exists within that small ether, that is to be sought for, that is to be understood.

2. And if they should say to him : ' Now with regard to that city of Brahman, and the palace in it, i. e. the small lotus of the heart, and the small ether within the heart, what is there within it that deserves to be sought for, or that is to be understood ? '

3. Then he should say: ' As large as this ether (all space) is, so large is that ether within the heart. Both heaven and earth are contained within it, both fire and air, both sun and moon, both lightning and stars ; and whatever there is of him (the Self) here in the world, and whatever is not (i. e. whatever has been or will be), all that is contained within it[1].'

4. And if they should say to him : ' If everything that exists is contained in that city of Brahman, all beings and all desires (whatever can be imagined or desired), then what is left of it, when old age reaches it and scatters it, or when it falls to pieces ? '

5. Then he should say: ' By the old age of the body, that (the ether, or Brahman within it) does not age ; by the death of the body, that (the ether, or Brahman within it) is not killed. That (the Brah-

---

an effect, seems to ordinary minds like a thing which is not. Therefore while the true philosopher, after acquiring the knowledge of the Highest Sat, becomes identified with it suddenly, like lightning, the ordinary mortal must reach it by slow degrees, and as a preparation for that higher knowledge which is to follow, the eighth Prapâ*th*aka, particularly the first portion of it, has been added to the teaching contained in the earlier books.

[1] The ether in the heart is really a name of Brahman. He is there, and therefore all that comes of him when he assumes bodily shapes, both what is and what is not, i. e. what is no longer or not yet ; for the absolute nothing is not intended here.

man) is the true Brahma-city (not the body[1]).   In
it all desires are contained.   It is the Self, free from
sin, free from old age, from death and grief, from
hunger and thirst, which desires nothing but what
it ought to desire, and imagines nothing but what it
ought to imagine.   Now as here on earth people
follow as they are commanded, and depend on the
object which they are attached to, be it a country or
a piece of land,

6. 'And as here on earth, whatever has been acquired by exertion, perishes, so perishes whatever is
acquired for the next world by sacrifices and other
good actions performed on earth.   Those who depart from hence without having discovered the
Self and those true desires, for them there is no
freedom in all the worlds.   But those who depart
from hence, after having discovered the Self and
those true desires[2], for them there is freedom in all
the worlds.

Second Kha*n*da.

1. 'Thus he who desires the world[3] of the fathers,
by his mere will the fathers come to receive him,
and having obtained the world of the fathers, he is
happy.

2. 'And he who desires the world of the mothers,
by his mere will the mothers come to receive him,

---

[1] I translate this somewhat differently from the commentator,
though the argument remains the same.

[2] True desires are those which we ought to desire, and the fulfilment of which depends on ourselves, supposing that we have
acquired the knowledge which enables us to fulfil them.

[3] World is the nearest approach to loka: it means life with the
fathers, or enjoying the company of the fathers.

and having obtained the world of the mothers, he is happy.

3. 'And he who desires the world of the brothers, by his mere will the brothers come to receive him, and having obtained the world of the brothers, he is happy.

4. 'And he who desires the world of the sisters, by his mere will the sisters come to receive him, and having obtained the world of the sisters, he is happy.

5. 'And he who desires the world of the friends, by his mere will the friends come to receive him, and having obtained the world of the friends, he is happy.

6. 'And he who desires the world of perfumes and garlands (gandhamâlya), by his mere will perfumes and garlands come to him, and having obtained the world of perfumes and garlands, he is happy.

7. 'And he who desires the world of food and drink, by his mere will food and drink come to him, and having obtained the world of food and drink, he is happy.

8. 'And he who desires the world of song and music, by his mere will song and music come to him, and having obtained the world of song and music, he is happy.

9. 'And he who desires the world of women, by his mere will women come to receive him, and having obtained the world of women, he is happy.

'Whatever object he is attached to, whatever object he desires, by his mere will it comes to him, and having obtained it, he is happy.

THIRD KHA*ND*A.

1. ' These true desires, however, are hidden by what is false; though the desires be true, they have a covering which is false. Thus, whoever belonging to us has departed this life, him we cannot gain back, so that we should see him with our eyes.

2. ' Those who belong to us, whether living or departed, and whatever else there is which we wish for and do not obtain, all that we find there (if we descend into our heart, where Brahman dwells, in the ether of the heart). There are all our true desires, but hidden by what is false[1]. As people who do not know the country, walk again and again over a gold treasure that has been hidden somewhere in the earth and do not discover it, thus do all these creatures day after day go into the Brahma-world (they are merged in Brahman, while asleep), and yet do not discover it, because they are carried away by untruth (they do not come to themselves, i. e. they do not discover the true Self in Brahman, dwelling in the heart).

3. ' That Self abides in the heart. And this is the etymological explanation. The heart is called h*ri*d-ayam, instead of h*ri*dy-ayam, i. e. He who is in the heart. He who knows this, that He is in the heart, goes day by day (when in sushupti, deep sleep) into heaven (svarga), i.e. into the Brahman of the heart.

4. ' Now that serene being[2] which, after having

---

[1] All the desires mentioned before are fulfilled, if we find their fulfilment in our Self, in the city of Brahman within our heart. There we always can possess those whom we have loved, only we must not wish to see them with our eyes; that would be a false covering to a true desire.

[2] Cf. *Kh.* Up. VIII, 12, 3.

risen from out this earthly body, and having reached the highest light (self-knowledge), appears in its true form, that is the Self,' thus he spoke (when asked by his pupils). This is the immortal, the fearless, this is Brahman. And of that Brahman the name is the True, Satyam,

5. This name Sattyam consists of three syllables, sat-tî-yam[1]. Sat signifies the immortal, t, the mortal, and with yam he binds both. Because he binds both, the immortal and the mortal, therefore it is yam. He who knows this goes day by day into heaven (svarga).

FOURTH KHANDA.

1. That Self is a bank[2], a boundary, so that these worlds may not be confounded. Day and night do not pass that bank, nor old age, death, and grief; neither good nor evil deeds. All evil-doers turn back from it, for the world of Brahman is free from all evil.

2. Therefore he who has crossed that bank, if blind, ceases to be blind; if wounded, ceases to be wounded; if afflicted, ceases to be afflicted. Therefore when that bank has been crossed, night becomes day indeed, for the world of Brahman is lighted up once for all[3].

3. And that world of Brahman belongs to those

---

[1] We ought probably to read Sattyam, and then Sat-tî-yam. The î in tî would then be the dual of an anubandha ï. Instead of yaddhi, I conjecture yatti. See Ait. Âranyaka II, 5, 5.

[2] Setu, generally translated by bridge, was originally a bank of earth (mridâdimaya), thrown up to serve as a pathway (pons) through water or a swamp. Such banks exist still in many places, and they serve at the same time as boundaries (maryâdâ) between fields belonging to different properties. Cf. Mait. Up. VII, 7; Kâth. Up. III, 2; Talav. Up. comm. p. 59; Mund. Up. II, 2, 5.

[3] Kh. Up. III, 11, 3.

only who find it by abstinence—for them there is freedom in all the worlds.

FIFTH KHA*ND*A.

1. What people call sacrifice (ya*g*ña), that is really abstinence (brahma*k*arya). For he who knows, obtains that (world of Brahman, which others obtain by sacrifice), by means of abstinence.

What people call sacrifice (ish*t*a), that is really abstinence, for by abstinence, having searched (ish-*t*vâ), he obtains the Self.

2. What people call sacrifice (sattrâya*n*a), that is really abstinence, for by abstinence he obtains from the Sat (the true), the safety (trâ*n*a) of the Self.

What people call the vow of silence (mauna), that is really abstinence, for he who by abstinence has found out the Self, meditates (manute).

3. What people call fasting (anâ*s*akâyana), that is really abstinence, for that Self does not perish (na na*s*yati), which we find out by abstinence.

What people call a hermit's life (ara*n*yâyana), that is really abstinence. Ara [1] and *N*ya are two lakes in the world of Brahman, in the third heaven from hence; and there is the lake Airammadîya, and the A*s*vattha tree, showering down Soma, and the city of Brahman (Hira*n*yagarbha) Aparâ*g*itâ [2], and the golden Prabhu-vimita (the hall built by Prabhu, Brahman).

Now that world of Brahman belongs to those who find the lakes Ara and *N*ya in the world of Brahman by means of abstinence; for them there is freedom in all the worlds [3].

---

[1] In the Kaush. Br. Up. I, 3, the lake is called Âra, at least according to the commentator.

[2] In the Kaush. Br. Up. Aparâ*g*ita is not pû*h*, but âyatanam.

[3] The fifth kha*nd*a is chiefly meant to recommend brahma*k*arya

SIXTH KHA*N*DA.

1. Now those arteries of the heart consist of a brown substance, of a white, blue, yellow, and red

---

or abstinence from all worldly enjoyments, enjoined on the brahma*k*ârin, the student, as a means of obtaining a knowledge of Brahman. But instead of showing that such abstinence is indispensable for a proper concentration of our intellectual faculties, we are told that abstinence is the same as certain sacrifices; and this is shown, not by arguments, but by a number of very far-fetched plays on words. These it is impossible to render in any translation, nay, they hardly deserve being translated. Thus abstinence is said to be identical with sacrifice, yag*ñ*a, because yo *g*ñâtâ, 'he who knows,' has a certain similarity with yag*ñ*a. Ish*t*a, another kind of sacrifice, is compared with esha*n*â, search; sattrâya*n*a with Sat, the True, the Brahman, and trâya*n*a, protection; mauna, silence, with manana, meditating (which may be right); anâ*s*akâyana, fasting, with na*s*, to perish, and ara*n*yâgana, a hermit's life, with ara, *n*ya, and ayana, going to the two lakes Ara and *N*ya, which are believed to exist in the legendary world of Brahman. Nothing can be more absurd. Having once struck the note of Brahmanic legends, such as we find it, for instance, in the Kaushîtaki-brâhma*n*a-upanishad, the author goes on. Besides the lakes Ara and *N*ya (in the Kaushîtaki-brâhma*n*a-upanishad we have only one lake, called Âra), he mentions the Airammadîya lake, and explains it as aira (irâ annam, tanmaya airo ma*n**d*as, tena pûr*n*am airam) and madîya, delightful. The A*s*vattha tree, which pours down Soma, is not tortured into anything else, except that Soma is explained as the immortal, or nectar. Aparâ*g*ita becomes the city of Brahman, because it can be conquered by no one except those who have practised abstinence. And the hall which elsewhere is called Vibhu‑pramita becomes Prabhuvimitam, or Prabhu-vinirmita, made by Prabhu, i.e. Brahman. All the fulfilled desires, as enumerated in kha*n**d*as 2–5, whether the finding again of our fathers and mothers, or entering the Brahmaloka with its lakes and palaces, must be taken, not as material (sthûla), but as mental only (mânasa). On that account, however, they are by no means considered as false or unreal, as little as dreams are. Dreams are false and unreal, relatively only, i. e. relatively to what we see, when we awake; but not in themselves. Whatever we see in waking, also, has been shown to be substance, and so is the sun brown, white, blue, yellow, and red.

2. As a very long highway goes to two places, to one at the beginning, and to another at the end, so do the rays of the sun go to both worlds, to this one and to the other. They start from the sun, and enter into those arteries; they start from those arteries, and enter into the sun.

3. And when a man is asleep, reposing, and at perfect rest, so that he sees no dream[1], then he has entered into those arteries. Then no evil touches him, for he has obtained the light (of the sun).

4. And when a man falls ill, then those who sit round him, say, 'Do you know me? Do you know me?' As long as he has not departed from this body, he knows them.

5. But when he departs from this body, then he departs upwards by those very rays (towards the worlds which he has gained by merit, not by knowledge); or he goes out while meditating on Om[2] (and thus securing an entrance into the Brahma-

---

false; because it consists of forms and names only; yet these forms and names have a true element in them, viz. the Sat. Before we know that Sat, all the objects we see in waking seem true; as dreams seem true in dreaming. But when once we awake from our waking by true knowledge, we see that nothing is true but the Sat. When we imagine we see a serpent, and then discover that it is a rope, the serpent disappears as false, but what was true in it, the rope, remains true.

[1] Svapna in Sanskrit is both somnus and somnium. Hence one might translate also, 'so that he is not aware that he is asleep,' which in some respects would seem even more appropriate in our passage; cf. VIII, 11, 1.

[2] According to the explanation given of the Om in the Upanishads, and more particularly in the Dahara-vidyâ contained in this Prapâthaka.

lóka).   And while his mind is failing, he is going to
the sun.   For the sun is the door of the world (of
Brahman).   Those who know, walk in; those who
do not know, are shut out.   There is this verse[1]:
' There are a hundred and one arteries of the heart;
one of them penetrates the crown of the head;
moving upwards by it a man reaches the immortal;
the others serve for departing in different directions,
yea, in different directions[2].'

SEVENTH KHANDA[3].

1. Pragâpati said: 'The Self which is free from sin,
free from old age, from death and grief, from hunger
and thirst, which desires nothing but what it ought
to desire, and imagines nothing but what it ought to
imagine, that it is which we must search out, that it
is which we must try to understand.   He who has
searched out that Self and understands it, obtains
all worlds and all desires.'

2. The Devas (gods) and Asuras (demons) both
heard these words, and said : ' Well, let us search
for that Self by which, if one has searched it out,
all worlds and all desires are obtained.'

Thus saying Indra went from the Devas, Virokana
from the Asuras, and both, without having communicated with each other, approached Pragâpati,

---

[1] Prasna Up. II, 1.

[2] The same verse occurs in the Katha 6, 16, and is frequently
quoted elsewhere, for instance, Mait. comm. p. 164. For vishvaṅṅ,
the right reading would seem to be vishvak.   In the Mait. Up. VI,
30, the Trishtubh are reduced to Anushtubh verses.   See also
Prasna Up. III, 6–7 ; Mund. Up. II, 2.

[3] Here the highest problem is treated again, the knowledge of
the true Self, which leads beyond the world of Brahmâ (masc.), and
enables the individual self to return into the Highest Self.

holding fuel in their hands, as is the custom for pupils approaching their master.

3. They dwelt there as pupils for thirty-two years. Then Pra*g*âpati asked them : ' For what purpose have you both dwelt here ? '

They replied : ' A saying of yours is being repeated, viz. "the Self which is free from sin, free from old age, from death and grief, from hunger and thirst, which desires nothing but what it ought to desire, and imagines nothing but what it ought to imagine, that it is which we must search out, that it is which we must try to understand. He who has searched out that Self and understands it, obtains all worlds and all desires." Now we both have dwelt here because we wish for that Self.'

Pra*g*âpati said to them : ' The person that is seen in the eye [1], that is the Self. This is what I have said. This is the immortal, the fearless, this is Brahman.'

They asked : ' Sir, he who is perceived in the water, and he who is perceived in a mirror, who is he ? '

He replied : ' He himself indeed is seen in all these [2].'

---

[1] The commentator explains this rightly. Pra*g*âpati means by the person that is seen in the eye, the real agent of seeing, who is seen by sages only, even with their eyes shut. His pupils, however, misunderstand him. They think of the person that is seen, not of the person that sees (Yoga-sûtras II, 6). The person seen in the eye is to them the small figure imaged in the eye, and they go on therefore to ask, whether the image in the water or in a mirror is not the Self.

[2] The commentators are at great pains to explain that Pra*g*âpati told no falsehood. He meant by purusha the personal element in the highest sense, and it was not his fault that his pupils took purusha for man or body.

EIGHTH KHANDA.

1. 'Look at your Self in a pan of water, and whatever you do not understand of your Self[1], come and tell me.'

They looked in the water-pan. Then Pragâpati said to them: 'What do you see?'

They said: 'We both see the self thus altogether, a picture even to the very hairs and nails.'

2. Pragâpati said to them: 'After you have adorned yourselves, have put on your best clothes and cleaned yourselves, look again into the water-pan.'

They, after having adorned themselves, having put on their best clothes and cleaned themselves, looked into the water-pan.

Pragâpati said: 'What do you see?'

3. They said: 'Just as we are, well adorned, with our best clothes and clean, thus we are both there, Sir, well adorned, with our best clothes and clean.'

Pragâpati said: 'That is the Self, this is the immortal, the fearless, this is Brahman.'

Then both went away satisfied in their hearts.

4. And Pragâpati, looking after them, said: 'They both go away without having perceived and without having known the Self, and whoever of these two[2], whether Devas or Asuras, will follow this doctrine (upanishad), will perish.'

Now Virokana, satisfied in his heart, went to the Asuras and preached that doctrine to them, that the self (the body) alone is to be worshipped, that the

---

[1] I take âtmana*h* as a genitive, governed by yad, not as an accusative plural.

[2] The commentator reads yatare for yata*h*.

self (the body) alone is to be served, and that he who worships the self and serves the self, gains both worlds, this and the next.

5. Therefore they call even now a man who does not give alms here, who has no faith, and offers no sacrifices, an Âsura, for this is the doctrine (upanishad) of the Asuras. They deck out the body of the dead with perfumes, flowers, and fine raiment by way of ornament, and think they will thus conquer that world[1].

NINTH KHANDA.

1. But Indra, before he had returned to the Devas, saw this difficulty. As this self (the shadow in the water)[2] is well adorned, when the body is well adorned, well dressed, when the body is well dressed, well cleaned, if the body is well cleaned, that self will also be blind, if the body is blind, lame, if the body is lame[3], crippled, if the body is crippled, and will perish in fact as soon as the body perishes. Therefore I see no good in this (doctrine).

2. Taking fuel in his hand he came again as a pupil to Pragâpati. Pragâpati said to him: 'Maghavat (Indra), as you went away with Virokana, satisfied in your heart, for what purpose did you come back?'

---

[1] This evidently refers to the customs and teaching of tribes not entirely conforming to the Brahmanic system. Whether the adorning of the dead body implies burial instead of burning, seems doubtful.

[2] The commentator remarks that though both Indra and Virokana had mistaken the true import of what Pragâpati said, yet while Virokana took the body to be the Self, Indra thought that the Self was the shadow of the body.

[3] Srâma, lame, is explained by the commentator as one-eyed, ekanetra.

He said : ' Sir, as this self (the shadow) is well
adorned, when the body is well adorned, well dressed,
when the body is well dressed, well cleaned, if the
body is well cleaned, that self will also be blind, if
the body is blind, lame, if the body is lame, crippled,
if the body is crippled, and will perish in fact as
soon as the body perishes.   Therefore I see no
good in this (doctrine).'

3. ' So it is indeed, Maghavat,' replied Pra*g*âpati ;
' but I shall explain him (the true Self) further to
you.   Live with me another thirty-two years.'

He lived with him another thirty-two years, and
then Pra*g*âpati said :

TENTH KHA*N*DA.

1. ' He who moves about happy in dreams, he is
the Self, this is the immortal, the fearless, this is
Brahman.'

Then Indra went away satisfied in his heart.   But
before he had returned to the Devas, he saw this
difficulty.   Although it is true that that self is not
blind, even if the body is blind, nor lame, if the
body is lame, though it is true that that self is not
rendered faulty by the faults of it (the body),

2. Nor struck when it (the body) is struck, nor
lamed when it is lamed, yet it is as if they struck
him (the self) in dreams, as if they chased him [1].

---

[1] I have adopted the reading vi*kkh*âyayanti, because it is the
most difficult, and therefore explains most easily the various corruptions, or it may be emendations, that have crept into the text.
*S*ankara explains vi*kkh*âdayanti by vidrâvayanti, and this shows
that he too must have read vi*kkh*âyayanti, for he could not have
explained vi*kkh*âdayanti, which means they uncover or they deprive
of their clothing, by vidrâvayanti, they drive away.   It is true that
vi*kkh*âyayanti may be explained in two ways ; it may be the causative of *kh*â, to cut, but this meaning is not very appropriate here,

He becomes even conscious, as it were, of pain, and sheds tears. Therefore I see no good in this.

3. Taking fuel in his hands, he went again as a pupil to Pra*g*âpati. Pra*g*âpati said to him : 'Maghavat, as you went away satisfied in your heart, for what purpose did you come back ?'

He said : 'Sir, although it is true that that self is not blind even if the body is blind, nor lame, if the body is lame, though it is true that that self is not rendered faulty by the faults of it (the body),

4. Nor struck when it (the body) is struck, nor lamed when it is lamed, yet it is as if they struck him (the self) in dreams, as if they chased him. He becomes even conscious, as it were, of pain, and sheds tears. Therefore I see no good in this.'

'So it is indeed, Maghavat,' replied Pra*g*âpati; 'but I shall explain him (the true Self) further to you. Live with me another thirty-two years.'

He lived with him another thirty-two years. Then Pra*g*âpati said :

---

and quite inadmissible in another passage where vi*kkh*âyayati occurs, whereas, if derived from vi*kh* (οἴχομαι) in a causative sense, *S*ankara could hardly have chosen a better explanation than vidrâvayanti, they make run away. The root vi*kh*, vi*kkh*âyayati is recognised in Pâ*n*ini III, 1, 28, and in the Dhâtupâ*th*a 28, 129, but it has hitherto been met with in this passage only, and in Br*i*hadâra*n*yaka Up. IV, 3, 20. Here also the author speaks of a man who imagines that people kill him or do him violence, or that an elephant chases him or that he falls into a pit. Here we have hastîva vi*kkh*âyayati, and *S*ankara, at least as printed by Dr. Roer, explains this by vi*kkh*âpayati, vi*kkh*âdayati, vidrâvayati; dhâvatîty artha*h*. Much better is Dvivedaganga's commentary, as published by Dr. Weber, *S*atap. Brâhm. p. 1145, Kadâ*k*id ena*m* hastî vi*kkh*âyayatîva vidrâvayatîva ; vi*kh*a gatau, gupûdhûpavi*kkh*ipa*n*ipanibhya âya iti (Pâ*n*. III, 1, 28) svârtha âyapratyaya*h*. In the Dictionary of Boehtlingk and Roth the derivation from *kh*â, to cut, is preferred ; see Nachträge, s. v. *kh*â.

Eleventh Khanda.

1. 'When a man being asleep, reposing, and at perfect rest[1], sees no dreams, that is the Self, this is the immortal, the fearless, this is Brahman.'

Then Indra went away satisfied in his heart. But before he had returned to the Devas, he saw this difficulty. In truth he thus does not know himself (his self) that he is I, nor does he know anything that exists. He is gone to utter annihilation. I see no good in this.

2. Taking fuel in his hand he went again as a pupil to Pragâpati. Pragâpati said to him : 'Maghavat, as you went away satisfied in your heart, for what purpose did you come back?'

He said : 'Sir, in that way he does not know himself (his self) that he is I, nor does he know anything that exists. He is gone to utter annihilation. I see no good in this.'

3. 'So it is indeed, Maghavat,' replied Pragâpati; 'but I shall explain him (the true Self) further to you, and nothing more than this[2]. Live here other five years.'

He lived there other five years. This made in all one hundred and one years, and therefore it is said that Indra Maghavat lived one hundred and one years as a pupil with Pragâpati. Pragâpati said to him :

Twelfth Khanda.

1. 'Maghavat, this body is mortal and always held by death. It is the abode of that Self which is

---

[1] See Kh. Up. VIII, 6, 3.

[2] Sankara explains this as meaning the real Self, not anything different from the Self.

immortal and without body[1]. When in the body (by
thinking this body is I and I am this body) the Self
is held by pleasure and pain. So long as he is in
the body, he cannot get free from pleasure and pain.
But when he is free of the body (when he knows
himself different from the body), then neither pleasure
nor pain touches him[2].

2. 'The wind is without body, the cloud, lightning, and thunder are without body (without hands,
feet, &c.) Now as these, arising from this heavenly
ether (space), appear in their own form, as soon as
they have approached the highest light,

3. 'Thus does that serene being, arising from this
body, appear in its own form, as soon as it has
approached the highest light (the knowledge of
Self[3]). He (in that state) is the highest person
(uttama pûrusha). He moves about there laughing
(or eating), playing, and rejoicing (in his mind), be it
with women, carriages, or relatives, never minding
that body into which he was born[4].

---

[1] According to some, the body is the result of the Self, the
elements of the body, fire, water, and earth springing from the
Self, and the Self afterwards entering them.

[2] Ordinary, worldly pleasure. Comm.

[3] The simile is not so striking as most of those old similes are.
The wind is compared with the Self, on account of its being for a
time lost in the ether (space), as the Self is in the body, and then
rising again out of the ether and assuming its own form as wind.
The chief stress is laid on the highest light, which in the one case
is the sun of summer, in the other the light of knowledge.

[4] These are pleasures which seem hardly compatible with the
state of perfect peace which the Self is supposed to have attained.
The passage may be interpolated, or put in on purpose to show
that the Self enjoys such pleasures as an inward spectator only,
without identifying himself with either pleasure or pain. He sees
them, as he says afterwards, with his divine eye. The Self per-

'Like as a horse attached to a cart, so is the spirit[1] (prâna, pragñâtman) attached to this body.

4. 'Now where the sight has entered into the void (the open space, the black pupil of the eye), there is the person of the eye, the eye itself is the instrument of seeing. He who knows, let me smell this, he is the Self, the nose is the instrument of smelling. He who knows, let me say this, he is the Self, the tongue is the instrument of saying. He who knows, let me hear this, he is the Self, the ear is the instrument of hearing.

5. 'He who knows, let me think this, he is the Self, the mind is his divine eye[2]. He, the Self, seeing these pleasures (which to others are hidden like a buried treasure of gold) through his divine eye, i. e. the mind, rejoices.

'The Devas who are in the world of Brahman meditate on that Self (as taught by Pragâpati to Indra, and by Indra to the Devas). Therefore all worlds belong to them, and all desires. He who knows that Self and understands it, obtains all worlds and all desires.' Thus said Pragâpati, yea, thus said Pragâpati.

---

ceives in all things his Self only, nothing else. In his commentary on the Taittirîya Upanishad (p. 45) Sankara refers this passage to Brahman as an effect, not to Brahman as a cause.

[1] The spirit, the conscious self, is not identical with the body, but only joined to it, like a horse, or driving it, like a charioteer. In other passages the senses are the horses; buddhi, reason, the charioteer; manas, mind, the reins. The spirit is attached to the cart by the ketana; cf. Ânandagñânagiri.

[2] Because it perceives not only what is present, but also what is past and future.

Thirteenth Khan*d*a [1].

1. From the dark (the Brahman of the heart) I come to the nebulous (the world of Brahman), from the nebulous to the dark, shaking off all evil, as a horse shakes his hairs, and as the moon frees herself from the mouth of Râhu [2]. Having shaken off the body, I obtain, self made and satisfied, the uncreated world of Brahman, yea, I obtain it.

Fourteenth Khan*d*a.

1. He who is called ether [3] (âkâ*s*a) is the revealer of all forms and names. That within which these forms and names are contained is the Brahman, the Immortal, the Self.

I come to the hall of Pra*g*âpati, to the house; I am the glorious among Brâhmans, glorious among princes, glorious among men [4]. I obtained that glory, I am glorious among the glorious. May I never go to the white, toothless, yet devouring, white abode [5]; may I never go to it.

---

[1] This chapter is supposed to contain a hymn of triumph.

[2] Râhu, in later times a monster, supposed to swallow the sun and moon at every solar or lunar eclipse. At first we only hear of the mouth or head of Râhu. In later times a body was assigned to him, but it had to be destroyed again by Vish*n*u, so that nothing remained of him but his head. Râhu seems derived from rah, to separate, to remove. From it raksh, to wish or strive to remove, to keep off, to protect, and in a different application rákshas, a tearing away, violence, rakshás, a robber, an evil spirit.

[3] Âkâ*s*a, ether or space, is a name of Brahman, because, like ether, Brahman has no body and is infinitely small.

[4] Here the three classes, commonly called castes, are clearly marked by the names of brâhma*n*a, râ*g*an, and vi*s*.

[5] Yoni*s*abditam pra*g*ananendriyam.

FIFTEENTH KHA*N*DA.

1. Brahmâ (Hira*n*yagarbha or Parame*s*vara) told this to Pra*g*âpati (Ka*s*yapa), Pra*g*âpati to Manu (his son), Manu to mankind. He who has learnt the Veda from a family of teachers, according to the sacred rule, in the leisure time left from the duties to be performed for the Guru, who, after receiving his discharge, has settled in his own house, keeping up the memory of what he has learnt by repeating it regularly in some sacred spot, who has begotten virtuous sons, and concentrated all his senses on the Self, never giving pain to any creature, except at the tîrthas[1] (sacrifices, &c.), he who behaves thus all his life, reaches the world of Brahman, and does not return, yea, he does not return.

---

[1] The commentator says that even travelling about as a mendicant causes pain, but that a mendicant is allowed to importune people for alms at tîrthas, or sacred places. Others explain this differently.

TALAVAKÂRA

OR

KENA-UPANISHAD.

TALAVAKÂRA-UPANISHAD.

FIRST KHANDA.

1. THE Pupil asks: 'At whose wish does the mind sent forth proceed on its errand? At whose command does the first breath go forth? At whose wish do we utter this speech? What god directs the eye, or the ear?'

2. The Teacher replies: 'It is the ear of the ear, the mind of the mind, the speech of speech, the breath of breath, and the eye of the eye. When freed (from the senses) the wise, on departing from this world, become immortal[1].

3. 'The eye does not go thither, nor speech, nor mind. We do not know, we do not understand, how any one can teach it.

4. 'It is different from the known, it is also above the unknown, thus we have heard from those of old, who taught us this[2].

5. 'That which is not expressed by speech and

---

[1] This verse admits of various translations, and still more various explanations. Instead of taking vâkam, like all the other words, as a nominative, we might take them all as accusatives, governed by atimukya, and sa u prânasya prânah as a parenthetical sentence. What is meant by the ear of the ear is very fully explained by the commentator, but the simplest acceptation would seem to take it as an answer to the preceding questions, so that the ear of the ear should be taken for him who directs the ear, i. e. the Self, or Brahman. This will become clearer as we proceed.

[2] Cf. Îsa Up. 11; 13.

by which speech is expressed, that alone know as
Brahman, not that which people here adore.

6. 'That which does not think by mind, and
by which, they say, mind is thought [1], that alone
know as Brahman, not that which people here
adore.

7. 'That which does not see by the eye, and by
which one sees (the work of) the eyes, that alone
know as Brahman, not that which people here
adore.

8. 'That which does not hear by the ear, and by
which the ear is heard, that alone know as Brahman,
not that which people here adore.

9. 'That which does not breathe by breath, and
by which breath is drawn, that alone know as Brahman, not that which people here adore.'

SECOND KHANDA.

1. The Teacher says: 'If thou thinkest I know
it well, then thou knowest surely but little, what is
that form of Brahman known, it may be, to thee [2]?'

2. The Pupil says: 'I do not think I know it
well, nor do I know that I do not know it.   He

---

[1] The varia lectio manaso matam (supported also by the commentary) is metrically and grammatically easier, but it may be, for
that very reason, an emendation.

[2] In order to obtain a verse, we must leave out the words tvam
yad asya deveshv atha nu mîmâmsyam eva.   They were probably
inserted, as an excuse for the third khanda treating of the relation
of Brahman to the Devas.   There is considerable variety in the
text, as handed down in the Sâma-veda and in the Atharva-veda,
which shows that it has been tampered with.   Daharam for dabhram
may be the older reading, as synezesis occurs again and again in
the Upanishads.

among us who knows this, he knows it, nor does he know that he does not know it [1].

3. 'He by whom it (Brahman) is not thought, by him it is thought; he by whom it is thought, knows it not. It is not understood by those who understand it, it is understood by those who do not understand it.

4. 'It is thought to be known (as if) by awakening, and (then) we obtain immortality indeed. By the Self we obtain strength, by knowledge we obtain immortality.

5. 'If a man know this here, that is the true (end of life); if he does not know this here, then there is great destruction (new births). The wise who have thought on all things (and recognised the Self in them) become immortal, when they have departed from this world.'

THIRD KHA*N*DA [2].

1. Brahman obtained the victory for the Devas. The Devas became elated by the victory of Brah-

---

[1] This verse has again been variously explained. I think the train of thought is this: We cannot know Brahman, as we know other objects, by referring them to a class and pointing out their differences. But, on the other hand, we do not know that we know him not, i. e. no one can assert that we know him not, for we want Brahman in order to know anything. He, therefore, who knows this double peculiarity of the knowledge of Brahman, he knows Brahman, as much as it can be known; and he does not know, nor can anybody prove it to him, that he does not know Brahman.

[2] This kha*n*da is generally represented as a later addition, but its prose style has more of a Brâhma*n*a character than the verses in the preceding kha*n*das, although their metrical structure is irregular, and may be taken as a sign of antiquity.

man, and they thought, this victory is ours only, this greatness is ours only.

2. Brahman perceived this and appeared to them. But they did not know it, and said: 'What sprite (yaksha or yakshya) is this?'

3. They said to Agni (fire): 'O *G*âtavedas, find out what sprite this is.' 'Yes,' he said.

4. He ran toward it, and Brahman said to him: 'Who are you?' He replied: 'I am Agni, I am *G*âtavedas.'

5. Brahman said: 'What power is in you?' Agni replied: 'I could burn all whatever there is on earth.'

6. Brahman put a straw before him, saying: 'Burn this.' He went towards it with all his might, but he could not burn it. Then he returned thence and said: 'I could not find out what sprite this is.'

7. Then they said to Vâyu (air): 'O Vâyu, find out what sprite this is.' 'Yes,' he said.

8. He ran toward it, and Brahman said to him: 'Who are you?' He replied: 'I am Vâyu, I am Mâtari*s*van.'

9. Brahman said: 'What power is in you?' Vâyu replied: 'I could take up all whatever there is on earth.'

10. Brahman put a straw before him, saying: 'Take it up.' He went towards it with all his might, but he could not take it up. Then he returned thence and said: 'I could not find out what sprite this is.'

11. Then they said to Indra: 'O Maghavan, find out what sprite this is.' He went towards it, but it disappeared from before him.

12. Then in the same space (ether) he came

towards a woman, highly adorned : it was Umâ, the daughter of Himavat [1]. He said to her : 'Who is that sprite ?'

FOURTH KHA*N*DA.

1. She replied : 'It is Brahman. It is through the victory of Brahman that you have thus become great.' After that he knew that it was Brahman.

2. Therefore these Devas, viz. Agni, Vâyu, and Indra, are, as it were, above the other gods, for they touched it (the Brahman) nearest [2].

3. And therefore Indra is, as it were, above the other gods, for he touched it nearest, he first knew it.

4. This is the teaching of Brahman, with regard to the gods (mythological) : It is that which now

---

[1] Umâ may here be taken as the wife of *S*iva, daughter of Himavat, better known by her earlier name, Pârvatî, the daughter of the mountains. Originally she was, not the daughter of the mountains or of the Himâlaya, but the daughter of the cloud, just as Rudra was originally, not the lord of the mountains, girî*s*a, but the lord of the clouds. We are, however, moving here in a secondary period of Indian thought, in which we see, as among Semitic nations, the manifested powers, and particularly the knowledge and wisdom of the gods, represented by their wives. Umâ means originally flax, from vâ, to weave, and the same word may have been an old name of wife, she who weaves (cf. duhit*ri*, spinster, and possibly wife itself, if O. H. G. wîb is connected with O. H. G. wëban). It is used almost synonymously with ambikâ, Taitt. Âr. p. 839. If we wished to take liberties, we might translate umâ haimavatî by an old woman coming from the Himavat mountains; but I decline all responsibility for such an interpretation.

[2] The next phrase was borrowed from § 3, without even changing the singular to the plural. As Indra only found out that it was Brahman, the original distinction between Indra and the other gods, who only came near to it, was quite justified. Still it might be better to adopt the var. lect. sa hy etat in § 2.

flashes forth in the lightning, and now vanishes again.

5. And this is the teaching of Brahman, with regard to the body (psychological): It is that which seems to move as mind, and by it imagination remembers again and again[1].

6. That Brahman is called Tadvana[2], by the name of Tadvana it is to be meditated on. All beings have a desire for him who knows this.

7. The Teacher: 'As you have asked me to tell you the Upanishad, the Upanishad has now

---

[1] I have translated these paragraphs very differently from *San*kara and other interpreters. The wording is extremely brief, and we can only guess the original intention of the Upanishad by a reference to other passages. Now the first teaching of Brahman, by means of a comparison with the gods or heavenly things in general, seems to be that Brahman is what shines forth suddenly like lightning. Sometimes the relation between the phenomenal world and Brahman is illustrated by the relation between bubbles and the sea, or lightning and the unseen heavenly light (Mait. Up. VI, 35). In another passage, *Kh*. Up. VIII, 12, 2, lightning, when no longer seen, is to facilitate the conception of the reality of things, as distinct from their perceptibility. I think, therefore, that the first simile, taken from the phenomenal world, was meant to show that Brahman is that which appears for a moment in the lightning, and then vanishes from our sight.

The next illustration is purely psychological. Brahman is proved to exist, because our mind moves towards things, because there is something in us which moves and perceives, and because there is something in us which holds our perceptions together (sankalpa), and revives them again by memory.

I give my translation as hypothetical only, for certainty is extremely difficult to attain, when we have to deal with these enigmatical sayings which, when they were first delivered, were necessarily accompanied by oral explanations.

[2] Tadvana, as a name of Brahman, is explained by ‘the desire of it,’ and derived from van, to desire, the same as vân*kh*.

been told you. We have told you the Brâhmî
Upanishad.

8. 'The feet on which that Upanishad stands are
penance, restraint, sacrifice; the Vedas are all its
limbs[1], the True is its abode.

9. 'He who knows this Upanishad, and has
shaken off all evil, stands in the endless, unconquerable[2] world of heaven, yea, in the world
of heaven.'

---

[1] It is impossible to adopt *S*ankara's first rendering, 'the Vedas
and all the Angas,' i.e. the six subsidiary doctrines. He sees
himself that sarvângâni stands in opposition to pratish*th*â and
âyatana, but seeing Veda and Anga together, no Brahman could
help thinking of the Vedângas.

[2] Might we read a*g*yeye for *g*yeye ? cf. *S*atap. Brâhm. XI, 5, 7, 1.

AITAREYA-ÂRA*N*YAKA.

AITAREYA-ÂRAÑYAKA.

FIRST ÂRAÑYAKA.

FIRST ADHYÂYA.

FIRST KHAÑDA.

1. Now follows the Mahâvrata ceremony.

2. After having killed Vritra, Indra became great. When he became great, then there was the Mahâvrata (the great work). This is why the Mahâvrata ceremony is called Mahâvrata.

3. Some people say: 'Let the priest make two (recitations with the offering of the) âgya (ghee) on that day,' but the right thing is one[1].

4. He who desires prosperity should use the hymn, pra vo devâyâgnaye (Rv. III, 13, 1).

5. He who desires increase should use the hymn, viso viso atithim (Rv. VIII, 74, 1).

---

[1] That it should be one only is proved from the types, i. e. from other sacrifices, that have to be followed in the performance of the Mahâvrata. The first type is the Agnishtoma, where one sastra is enjoined as âgyasastra, viz. pra vo devâyâgnaye. In the Visvagit, which has to follow the Agnishtoma, another hymn is put in its place, viz. agnim naro dîdhitibhih. In the Mahâvrata, which has to follow the Visvagit, some people recommend the use of both these hymns. But that is wrong, for there must be in the sacrifices which follow the Agnishtoma twelve sastras altogether; and if there were two here, instead of one, we should get a total of thirteen.

6. The people (viṣaℏ) indeed are increase[1], and therefore he (the sacrificer) becomes increased.

7. But (some say), there is the word atithim (in that hymn, which means a guest or stranger, asking for food). Let him not therefore take that hymn. Verily, the atithi (stranger) is able[2] to go begging.

8. 'No,' he said, 'let him take that hymn.

9. 'For he who follows the good road and obtains distinction, he is an atithi (guest)[3].

10. 'They do not consider him who is not so, worthy to be (called) an atithi (guest).

11. 'Therefore let him by all means take that hymn.'

12. If he takes that hymn, let him place the (second) tristich, âganma vṛitrahantamam, 'we came near to the victorious,' first.

13. For people worship the whole year (performing the Gavâmayana sacrifice) wishing for this day (the last but one)—they do come near.

14. The (next following) three tristichs begin with an Anushtubh[4]. Now Brahman is Gâyatrî, speech is Anushtubh. He thus joins speech with Brahman.

15. He who desires glory should use the hymn, abodhy agniℏ samidhâ ǥanânâm (Rv. V, 1, 1).

---

[1] The word viṣaℏ, which occurs in the hymn, means people. The commentator says that because the Vaiṣyas or tradespeople increase their capital, therefore they are called increase.

[2] Able, or liable; cf. Ait. Âr. II, 3, 5, 7.

[3] Atithi is here explained by yo bhavati, and bhavati is explained as walking on the good road. One expects yo vâ atati. The obtaining of distinction is probably derived from ati, above, in atithi.

[4] In the first and second the Anushtubh is followed by two Gâyatrîs.

16. He who desires offspring and cattle should use the hymn, hotâ*g*anish*t*a *k*etana*h* (Rv. II, 5, 1).

SECOND KHA*N*DA.

1. He who desires proper food[1] should use the hymn, agnim naro dîdhitibhi*h* (Rv. VII, 1, 1)[2].

2. Verily, Agni (fire) is the eater of food.

In the other (recitations accompanying the) offerings of â*g*ya (where Agni is likewise mentioned) the worshippers come more slowly near to Agni (because the name of Agni does not stand at the beginning of the hymn). But here a worshipper obtains proper food at once, he strikes down evil at once.

3. Through the words (occurring in the second foot of the first verse), hasta*k*yuti *g*anayanta, 'they caused the birth of Agni by moving their arms,' the hymn becomes endowed with (the word) birth. Verily, the sacrificer is born from this day of the sacrifice, and therefore the hymn is endowed with (the word) birth.

4. There are four metrical feet (in the Trish*t*ubh verses of this hymn). Verily, cattle have four feet, therefore they serve for the gaining of cattle.

5. There are three metrical feet (in the Virâ*g* verses of this hymn). Verily, three are these three-

---

[1] Annâdyam is always explained as food, here as anna*m* tad âdyam *k*a. It must be so translated here and elsewhere (I, 2, 10), though it is often an abstract of annâda, an eater of food, a healthy man.

[2] This hymn is prescribed in the Vi*s*va*g*it sacrifice, and taken over to the Mahâvrata, according to rule. It is used, however, both as obligatory and as optional at the same time, i. e. it is an essential part of the sacrifice, and at the same time to be used by those who wish for proper food.

fold worlds.   Therefore they serve for the conquest
of the worlds.

6. These (the Trish*t*ubh and Virâg* verses of the
hymn) form two metres, which form a support (pratish*th*â).   Verily, man is supported by two (feet),
cattle by four feet.   Therefore this hymn places the
sacrificer who stands on two feet among cattle which
stand on four.

7. By saying them straight on there are twenty-
five verses in this hymn.   Man also consists of
twenty-five.   There are ten fingers on his hands,
ten toes on his feet, two legs, two arms, and the
trunk (âtman) the twenty-fifth.   He adorns that
trunk, the twenty-fifth, by this hymn.

8. And then this day (of the sacrifice) consists of
twenty-five, and the Stoma hymn of that day consists of twenty-five[1] (verses); it becomes the same
through the same.   Therefore these two, the day
and the hymn, are twenty-five[2].

9. These twenty-five verses, by repeating the
first thrice and the last thrice, become thirty less
one.   This is a Virâg* verse (consisting of thirty
syllables), too small by one.   Into the small (heart)
the vital spirits are placed, into the small stomach
food is placed[3], therefore this Virâg*, small by one,
serves for the obtainment of those desires.

10. He who knows this, obtains those desires.

11. The verses (contained in the hymn agnim
naro dîdhitibhi*h*) become the B*ri*hatî[4] metre and

---

[1] Cf. Ait. Âr. I, 1, 4, 21; II, 3, 4, 2.
[2] The plural after the dual is explained by the fact that the
hymn means the twenty-five verses.
[3] Cf. I, 3, 7, 5.
[4] The hymn consists of eighteen Virâg* and seven Trish*t*ubh

the Virâg metre, (they become) the perfection which belongs to that day (the mahâvrata). Then they also become Anushṭubh [1], for the offerings of âgya (ghee) dwell in Anushṭubhs [2].

THIRD KHANDA [3].

1. Some say: 'Let him take a Gâyatrî hymn for the Pra-uga. Verily, Gâyatrî is brightness and glory of countenance, and thus the sacrificer becomes bright and glorious.'

2. Others say: 'Let him take a Ushṇih hymn for the Pra-uga. Verily, Ushṇih is life, and thus the sacrificer has a long life.'

Others say: 'Let him take an Anushṭubh hymn

---

verses. Therefore the eighteen Virâg verses remain what they are, only that the first is repeated three times, so that we have twenty Virâg verses. The seven Trishṭubhs, by repeating the last three times, become nine. We then take eight syllables away from each verse, thus changing them into nine Brihatî verses. The nine times eight syllables, which were taken off, give us seventy-two syllables, and as each Brihatî consists of thirty-six syllables, two Brihatîs.

[1] The change of the first verse, which is a Virâg of thirty-three syllables, into an Anushṭubh is produced by a still easier process. The first Virâg consists here of thirty-three syllables, the Anushṭubh should have thirty-two. But one or two syllables more or less does not destroy a metre, according to the views of native metricians. The Virâg itself, for instance, should have thirty syllables, and here has thirty-three. Therefore if changed into an Anushṭubh, it simply has one syllable over, which is of no consequence. Comm.

[2] Cf. Ait. Âr. I, 1, 1, 4.

[3] Thus far the hymn which has to be recited by the Hotri priest, after the eating of the ritugrahas, has been considered. What follows next is the so-called Pra-uga hymn, consisting of seven trikas, which the Hotri has to recite after the Visvedeva-graha. Different Sâkhâs recommend hymns of different metres, our Sâkhâ fixes on the Gâyatrî.

for the Pra-uga. Verily, Anush*t*ubh is valour, and
it serves for obtaining valour.'

Others say: 'Let him take a B*ri*hatî hymn for
the Pra-uga. Verily, B*ri*hatî is fortune, and thus
the sacrificer becomes fortunate.'

Others say: 'Let him take a Pańkti hymn for
the Pra-uga. Verily, Pańkti is food, and thus the
sacrificer becomes rich in food.'

Others say: 'Let him take a Trish*t*ubh hymn for
the Pra-uga. Verily, Trish*t*ubh is strength, and thus
the sacrificer becomes strong.'

Others say: 'Let him take a *G*agatî hymn for the
Pra-uga. Verily, cattle is *G*agatî-like, and thus the
sacrificer becomes rich in cattle.'

3. But we say: 'Let him take a Gâyatrî hymn
only. Verily, Gâyatrî is Brahman, and that day
(the mahâvrata) is (for the attainment of) Brahman.
Thus he obtains Brahman by means of Brahman.

4. 'And it must be a Gâyatrî hymn by Madhu-
*kkh*andas,

5. 'For Madhu*kkh*andas is called Madhu*kkh*andas,
because he wishes (*kh*andati) for honey (madhu) for
the *R*ishis.

6. 'Now food verily is honey, all is honey, all
desires are honey, and thus if he recites the hymn
of Madhu*kkh*andas, it serves for the attainment of
all desires.

7. 'He who knows this, obtains all desires.'

This (Gâyatrî pra-uga), according to the one-day
(ekâha) ceremonial[1], is perfect in form[2]. On that day
(the mahâvrata) much is done now and then which

---

[1] It is copied from the Vi*s*va*g*it, and that from the Agnish*t*oma.

[2] Nothing is wanting for its performance, if one only follows the
rules given in the Agnish*t*oma.

has to be hidden [1], and has to be atoned for (by recitation of hymns). Atonement (*s*ânti) is rest, the
one-day sacrifice. Therefore at the end of the year
(on the last day but one of the sacrifice that lasts
a whole year) the sacrificers rest on this atonement
as their rest.

8. He who knows this rests firm, and they also
for whom a Hot*ri* priest who knows this, recites
this hymn.

FOURTH KHA*N*DA [2].

1. Rv. I, 2, 1–3. Vâyav â yâhi dar*s*ateme somâ
ara*m* k*ri*tâ*h*, 'Approach, O Vâyu, conspicuous, these
Somas have been made ready.' Because the word
ready occurs in these verses, therefore is this day
(of the sacrifice) ready (and auspicious) for the
sacrificer and for the gods.

2. Yes, this day is ready (and auspicious) to him
who knows this, or for whom a Hot*ri* priest who
knows this, recites.

3. Rv. I, 2, 4–6. Indravâyû ime sutâ, â yâtam
upa nishk*ri*tam, 'Indra and Vâyu, these Somas are
prepared, come hither towards what has been prepared.' By nishk*ri*ta, prepared, he means what has
been well prepared (sa*m*sk*ri*ta).

4. Indra and Vâyu go to what has been prepared
by him who knows this, or for whom a Hot*ri* priest
who knows this, recites.

---

[1] Dâsî*nri*tya-bahubhûtamaithuna-brahma*k*âripu*ms*ka*l*îsampravâ-
dâdikam. See Rajendralal Mitra, Introduction to his edition of the
Aitareya-âra*n*yaka, p. 25. It might be better to join ekâha*h* with
*s*ântyâm, but even then the argumentation is not quite clear.

[2] Next follows a list of the verses which form the seven *tri*kas
(groups of three verses) of the Pra-uga hymn, with occasional
remarks on certain words.

5. Rv. I, 2, 7. Mitra*m* huve pûtadaksham, dhiya*m* gh*r*itâ*k*îm sâdhantâ, 'I call Mitra of holy strength; (he and Varu*n*a) they fulfil the prayer accompanied with clarified butter.' Verily, speech is the prayer accompanied with clarified butter.

6. Speech is given to him who knows this, or for whom a Hot*r*i priest who knows this, recites.

7. Rv. I, 3, 1. A*s*vinâ ya*g*varîr isha*h*, 'O A*s*vinau, (eat) the sacrificial offerings.' Verily, the sacrificial offerings are food, and this serves for the acquirement of food.

8. Rv. I, 3, 3. Â yâta*m* rudravartanî, 'Come hither, ye Rudravartanî.'

9. The A*s*vinau go to the sacrifice of him who knows this, or for whom a Hot*r*i priest who knows this, recites.

10. Rv. I, 3, 4–6. Indrâ yâhi *k*itrabhâno, indrâ yâhi dhiyeshita*h*, indrâ yâhi tûtu*g*âna, 'Come hither, Indra, of bright splendour, Come hither, Indra, called by prayer, Come hither, Indra, quickly!' Thus he recites, Come hither, come hither!

11. Indra comes to the sacrifice of him who knows this, or for whom a Hot*r*i priest who knows this, recites.

12. Rv. I, 3, 7. Omâsa*s* *k*arsha*n*îdh*r*ito vi*s*ve devâsa â gata, 'Vi*s*ve Devas, protectors, supporters of men, come hither!'

13. Verily, the Vi*s*ve Devas come to the call of him who knows this, or for whom a Hot*r*i priest who knows this, recites.

14. Rv. I, 3, 7. Dâ*s*vâ*m*so dâ*s*usha*h* sutam, 'Come ye givers to the libation of the giver!' By dâ*s*usha*h* he means dadusha*h*, i. e. to the libation of every one that gives.

15. The gods fulfil his wish, with whatever wish he recites this verse,

16. (The wish of him) who knows this, or for whom a Hot*ri* priest who knows this, recites.

17. Rv. I, 3, 10. Pâvakâ na*h* sarasvatî ya*gñam* vash*t*u dhiyâvasu*h*, 'May the holy Sarasvatî accept our sacrifice, rich in prayer!' Speech is meant by 'rich in prayer.'

18. Speech is given to him who knows this, or for whom a Hot*ri* priest who knows this, recites.

19. And when he says, 'May she accept our sacrifice!' what he means is, '"May she carry off our sacrifice!'

20. If these verses are recited straight on, they are twenty-one. Man also consists of twenty-one. There are ten fingers on his hands, ten toes on his feet, and the trunk the twenty-first. He adorns that trunk, the twenty-first, by this hymn.

21. By repeating the first and the last verses thrice, they become twenty-five. The trunk is the twenty-fifth, and Pra*g*âpati is the twenty-fifth. There are ten fingers on his hands, ten toes on his feet, two legs, two arms, and the trunk the twenty-fifth. He adorns that trunk, the twenty-fifth, by this hymn[1].

Now this day consists of twenty-five, and the Stoma hymn of that day consists of twenty-five: it becomes the same through the same. Therefore these two, the day and the hymn, are twenty-five, yea, twenty-five.

---

[1] Cf. I, 1, 2, 7; I, 3, 5, 7.

SECOND ADHYÂYA.

First Kha*nd*a [1].

1. The two *tri*kas, Rv. VIII, 68, 1–3, â tvâ
ratha*m* yathotaye, and Rv. VIII, 2, 1–3, ida*m* vaso
sutam andha*h*, form the first˙ (pratipad) and the
second (anu*k*ara) of the Marutvatîya hymn.

2. Both, as belonging to the one-day ceremonial [2],
are perfect in form. On that day much is done
now and then which has to be hidden, and has to
be atoned for. Atonement is rest, the one-day
sacrifice. Therefore at the end of the year the
sacrificers rest on this atonement as their rest. He
who knows this rests firm, and they also for whom
a Hot*ri* priest who knows this, recites this hymn [3].

3. In the second verse of (the Pragâtha [4]), indra
nedîya ed ihi, pra sû tirâ sa*k*îbhir ye ta ukthina*h*
(Rv. VIII, 53, 5, 6), there occurs the word ukthina*h*,
reciters of hymns [5]. Verily, this day (the mahâvrata)
is an uktha (hymn), and as endowed with an uktha,
the form of this day is perfect.

4. In the first verse (of another Pragâtha) the
word vîra, strong, occurs (Rv. I, 40, 3), and as
endowed with the word vîra, strong, the form of
this day is perfect.

---

[1] In the first adhyâya the two hymns to be recited by the Hot*ri*
priest at the morning-libation (the â*g*ya and pra-uga *s*astra) have
been considered. Now follows the Marutvatîya hymn, to be
recited by the Hot*ri* priest at the noon-libation.

[2] Taken from the Agnish*t*oma.

[3] Cf. I, 1, 3, 7–8.

[4] All these Pragâthas consist of two verses expanded into a
*tri*ka.

[5] Hotrâdaya ukthina*h* *s*astri*n*a*h*.

5. In the second verse (of another Pragâtha) the word suvîryam, strength, occurs (Rv. I. 40, 1), and as endowed with the word suvîrya, strength, the form of this day is perfect.

6. In the first verse (of another Pragâtha) the word ukthyam, to be hymned, occurs (Rv. I, 40, 5). Verily, this day is an uktha, and as endowed with an uktha, the form of this day is perfect.

7. In the (Dhayyâ) verse agnir netâ (Rv. III, 20, 4) the word vritrahâ, killer of Vritra, occurs. The killing of Vritra is a form (character) of Indra, this day (the mahâvrata) belongs to Indra, and this is the (perfect) form of that day.

8. In the (Dhayyâ) verse tvam soma kratubhih sukratur bhûh (Rv. I, 91, 2) the word vrishâ[1], powerful, occurs. Powerful is a form (character) of Indra, this day belongs to Indra, and this is the (perfect) form of that day.

9. In the (Dhayyâ) verse pinvanty apah (Rv. I, 64, 6) the word vâginam, endowed with food, occurs. Endowed with food is a form (character) of Indra, this day belongs to Indra, and this is the (perfect) form of that day.

10. In the same verse the word stanayantam, thundering, occurs. Endowed with thundering is a form (character) of Indra, this day belongs to Indra, and this is the (perfect) form of that day.

11. In (the Pragâtha) pra va indrâya brihate (Rv. VIII, 89, 3) (the word brihat occurs). Verily, brihat is mahat (great), and as endowed with mahat, great, the form of this day (mahâvrata) is perfect.

12. In (the Pragâtha) brihad indrâya gâyata (Rv.

---

[1] Cf. I, 2, 2, 14.

VIII, 89, 1) (the word br*i*hat occurs). Verily, br*i*hat is mahat (great), and as endowed with mahat, the form of this day is perfect.

13. In (the Pragâtha) naki*h* sudâso ratham pary âsa na rîramad (Rv. VII, 32, 10) the words paryâsa (he moved round) and na rîramad (he did not enjoy) occur, and as endowed with the words paryasta and rânti the form of this day is perfect [1].

He recites all (these) Pragâthas, in order to obtain all the days (of the sacrifice), all the Ukthas [2], all the Prish*th*as [3], all the *S*astras [4], all the Pra-ugas [5], and all the Savanas (libations).

SECOND KHAN̄DA [6].

1. He recites the hymn, asat su me *g*arita*h* sâbhi-vega*h* (Rv. X, 27, 1), (and in it the word) satya-dhv*ri*tam, the destroyer of truth. Verily, that day

---

[1] Because the performance of the Mahâvrata sacrifice moves the worshipper round to another world and gives him enjoyment. Comm. It is difficult to surpass the absurdity of these explanations. Na rîramat means no one stopped the chariot of Sudâs. But even if it meant that no one rejoiced through the chariot of Sudâs, it would be difficult to see how the negative of enjoyment, mentioned in the hymn, could contribute to the perfection of a sacrifice which is to confer positive enjoyment on the worshipper.

[2] The stotras following after the Ya*g*ñâya*g*ñîya Sâman, serving for the ukthya-kratus.

[3] The stotras of the noon-libation, to be performed with the Rathantara, Br*i*hat, and other Sâmans.

[4] The *s*astras, recitations, accompanying the oblations of â*g*ya.

[5] The pra-ugas, a division of *s*astras, described above.

[6] The type after which the Marutvatîya-*s*astra is to be performed is the *K*aturvi*m*sa day. Hitherto (from â tvâ ratham to naki*h* sudâsa*h*), all that is taken over from the type to the modification, i. e. the Marutvatîya, has been explained. Now follow the verses which are new and peculiar to the Marutvatîya of the Mahâvrata.

is truth, and as endowed with the word satya, truth, the form of this day is perfect [1].

2. That hymn is composed by Vasukra. Verily, Vasukra is Brahman, and that day is Brahman. Thus he obtains Brahman by means of Brahman [2].

3. Here they say: 'Why then is that Marutvatîya hymn completed by the hymn of Vasukra?' Surely because no other *Ri*shi but Vasukra brought out a Marutvatîya hymn, or divided it properly [3]. There fore that Marutvatîya hymn is completed by the hymn of Vasukra.

4. That hymn, asat su me, is not definitely ad-dressed to any deity, and is therefore supposed to be addressed to Pra*g*âpati. Verily, Pra*g*âpati is indefinite, and therefore the hymn serves to win Pra*g*âpati.

5. Once in the hymn (Rv. X, 27, 22) he defines Indra (indrâya sunvat); therefore it does not fall off from its form, as connected with Indra.

6. He recites the hymn (Rv. VI, 17, 1) pibâ somam abhi yam ugra tarda*h*.

7. In the verse ûrvam gavyam mahi gri*n*âna indra the word mahi, great, occurs. Endowed with the word mahat, the form of this day is perfect.

8. That hymn is composed by Bharadvâ*g*a, and Bharadvâ*g*a was he who knew most, who lived longest, and performed the greatest austerities among the *Ri*shis, and by this hymn he drove away evil. Therefore if he recites the hymn of Bharadvâ*g*a,

---

[1] The commentator endeavours to make the meaning more natural by taking in the word prahantâ, he who kills the destroyer of truth. But considering the general character of these remarks, this is hardly necessary.

[2] Cf. I, 1, 3, 3.

[3] By separating the first tri*k*a from the second, and so forth.

then, after having driven away evil, he becomes
learned, long-lived, and full of austerities.

9. He recites the hymn kayâ _s_ubhâ savayasa_h_
sanîlâ_h_ (Rv. I, 165, 1).

10. In the verse â _s_âsate prati haryanty ukthâ
(Rv. I, 165, 4) the word ukthâ occurs. Verily, that
day (the mahâvrata) is uktha (hymn). Endowed with
the word uktha, the form of this day becomes perfect.

11. That hymn is called Kayâ_s_ubhîya[1]. Verily,
that hymn, which is called Kayâ_s_ubhîya, is mutual
understanding and it is lasting. By means of it
Indra, Agastya, and the Maruts came to a mutual
understanding. Therefore, if he recites the Kayâ-
_s_ubhîya hymn, it serves for mutual understanding.

12. The same hymn is also long life. Therefore,
if the sacrificer is dear to the Hot_ri_, let him recite
the Kayâ_s_ubhîya hymn for him.

13. He recites the hymn marutvâ_n_ indra v_ri_shabo
ra_n_âya (Rv. III, 47, 1).

14. In it the words indra v_ri_shabha (powerful)
occur. Verily, powerful is a form of Indra[2], this
day belongs to Indra, and this is the perfect form
of that day.

15. That hymn is composed by Vi_s_vâmitra. Verily,
Vi_s_vâmitra was the friend (mitra) of all (vi_s_va).

16. Everybody is the friend of him who knows
this, and for whom a Hot_ri_ priest who knows this,
recites this hymn.

17. The next hymn, _g_anish_th_â ugra_h_ sahase tu-
râya (Rv. I, 73, 1), forms a Nividdhâna[3], and,

---

[1] Cf. Ait. Brâhm. V, 16.   [2] Cf. Ait. Âr. II, 2, 1, 8.

[3] The hymn consists of eleven verses. In the middle, after the
sixth verse, nivids or invocations, such as indro marutvân, are inserted, and therefore it is called a nividdhâna hymn.

according to the one-day (ekâha) ceremonial, is perfect in form.   On that day much is done now and then which has to be hidden, and has to be atoned for (by recitation of hymns).   Atonement is rest, the one-day sacrifice.   Therefore at the end of the year (on the last day but one of the sacrifice that lasts a whole year) the sacrificers rest on this atonement as their rest.

He who knows this rests firm, and they also for whom a Hot*ri* priest who knows this, recites this hymn [1].

18. These, if recited straight on, are ninety-seven verses [2].   The ninety are three Virâ*g*, each consisting of thirty, and then the seven verses which are over. Whatever is the praise of the seven, is the praise of ninety also.

---

[1] With this hymn the Marutvatîya-*s*astra is finished.   All the hymns from â tvâ ratham to asat su me *g*aritar are simply taken over from the *K*aturvim*s*a ceremonial, the rest are peculiar to the Mahâvrata day, the day preceding the Udayanîya or final day of the Gavâmayana sattra.   All this is more fully described in the fifth Âra*n*yaka (V, 1, 1, 8), containing the Sûtras or rules of *S*aunaka, while the earlier Âra*n*yakas are reckoned as Brâhma*n*as, and are therefore mixed up with matters not actually required for the performance of the sacrifice.

[2] The first Stotriya and Ânurûpa

tri*k*as =	.	.	.	.	6 (I, 2, 1, 1).

The six Pragâthas, each of 2 verses
   raised to 3 (but the text gives

seven Pragâthas) =	.	.	18 (I, 2, 1, 3; 4; 5; 6; 11; 12; 13).
Three Dhâyyâs =	.	.	.	3 (I, 2, 1, 7; 8; 9).
Asat su =	.	.	.	.	24 (I, 2, 2, 1).
Pibâ somam =	.	.	.	15 (I, 2, 2, 6).
Kayâ *s*ubhâ =	.	.	.	15 (I, 2, 2, 9).
Marutvâ*n* indra =	.	.	5 (I, 2, 2, 13).
*G*anish*th*â ugra*h* =	.	.	11 (I, 2, 2, 17).

19. By repeating the first and last verses three times each, they become one hundred and one verses.

20. There are five fingers, of four joints each, two pits (in the elbow and the arm), the arm, the eye, the shoulder-blade; this makes twenty-five. The other three parts have likewise twenty-five each [1]. That makes a hundred, and the trunk is the one hundred and first.

21. Hundred is life, health, strength, brightness. The sacrificer as the one hundred and first rests in life, health, strength, and brightness.

22. These verses become Trish/ubh [2], for the noonday-libation consists of Trish/ubh verses.

THIRD KHAN̄DA [3].

1. They say: 'What is the meaning of preṅkha, swing?' Verily, he is the swing, who blows (the wind). He indeed goes forward (pra + iṅkhate) in these worlds, and that is why the swing is called preṅkha.

2. Some say, that there should be one plank, because the wind blows in one way, and it should be like the wind.

3. That is not to be regarded.

4. Some say, there should be three planks, because there are these three threefold worlds, and it should be like them.

---

[1] The left side as well as the right, and then the left and right side of the lower body. Thus we have twenty joints of the five toes, a thigh, a leg, and three joints, making twenty-five on each side.

[2] Approach the Trish/ubh metre of the last hymn. Comm.

[3] After having considered the Marutvatîya, he proceeds to consider the Nishkevalya. This has to be recited by the Hotr̄i while sitting on a swing.

5. That is not to be regarded.

6. Let there be two, for these two worlds (the earth and heaven) are seen as if most real, while the ether (space) between the two is the sky (antariksha). Therefore let there be two planks.

7. Let them be made of Udumbara wood. Verily, the Udumbara tree is sap and eatable food, and thus it serves to obtain sap and eatable food.

8. Let them be elevated in the middle (between the earth and the cross-beam). Food, if placed in the middle, delights man, and thus he places the sacrificer in the middle of eatable food.

9. There are two kinds of rope, twisted towards the right and twisted towards the left. The right ropes serve for some animals, the left ropes for others. If there are both kinds of rope, they serve for the attainment of both kinds of cattle.

10. Let them be made of Darbha (Kusa grass), for among plants Darbha is free from evil, therefore they should be made of Darbha grass.

FOURTH KHANDA.

1. Some say: ' Let the swing be one ell (aratni) above the ground, for by that measure verily the Svarga worlds are measured.' That is not to be regarded.

2. Others say : ' Let it be one span (prâdesa), for by that measure verily the vital airs were measured.' That is not to be regarded [1].

3. Let it be one fist (mushti), for by that measure verily all eatable food is made, and by that measure

---

[1] They rise one span above the heart, and they proceed one span from out the mouth. Comm.

all eatable food is taken; therefore let it be one fist above the ground.

4. They say: 'Let him mount the swing from east to west, like he who shines; for the sun mounts these worlds from east to west.' That is not to be regarded.

5. Others say: 'Let him mount the swing sideways, for people mount a horse sideways[1], thinking that thus they will obtain all desires.' That is not to be regarded.

6. They say: 'Let him mount the swing[2] from behind, for people mount a ship from behind, and this swing is a ship in which to go to heaven.' Therefore let him mount it from behind.

7. Let him touch the swing with his chin (*kh*u-buka). The parrot (*s*uka) thus mounts a tree, and he is of all birds the one who eats most food. Therefore let him touch it with his chin.

8. Let him mount the swing with his arms[3]. The hawk swoops thus on birds and on trees, and he is of all birds the strongest. Therefore let him mount with his arms.

9. Let him not withdraw one foot (the right or left) from the earth, for fear that he may lose his hold.

10. The Hot*ri* mounts the swing, the Udgât*ri* the seat made of Udumbara wood. The swing is masculine, the seat feminine, and they form a union. Thus he makes a union at the beginning of the uktha in order to get offspring.

---

[1] Here we have clearly riding on horseback.

[2] While the swing points to the east, let him stand west, and thus mount.

[3] The fore-arms, from the elbow to the end, the aratnî. Comm.

11. He who knows this, gets offspring and cattle.

12. Next the swing is food, the seat fortune. Thus he mounts and obtains food and fortune.

13. The Hotrakas (the Prasâstri, Brâhmanâkkhamsin, Potri, Neshtri, Agnîdhra, and Akkhâvâka) together with the Brahman sit down on cushions made of grass, reeds, leaves, &c.

14. Plants and trees, after they have grown up, bear fruit. Thus if the priests mount on that day altogether (on their seats), they mount on solid and fluid as their proper food. Therefore this serves for the attainment of solid as proper food [1].

15. Some say: 'Let him descend after saying vashat [2].' That is not to be regarded. For, verily, that respect is not shown which is shown to one who does not see it [3].

16. Others say: 'Let him descend after he has taken the food in his hand.' That is not to be regarded. For, verily, that respect is not shown which is shown to one after he has approached quite close.

17. Let him descend after he has seen the food. For, verily, that is real respect which is shown to one when he sees it. Only after having actually

---

[1] One expects ishah before ûrgah, but it is wanting in both text and commentary, and in other MSS. also.

[2] The word by which the Hotri invites the Adhvaryu to offer the oblation to the gods. The descending from the swing belongs, of course, to a later part of the sacrifice.

[3] It is supposed that the Hotri rises from the swing to show respect to the sacrificial food, when it is brought near. But as it is not brought near, immediately after the Hotri has finished his part with the word vashat, the food could not see the Hotri rise, and this mark of respect, intended for the food, would thus be lost.

seen the food (that is brought to the sacrifice), let him descend from the swing.

18. Let him descend turning towards the east, for in the east the seed of the gods springs up[1]. Therefore let him rise turning towards the east, yea, turning towards the east.

THIRD ADHYÂYA.

First Khan̄da.

1. Let him begin this day[2] with singing ' Him,' thus they say.

2. Verily, the sound Him is Brahman, that day also is Brahman. He who knows this, obtains Brahman even by Brahman.

3. As he begins with the sound Him, surely that masculine sound of Him and the feminine *Rik* (the verse) make a couple. Thus he makes a couple at the beginning of the hymn in order to get offspring[3]. He who knows this, gets cattle and offspring.

4. Or, as he begins with the sound Him, surely like a wooden spade, so the sound Him serves to dig up Brahman (the sap of the Veda). And as a man wishes to dig up any, even the hardest soil, with a spade, thus he digs up Brahman.

5. He who knows this digs up, by means of the sound Him, everything he may desire.

6. If he begins with the sound Him, that sound is the holding apart of divine and human speech.

---

[1] Should it be devareta*h* sampra*g*âyate, or devaretasam pra*g*âyate?
[2] The Nishkevalya-*s*astra, of the noon-libation; cf. I, 2, 2, 1.
[3] Cf. I, 2, 4, 10.

Therefore, he who begins, after having uttered the sound Him, holds apart divine and human speech [1].

SECOND KHA*N*DA.

1. And here they ask : 'What is the beginning of this day?' Let him say: 'Mind and speech [2].'

2. All desires dwell in the one (mind), the other yields all desires.

3. All desires dwell in the mind, for with the mind he conceives all desires.

4. All desires come to him who knows this.

5. Speech yields all desires, for with speech he declares all his desires.

6. Speech yields all desires to him who knows this.

7. Here they say: 'Let him not begin this day with a *Rik*, a Ya*g*us, or a Sâman verse (divine speech), for it is said, he should not start with a *Rik*, a Ya*g*us, or a Sâman [3].'

8. Therefore, let him say these Vyâh*ri*tis (sacred interjections) first.

9. These interjections Bhûs, Bhuvas, Svar are the three Vedas, Bhûs the *Rig*-veda, Bhuvas the Ya*g*ur-veda, Svar the Sâma-veda. Therefore (by

---

[1] Human speech is the ordinary speech, divine speech that of the Veda. Thus between the hymns, or the divine speech, and the ordinary language of conversation the sound Him is interposed as a barrier.

[2] Mind, to think about the hymns which have to be recited; speech, to recite them without a flaw.

[3] It is doubtful whether neyâd *rikah* and apaga*kkh*et can have this meaning. However, what is intended is clear, viz. that the priest, even after having uttered the sound Him, should not immediately begin with verses from the Vedas, but should intercalate the three syllables bhûr bhuva*h* svar, or, if taken singly, bhûs, bhuvas, svar.

intercalating these) he does not begin simply with a
Rik, Ya*g*us, or Sâman verse, he does not start with
a *Rik*, Ya*g*us, or Sâman verse.

THIRD KHA*N*DA.

1. He begins with tad, this, (the first word of the
first hymn, tad id âsa). Verily 'this, this' is food,
and thus he obtains food.

2. Pra*g*âpati indeed uttered this as the first word,
consisting of one or two syllables, viz. tata and tâta
(or tat)[1]. And thus does a child, as soon as he
begins to speak, utter the word, consisting of one
or two syllables, viz. tata and tâta (or tat). With
this very word, consisting of tat or tatta, he begins.

3. This has been said by a *Ri*shi (Rv. X, 71, 1)[2]:—

4. 'O B*ri*haspati, the first point of speech;'— for
this is the first and highest point of speech.

5. 'That which you have uttered, making it a
name;'—for names are made by speech.

---

[1] Tata and tâta are used both by children in addressing their
parents, and by parents in addressing their children. If tat is
call d the very same word, eva is used in the sense of iva.

[2] The verse is cited to confirm the meaning of tat, the first word
of the first hymn (tad id âsa), as explained before. It was said
that tat was the first name applied to a child. Now, according to
Â*s*valâyana G*ri*hya-sûtra I, 16, 8, a name is given to a child at the
time of its birth, a name which no one knows except father and
mother, till the time when he is initiated by a Guru. This is called
the abhivadanîya name. In allusion to this custom it is said here
that tata is the secret name of the child, which becomes publicly
known at a later time only. Of course the interpretation of the
verse in that sense is unnatural, but quite in keeping with the
general character of the Âra*n*yaka. I doubt whether even the commentator understood what was intended by the author, and whether
the gods who enter the body are supposed to know the name, or
whether the name refers to these gods, or, it may be, to tad, the
Brahman.

6. ' That (name) which was the best and without
a flaw ;'—for this is the best and without a flaw.

7. ' That which was hidden by their love, is made
manifest;'—for this was hidden in the body, viz. those
deities (which enter the body, Agni as voice, entering
the mouth, &c.) ; and that was manifest among the
gods in heaven.   This is what was intended by the
verse.

FOURTH KHA*N*DA[1].

1. He begins with : ' That indeed was the oldest
in the worlds [2];'—for that (the Brahman) is verily the
oldest in the worlds.

2. 'Whence was born the fierce one, endowed
with brilliant force;'—for from it was born the fierce
one, who is endowed with brilliant force.

3. 'When born he at once destroys the enemies;'—
for he at once when born struck down the evil one.

4. ' He after whom all friends rejoice;'—verily all
friends are the creatures, and they rejoice after him,
saying, ' He has risen, he has risen[3].'

5. ' Growing by strength, the almighty[4];'—for he
(the sun) does grow by strength, the almighty.

6. ' He, as enemy, causes fear to the slave;'—for
everything is afraid of him.

7. 'Taking the breathing and the not-breathing;'—
this means the living and the lifeless.

8. ' Whatever has been offered at feasts came to
thee;'—this means everything is in thy power.

9. 'All turn their thought also on thee[5];'—this

---

[1] He now explains the first hymn of the Nishkevalya, which is
called the Râ*g*ana.

[2] Rv. X, 120, 1.   [3] The sun and the fire.

[4] Rv. X, 120, 2.   [5] Rv. X, 120, 3.

means all these beings, all minds, all thoughts also turn to thee.

10. 'When these two become three protectors;'— i. e. when these two united beget offspring.

11. He who knows this, gets offspring and cattle.

12. 'Join what is sweeter than sweet (offspring) with the sweet (the parents);'—for the couple (father and mother) is sweet, the offspring is sweet, and he thus joins the offspring with the couple.

13. 'And this (the son, when married) being very sweet, conquered through the sweet;'—i.e. the couple is sweet, the offspring is sweet, and thus through the couple he conquers offspring[1].

14. This is declared by a Rishi[2]: 'Because he (Pragâpati) raised his body (the hymn tad id âsa or the Veda in general) in the body (of the sacrificer)' (therefore that Nishkevalya hymn is praised); —i. e. this body, consisting of the Veda, in that corporeal form (of the sacrificer).

15. 'Then let this body indeed be the medicine of that body;'—i. e. this body, consisting of the Veda, of that corporeal form (of the sacrificer).

16. Of this (the first foot of Rv. X, 120, 1) the eight syllables are Gâyatrî, the eleven syllables are Trishṭubh, the twelve syllables are Gagatî, the ten syllables are Virâg. The Virâg, consisting of ten syllables, rests in these three metres[3].

17. The word purusha, consisting of three syllables, that indeed goes into the Virâg[4].

---

[1] All these are purely fanciful interpretations.

[2] Not to be found in our Sâkhâ of the Rig-veda.

[3] These metres are obtained by a purely arbitrary counting of syllables in the hymn tadidâsa, which really consists of Trishṭubh verses.

[4] If we simply count syllables, the first and second feet of the

18. Verily, these are all metres, these (Gâyatrî, Trish*t*ubh, *G*agatî) having the Virâ*g* as the fourth. In this manner this day is complete in all metres to him who knows this.

FIFTH KHA*N*DA.

1. He extends these (verses) by (interpolating) the sound[1]. Verily, the sound is purusha, man. Therefore every man when he speaks, sounds loud, as it were.

2. At the end of each foot of the first verse of the hymn tad id âsa, he inserts one foot of the second verse of hymn Rv. VIII, 69, nada*m* va odatînâm, &c. Thus the verse is to be recited as follows :

Tad id âsa bhuvaneshu *g*yesh*th*am pu
    nada*m* va odatînâm,
Yato *g*ag*ñ*a ugras tveshanr*im*n*o*   ru
    nada*m* yoyuvatînâm,
Sadyo *g*ag*ñ*âno ni ri*n*âti *s*atrûn
    pati*m* vo aghnyânâm,
Anu ya*m* vi*s*ve madanti ûmâ*h*   sho
    dhenûnâm ishudhyasi.

first verse consist of ten syllables only, the fourth of nine or ten. In order to bring them to the right number, the word purusha is to be added to what is a Virâ*g*, i.e. to the first, the second, and fourth feet. We thus get :

    tad id âsa bhuvaneshu *g*yesh*th*am pu
    yato *g*ag*ñ*a ugras tveshanr*im*n*o*   ru
    sadyo *g*ag*ñ*âno ni ri*n*âti *s*atrûn
    anu ya*m* vi*s*ve madanti ûmâ*h*   sha*h*.

Cf. Ait. Âr. V, 1, 6.

[1] The sound, nada, is really a verse beginning with nadam, and which is interpolated after the syllables pu ru sha*h*.

In nada*m* va odatînâm (Rv. VIII, 69, 2), odatî [1] are the waters in heaven, for they water all this; and they are the waters in the mouth, for they water all good food.

3. In nada*m* yoyuvatînâm (Rv. VIII, 69, 2), yoyuvatî are the waters in the sky, for they seem to inundate; and they are the waters of perspiration, for they seem to run continually.

4. In pati*m* vo aghnyânâm (Rv. VIII, 69, 2), aghnyâ are the waters which spring from the smoke of fire, and they are the waters which spring from the organ.

5. In dhenûnâm ishudhyasi (Rv. VIII, 69, 2), the dhenu (cows) are the waters, for they delight all this; and ishudhyasi means, thou art food.

6. He extends a Trish*t*ubh and an Anush*t*ubh [2]. Trish*t*ubh is the man, Anush*t*ubh the wife, and they make a couple. Therefore does a man, after having found a wife, consider himself a more perfect man.

7. These verses, by repeating the first three times, become twenty-five. The trunk is the twenty-fifth, and Pra*g*âpati is the twenty-fifth [3]. There are ten fingers on his hands, ten toes on his feet, two legs, two arms, and the trunk the twenty-fifth. He adorns that trunk as the twenty-fifth. Now this day consists of twenty-five, and the Stoma hymn of that day consists of twenty-five: it becomes the same

---

[1] The nasal pluta on iti is explained as pâdapratîkagraha*n*e 'tyantamâdarârtha*h*. Cf. Ait. Âr. II, 1, 4, 3.

[2] Tad id âsa is a Trish*t*ubh, nada*m* va*h* an Anush*t*ubh.

[3] Cf. I, 1, 2, 7; I, 1, 4, 21.

through the same.   Therefore the two, the day and the hymn, are twenty-five [1].

Sixth Khanda.

This is an exact repetition of the third khanda. According to the commentator, the third khanda was intended for the glory of the first word tad, while the sixth is intended for the glory of the whole hymn.

Seventh Khanda.

1. He begins with the hymn, Tad id âsa bhuvaneshu gyeshtham (Rv. X, 120). Verily, gyeshtha, the oldest, is mahat, great. Endowed with mahat the form of this day is perfect.

2. Then follows the hymn, Tâm su te kîrtim maghavan mahitvâ (Rv. X, 54), with the auspicious word mahitvâ.

3. Then follows the hymn, Bhûya id vavridhe vîryâya (Rv. VI, 30), with the auspicious word vîrya.

4. Then follows the hymn, Nrinâm u tvâ nritamam gobhir ukthaih (Rv. I, 51, 4), with the auspicious word uktha.

5. He extends the first two pâdas, which are too small, by one syllable (Rv. X, 120, 1 a, and Rv. VIII, 69, 2 a) [2].   Into the small heart the vital spirits are placed, into the small stomach food is placed.   It

---

[1] The number is obtained as follows:

1. Tad id âsa (Rv. X, 120)=	.	.	9 verses
2. Tâm su te kîrtim (Rv. X, 54)=	.	6	,,
3. Bhûya id vavridhe (Rv. VI, 30)=	.	5	,,
4. Nrinâm u tvâ (Rv. I, 51, 4)=	.	.	3	,,

23 + 2 = 25

[2] Cf. I, 1, 2, 9.

serves for the attainment of these desires.   He who knows this, obtains these desires.

6. The two feet, each consisting of ten syllables (Rv. X, 120, 1 a, b), serve for the gaining of both kinds of food[1], of what has feet (animal food), and what has no feet (vegetable food).

7. They come to be of eighteen syllables each[2]. Of those which are ten, nine are the prânas (openings of the body)[3], the tenth is the (vital) self. This is the perfection of the (vital) self. Eight syllables remain in each. He who knows them, obtains whatever he desires.

EIGHTH KHANDA.

1. He extends (these verses) by (interpolating) the sound[4]. Verily, breath (prâna) is sound. Therefore every breath when it sounds, sounds loud, as it were.

2. The verse (VIII, 69, 2) nadam va odatînâm, &c., is by its syllables an Ushnih[5], by its feet an Anushtubh[6]. Ushnih is life, Anushtubh, speech. He thus places life and speech in him (the sacrificer.)

3. By repeating the first verse three times, they

---

[1] Because Virâg, a foot of ten syllables, is food.

[2]
Rv. X, 120, 1 a= .	.	10
Rv. VIII, 69, 2 a=	.	7
Syllable pu=	. .	1
		18

[3] Seven in the head and two in the body; sapta vai sîrshanyâh prânâ dvâv avâñkâv iti.

[4] Cf. I, 3, 5, 1.

[5] Each pâda has seven syllables, the third only six; but a seventh syllable is gained by pronouncing the y as i. Comm.

[6] Because it has four pâdas.

become twenty-five.   The trunk is the twenty-fifth,
and Pra*g*âpati is the twenty-fifth.   There are ten
fingers on his hands, ten toes on his feet, two legs,
two arms, and the trunk the twenty-fifth.   He
adorns that trunk as the twenty-fifth.   Now this day
consists of twenty-five, and the Stoma hymn of that
day consists of twenty-five : it becomes the same
through the same.   Therefore the two, the day and
the hymn, are twenty-five.   This is the twenty-fifth
with regard to the body.

4. Next, with regard to the deities : The eye, the
ear, the mind, speech, and breath, these five deities
(powers) have entered into that person (purusha),
and that person entered into the five deities.   He is
wholly pervaded there with his limbs to the very
hairs and nails.   Therefore all beings to the very
insects are born as pervaded (by the deities or
senses)[1].

5. This has been declared by a *R*ishi (Rv. X,
114, 8):—

6. 'A thousandfold are these fifteen hymns;'—for
five arise from ten[2].

7. 'As large as heaven and earth, so large is
it;'—verily, the self (*g*îvâtman) is as large as heaven
and earth.

8. 'A thousandfold are the thousand powers[3];'—

---

[1] The commentator takes this in a different sense, explaining
atra, there, as the body pervaded by the person, yet afterwards
stating that all beings are born, pervaded by the senses.

[2] The commentator explains ukthâ, hymns, as members or organs.
They are the five, and they spring from the ten, i. e. from the five
elements (earth, water, fire, wind, and ether), forming part of the
father and mother each, and therefore called ten, *q*r a decade.
Da*s*ata*h* is explained by bhûtada*s*akât.

[3] The application of the senses to a thousand different objects.

by saying this the poet pleases the hymns (the senses), and magnifies them.

9. 'As far as Brahman reaches, so far reaches speech;'—wherever there is Brahman, there is a word; and wherever there is a word, there is Brahman, this was intended.

10. The first of the hymns among all those hymns has nine verses. Verily, there are nine prânas (openings), and it serves for their benefit.

11. Then follows a hymn of six verses. Verily, the seasons are six, and it serves to obtain them.

12. Then follows a hymn of five verses. Verily, the Pankti consists of five feet. Verily, Pankti is food, and it serves for the gaining of proper food.

13. Then follows a tristich. Three are these threefold worlds, and it serves to conquer them.

14. These verses become Brihatîs[1], that metre being immortal, leading to the world of the Devas. That body of verses is the trunk (of the bird represented by the whole sastra), and thus it is. He who knows this comes by this way (by making the verses the trunk of the bird) near to the immortal Self, yea, to the immortal Self[2].

---

[1] Each foot of the Trishtubh has eleven syllables, to which seven are added from the Nada hymn. This gives eighteen syllables for each pâda. Two pâdas therefore give thirty-six syllables, and this is a Brihatî. In this manner the twenty-three verses of the hymns yield forty-six Brihatîs. Comm.

[2] He obtains a birth among the gods by means of this Mahâvrata ceremonial, if performed with meditation and a right understanding of its hidden meaning.

FOURTH ADHYÂYA.

FIRST KHAÑDA.

1. Next comes the Sûdadohas[1] verse. Sûdadohas is breath, and thereby he joins all joints with breath.

2. Next follow the neck verses. They recite them as Ushñih, according to their metre[2].

3. Next comes (again) the Sûdadohas verse. Sûdadohas is breath, and thereby he joins all joints with breath.

4. Next follows the head. That is in Gâyatrî verses. The Gâyatrî is the beginning of all metres[3]; the head the first of all members. It is in Arkavat verses (Rv. I, 7, 1–9)[4]. Arka is Agni. They are nine verses. The head consists of nine pieces. He recites the tenth verse, and that is the skin and the hairs on the head. It serves for reciting one verse more than (the nine verses contained in) the Stoma[5].

---

[1] The Nishkevalya-*sastra* is represented in the shape of a bird, consisting of trunk, neck, head, vertebrae, wings, tail, and stomach. Before describing the hymns which form the neck, another hymn has to be mentioned, called Sûdadohas, which has to be recited at the end of the hymns, described before, which form the trunk. Sûdadohas is explained as 'yielding milk,' and because that word occurs in the verse, the verse is called Sûdadohas. It follows on the Nada verse, Rv. VIII, 69, 3. Cf. Ait. Âr. I, 5, 1, 7.

[2] They occur in another *sâkhâ*, and are to be recited such as they are, without any insertions. They are given by *S*aunaka, Ait. Âr. V, 2, 1.

[3] It was created from the mouth of Pra*g*âpati.

[4] They are called so, because the word arka occurs in them.

[5] The chanters of the Sâma-veda make a Triv*ri*t Stoma of this hymn, without any repetitions, leaving out the tenth verse. The reciters of the Rig-veda excel them therefore by reciting a tenth verse. This is called ati*sam*sanam (or -nâ).

These form the Triv*ri*t Stoma and the Gâyatrî
metre, and whatever there exists, all this is produced after the production of this Stoma and this
metre.   Therefore the recitation of these head-
hymns serves for production.

5. He who knows this, gets offspring and cattle.

6. Next comes the Sûdadohas verse.   Verily,
Sûdadohas is breath, and thereby he joins all joints
with breath.

7. Next follow the vertebrae[1] (of the bird).
These verses are Virâ*g* (shining).   Therefore man
says to man, 'Thou shinest above us;' or to a stiff
and proud man, 'Thou carriest thy neck stiff.'   Or
because the (vertebrae of the neck) run close together, they are taken to be the best food.   For Virâ*g*
is food, and food is strength.

8. Next comes the Sûdadohas verse.   Sûdadohas
is breath, and thereby he joins all joints with breath.

---

[1] Vi*g*avas may be a singular, and the commentator seems to
take it as such in his first explanation.   The text, tâ virâ*g*o bhavanti, proves nothing, because it could not be sa virâ*g*o bhavanti,
nor even sa virâ*d* bhavati.   Possibly the word may occur in both
forms, vi*g*u, plural vi*g*ava*h*, and vi*g*ava*h*.   In a somewhat similar
way we find grîvâ and grîvâ*h*, folia and la feuille.   On p. 109,
the commentator speaks of vi*g*avabhâga, and again, p. 110, pa-
kshamûlarûpâ vi*g*avâ abhihitâ*h*.   He, however, explains its meaning
rightly, as the root of the wings, or rather the lower bones of the
neck.   Grîvâ*h*, plural, were originally the vertebrae of the neck.
The paragraph, though very empty, contains at least some interesting forms of language.   First vi*g*u, vertebrae, then the partici-
ples duta and sambâ*lh*atama, and lastly the verb pratya*k*, the last
probably used in the sense of to bring near, to represent, with the
superlative adverb annatamâm (Pâ*n*. V, 4, 11), i. e. they are represented as if they brought the best food.

SECOND KHA*N*DA.

1. Next follows the right wing. It is this world (the earth), it is this Agni, it is speech, it is the Rathantara [1], it is Vasish*th*a, it is a hundred [2]. These are the six powers (of the right wing) [3]. The Sampâta hymn (Rv. IV, 20) serves indeed for obtaining desires and for firmness. The Pankti verse (Rv. I, 80, 1) serves for proper food.

2. Next comes the Sûdadohas verse. Sûdadohas is breath, thereby he joins all joints with breath.

3. Next follows the left wing. It is that world (heaven), it is that sun, it is mind, it is the B*ri*hat, it

---

[1] Rathantara is the name of the whole number of hymns to be recited at this part of the sacrifice. It was made by Vasish*th*a, and consists of one hundred verses.

[2]
1. Stotriya, abhi tvâ *s*ûra nonuma*h* (Rv. VII, 32, 22)	2 (3)
2. Anurûpa, abhi tvâ pûrvapîtaye (Rv. VIII, 3, 7)	2 (3)
3. Indrasya nu (Rv. I, 32)	15
4. Tve ha (Rv. VII, 18, 1–15) . . .	15
5. Yas tigma (Rv. VII, 19)	11
6. Ugro *g*ag*ñ*e (Rv. VII, 20)	10
7. Ud u (Rv. VII, 23)	6
8. Â te maha*h* (Rv. VII, 25)	6
9. Na soma*h* (Rv. VII, 26)	5
10. Indra*m* nara*h* (Rv. VII, 27) . . .	5
11. Brahmâ *n*a*h* (Rv. VII, 28)	5
12. Ayam soma*h* (Rv. VII, 29) . . .	5
13. Â na indra*h* (Rv. IV, 20)	11
	98 (100)
14. Itthâ hi (Rv. I, 80, 1)	1
	99 (101)

These hymns and verses are given Ait. Âr. V, 2, 2, 1. Here we also learn that hymn Rv. IV, 20, is called Sampâta, and that the last verse is a Pankti.

[3] The six powers are earth, Agni, speech, Rathantara, Vasish*th*a, and a hundred.

is Bharadvâ*g*a, it is a hundred[1]. These are the
six powers (of the left wing). The Sampâta hymn
(Rv. IV, 23) serves indeed for obtaining desires
and for firmness. The Pañkti verse (Rv. I, 81, 1)
serves for proper food.

4. These two (the right and the left wings) are
deficient and excessive[2]. The B*ri*hat (the left wing)
is man, the Rathantara (the right wing) is woman.
The excess belongs to the man, the deficiency to the
woman. Therefore they are deficient and excessive.

5. Now the left wing of a bird is verily by one
feather better, therefore the left wing is larger by
one verse.

---

[1] The hundred verses are given Ait. Âr. V, 2, 2, 5.

1. Stotriya, tvâm id dhi (Rv. VI, 46, 1)	.	.	2 (3)
2. Anurûpa, tva*m* hy ehi (Rv. VIII, 61, 7)	.	.	2 (3)
3. Tam u sh*t*uhi (Rv. VI, 18)	.	.	15
4. Suta it tvam (Rv. VI, 23)	.	.	˙ 10
5. V*ri*shâ mada*h* (Rv. VI, 24)	.	.	10
6. Yâ ta ûti*h* (Rv. VI, 25)	.	.	9
7. Abhûr eka*h* (Rv. VI, 31)	.	.	5
8. Apûrvyâ (Rv. VI, 32)	.	.	5
9. Ya o*g*ish*th*ah (Rv. VI, 33)	.	.	5
10. Sa*m* *k*a tve (Rv. VI, 34)	.	.	5
11. Kadâ bhuvan (Rv. VI, 35)	.	.	5
12. Satrâ madâsa*h* (Rv. VI, 36)	.	.	5
13. Arvâg ratham (Rv. VI, 37)	.	.	5
14. Apâd (Rv. VI, 38)	.	.	5
15. Kathâ mahân (Rv. IV, 23)	.	.	11

99 (101)

16. Indro madâya (Rv. I, 81, 1)   .   .   .   1

100 (102)

Though there are said to be 100 verses before the Pañkti
(No. 16), I can get only 99 or 101. See the following note.

[2] The right wing is deficient by one verse, the left wing exceeds
by one verse. I count 99 or 101 verses in the right, and 100 or 102
in the left wing.

6. Next comes the Sûdadohas verse. Sûdadohas is breath, and thereby he joins all joints with breath.

7. Next follows the tail. They are twenty-one Dvipadâ verses[1]. For there are twenty-one backward feathers in a bird.

8. Then the Ekavimsa is the support of all Stomas, and the tail the support of all birds[2].

9. He recites a twenty-second verse. This is made the form of two supports. Therefore all birds support themselves on their tail, and having supported themselves on their tail, they fly up. For the tail is a support.

10. He (the bird and the hymn) is supported by two decades which are Virâg. The man (the sacrificer) is supported by the two Dvipadâs, the twenty-first and twenty-second. That which forms the bird serves for the attainment of all desires; that which forms the man, serves for his happiness, glory, proper food, and honour.

11. Next comes a Sûdadohas verse, then a Dhayyâ, then a Sûdadohas verse. The Sûdadohas is a man, the Dhayyâ a woman, therefore he recites the Dhayyâ as embraced on both sides by the Sûdadohas. Therefore does the seed of both, when it is effused, obtain oneness, and this with regard to the

---

[1] These verses are given Ait. Âr. V, 2, 2, 9.

1. Imâ nu kam (Rv. X, 157)	.	.	.	.	5
2. Â yâhi (Rv. X, 172)	.	.	.	.	4
3. Pra va indrâya &c. (not in the Sâkalya-samhitâ)				9
4. Esha brahmâ &c. (not in the Sâkalya-samhitâ)				3

21

[2] The other Stomas of the Agnishtoma are the Trivrit, Pañkadasa, Saptadasa, the Ekavimsa being the highest. Cf. I, 5, 1, 3.

woman only.   Hence birth takes place in and from
the woman.   Therefore he recites that Dhayyâ in
that place [1].

THIRD KHAN̄DA.

1. He recites the eighty tristichs of Gâyatrîs [2].
Verily, the eighty Gâyatrî tristichs are this world
(earth).   Whatever there is in this world of glory,
greatness, wives, food, and honour, may I obtain it,
may I win it, may it be mine.

2. Next comes the Sûdadohas verse.   Sûdadohas
verily is breath.   He joins this world with breath.

3. He recites the eighty tristichs of Br̄ihatîs.
Verily, the eighty Br̄ihatî tristichs are the world of
the sky.   Whatever there is in the world of the sky
of glory, greatness, wives, food, and honour, may I
obtain it, may I win it, may it be mine.

4. Next comes the Sûdadohas verse.   Sûdadohas
verily is breath.   He joins the world of the sky
with breath.

5. He recites the eighty tristichs of Ushn̄ih.   Verily, the eighty Ushn̄ih tristichs are that world, the
heaven.   Whatever there is in that world of glory,
greatness, wives, food, and honour, also the divine
being of the Devas (Brahman), may I obtain it, may
I win it, may it be mine.

6. Next comes the Sûdadohas verse.   Sûdadohas
verily is the breath.   He joins that world with
breath, yea, with breath.

---

[1] Asmin viḡavabhâge. Comm.
[2] These and the following verses form the food of the bird.
Comm. The verses themselves are given by S̄aunaka in the fifth
Âran̄yaka.

FIFTH ADHYÂYA.

FIRST KHA*N*DA.

1. He recites the Va*s*a hymn[1], wishing, May everything be in my power.

2. They (its verses) are twenty-one[2], for twenty-one are the parts (the lungs, spleen, &c.) in the belly.

3. Then the Ekavi*ms*a is verily the support of all Stomas, and the belly the support of all food.

4. They consist of different metres. Verily, the intestines are confused, some small, some large.

5. He recites them with the pra*n*ava[3], according to the metre[4], and according to rule[5]. Verily, the intestines are according to rule, as it were; some shorter, some longer.

6. Next comes the Sûdadohas verse. Sûdadohas verily is breath. He joins the joints with breath.

7. After having recited that verse twelve times he

---

[1] Having recited the verses which form the body, neck, head, wings, and tail of the bird, also the food intended for the bird, he now describes the Va*s*a hymn, i. e. the hymn composed by Va*s*a, Rv. VIII, 46. That hymn takes the place of the stomach, which receives the food intended for the bird. Cf. Ait. Âr. V, 2, 5. In I, 5, 2, 4 it is called a Nivid.

[2] Verses 1–20 of the Va*s*a hymn, and one Sûdadohas.

[3] Pra*n*âvam means 'with pra*n*ava,' i. e. inserting Om in the proper places.

[4] According as the metres of the different verses are fixed by *S*aunaka, Ait. Âr. V, 2, 5, who says that verse 15 is Dvipadâ, and that the last four words, nûnam atha, form an Ekapadâ.

[5] According to rule, i. e. so that they should come right as Â*s*valâyana has prescribed the recitation of Dvipadâ and Ekapadâ verses. In a Dvipadâ there should be a stop after the first foot, and Om at the end of the second. In an Ekapadâ there should be Om at the beginning and at the end.

leaves it off there.   These prânas are verily twelve-
fold, seven in the head, two on the breast, three
below.   In these twelve places the prânas are contained, there they are perfect.   Therefore he leaves
it off there [1].

8. The hymn indrâgnî yuvam su nah (Rv. VIII,
40) forms the two thighs (of the bird) belonging to
Indra and Agni, the two supports with broad bones.

9. These (verses) consist of six feet, so that they
may stand firm.   Man stands firm on two feet,
animals on four.   He thus places man (the sacrificer), standing on two feet, among four-footed
cattle.

10. The second verse has seven feet, and he
makes it into a Gâyatrî and Anushtubh.   Gâyatrî is
Brahman, Anushtubh is speech; and he thus puts
together speech with Brahman.

11. He recites a Trishtubh at the end.   Trishtubh
is strength, and thus does he come round animals
by strength.   Therefore animals come near where
there is strength (of command, &c.); they come to
be roused and to rise up, (they obey the commands
of a strong shepherd.)

SECOND KHANDA.

1. When he recites the Nishkevalya hymn addressed to Indra (Rv. X, 50), pra vo mahe, he inserts
a Nivid [2] (between the fourth and fifth verses).   Thus
he clearly places strength in himself (in the sastra,
in the bird, in himself).

2. They are Trishtubhs and Gagatîs.

---

[1] He repeats the Sûdadohas verse no more. Comm.
[2] Sentences like indro devah somam pibatu.

3. There they say: 'Why does he insert a Nivid among mixed Trishtubhs and Gagatis[1]?' But surely one metre would never support the Nivid of this day, nor fill it: therefore he inserts the Nivid among mixed Trishtubhs and Gagatis.

4. Let him know that this day has three Nivids: the Vasa hymn is a Nivid, the Vâlakhilyas[2] are a Nivid, and the Nivid itself is a Nivid. Thus let him know that day as having three Nivids.

5. Then follow the hymns vane na vâ (Rv. X, 29) and yo gâta eva (Rv. II, 12). In the fourth verse of the former hymn occur the words anne samasya yad asan manîshâh, and they serve for the winning of proper food.

6. Then comes an insertion. As many Trishtubh and Gagatî verses[3], taken from the ten Mañdalas and addressed to Indra, as they insert (between the two above-mentioned hymns), after changing them into Brihatîs, so many years do they live beyond the (usual) age (of one hundred years). By this insertion age is obtained.

7. After that he recites the Saganîya hymn, wishing that cattle may always come to his offspring.

8. Then he recites the Târkshya hymn[4]. Târkshya is verily welfare, and the hymn leads to welfare. Thus (by reciting the hymn) he fares well[5].

---

[1] According to the Prakriti of the Agnishtoma they ought to be all Trishtubhs. Comm.

[2] These hymns occur in the eighty Brihatî tristichs.

[3] From the Samhitâ, which consists of ten thousand verses. Comm.

[4] Rv. X, 178. Târksha Garuda being the deity of the hymn, it is called Târkshya.

[5] Cf. I, 5, 3, 13.

9. Then he recites the Ekapadâ (indro vi*sv*a*m* vi râ*g*ati), wishing, May I be everything at once, and may I thus finish the whole work of metres[1].

10. In reciting the hymn indra*m* vi*sv*â avîv*ri*dhan (Rv. I, 11) he intertwines the first seven verses by intertwining their feet[2]. There are seven prâ*n*as (openings) in the head, and he thus places seven prâ*n*as in the head. The eighth verse (half-verse) he does not intertwine[3]. The eighth is speech, and he thinks, May my speech never be intertwined with the other prâ*n*as. Speech therefore, though dwelling in the same abode as the other prâ*n*as, is not intertwined with them.

11. He recites the Virâ*g* verses[4]. Verily, Virâ*g* verses are food, and they thus serve for the gaining of food.

12. He ends with the hymn of Vasish*th*a[5], wishing, May I be Vasish*th*a!

13. But let him end with the fifth verse, esha stomo maha ugrâya vâhe, which, possessing the word mahat, is auspicious.

14. In the second foot of the fifth verse the word dhuri occurs. Verily, dhu*h* (the place where the horse is fastened to the car) is the end (of the car). This day also is the end (of the sacrifice which lasts a whole year)[6]. Thus the verse is fit for the day.

---

[1] The Ekapadâ forms the last metre in this ceremony.

[2] The first and last half-verses of the hymn are not to be intertwined. Of the remaining fourteen half-verses he joins, for instance, the fourth foot of the first verse with the second foot of the second verse, and so on. Comm.

[3] Because nothing more follows. Comm.

[4] Rv. VII, 22, 1–6.   [5] Rv. VII, 24.

[6] The last day is the udayanîyâtirâtra. Comm.

15. In the third foot the word arka is auspicious.

16. The last foot is: 'Make our glory high as heaven over heaven.' Thus wherever Brahmanic speech is uttered, there his glory will be, when he who knows this finishes with that verse. Therefore let a man who knows this, finish (the Nishkevalya) with that verse.

THIRD KHA*N*DA [1].

1. Tat savitur v*ri*n*î*mahe (Rv. V, 82, 1–3) and adyâ no deva savitar (Rv. V, 82, 4–6) are the beginning (pratipad) and the next step (anu*k*ara) of the Vai*s*vadeva hymn, taken from the Ekâha ceremonial and therefore proper [2].

2. On that day [3] much is done now and then which has to be hidden, and has to be atoned for. Atonement is rest, the one-day sacrifice. Therefore at the end of the year the sacrificers rest on this atonement as their rest. He who knows this rests firm, and they also for whom a Hot*ri* priest who knows this, recites this hymn.

3. Then (follows) the hymn addressed to Savit*ri*, tad devasya savitur vâryam mahat (Rv. IV, 53). Verily, mahat, great, (in this foot) is the end [4]. This day too is the end. Thus the verse is fit for the day.

---

[1] After finishing the Nishkevalya of the noon-libation, he explains the vai*s*vadeva*s*astra of the third libation.

[2] The norm of the Mahâvrata is the Vi*s*va*g*it, and the norm of that, the Agnish*t*oma Ekâha. The verses to be used for the Vai*s*vadeva hymn are prescribed in those normal sacrifices, and are here adopted.

[3] Cf. Ait. Âr. I, 2, 1, 2.

[4] Nothing higher than the great can be wished for or obtained. Comm.

4. The hymn katarâ pûrvâ katarâ parâyo*h* (Rv. I, 185), addressed to Dyâvâp*ri*thivî, is one in which many verses have the same ending. Verily, this day also (the mahâvrata) is one in which many receive the same reward [1]. Thus it is fit for the day.

5. The hymn ana*s*vo *g*âto anabhîsur ukthya*h* (Rv. IV, 36) is addressed to the *Ri*bhus.

6. In the first verse the word tri (*k*akra*h*) occurs, and trivat [2] is verily the end. This day also is the end (of the sacrifice). Thus the verse is fit for the day.

7. The hymn asya vâmasya palitasya hotu*h* (Rv. I, 164), addressed to the Vi*s*vedevas, is multiform. This day also is multiform [3]. Thus the verse is fit for the day.

8. He recites the end of it, beginning with gaurîr mimâya (Rv. I, 164, 41).

9. The hymn â no bhadrâ*h* kratavo yantu vi*s*vata*h* (Rv. I, 89), addressed to the Vi*s*vedevas, forms the Nividdhâna, taken from the Ekâha ceremonial, and therefore proper.

10. On that day much is done now and then which has to be hidden, and has to be atoned for. Atonement is rest, the one-day sacrifice. Therefore at the end of the year the sacrificers rest on this atonement as their rest. He who knows this rests firm, and they also for whom a Hot*ri* priest who knows this, recites this hymn.

11. The hymn vai*s*vânarâya dhisha*n*âm *ri*ta-

---

[1] All who perform the ceremony obtain Brahman. Cf. § 12.

[2] The third wheel, in addition to the usual two wheels, forms the end of a carriage, as before the dhu*h*, cf. I, 5, 2, 14. This day also is the end.

[3] Consisting of Vedic hymns and dances, &c. Comm.

vṛidhe (Rv. III, 2) forms the beginning of the Âgnimâruta. Dhishaṇâ, thought, is verily the end, this day also is the end. Thus it is fit for the day.

12. The hymn prayagyavo maruto bhrâgadṛishṭa-yaḥ (Rv. V, 55), addressed to the Maruts, is one in which many verses have the same ending. Verily, this day also is one in which many receive the same reward. Thus it is fit for the day [1].

13. He recites the verse gâtavedase sunavâma somam (Rv. I, 99, 1), addressed to Gâtavedas, before the (next following) hymn. That verse addressed to Gâtavedas is verily welfare, and leads to welfare. Thus (by reciting it) he fares well [2].

14. The hymn imam stomam arhate gâtavedase (Rv. I, 94), addressed to Gâtavedas, is one in which many verses have the same ending. Verily, this day also (the mahâvrata) is one in which many receive the same reward. Thus it is fit for the day, yea, it is fit for the day.

---

[1] Cf. § 4.   [2] Cf. I, 5, 2, 8.

SECOND ÂRAⁿYAᐧKA.

FIRST ADHYÂYA.

First Khaⁿda.

With the second Âraⁿyaka the Upanishad begins. It comprises the second and third Âraⁿyakas, and may be said to consist of three divisions, or three Upanishads. Their general title is Bahvrika-upanishad, sometimes Mahaitareya-upanishad, while the Upanishad generally known as Aitareya-upanishad comprises the 4th, 5th, and 6th adhyâyas only of the second Âraⁿyaka.

The character of the three component portions of the Upanishad can best be described in Saṅkara's own words (Âr. III, 1, 1, Introd. p. 306): 'There are three classes of men who want to acquire knowledge. The highest consists of those who have turned away from the world, whose minds are fixed on one subject and collected, and who yearn to be free at once. For these a knowledge of Brahman is intended, as taught in the Ait. Âr. II, 4-6. The middle class are those who wish to become free gradually by attaining to the world of Hiraⁿyagarbha. For them the knowledge and worship of Prâna (breath and life) is intended, as explained in the Ait. Âr. II, 1-3. The lowest class consists of those who do not care either for immediate or gradual freedom, but who desire nothing but offspring, cattle, &c. For these the meditative worship of the Samhitâ is intended, as explained in the third Âraⁿyaka. They cling too strongly to the letter of the sacred text to be able to surrender it for a knowledge either of Prâⁿa (life) or of Brahman.'

The connexion between the Upanishad or rather the three Upanishads and the first Âraⁿyaka seems at first sight very slight. Still we soon perceive that it would be impossible to understand the first Upanishad, without a previous knowledge of the Mahâvrata ceremony as described in the first Âraⁿyaka.

On this point too there are some pertinent remarks in Saṅkara's commentary on the Âraⁿyaka II, 1, 2. 'Our first duty,' he says, 'consists in performing sacrifices, such as are described in the first portion of the Veda, the Samhitâs, Brâhmaⁿas, and, to a certain extent, in the Âraⁿyakas also. Afterwards arises a desire for knowledge, which cannot be satisfied except a man has first attained complete concentration of thought (ekâgratâ). In order to acquire that concentration, the performance of certain upâsanas or meditations is enjoined, such as we find described in our Upanishad, viz. in Âr. II, 1–3.'

This meditation or, as it is sometimes translated, worship is of two kinds, either brahmopâsana or pratîkopâsana. Brahmopâsana or meditation on Brahman consists in thinking of him as distinguished by certain qualities. Pratîkopâsana or meditation on symbols consists in looking upon certain worldly objects as if they were Brahman, in order thus to withdraw the mind from the too powerful influence of external objects.

These objects, thus lifted up into symbols of Brahman, are of two kinds, either connected with sacrifice or not. In our Upanishad we have to deal with the former class only, viz. with certain portions of the Mahâvrata, as described in the first Âra*n*yaka. In order that the mind may not be entirely absorbed by the sacrifice, it is lifted up during the performance from the consideration of these sacrificial objects to a meditation on higher objects, leading up at last to Brahman as prâ*n*a or life.

This meditation is to be performed by the priests, and while they meditate they may meditate on a hymn or on a single word of it as meaning something else, such as the sun, the earth, or the sky, but not vice versâ. And if in one *S*âkhâ, as in that of the Aitareyins, for instance, a certain hymn has been symbolically explained, the same explanation may be adopted by another *S*âkhâ also, such as that of the Kaushîtakins. It is not necessary, however, that every part of the sacrifice should be accompanied by meditation, but it is left optional to the priest in what particular meditation he wishes to engage, nor is even the time of the sacrifice the only right time for him to engage in these meditations.

1. This is the path : this sacrifice, and this Brahman. This is the true [1].

2. Let no man swerve from it, let no man transgress it.

---

[1] Comm. The path is twofold, consisting of works and knowledge. Works or sacrifices have been described in the Sa*m*hitâ, the Brâhma*n*a, and the first Âra*n*yaka. Knowledge of Brahman forms the subject of the second and third Âra*n*yakas. The true path is that of knowledge.

3. For the old (sages) did not transgress it, and those who did transgress, became lost.

4. This has been declared by a *Ri*shi (Rv. VIII, 101, 14): 'Three (classes of) people transgressed, others settled down round about the venerable (Agni, fire); the great (sun) stood in the midst of the worlds, the blowing (Vâyu, air) entered the Harits (the dawns, or the ends of the earth).'

5. When he says: 'Three (classes of) people transgressed,' the three (classes of) people who transgressed are what we see here (on earth, born again) as birds, trees, herbs, and serpents [1].

6. When he says: 'Others settled down round about the venerable,' he means those who now sit down to worship Agni (fire).

7. When he says: 'The great stood in the midst of the worlds,' the great one in the midst of the world is meant for this Âditya, the sun.

8. When he says: 'The blowing entered the Harits,' he means that Vâyu, the air, the purifier, entered all the corners of the earth [2].

SECOND KHA*N*DA.

1. People say: 'Uktha, uktha,' hymns, hymns! (without knowing what uktha, hymn [3], means.) The

---

[1] Va*n*gâ*h* is explained by vanagatâ v*ri*kshâ*h*; avagadhâ*h* is explained by vrîhiyavâdyâ oshadhaya*h*; îrapâdâ*h* is explained by ura*h*-pâdâ*h* sarpâ*h*. Possibly they are all old ethnic names, like Va*n*ga, *K*era, &c. In Ânandatîrtha's commentary vayâ*m*si are explained by Pi*s*â*k*a, Va*n*gâvagadhas by Râkshasa, and Îrapâdas by Asuras.

[2] Three classes of men go to Naraka (hell); the fourth class, full of faith and desirous of reaching the highest world, worships Agni, Vâyu, and other gods. Comm.

[3] The Comm. explains uktha as that from whence the favour of the gods arises, uttish*th*aty anena devatâprasâda iti vyutpatte*h*.

hymn is truly (to be considered as) the earth, for from it all whatsoever exists arises.

2. The object of its praise is Agni (fire), and the eighty verses (of the hymn) are food, for by means of food one obtains everything.

3. The hymn is truly the sky, for the birds fly along the sky, and men drive following the sky. The object of its praise is Vâyu (air), and the eighty verses (of the hymn) are food, for by means of food one obtains everything.

4. The hymn is truly the heaven, for from its gift (rain) all whatsoever exists arises. The object of its praise is Âditya (the sun), and the eighty verses are food, for by means of food one obtains everything.

5. So much with reference to the gods (mythological); now with reference to man (physiological).

6. The hymn is truly man. He is great, he is Pragâpati. Let him think, I am the hymn.

7. The hymn is his mouth, as before in the case of the earth.

8. The object of its praise is speech, and the eighty verses (of the hymn) are food, for by means of food he obtains everything.

9. The hymn is the nostrils, as before in the case of the sky.

10. The object of its praise is breath, and the eighty verses (of the hymn) are food, for by means of food he obtains everything.

11. The slight bent (at the root) of the nose is, as it were, the place of the brilliant (Âditya, the sun).

The object is now to show that the uktha or hymn used at the Mahâvrata ceremony has a deeper meaning than it seems to have, and that its highest aim is Brahman; not, however, the highest Brahman, but Brahman considered as life (prâna).

12. The hymn is the forehead, as before in the case of heaven. The object of its praise is the eye, and the eighty verses (of the hymn) are food, for by means of food he obtains everything.

13. The eighty verses (of the hymn) are alike food with reference to the gods as well as with reference to man. For all these beings breathe and live by means of food indeed. By food (given in alms, &c.) he conquers this world, by food (given in sacrifice) he conquers the other. Therefore the eighty verses (of the hymn) are alike food, with reference to the gods as well as with reference to man.

14. All this that is food, and all this that consumes food, is only the earth, for from the earth arises all whatever there is.

15. And all that goes hence (dies on earth), heaven consumes it all; and all that goes thence (returns from heaven to a new life) the earth consumes it all.

16. That earth is thus both food and consumer.

He also (the true worshipper who meditates on himself as being the uktha) is both consumer and consumed (subject and object[1]). No one possesses that which he does not eat, or the things which do not eat him[2].

---

[1] As a master who lives by his servants, while his servants live by him. Comm.

[2] I have translated these paragraphs, as much as possible, according to the commentator. I doubt whether, either in the original or in the interpretation of the commentator, they yield any very definite sense. They are vague speculations, vague, at least, to us, though intended by the Brahmans to give a deeper meaning to certain ceremonial observances connected with the Mahâvrata. The uktha, or hymn, which is to be meditated on, as connected with the sacrifice, is part of the Mahâvrata, an important ceremony, to be

THIRD KHA*N*DA.

1. Next follows the origin of seed. The seed of Pra*g*âpati are the Devas (gods). The seed of the Devas is rain. The seed of rain are herbs. The seed of herbs is food. The seed of food is seed. The seed of seed are creatures. The seed of creatures is the heart. The seed of the heart is the mind. The seed of the mind is speech (Veda). The seed of speech is action (sacrifice). The action done (in a former state) is this man, the abode of Brahman.

2. He (man) consists of food (irâ), and because he consists of food (irâmaya), he consists of gold (hira*n*maya [1]). He who knows this becomes golden in the other world, and is seen as golden (as the sun) for the benefit of all beings.

performed on the last day but one (the twenty-fourth) of the Gavâmayana sacrifice. That sacrifice lasts a whole year, and its performance has been fully described in the Brâhma*n*as and Âra*n*yakas. But while the ordinary performer of the Mahâvrata has simply to recite the uktha or nishkevalya-*s*astra, consisting of eighty verses (*tri*ka) in the Gâyatrî, Br*i*hatî, and Ush*n*ih metres, the more advanced worshipper (or priest) is to know that this uktha has a deeper meaning, and is to meditate on it as being the earth, sky, heaven, also as the human body, mouth, nostrils, and forehead. The worshipper is in fact to identify himself by meditation with the uktha in all its senses, and thus to become the universal spirit or Hira*n*yagarbha. By this process he becomes the consumer and consumed, the subject and object, of everything, while another sacrificer, not knowing this, remains in his limited individual sphere, or, as the text expresses it, does not possess what he cannot eat (perceive), or what cannot eat him (perceive him). The last sentence is explained differently by the commentator, but in connexion with the whole passage it seems to me to become more intelligible, if interpreted as I have proposed to interpret it.

[1] Play on words. Comm.

FOURTH KHA*N*DA.

1. Brahman (in the shape of prâ*n*a, breath) entered into that man by the tips of his feet, and because Brahman entered (prâpadyata) into that man by the tips of his feet, therefore people call them the tips of the feet (prapada), but hoofs and claws in other animals.

2. Then Brahman crept up higher, and therefore they were (called)[1] the thighs (ûrû).

3. Then he said: 'Grasp wide,' and that was (called) the belly (udara).

4. Then he said: 'Make room for me,' and that was (called) the chest (uras).

5. The *S*ârkarâkshyas meditate on the belly as Brahman, the Âru*n*is on the heart[2]. Both (these places) are Brahman indeed[3].

6. But Brahman crept upwards and came to the head, and because he came to the head, therefore the head is called head[4].

7. Then these delights alighted in the head, sight, hearing, mind, speech, breath.

8. Delights alight on him who thus knows, why the head is called head.

9. These (five delights or senses) strove together, saying: 'I am the uktha (hymn), I am the uktha[5].' 'Well,' they said, 'let us all go out from

---

[1] These are all plays on words. Comm.

[2] This does not appear to be the case either in the *Kh.* Up. V, 15; 17, or in the *S*atapatha-brâhma*n*a X, 6, 1.

[3] The pluti in tâ3i is explained as *s*âstrîyaprasiddhyarthâ.

[4] All puns, as if we were to say, because he hied up to the head, therefore the head was called head.

[5] Each wished to be identified with the uktha, as it was said before that the human body, mouth, nostrils, forehead were to be identified with the uktha. Cf. Kaush. Up. III, 3.

this body; then on whose departure this body shall fall, he shall be the uktha among us[1].'

10. Speech went out, yet the body without speaking remained, eating and drinking.

Sight went out, yet the body without seeing remained, eating and drinking.

Hearing went out, yet the body without hearing remained, eating and drinking.

Mind went out, yet the body, as if blinking, remained, eating and drinking.

Breath went out, then when breath was gone out, the body fell.

11. It was decayed, and because people said, it decayed, therefore it was (called) body (sarîra). That is the reason of its name.

12. If a man knows this, then the evil enemy who hates him decays, or the evil enemy who hates him is defeated.

13. They strove again, saying: 'I am the uktha, I am the uktha.' 'Well,' they said, 'let us enter that body again; then on whose entrance this body shall rise again, he shall be the uktha among us.'

14. Speech entered, but the body lay still. Sight entered, but the body lay still. Hearing entered, but the body lay still. Mind entered, but the body lay still. Breath entered, and when breath had entered, the body rose, and it became the uktha.

15. Therefore breath alone is the uktha.

16. Let people know that breath is the uktha indeed.

17. The Devas (the other senses) said to breath: 'Thou art the uktha, thou art all this, we are thine, thou art ours.'

---

[1] Cf. *Kh.* Up. V, 1; *Brih.* Up. VI, 1; Kaush. Up. II, 12–14; III, 2; Prasna Up. II, 1.

18. This has also been said by a *Ri*shi (Rv. VIII, 92, 32): 'Thou art ours, we are thine.'

FIFTH KHA*N*DA.

1. Then the Devas carried him (the breath) forth, and being carried forth, he was stretched out, and when people said, ' He was stretched out,' then it was in the morning ; when they said, ' He is gone to rest,' then it was in the evening. Day, therefore, is the breathing up, night the breathing down [1].

2. Speech is Agni, sight that Âditya (sun), mind the moon, hearing the Di*s* (quarters): this is the prahitâ*m* sa*m*yoga [2], the union of the deities as sent forth. These deities (Agni, &c.) are thus in the body, but their (phenomenal) appearance yonder is among the deities—this was intended.

3. And Hira*n*yadat Vaida also, who knew this (and who by his knowledge had become Hira*n*ya-garbha or the universal spirit), said : ' Whatever they do not give to me, they do not possess themselves.' I know the prahitâ*m* sa*m*yoga, the union of the deities, as entered into the body [3]. This is it.

---

[1] All these are plays on words, prâtar being derived from prâtâyi, sâyam from samâgât. The real object, however, is to show that breath, which is the uktha, which is the worshipper, is endowed with certain qualities, viz. time, speech, &c.

[2] The meaning is, that the four deities, Agni, Âditya, Moon, and the Di*s* proceed from their own places to dwell together in the body of man, and that this is called the prahitâ*m* sa*m*yoga*h*. Prahit is explained as prahita, placed, sent. It is probably formed from hi, not from dhâ. Prahito*h* sa*m*yo*g*anam is the name of a Sâman, Ind. Stud. III, 225. As Devas or gods they appear each in its own place. The whole passage is very obscure.

[3] All this is extremely obscure, possibly incorrect. For yam, unless it refers to some other word, we expect yan. For dadyu*h* one expects dadyât. What is intended is that Hira*n*yadat had

4. To him who knows this all creatures, without being constrained, offer gifts.

5. That breath is (to be called) sattya (the true), for sat is breath, ti is food, yam is the sun[1]. This is threefold, and threefold the eye also may be called, it being white, dark, and the pupil. He who knows why true is true (why sattya is sattya), even if he should speak falsely, yet what he says is true.

SIXTH KHAÑDA.

1. Speech is his (the breath's) rope, the names the knots[2]. Thus by his speech as by a rope, and by his names as by knots, all this is bound. For all this are names indeed, and with speech he calls everything.

2. People carry him who knows this, as if they were bound by a rope.

3. Of the body of the breath thus meditated on, the Ushñih verse forms the hairs, the Gâyatrî the skin, the Trishtubh the flesh, the Anushtubh the muscles, the Gagatî the bone, the Pañkti the marrow, the Brihatî the breath[3] (prâña). He is covered with the verses (khandas, metres). Because he is thus covered with verses, therefore they call them khandas (coverings, metres).

4. If a man knows the reason why khandas are called khandas, the verses cover him in whatever place he likes against any evil deed.

---

through meditation acquired identity with the universal spirit, and that therefore he might say that whatever was not surrendered to him did not really belong to anybody. On Hirañyadat, see Ait. Brâhm. III, 6.

[1] Cf. *Kh*. Up. VIII, 3, 5.

[2] The rope is supposed to be the chief rope to which various smaller ropes are attached for fastening animals.

[3] Here conceived as the air breathed, not as the deity. Comm.

5. This is said by a *Ri*shi (Rv. I, 164, 13):—

6. 'I saw (the breath) as a guardian, never tiring, coming and going on his ways (the arteries). That breath (in the body, being identified with the sun among the Devas), illuminating the principal and intermediate quarters of the sky, is returning constantly in the midst of the worlds.'

He says: 'I saw a guardian,' because he, the breath, is a guardian, for he guards everything.

7. He says: 'Never tiring,' because the breath never rests.

8. He says: 'Coming and going on his ways,' because the breath comes and goes on his ways.

9. He says: 'Illuminating the principal and intermediate,' because he illuminates these only, the principal and intermediate quarters of the sky.

10. He says: 'He is returning constantly in the midst of the worlds,' because he returns indeed constantly in the midst of the worlds.

11. And then, there is another verse (Rv. I, 55, 81): 'They are covered like caves by those who make them,'

12. For all this is covered indeed by breath.

13. This ether is supported by breath as B*ri*hatî, and as this ether is supported by breath as B*ri*hatî, so one should know that all things, not excepting ants, are supported by breath as B*ri*hatî.

SEVENTH KHA*N*DA.

1. Next follow the powers of that Person [1].

2. By his speech earth and fire were created.

---

[1] The purusha, as described before in the second chapter, is the Pra*g*âpati or universal spirit with whom the worshipper is to identify himself by meditation. The manifestations of his power consist in creating the earth, fire, the sky, the air, heaven, the sun.

Herbs are produced on the earth, and Agni (fire) makes them ripe and sweet. 'Take this, take this,' thus saying do earth and fire serve their parent, speech.

3. As far as the earth reaches, as far as fire reaches, so far does his world extend, and as long as the world of the earth and fire does not decay, so long does his world not decay who thus knows this power of speech.

4. By breath (in the nose) the sky and the air were created. People follow the sky, and hear along the sky, while the air carries along pure scent. Thus do sky and air serve their parent, the breath.

As far as the sky reaches, as far as the air reaches, so far does his world extend, and as long as the world of the sky and the air does not decay, so long does his world not decay who thus knows this power of breath.

5. By his eye heaven and the sun were created. Heaven gives him rain and food, while the sun causes his light to shine. Thus do the heaven and the sun serve their parent, the eye.

As far as heaven reaches and as far as the sun reaches, so far does his world extend, and as long as the world of heaven and the sun does not decay, so long does his world not decay who thus knows the power of the eye.

6. By his ear the quarters and the moon were created. From all the quarters they come to him, and from all the quarters he hears, while the moon produces for him the bright and the dark halves for the sake of sacrificial work. Thus do the quarters and the moon serve their parent, the ear.

As far as the quarters reach and as far as the

moon reaches, so far does his world extend, and as
long as the world of the quarters and the moon does
not decay, so long does his world not decay who
thus knows the power of the ear.

7. By his mind the water and Varu*n*a were
créated. Water yields to him faith (being used for
sacred acts), Varu*n*a keeps his offspring within the
law. Thus do water and Varu*n*a serve their parent,
the mind.

As far as water reaches and as far as Varu*n*a
reaches, so far does his world extend, and as long
as the world of water and Varu*n*a does not decay,
so long does his world not decay who thus knows
the power of the mind.

Eighth Kha*n*da [1].

1. Was it water really ? Was it water ? Yes,
all this was water indeed. This (water) was the root
(cause), that (the world) was the shoot (effect). He
(the person) is the father, they (earth, fire, &c.) are
the sons. Whatever there is belonging to the son,
belongs to the father ; whatever there is belonging to
the father, belongs to the son. This was intended[2].

2. Mahidâsa Aitareya, who knew this, said : ‘ I
know myself (reaching) as far as the gods, and I
know the gods (reaching) as far as me. For these

---

[1] Having described how Prâ*n*a, the breath, and his companions
or servants created the world, he now discusses the question of
the material cause of the world out of which it was created.
Water, which is said to be the material of the world, is explained
by the commentator to mean here the five elements.

[2] Cause and effect are not entirely separated, therefore water,
as the elementary cause, and earth, fire, &c., as its effect, are one ;
likewise the worshipper, as the father, and the earth, fire, &c. as his
sons, as described above. Mûla and tûla, root and shoot, are evidently chosen for the sake of the rhyme, to signify cause and effect.

gods receive their gifts from hence, and are supported from hence.'

3. This is the mountain[1], viz. eye, ear, mind, speech, and breath. They call it the mountain of Brahman.

4. He who knows this, throws down the evil enemy who hates him; the evil enemy who hates him is defeated.

5. He (the Prâ*n*a, identified with Brahman) is the life, the breath; he is being (while the *g*îvâtman remains), and not-being (when the *g*îvâtman departs).

6. The Devas (speech, &c.) worshipped him (prâ*n*a) as Bhûti or being, and thus they became great beings. And therefore even now a man who sleeps, breathes like bhûrbhu*h*.

7. The Asuras worshipped him as Abhûti or not-being, and thus they were defeated.

8. He who knows this, becomes great by himself, while the evil enemy who hates him, is defeated.

9. He (the breath) is death (when he departs), and immortality (while he abides).

10. And this has been said by a *R*i*s*hi (Rv. I, 164, 38) :—

11. 'Downwards and upwards he (the wind of the breath) goes, held by food;'—for this up-breathing, being held back by the down-breathing, does not move forward (and leave the body altogether).

12. 'The immortal dwells with the mortal;'—for through him (the breath) all this dwells together, the bodies being clearly mortal, but this being (the breath), being immortal.

---

[1] Prâ*n*a is called the giri*h*, because it is swallowed or hidden by the other senses (gira*n*ât). Again a mere play of words, intended to show that Brahman under the form of Prâ*n*a, or life, is to be meditated on.

13. 'These two (body and breath) go for ever in different directions (the breath moving the senses of the body, the body supporting the senses of the breath : the former going upwards to another world, the body dying and remaining on earth). They increase the one (the body), but they do not increase the other,' i. e. they increase these bodies (by food), but this being (breath) is immortal.

14. He who knows this becomes immortal in that world (having become united with Hiraṇyagarbha), and is seen as immortal (in the sun) by all beings, yea, by all beings.

SECOND ADHYÂYA[1].

First Khaṇḍa.

1. He (the sun), who shines, honoured this world (the body of the worshipper, by entering into it), in the form of man[2] (the worshipper who meditates on breath). For he who shines (the sun) is (the same as) the breath. He honoured this (body of the worshipper) during a hundred years, therefore there are a hundred years in the life of a man. Because he honoured him during a hundred years, therefore there are (the poets of the first Maṇḍala of the Rig-veda, called) the Satarḳin, (having honour for a

---

[1] In the first adhyâya various forms of meditating on Uktha, conceived as Prâṇa (life), have been declared. In the second some other forms of meditation, all extremely fanciful, are added. They are of interest, however, as showing the existence of the hymns of the Rig-veda, divided and arranged as we now possess them, at the time when this Âraṇyaka was composed.

[2] The identity of the sun and of breath as living in man has been established before. It is the same power in both, conceived either adhidaivatam (mythological) or adhyâtmam (physiological).

hundred years.) Therefore people call him who is really Prâña (breath), the Satarkin poets [1].

2. He (breath) placed himself in the midst of all whatsoever exists. Because he placed himself in the midst of all whatsoever exists, therefore there are (the poets of the second to the ninth Mañdala of the Rig-veda, called) the Mâdhyamas. Therefore people call him who is really Prâña (breath), the Mâdhyama poets.

3. He as up-breathing is the swallower (gritsa), as down-breathing he is delight (mada). Because as up-breathing he is swallower (gritsa) and as down-breathing delight (mada), therefore there is (the poet of the second Mañdala of the Rig-veda, called) Gritsamada. Therefore people call him who is really Prâña (breath), Gritsamada.

4. Of him (breath) all this whatsoever was a friend. Because of him all (visvam) this whatsoever was a friend (mitram), therefore there is (the poet of the third Mañdala of the Rig-veda, called) Visvâmitra. Therefore people call him who is really Prâña (breath), Visvâmitra.

5. The Devas (speech, &c.) said to him (the breath) : 'He is to be loved by all of us.' Because the Devas said of him, that he was to be loved (vâma) by all of them, therefore there is (the poet of the fourth Mañdala of the Rig-veda, called) Vâmadeva. Therefore people call him who is really Prâña (breath), Vâmadeva.

6. He (breath) guarded all this whatsoever from evil. Because he guarded (atrâyata) all this whatso-

---

[1] The real ground for the name is that the poets of the first Mañdala composed on an average each about a hundred Rik verses.

ever from evil, therefore there are (the poets of the
fifth Maṇḍala of the Rig-veda, called) Atrayaḥ.
Therefore people call him who is really Prâṇa
(breath), Atrayaḥ.

SECOND KHAṆDA.

1. He (breath) is likewise a Bibhradvâga (bringer
of offspring). Offspring is vâga, and he (breath)
supports offspring. Because he supports it, therefore there is (the poet of the sixth Maṇḍala of the
Rig-veda, called) Bharadvâga. Therefore people
call him who is really Prâṇa (breath), Bharadvâga.

2. The Devas (speech, &c.) said to him : 'He it
is who chiefly causes us to dwell on earth.' Because
the Devas said of him, that he chiefly caused them
to dwell on earth, therefore there is (the poet of the
seventh Maṇḍala of the Rig-veda, called) Vasishṭha.
Therefore people call him who is really Prâṇa
(breath), Vasishṭha [1].

3. He (breath) went forth towards [2] all this whatsoever. Because he went forth toward all this whatsoever, therefore there are (the poets of the eighth
Maṇḍala of the Rig-veda, called) the Pragâthas.
Therefore people call him who is really Prâṇa
(breath), the Pragâthas.

4. He (breath) purified all this whatsoever. Because he purified all this whatsoever, therefore there

---

[1] I translate in accordance with the commentator, and probably
with the intention of the author. The same etymology is repeated
in the commentary on II, 2, 4, 2. It would be more natural to
take vasishṭha in the sense of the richest.

[2] This is the interpretation of the commentator, and the pre-
position abhi seems to show that the author too took that view
of the etymology of pragâtha.

are (the hymns and also the poets [1] of the ninth Mañdala of the Rig-veda, called) the Pavamânîs. Therefore people called him who is really Prâña (breath), the Pavamânîs.

5. He (breath) said: 'Let me be everything whatsoever, small (kshudra) and great (mahat), and this became the Kshudrasûktas and Mahâsûktas.' Therefore there were (the hymns and also the poets of the tenth Mañdala of the Rig-veda, called) the Kshudrasûktas (and Mahâsûktas). Therefore people call him who is really Prâña (breath), the Kshudrasûktas (and Mahâsûktas).

6. He (breath) said once: 'You have said what is well said (su-ukta) indeed. This became a Sûkta (hymn).' Therefore there was the Sûkta. Therefore people call him who is really Prâña (breath), Sûkta [2].

7. He (breath) is a *Rik* (verse), for he did honour [3] to all beings (by entering into them). Because he did honour to all beings, therefore there was the *Rik* verse. Therefore people call him who is really Prâña (breath), *Rik*.

8. He (breath) is an Ardharka (half-verse), for he did honour to all places (ardha) [4]. Because he did honour to all places, therefore there was the Ardharka. Therefore people call him who is really Prâña (breath), Ardharka.

---

[1] It seems, indeed, as if in the technical language of the Brahmans, the poets of the ninth Mañdala were sometimes called Pavamânîs, and the hymns of the tenth Mañdala Kshudrasûktas and Mahâsûktas (masc.) Cf. Ârsheya-brâhmaña, ed. Burnell, p. 42.

[2] The poet also is called Sûkta, taddrashtâpi sûktanâmako 'bhût. Comm.

[3] I translate according to the commentator.

[4] Ardha means both half and place.

9. He (breath) is a Pada (word) [1], for he got into all these beings. Because he got (pâdi) into all these beings, therefore there was the Pada (word). Therefore people call him who is really Prâna (breath), Pada.

10. He (breath) is an Akshara (syllable), for he pours out (ksharati) gifts to all these beings, and without him no one can pour out (atiksharati) gifts. Therefore there was the Akshara (syllable). Therefore people call him who is really Prâna (breath), Akshara [2].

11. Thus all these *Rik* verses, all Vedas, all sounds [3] are one word, viz. Prâna (breath). Let him know that Prâna is all *Rik* verses.

THIRD KHANDA.

1. While Visvâmitra was going to repeat the hymns of this day (the mahâvrata), Indra sat down near him [4]. Visvâmitra (guessing that Indra wanted food) said to him, ' This (the verses of the hymn) is food,' and repeated the thousand B*ri*hatî verses [5].

---

[1] It may also be intended for pâda, foot of a verse.

[2] The Prâna (breath) is to be meditated on as all hymns, all poets, all words, &c. Comm.

[3] All aspirated sonant consonants. Comm.

[4] Upanishasasâda, instead of upanishasâda. The mistake is probably due to a correction, sa for sha; the commentator, however, considers it as a Vedic license. Sakâro 'dhikas *kh*ândasa*h*.

[5] These are meant for the Nishkevalya hymn recited at the noon-libation of the Mahâvrata. That hymn consists of ten parts, corresponding, as we saw, to ten parts of a bird, viz. its body, neck, head, root of wings, right wing, left wing, tail, belly, chest, and thighs. The verses corresponding to these ten parts, beginning with tad id âsa bhuvaneshu *gy*esh*th*am, are given in the first Âra*ny*aka, and more fully in the fifth Âra*ny*aka by *S*aunaka.

By means of this he went to the delightful home of Indra (Svarga).

2. Indra said to him : ' *Ri*shi, thou hast come to my delightful home. *Ri*shi, repeat a second hymn [1].' Vi*s*vâmitra (guessing that Indra wanted food) said to him, ' This (the verses of the hymn) is food,' and repeated the thousand B*ri*hatî verses. By means of this he went to the delightful home of Indra (Svarga).

3. Indra said to him : ' *Ri*shi, thou hast come to my delightful home. *Ri*shi, repeat a third hymn.' Vi*s*vâmitra (guessing that Indra wanted food) said to him, ' This (the verses of the hymn) is food,' and repeated the thousand B*ri*hatî verses. By means of this he went to the delightful home of Indra (Svarga).

4. Indra said to him : ' *Ri*shi, thou hast come to my delightful home. I grant thee a boon.' Vi*s*vâmitra said : 'May I know thee.' Indra said : ' I am Prâ*n*a (breath), O *Ri*shi, thou art Prâ*n*a, all things are Prâ*n*a. For it is Prâ*n*a who shines as the sun, and I here pervade all regions under that form. This food of mine (the hymn) is my friend and my support (dakshi*n*a). This is the food prepared by Vi*s*vâmitra. I am verily he who shines (the sun).'

Though they consist of many metres, yet, when one counts the syllables, they give a thousand B*ri*hatî verses, each consisting of thirty-six syllables.

[1] Although the Nishkevalya is but one hymn, consisting of eighty tri*k*as, yet as these eighty tri*k*as were represented as three kinds of food (see Ait. Âr. II, 1, 2, 2–4), the hymn is represented as three hymns, first as eighty Gâyatrî tri*k*as, then as eighty B*ri*hatî tri*k*as, lastly as eighty Ush*n*ih tri*k*as.

FOURTH KHANDA.

1. This then becomes perfect as a thousand of Brihatî verses. Its consonants[1] form its body, its voice[2] (vowels) the soul[3], its sibilants[4] the air of the breath.

2. He who knew this became Vasish*th*a, he took this name from thence[5].

3. Indra verily declared this to Visvâmitra, and Indra verily declared this to Bharadvâ*g*a. Therefore Indra is invoked by him as a friend[6].

4. This becomes perfect as a thousand of Brihatî verses[7], and of that hymn perfect with a thousand Brihatî verses, ·there are 36,000 syllables[8]. So many are also the thousands of days of a hundred years (36,000). With the consonants they fill the nights, with the vowels the days.

5. This becomes perfect as a thousand of Brihatî verses. He who knows this, after this thousand of Brihatîs thus accomplished, becomes full of knowledge, full of the gods, full of Brahman, full of the immortal, and then goes also to the gods.

6. What I am (the worshipper), that is he (sun); what he is, that am I.

---

[1] Vyañ*g*anâni, explained by kâdini.

[2] Ghosha, explained by aspirated sonant consonants.

[3] Âtmâ, explained by madhya*s*arîram.

[4] Sashasahâ*h*. Comm.

[5] He became Prâ*n*a, and because Prâ*n*a causes all to dwell, or covers all (vâsayati), therefore the *Ri*shi was called Vasish*th*a. Comm. Cf. Ait. Âr. II, 2, 2, 2.

[6] At the Subrahma*ny*â ceremony in the Soma sacrifices, the invocations are, Indra â ga*kkh*a, hariva â ga*kkh*a.

[7] Cf. Ait. Âr. II, 3, 8, 8.

[8] Each Brihatî has thirty-six syllables.

7. This has been said by a *Ri*shi (Rv. I, 115, 1):
' The sun is the self of all that moves and rests.'

8. Let him look to that, let him look to that!

THIRD ADHYÂYA [1].

FIRST KHA*N*DA.

1. He who knows himself as the fivefold hymn (uktha), the emblem of Prâ*n*a (breath), from whence all this springs [2], he is clever. These five are the earth, air, ether, water, and fire (*g*yotis). This is the self, the fivefold uktha. For from him all this springs, and into him it enters again (at the dissolution of the world). He who knows this, becomes the refuge of his friends.

2. And to him who knows the food (object) and the feeder (subject) in that uktha, a strong son is born, and food is never wanting. Water and earth are food, for all food consists of these two. Fire and air are the feeder, for by means of them [3] man eats all food. Ether is the bowl, for all this is poured into the ether. He who knows this, becomes the bowl or support of his friends.

3. To him who knows the food and the feeder in that uktha, a strong son is born, and food is never wanting. Herbs and trees are food, animals the feeder, for animals eat herbs and trees.

4. Of them again those who have teeth above

---

[1] In this adhyâya some more qualities are explained belonging to the Mahâvrata ceremonial and the hymns employed at it, which can be meditated on as referring to Prâ*n*a, life.

[2] Because the world is the result or reward for performing a meditation on the uktha. Comm.

[3] The digestive fire is lighted by the air of the breath. Comm.

and below, shaped after the likeness of man, are feeders, the other animals are food. Therefore these overcome the other animals, for the eater is over the food.

5. He who knows this is over his friends.

SECOND KHAÍVDA[1].

1. He who knows the gradual development of the self in him (the man conceived as the uktha), obtains himself more development.

2. There are herbs and trees and all that is animated, and he knows the self gradually developing in them. For in herbs and trees sap only is seen[2], but thought (*k*itta) in animated beings.

3. Among animated beings again the self develops gradually, for in some sap (blood) is seen (as well as thought), but in others thought is not seen.

4. And in man again the self develops gradually, for he is most endowed with knowledge. He says what he has known, he sees what he has known[3]. He knows what is to happen to-morrow, he knows heaven and hell. By means of the mortal he desires the immortal—thus is he endowed.

5. With regard to the other animals hunger and thirst only are a kind of understanding. But they do not say what they have known, nor do they see

---

[1] This treats of the gradual development of life in man, particularly of the development of a thinking soul (*k*aitanya).

[2] In stones there is not even sap, but only being, sattâ. Comm.

[3] What he has known yesterday he remembers, and is able to say before men, I know this. And when he has known a thing he remembers it, and goes to the same place to see it again. Comm.

what they have known. They do not know what
is to happen to-morrow, nor heaven and hell. They
go so far and no further, for they are born according
to their knowledge (in a former life).

THIRD KHA*N*DA.

1. That man (conceived as uktha) is the sea,
rising beyond the whole world[1]. Whatever he
reaches, he wishes to go beyond[2]. If he reaches the
sky, he wishes to go beyond.

2. If he should reach that (heavenly) world, he
would wish to go beyond.

3. That man is fivefold. The heat in him is fire;
the apertures (of the senses) are ether; blood, mucus,
and seed are water ; the body is earth ; breath is air.

4. That air is fivefold, viz. up-breathing, down-
breathing, back-breathing, out-breathing, on-breathing. The other powers (devatâs), viz. sight, hearing,
mind, and speech, are comprised under up-breathing
and down-breathing. For when breath departs, they
also depart with it.

5. That man (conceived as uktha) is the sacrifice,
which is a succession now of speech and now of
thought. That sacrifice is fivefold, viz. the Agnihotra, the new and full moon sacrifices, the four-
monthly sacrifices, the animal sacrifice, the Soma
sacrifice. The Soma sacrifice is the most perfect of
sacrifices, for in it these five kinds of ceremonies
are seen : the first which precedes the libations (the
Dîkshâ, &c.), then three libations, and what follows
(the Avabh*ri*tha, &c.) is the fifth.

---

[1] Bhûloka. Comm.
[2] Should it not be aty enan manyate ?

FOURTH KHA*N*DA.

1. He who knows one sacrifice above another, one day above another, one deity above the others, he is clever. Now this great uktha (the nishke-valya-*s*astra) is the sacrifice above another, the day above another, the deity above others [1].

2. This uktha is fivefold. With regard to its being performed as a Stoma (chorus), it is Triv*ri*t, Pañ*k*ada*s*a, Saptada*s*a, Ekavi*m*sa, and Pañ*k*avi*m*sa. With regard to its being performed as a Sâman (song), it is Gâyatra, Rathantara, B*ri*hat, Bhadra, and Râ*g*ana. With regard to metre, it is Gâyatrî, Ush*n*ih, B*ri*hatî, Trish*t*ubh, and Dvipadâ. And the explanation (given before in the Âra*n*yaka) is that it is the head, the right wing, the left wing, the tail, and the body of the bird [2].

---

[1] The uktha is to be conceived as prâ*n*a, breath or life, and this prâ*n*a was shown to be above the other powers (devatâs), speech, hearing, seeing, mind. The uktha belongs to the Mahâvrata day, and that is the most important day of the Soma sacrifice. The Soma sacrifice, lastly, is above all other sacrifices.

[2] All these are technicalities connected with the singing and reciting of the uktha. The commentator says: The stoma is a collection of single *Rik* verses occurring in the *trik*as which have to be su*n*g. The Triv*ri*t stoma, as explained in the Sâma-brâhma*n*a, is as follows: There are three Sûktas, each consisting of three verses, the first being upâsmai gâyata, S. V. Uttarâr*k*ika I, 1, 1 = Rv. IX, 11. The Udgât*ri* first sings the first three verses [a] in each hymn. This is the first round. He then sings the three middle verses in each hymn. This is the second round. He lastly sings the last three verses in each h*y*mn. This is the third round. This song is called Udyatî.

The Pañ*k*ada*s*a stoma is formed out of one Sûkta only, consisting of three verses. In the first round he sings the first verse

---

[a] Hiṅk*ri* with dative is explained as gai with accusative.

3. He performs the Prastâva in five ways, he performs the Udgîtha in five ways, he performs the

---

three times, the second and third once. In the second round he sings the middle verse three times, in the third round he sings the last verse three times. This song is called Vish/uti.

The Saptadaṣa stoma is formed in the same manner, only that in the first round he sings the first verse three times, in the second the middle verse three times, in the third round the middle and last verses three times. This song is called Daṣasapta.

The Ekaviṃsa stoma is formed in the same manner, only that in the first round he sings the last verse once, in the second the first verse once, in the third the middle verse once, while the other verses are each repeated three times. This song is called Saptasaptinî.

The Pañ*kaviṃsa stoma is formed in the same manner, only that in the first round he sings the first verse three times, the second four times, the last once; in the second round the first once, the second three times, the third four times; in the third round the first five times, the second once, the last three times; or he sings in the third round the first verse four times, the second twice, the last three times.

Sâyaṇa in his commentary on the Ait. Âr. takes the Trivṛit stoma to be formed out of three hymns, each consisting of three verses, while he says that the other stomas are formed out of one hymn only. B. and R., s. v. trivṛit, state that this stoma consists of verses 1, 4, 7; 2, 5, 8; and 3, 6, 9 of the Rig-veda hymn IX, 11, but, according to Sâyaṇa, the stoma consists (1) of the first verses of the three Sûktas, upâsmai gâyata, davidyutatyâ, and pavamânasya at the beginning of the Sâma-veda-Uttarâr*ika, (2) of the second, (3) of the third verses of the same three hymns. Mahîdhâra (Yv. X, 9) takes the same view, though the MSS. seem to have left out the description of the second paryâya, while Sâyaṇa in his commentary to the Tân*dya-brâhmaṇa seems to support the opinion of B. and R. There is an omission, however, in the printed text of the commentary, which makes it difficult to see the exact meaning of Sâyaṇa.

The Pañ*kadaṣa stoma is well described by Sâyaṇa, Tân*dya Br. II, 4. Taking the Sûkta agna â yâhi (Uttarârkika 1, 1, 4 = Rv. VI, 16, 10–12), he shows the stoma to consist of (1) verse 1 × 3, 2, 3; (2) verse 1, 2 × 3, 3; (3) verse 1, 2, 3 × 3.

The five Sâmans are explained by the commentator. The

Pratihâra in five ways, he performs the Upadrava in five ways, he performs the Nidhana in five ways [1]. All this together forms one thousand Stobhas, or musical syllables [2].

4. Thus also are the *Rik* verses, contained in the Nishkevalya, recited (by the Hot*ri*) in five orders. What precedes the eighty *trik*as, that is one order, then follow the three sets of eighty *trik*as each, and what comes after is the fifth order [3].

Gâyatra is formed out of the *Rik* (III, 62, 10) tat savitur vare*n*yam. The Rathantara is formed out of the *Rik* (VII, 32, 22) abhi tvâ *s*ûra nonuma. The Br*i*hat is formed out of the *Rik* (VI, 46, 1) tvâm id dhi havâmahe. The Bhadra is formed out of the *Rik* (X, 157, 1) imâ nu kam. The Râgana is formed out of the *Rik* (VII, 27, 1) indra*m* naro nemadhitâ.

The metres require no explanation.

In identifying certain portions of the Nishkevalya hymn with a bird, the head of the bird corresponds to the hymns indram id gâthina*h*, &c.; the right wing to the hymns abhi tvâ *s*ûra, &c.; the left wing to the hymns tvâm id dhi, &c.; the tail to the hymns imâ nu ka*m*, &c.; the body to the hymns tad id âsa, &c. All this was explained in the first Âra*n*yaka.

[1] The Sâmagas sing the Râgana at the Mahâvrata, and in that Sâman there are, as usual, five parts, the Prastâva, Udgîtha, Pratihâra, Upadrava, and Nidhana. The Prastot*ri*, when singing the Prastâva portions, sings them five times. The Udgât*ri* and Pratihart*ri* sing their portions, the Udgîtha and Pratihâra, five times. The Udgât*ri* again sings the Upadrava five times. And all the Udgât*ri*s together sing the Nidhana five times.

[2] The Stobha syllables are syllables without any meaning, added when verses have to be sung, in order to have a support for the music. See *Kh.* Up. I, 13. In singing the five Sâmans, each five times, one thousand of such Stobha syllables are required.

[3] There are in the Nishkevalya hymn, which the Hot*ri* has to recite, three sets of eighty *trik*as each. The first, consisting of Gâyatrîs, begins with mahâ*n* indro ya o*g*asâ. The second, consisting of Br*i*hatîs, begins with mâ *k*id anyad. The third, consisting of Ush*n*ihs, begins with ya indra somapâtama. These three sets form the food of the bird, as the emblem of the *s*astra. The hymns

5. This (the hymns of this *S*astra) as a whole (if properly counted with the Stobha syllables) comes to one thousand (of B*ri*hatî verses). That (thousand) is the whole, and ten, ten is called the whole. For number is such (measured by ten). Ten tens are a hundred, ten hundreds are a thousand, and that is the whole. These are the three metres (the tens, pervading everything). And this food also (the three sets of hymns being represented as food) is threefold, eating, drinking, and chewing. He obtains that food by those (three numbers, ten, hundred, and thousand, or by the three sets of eighty t*ri*kas).

FIFTH KHAⁿDA.

1. This (nishkevalya-*s*astra) becomes perfect as a thousand of B*ri*hatî verses.

2. Some teachers (belonging to a different *S*âkhâ) recognise a thousand of different metres (not of B*ri*hatîs only). They say: 'Is another thousand (a thousand of other verses) good? Let us say it is good.'

3. Some say, a thousand of Trish*t*ubh verses, others a thousand of *G*agatî verses, others a thousand of Anush*t*ubh verses.

4. This has been said by a *Ri*shi (Rv. X, 124, 9):—

5. 'Poets through their understanding discovered Indra dancing an Anush*t*ubh.' This is meant to say: They discovered (and meditated) in speech (called Anush*t*ubh)—at that time (when they wor-

---

which precede these, form the body, head, and wings of the bird. This is one order. Then follow the three sets of eighty t*ri*kas each; and lastly, the fifth order, consisting of the hymns which form the belly and the legs of the bird.

shipped the uktha)—the Prâna (breath) connected
with Indra.

6. He (who takes the recited verses as Anushtubhs) is able to become celebrated and of good
report.

7. No! he says; rather is such a man liable to
die before his time. For that self (consisting of
Anushtubhs) is incomplete. For if a man confines
himself to speech, not to breath, then driven by his
mind, he does not succeed with speech [1].

8. Let him work towards the Brihatî, for the
Brihatî (breath) is the complete self.

9. That self (gîvâtman) is surrounded on all sides
by members. And as that self is on all sides surrounded by members, the Brihatî also is on all sides
surrounded by metres [2].

10. For the self (in the heart) is the middle of
these members, and the Brihatî is the middle of the
metres.

11. 'He is able to become celebrated and of good

---

[1] This passage is obscure, and probably corrupt. I have
followed the commentator as much as possible. He says: 'If
the Hotri priest proceeds with reciting the sastra, looking to the
Anushtubh, which is speech, and not to the thousand of Brihatîs
which are breath, then, neglecting the Brihatî (breath), and
driven by his mind to the Anushtubh (speech), he does not by his
speech obtain that sastra. For in speech without breath the Hotri
cannot, through the mere wish of the mind, say the sastra, the
activity of all the senses being dependent on breath.' The commentator therefore takes vâgabhi for vâkam abhi, or for some old
locative case formed by abhi. He also would seem to have read
prâne na. One might attempt another construction, though it is
very doubtful. One might translate, 'For that self, which is speech,
is incomplete, because he understands if driven to the mind by
breath, not (if driven) by speech.'

[2] Either in the sastra, or in the list of metres, there being some
that have more, others that have less syllables.

report, but (the other) able to die before his time,'
thus he said.   For the Brihatî is the complete self,
therefore let him work towards the Brihatî (let him
reckon the sastra recitation as a thousand Brihatîs).

SIXTH KHANDA.

1. This (nishkevalya-sastra) becomes perfect as
a thousand of Brihatî verses.   In this thousand of
Brihatîs there are one thousand one hundred and
twenty-five Anushtubhs.   For the smaller is contained in the larger.

2. This has been said by a Rishi (Rv. VIII, 76,
12):—

3. 'A speech of eight feet;'—because there are
eight feet of four syllables each in the Anushtubh.

4. 'Of nine corners;'—because the Brihatî becomes nine-cornered (having nine feet of four syllables each).

5. 'Touching the truth;'—because speech (Anushtubh) is truth, touched by the verse (Brihatî)[1].

6. 'He (the Hotri) makes the body out of Indra;'—
for out of this thousand of Brihatî verses turned
into Anushtubhs, and therefore out of Prâna as
connected with Indra[2], and out of the Brihatî (which
is Prâna), he makes speech, that is Anushtubh, as a
body[3].

7. This Mahaduktha is the highest development

---

[1] Vâk, speech, taking the form of Anushtubh, and being joined
with the Rik, or the Brihatî, touches the true, i. e. Prâna, breath,
which is to be meditated on under the form of the Brihatî.   Comm.

[2] Cf. Ait. Âr. II, 2, 3, 4.

[3] Because the Anushtubh is made out of the Brihatî, the Brihatî
being breath, therefore the Anushtubh is called its body.

of speech, and it is fivefold, viz. measured, not measured, music, true, and untrue.

8. A *Rik* verse, a gâthâ¹, a kumbyâ² are measured (metrical). A Ya*g*us line, an invocation, and
general remarks³, these are not measured (they are
in prose). A Sâman, or any portion (parvan) of it, is
music. Om is true, Na is untrue.

9. What is true (Om) is the flower and fruit of
speech. He is able to become celebrated and of
good report, for he speaks the true (Om), the flower
and fruit of speech.

10. Now the untrue is the root⁴ of speech, and as
a tree whose root is exposed dries up and perishes,
thus a man who says what is untrue exposes his
root, dries up and perishes. Therefore one should
not say what is untrue, but guard oneself from it.

11. That syllable Om (yes) goes forward (to the
first cause of the world) and is empty. Therefore if
a man says Om (yes) to everything, then that (which
he gives away) is wanting to him here⁵. If he says
Om (yes) to everything, then he would empty himself, and would not be capable of any enjoyments.

12. That syllable Na (no) is full for oneself⁶. If
a man says No to everything, then his reputation

---

¹ A gâthâ is likewise in verse, for instance, prâta*h* prâtar
an*ri*ta*m* te vadanti.

² A kumbyâ is a metrical precept, such as, brahma*k*âryasyâpo-
*s*âna*m* karma kuru, divâ mâ svâpsî*h*, &c.

³ Such as arthavâdas, explanatory passages, also gossip, such as
is common in the king's palace, laughing at people, &c.

⁴ As diametrically opposed to the flowers and fruits which
represent the true. Comm.

⁵ Then that man is left empty here on earth for that enjoyment.
Comm.

⁶ He who always says No, keeps everything to himself.

would become evil, and that would ruin him even here.

13. Therefore let a man give at the proper time only, not at the wrong time. Thus he unites the true and the untrue, and from the union of those two he grows, and becomes greater and greater.

14. He who knows this speech of which this (the mahaduktha) is a development, he is clever. A is the whole of speech, and manifested through different kinds of contact (mutes) and of wind (sibilants), it becomes manifold and different.

15. Speech if uttered in a whisper is breath, if spoken aloud, it is body. Therefore (if whispered) it is almost hidden, for what is incorporeal is almost hidden, and breath is incorporeal. But if spoken aloud, it is body, and therefore it is perceptible, for body is perceptible.

Seventh Khanda.

1. This (nishkevalya-sastra) becomes perfect as a thousand of Brihatîs. It is glory (the glorious Brahman, not the absolute Brahman), it is Indra. Indra is the lord of all beings. He who thus knows Indra as the lord of all beings, departs from this world by loosening the bonds of life [1]—so said Mahidâsa Aitareya. Having departed he becomes Indra (or Hiranyagarbha) and shines in those worlds [2].

---

[1] The commentator explains visrasâ by 'merging his manhood in the identity with all,' and doing this while still alive. Visras is the gradual loosening of the body, the decay of old age, but here it has the meaning of vairâgya rather, the shaking off of all that ties the Self to this body or this life.

[2] The fourteen worlds in the egg of Brahman. Comm. Some hold that he who enters on this path, and becomes deity, does not

2. And with regard to this they say: 'If a man obtains the other world in this form (by meditating on the prâna, breath, which is the uktha, the hymn of the mahâvrata), then in what form does he obtain this world[1]?'

3. Here the blood of the woman is a form of Agni (fire); therefore no one should despise it. And the seed of the man is a form of Âditya (sun); therefore no one should despise it. This self (the woman) gives her self (skin, blood, and flesh) to that self (fat, bone, and marrow), and that self (man) gives his self (fat, bone, and marrow) to this self (skin, blood, and flesh). Thus[2] these two grow together. In this form (belonging to the woman and to fire) he goes to that world (belonging to the man and the sun), and in that form (belonging to man and the sun) he goes to this world (belonging to the woman and to fire[3]).

EIGHTH KHANDA.

1. Here (with regard to obtaining Hiranyagarbha) there are these Slokas:

---

arrive at final liberation. Others, however, show that this identification with the uktha, and through it with the prâna (breath) and Hiranyagarbha, is provisional only, and intended to prepare the mind of the worshipper for the reception of the highest knowledge of Brahman.

[1] The last line on page 246 should, I think, be the penultimate line of page 247.

[2] The body consists of six elements, and is hence called shâtkausika. Of these, three having a white appearance (fat, bone, and marrow), come from the sun and from man; three having a red appearance, come from fire and from the woman.

[3] It is well therefore to shake off this body, and by meditating on the uktha to obtain identity with Hiranyagarbha. Comm.

2. The fivefold body into which the indestructible (prâ*n*a, breath) enters, that body which the harnessed horses (the senses) draw about, that body where the true of the true (the highest Brahman) follows after, in that body (of the worshipper) all gods[1] become one.

3. That body into which goes the indestructible (the breath) which we have joined (in meditation), proceeding from the indestructible (the highest Brahman), that body which the harnessed horses (the senses) draw about, that body where the true of the true follows after, in that body all gods become one.

4. After separating themselves from the Yes and No of language, and of all that is hard and cruel, poets have discovered (what they sought for); dependent on names they rejoiced in what had been revealed[2].

5. That in which the poets rejoiced (the revealed nature of prâ*n*a, breath), in it the gods exist all joined together. Having driven away evil by means of that Brahman (which is hidden in prâ*n*a), the enlightened man goes to the Svarga world (becomes one with Hira*n*yagarbha[3], the universal spirit).

6. No one wishing to describe him (prâ*n*a, breath) by speech, describes him by calling him 'woman,' 'neither woman nor man,' or 'man' (all such names applying only to the material body, and not to prâ*n*a or breath).

---

[1] The worshipper identifies himself by meditation with prâ*n*a, breath, which comprehends all gods. These gods (Agni and the rest) appear in the forms of speech, &c. Comm.

[2] The prâ*n*a, breath, and their identity with it through meditation or worship. Comm.

[3] Sarvâhammânî hira*n*yagarbha iti *s*rute*h*. Comm.

7. Brahman (as hidden beneath prâna) is called the A; and the I (ego) is gone there (the worshipper should know that he is uktha and prâna).

8. This becomes perfect as a thousand of Brihatî verses, and of that hymn, perfect with a thousand Brihatî verses, there are 36,000 syllables. So many are also the thousands of days of human life[1]. By means of the syllable of life (the a) alone (which is contained in that thousand of hymns) does a man obtain the day of life (the mahâvrata day, which completes the number of the days in the Gavâmayana sacrifice), and by means of the day of life (he obtains) the syllable of life.

9. Now there is a chariot of the god (prâna) destroying all desires (for the worlds of Indra, the moon, the earth, all of which lie below the place of Hiranyagarbha). Its front part (the point of the two shafts of the carriage where the yoke is fastened) is speech, its wheels the ears, the horses the eyes, the driver the mind. Prâna (breath) mounts that chariot (and on it, i. e. by means of meditating on Prâna, he reaches Hiranyagarbha).

10. This has been said by a Rishi (Rv. X, 39, 12):—

11. 'Come hither on that which is quicker than mind,' and (Rv. VIII, 73, 2) 'Come hither on that which is quicker than the twinkling of an eye,' yea, the twinkling of an eye[2].

---

[1] Cf. II, 2, 4, 4.

[2] The commentator remarks that the worship and meditation on the uktha as prâna, as here taught, is different from the prânavidyâ, the knowledge of prâna, taught in the Khândogya, the Brihadâranyaka, &c., where prâna or life is represented as the object of meditation, without any reference to the uktha or other portions of the Mahâvrata ceremony. He enjoins that the meditation on

the uktha as prâ*n*a should be continued till the desired result, the identification of the worshipper with prâ*n*a, is realised, and that it should afterwards be repeated until death, because otherwise the impression might vanish, and the reward of becoming a god, and going to the gods, be lost.   Nor is the worship to be confined to the time of the sacrifice, the Mahâvrata, only, but it has to be repeated mentally during life.   There are neither certain postures required for it, nor certain times and places.   At the time of death, however, he who has become perfect in this meditation on uktha, as the emblem of prâ*n*a, will have his reward.   Up to a certain point his fate will be the same as that of other people.   The activity of the senses will be absorbed in the mind, the activity of the mind in breath, breath in the activity of life, life with breath in the five elements, fire, &c., and these five elements will be absorbed up to their seed in the Paramâtman or Highest Self.   This ends the old birth.   But then the subtile body, having been absorbed in the Highest Self, rises again in the lotus of the heart, and passing out by the channel of the head, reaches a ray of the sun, whether by day or by night, and goes at the northern or southern course of the sun to the road of Ar*k*is or light.   That Ar*k*is, light, and other powers carry him on, and led by these he reaches the Brahma-loka, where he creates to himself every kind of enjoyment, according to his wish. He may create for himself a material body and enjoy all sorts of pleasures, as if in a state of waking, or he may, without such a body, enjoy all pleasures in mind only, as if in a dream.   And as he creates these various bodies according to his wish, he creates also living souls in each, endowed with the internal organs of mind, and moves about in them, as he pleases.   In fact this world is the same for the devotee (yogin) and for the Highest Self, except that creative power belongs truly to the latter only.   At last the devotee gains the highest knowledge, that of the Highest Self in himself, and then, at the dissolution of the Brahma-loka, he obtains complete freedom with Brahman.

FOURTH ADHYÂYA.

First Khanda.

With this adhyâya begins the real Upanishad, best known under the name of the Aitareya-upanishad, and often separately edited, commented on, and translated. If treated separately, what we call the fourth adhyâya of the second Âra*n*yaka, becomes the first adhyâya of the Upanishad, sometimes also, by counting all adhyâyas from the beginning of the Aitareya-âra*n*yaka, the ninth. The divisions adopted by Sâya*n*a, who explains the Upanishad as part of the Âra*n*yaka, and by *S*ankara, who explains it independently, vary, though Sâya*n*a states that he follows in his commentary on the Upanishad the earlier commentary of *S*ankara. I have given the divisions adopted by Sâya*n*a, and have marked those of *S*ankara's by figures in parentheses, placed at the end of each paragraph. The difference between this Upanishad and the three preceding adhyâyas is easily perceived. Hitherto the answer to the question, Whence this world? had been, From Prâ*n*a, prâ*n*a meaning breath and life, which was looked upon for a time as a sufficient explanation of all that is. From a psychological point of view this prâ*n*a is the conscious self (prag*ñ*âtman); in a more mythological form it appears as Hira*n*yagarbha, 'the golden germ,' sometimes even as Indra. It is one of the chief objects of the prâ*n*avidyâ, or life-knowledge, to show that the living principle in us is the same as the living principle in the sun, and that by a recognition of their identity and of the true nature of prâ*n*a, the devotee, or he who has rightly meditated on prâ*n*a during his life, enters after death into the world of Hira*n*yagarbha.

This is well expressed in the Kaushîtaki-upanishad III, 2, where Indra says to Pratardana: 'I am Prâ*n*a; meditate on me as the conscious self (prag*ñ*âtman), as life, as immortality. Life is prâ*n*a, prâ*n*a is life. Immortality is prâ*n*a, prâ*n*a is immortality. By prâ*n*a he obtains immortality in the other world, by knowledge (prag*ñ*â) true conception. Prâ*n*a is consciousness (prag*ñ*â), consciousness is prâ*n*a.'

This, however, though it may have satisfied the mind of the Brahmans for a time, was not a final solution. That final solution of the problem not simply of life, but of existence, is given in the Upanishad which teaches that Âtman, the Self, and not Prâ*n*a, Life, is the last and only cause of everything. In some places this doctrine is laid down in all its simplicity.   Our true self, it is said, has its true being in the Highest Self only.   In other passages, however, and nearly in the whole of this Upanishad, this simple doctrine is mixed up with much that is mythological, fanciful, and absurd, arthavâda, as the commentators call it, but as it might often be more truly called, anarthavâda, and it is only towards the end that the identity of the self-conscious self with the Highest Self or Brahman is clearly enuntiated.

Adoration to the Highest Self.   Hari, Om!

1. Verily, in the beginning [1] all this was Self, one only; there was nothing else blinking [2] whatsoever.

2. He thought: 'Shall I send forth worlds?' (1) He sent forth these worlds,

3. Ambhas (water), Marî*k*i (light), Mara (mortal), and Ap (water).

4. That Ambhas (water) is above the heaven, and it is heaven, the support.   The Marî*k*is (the lights) are the sky.   The Mara (mortal) is the earth, and the waters under the earth are the Ap world [3]. (2)

---

[1] Before the creation.   Comm.

[2] Blinking, mishat, i. e. living ; cf. Rv. X, 190, 2, vi*s*vasya mishato va*s*î, the lord of all living.   Sâya*n*a seems to take mishat as a 3rd pers. sing.

[3] The names of the four worlds are peculiar.   Ambhas means water, and is the name given to the highest world, the waters above the heaven, and heaven itself.   Marî*k*is are rays, here used as a name of the sky, antariksha.   Mara means dying, and the earth is called so, because all creatures living there must die.   Ap is water, here explained as the waters under the earth.   The usual division of the world is threefold, earth, sky, and heaven.   Here it is fourfold, the fourth division being the water round the earth, or, as the commentator says, under the earth.   Ambhas was probably intended for the highest heaven (dyaus), and was then explained both as what is above the heaven and as heaven itself, the support. If we translate, like *S*ankara and Colebrooke, 'the water is the region above the heaven which heaven upholds,' we should lose heaven altogether, yet heaven, as the third with sky and earth, is essential in the Indian view of the world.

5. He thought: 'There are these worlds; shall I send forth guardians of the worlds?'

He then formed the Purusha (the person)[1], taking him forth from the water[2]. (3)

6. He brooded on him[3], and when that person had thus been brooded on, a mouth burst forth[4] like an egg. From the mouth proceeded speech, from speech Agni (fire)[5].

Nostrils burst forth. From the nostrils proceeded scent (prâ*n*a)[6], from scent Vâyu (air).

Eyes burst forth. From the eyes proceeded sight, from sight Âditya (sun).

Ears burst forth. From the ears proceeded hearing, from hearing the Di*s* (quarters of the world).

Skin burst forth. From the skin proceeded hairs (sense of touch), from the hairs shrubs and trees.

The heart burst forth. From the heart proceeded mind, from mind *K*andramas (moon).

The navel burst forth. From the navel proceeded the Apâna (the down-breathing)[7], from Apâna death.

---

[1] Purusha; an embodied being, Colebrooke; a being of human shape, Röer; purushâkâram virâ*t*pi*nd*am, Sâya*n*a.

[2] According to the commentator, from the five elements, beginning with water. That person is meant for the Virâ*g*.

[3] Tap, as the commentator observes, does not mean here and in similar passages to perform austerities (tapas), such as the K*rikkh*ra, the *K*ândrâya*n*a, &c., but to conceive and to will and to create by mere will. I have translated it by brooding, though this expresses a part only of the meaning expressed by tap.

[4] Literally, was opened.

[5] Three things are always distinguished here—the place of each sense, the instrument of the sense, and the presiding deity of the sense.

[6] Prâ*n*a, i. e. ghrâ*n*endriya, must be distinguished from the prâ*n*a, the up-breathing, one of the five prâ*n*as, and likewise from the prâ*n*a as the principle of life.

[7] The Apâna, down-breathing, is generally one of the five vital airs

The generative organ burst forth. From the organ proceeded seed, from seed water. (4)

SECOND KHA*N*DA.

1. Those deities (devatâ), Agni and the rest, after they had been sent forth, fell into this great ocean [1].

Then he (the Self) besieged him, (the person) with hunger and thirst.

2. The deities then (tormented by hunger and thirst) spoke to him (the Self): 'Allow us a place in which we may rest and eat food [2].' (1)

He led a cow towards them (the deities). They said: 'This is not enough.' He led a horse towards them. They said: 'This is not enough.' (2)

He led man [3] towards them. Then they said: 'Well done [4], indeed.' Therefore man is well done.

3. He said to them: 'Enter, each according to his place.' (3)

4. Then Agni (fire), having become speech, entered the mouth. Vâyu (air), having become scent, entered the nostrils. Âditya (sun), having become sight, entered the eyes. The Di*s* (regions), having become hearing, entered the ears. The shrubs and trees, having become hairs, entered the skin. *K*andramas (the moon), having become mind, entered

---

which are supposed to keep the body alive. In our place, however, apâna is deglutition and digestion, as we shall see in II, 4, 3, 10.

[1] They fell back into that universal being from whence they had sprung, the first created person, the Virâ*g*. Or they fell into the world, the last cause of which is ignorance.

[2] To eat food is explained to mean to perceive the objects which correspond to the senses, presided over by the various deities.

[3] Here purusha is different from the first purusha, the universal person. It can only be intended for intelligent man.

[4] Suk*ri*ta, well done, virtue; or, if taken for svak*ri*ta, self-made.

the heart. Death, having become down-breathing, entered the navel. The waters, having become seed, entered the generative organ. (4)

5. Then Hunger and Thirst spoke to him (the Self) : ' Allow us two (a place).' He said to them : ' I assign you to those very deities there, I make you co-partners with them.' Therefore to whatever deity an oblation is offered, hunger and thirst are co-partners in it. (5)

THIRD KHA*N*DA.

1. He thought : ' There are these worlds and the guardians of the worlds. Let me send forth food for them.' (1)

He brooded over the water [1]. From the water thus brooded on, matter [2] (mûrti) was born. And that matter which was born, that verily was food [3]. (2)

2. When this food (the object matter) had thus been sent forth, it wished to flee [4], crying and turning away. He (the subject) tried to grasp it by speech. He could not grasp it by speech. If he had grasped it by speech, man would be satisfied by naming food. (3)

He tried to grasp it by scent (breath). He could not grasp it by scent. If he had grasped it by scent, man would be satisfied by smelling food. (4)

He tried to grasp it by the eye. He could not

---

[1] The water, as mentioned before, or the five elements.

[2] Mûrti, for mûrtti, form, Colebrooke; a being of organised form, Röer ; vrîhiyavâdirûpâ mûshakâdirûpâ *k*a mûrti*h*, i. e. vegetable food for men, animal food for cats, &c.

[3] Offered food, i. e. objects for the Devatâs and the senses in the body.

[4] Atya*g*ighâ*m*sat, ati*s*ayena hantu*m* gantum ai*kkh*at. Sâya*n*a.

grasp it by the eye.   If he had grasped it by the eye, man would be satisfied by seeing food. (5)

He tried to grasp it by the ear.   He could not grasp it by the ear.   If he had grasped it by the ear, man would be satisfied by hearing food. (6)

He tried to grasp it by the skin.   He could not grasp it by the skin.   If he had grasped it by the skin, man would be satisfied by touching food. (7)

He tried to grasp it by the mind.   He could not grasp it by the mind.   If he had grasped it by the mind, man would be satisfied by thinking food. (8)

He tried to grasp it by the generative organ. He could not grasp it by the organ.   If he had grasped it by the organ, man would be satisfied by sending forth food. (9)

He tried to grasp it by the down-breathing (the breath which helps to swallow food through the mouth and to carry it off through the rectum, the pâyvindriya).   He got it.

3. Thus it is Vâyu (the getter [1]) who lays hold of food, and the Vâyu is verily Annâyu (he who gives life or who lives by food). (10)

4. He thought : ' How can all this be without me ? '

5. And then he thought : ' By what way shall I get there [2] ? '

6. And then he thought : ' If speech names, if scent smells, if the eye sees, if the ear hears, if the skin feels, if the mind thinks, if the off-breathing digests, if the organ sends forth, then what am I ? ' (11)

---

[1] An attempt to derive vâyu from vî, to get.

[2] Or, by which of the two ways shall I get in, the one way being from the top of the foot (cf. Ait. Âr. II, 1, 4, 1), the other from the skull ? Comm.

7. Then opening the suture of the skull, he got in by that door.

8. That door is called the Vidriti (tearing asunder), the Nândana (the place of bliss).

9. There are three dwelling-places for him, three dreams; this dwelling-place (the eye), this dwelling-place (the throat), this dwelling-place (the heart)[1]. (12)

10. When born (when the Highest Self had entered the body) he looked through all things, in order to see whether anything wished to proclaim here another (Self). He saw this person only (himself) as the widely spread Brahman. 'I saw it,' thus he said[2]; (13)

Therefore he was Idam-dra (seeing this).

11. Being Idamdra by name, they call him Indra mysteriously. For the Devas love mystery, yea, they love mystery. (14)

---

[1] Passages like this must always have required an oral interpretation, but it is by no means certain that the explanation given in the commentaries represents really the old traditional interpretation. Sâyana explains the three dwelling-places as the right eye, in a state of waking; as the throat, in a state of dreaming; as the heart, in a state of profound sleep. Sankara explains them as the right eye, the inner mind, and the ether in the heart. Sâyana allows another interpretation of the three dwelling-places being the body of the father, the body of the mother, and one's own body. The three dreams or sleeps he explains by waking, dreaming, and profound sleep, and he remarks that waking too is called a dream as compared with the true awakening, which is the knowledge of Brahman. In the last sentence the speaker, when repeating three times 'this dwelling-place,' is supposed to point to his right eye, the throat, and the heart. This interpretation is supported by a passage in the Brahma-upanishad, Netre gâgaritam vidyât kanthe svapnam samâdiset, sushuptam hridayasya tu.

[2] In this passage, which is very obscure, Sankara fails us, either because, as Ânandagñâna says, he thought the text was too easy to require any explanation, or because the writers of the MSS. left out

FIFTH ADHYÂYA.

First Kha*n*da.

1. Let the women who are with child move away[1]!

2. Verily, from the beginning he (the self) is in man as a germ, which is called seed.

3. This (seed), which is strength gathered from all the limbs of the body, he (the man) bears as self in his self (body). When he commits the seed to the woman, then he (the father) causes it to be born. That is his first birth. (1)

4. That seed becomes the self of the woman, as

the passage. Ânanda*g*ñâna explains: 'He looked through all creatures, he identified himself with them, and thought he was a man, blind, happy, &c.; or, as it is elsewhere expressed, he developed forms and names. And how did this mistake arise? Because he did not see the other, the true Self;' or literally, 'Did he see the other Self?' which is only a figure of speech to convey the meaning that he did not see it. The particle iti is then to be taken in a causal sense, (i.e. he did so, because what else could he have wished to proclaim?) But he allows another explanation, viz. 'He considered all beings, whether they existed by themselves or not, and after having considered, he arrived at the conclusion, What shall I call different from the true Self?' The real difficulties, however, are not removed by these explanations. First of all, we expect vâvadisham before iti, and secondly, unless anyam refers to âtmânam, we expect anyad. My own translation is literal, but I am not certain that it conveys the true meaning. One might understand it as implying that the Self looked about through all things, in order to find out, 'What does wish to proclaim here another Self?' And when he saw there was nothing which did not come from himself, then he recognised that the Purusha, the person he had sent forth, or, as we should say, the person he had created, was the developed Brahman, was the Âtman, was himself. Sâya*n*a explains vâvadishat by vadishyâmi, but before iti the third person cannot well refer to the subject of vyaikshat.

[1] Some MSS. begin this adhyâya with the sentence apakrâmantu garbhi*n*ya*h*, may the women who are with child walk away! It is counted as a paragraph.

if one of her own limbs. Therefore it does not injure her.

5. She nourishes his (her husband's) self (the son) within her. (2)   She who nourishes, is to be nourished.

6. The woman bears the germ.   He (the father) elevates the child even before the birth, and immediately after [1].

7. When he thus elevates the child both before and after his birth, he really elevates his own self,

8. For the continuation of these worlds (men). For thus are these worlds continued.

9. This is his second birth. (3)

10. He (the son), being his self, is then placed in his stead for (the performance of) all good works.

11. But his other self (the father), having done all he has to do, and having reached the full measure of his life, departs.

12. And departing from hence he is born again. That is his third birth.

13. And this has been declared by a *Ri*shi (Rv. IV, 27, 1): (4)

14. 'While dwelling in the womb, I discovered all the births of these Devas. A hundred iron strongholds kept me, but I escaped quickly down like a falcon.'

15. Vâmadeva, lying in the womb, has thus declared this. (5)

And having this knowledge he stepped forth, after this dissolution of the body, and having obtained all his desires in that heavenly world, became immortal, yea, he became immortal. (6)

---

[1] By nourishing the mother, and by performing certain ceremonies both before and after the birth of a child.

SIXTH ADHYÂYA.

First Kha*n*da.

1. Let the women go back to their place.

2. Who is he whom[1] we meditate on as the Self? Which[2] is the Self?

3. That by which we see (form), that by which we hear (sound), that by which we perceive smells, that by which we utter speech, that by which we distinguish sweet and not sweet, (1) and what comes from the heart and the mind, namely, perception, command, understanding, knowledge, wisdom, seeing, holding, thinking, considering, readiness (or suffering), remembering, conceiving, willing, breathing, loving, desiring?

4. No, all these are various names only of knowledge (the true Self). (2)

5. And that Self, consisting of (knowledge), is Brahman (m.)[3], it is Indra, it is Pra*g*âpati[4]. All these Devas, these five great elements, earth, air, ether, water, fire, these and those which are, as it were, small and mixed[5], and seeds of this kind and that kind, born from eggs, born from the womb, born from heat, born from germs[6], horses, cows, men, elephants, and whatsoever breathes, whether walking or flying, and what is immoveable—all that is led (produced) by knowledge (the Self).

6. It rests on knowledge (the Self).   The world

---

[1] I read ko yam instead of ko 'yam.

[2] Or, Which of the two, the real or the phenomenal, the nirupâdhika or sopâdhika?

[3] Hira*n*yagarbha. Comm.   [4] Virâ*g*. Comm.

[5] Serpents, &c., says the commentary.

[6] Cf. *Kh.* Up. VI, 3, 1, where the sveda*g*a, born from heat or perspiration, are not mentioned.

is led (produced) by knowledge (the Self). Knowledge is its cause [1].

7. Knowledge is Brahman. (3)

8. He (Vâmadeva), having by this conscious self
stepped forth from this world, and having obtained
all desires in that heavenly world, became immortal,
yea, he became immortal. Thus it is, Om. (4)

SEVENTH ADHYÂYA [2].

FIRST KHA*N*DA.

1. My speech rests in the mind, my mind rests in
speech [3]. Appear to me (thou, the Highest Self)!
You (speech and mind) are the two pins [4] (that hold
the wheels) of the Veda. May what I have learnt
not forsake me [5]. I join day and night with what I
have learnt [6]. I shall speak of the real, I shall speak
the true. May this protect me, may this protect
the teacher! May it protect me, may it protect the
teacher, yea, the teacher!

---

[1] We have no words to distinguish between pra*g*ñâ, state of
knowing, and pra*g*ñâna, act of knowing. Both are names of the
Highest Brahman, which is the beginning and end (pratish*th*â) of
everything that exists or seems to exist.

[2] This seventh adhyâya contains a propitiatory prayer (*s*ântikaro
mantra*h*). It is frequently left out in the MSS. which contain the
Aitareya-upanishad with *S*ankara's commentary, and Dr. Röer has
omitted it in his edition. Sâya*n*a explains it in his commentary on
the Aitareya-âra*n*yaka; and in one MS. of *S*ankara's commentary
on the Aitareya-upanishad, which is in my possession, the seventh
adhyâya is added with the commentary of Mâdhavâmâtya, the
Â*g*ñâpâlaka of Vîrabukka-mahârâ*g*a.

[3] The two depend on each other.

[4] Â*n*î, explained by the commentator as ânayanasamartha.

[5] Cf. *Kh*. Up. IV, 2, 5.

[6] I repeat it day and night so that I may not forget it.

THIRD ÂRA*N*YAKA[1].

FIRST ADHYÂYA.

FIRST KHA*ND*A.

1. Next follows the Upanishad of the Sa*m*hitâ[2].

2. The former half is the earth, the latter half the heaven, their union the air[3], thus says Mâ*nd*u-keya; their union is the ether, thus did Mâkshavya teach it.

3. That air is not considered[4] independent[5], therefore I do not agree with his (Ma*nd*ûka's) son.

4. Verily, the two are the same, therefore air is

---

[1] This last portion of the Upanishad is found in the MS. discovered by Dr. Bühler in Kashmir, and described by him in the Journal of the Bombay Branch of the Royal Asiatic Society, 1877, p. 36. I have collated it, so far as it was possible to read it, many lines being either broken off altogether, or almost entirely obliterated.

[2] Sa*m*hitâ is the sacred text in which all letters are closely joined. The joining together of two letters is called their sa*m*hitâ; the first letter of a joined group the pûrvarûpa (n.), the second the uttararûpa. For instance, in agnim î*l*e the m is pûrvarûpa, the î uttararûpa, and mî their sa*m*hitâ or union.

[3] As in worshipping the *S*âlagrâma stone, we really worship Vish*n*u, so we ought to perceive the earth, the heaven, and the air when we pronounce the first and the second letters of a group, and that group itself.

[4] Mene has here been taken as 3rd pers. sing. perf. passive. The commentator, however, explains it as an active verb, ni*sk*itavân.

[5] Because it is included in the ether, not the ether in the air. Comm.

considered independent, thus says Âgastya. For it
is the same, whether they say air or ether [1].

5. So far with reference to deities (mythologically);
now with reference to the body (physiologically) :

6. The former half is speech, the latter half is
mind, their union breath (prâ*n*a), thus says *S*ûravîra [2]
Mâ*nd*ukeya.

7. But his eldest son said : The former half is
mind, the latter half speech. For we first conceive
with the mind indeed [3], and then we utter with speech.
Therefore the former half is indeed mind, the latter
half speech, but their union is really breath.

8. Verily, it is the same with both, the father
(Mâ*nd*ukeya) and the son [4].

9. This (meditation as here described), joined [5]
with mind, speech, and breath, is (like) a chariot
drawn by two horses and one horse between them
(prash*t*ivâhana).

10. And he who thus knows this union, becomes
united with offspring, cattle, fame, glory of countenance, and the world of Svarga. He lives his
full age.

11. Now all this comes from the Mâ*nd*ukeyas.

SECOND KHA*ND*A.

1. Next comes the meditation as taught by
*S*âkalya.

---

[1] Both views are tenable, for it is not the actual air and ether
which are meditated on, but their names, as declared and explained
in this peculiar act of worship. We should read âkâ*sas*keti, a reading
confirmed both by the commentary and by the Kashmir MS.

[2] The man among heroes. Comm.

[3] The Kashmir MS. reads manasaivâgre.

[4] Both views are admissible. Comm.

[5] Prâ*n*asa*m*hita*h*, Kashmir MS.

2. The first half is the earth, the second half heaven, their uniting the rain, the uniter Parg'anya [1].

3. And so it is when he (Parg'anya) rains thus strongly, without ceasing, day and night [2],

4. Then they say also (in ordinary language), 'Heaven and earth have come together.'

5. So much with regard to the deities; now with regard to the body:—

6. Every man is indeed like an egg [3]. There are two halves [4] (of him), thus they say: 'This half is the earth, that half heaven.' And there between them is the ether (the space of the mouth), like the ether between heaven and earth. In this ether there (in the mouth) the breath is fixed, as in that other ether the air is fixed. And as there are those three luminaries (in heaven), there are these three luminaries in man.

7. As there is that sun in heaven, there is this eye in the head. As there is that lightning in the sky, there is this heart in the body; as there is that fire on earth, there is this seed in the member.

8. Having thus represented the self (body) as the whole world, S'âkalya said: This half is the earth, that half heaven.

9. He who thus knows this union, becomes united with offspring, cattle, fame, glory of coun-

---

[1] If i is followed by a, the i is changed to y, and both are united as ya. Here a is the cause which changes i into y. Thus Parg'anya, the god of rain, is the cause which unites earth and heaven into rain. Comm.

[2] When it rains incessantly, heaven and earth seem to be one in rain.

[3] Ândam, andasadrisam. Comm.

[4] The one half from the feet to the lower jaw, the other half from the upper jaw to the skull. Comm.

tenance, and the world of Svarga. He lives his full age.

THIRD KHA*N*DA[1].

1. Next come the reciters of the Nirbhu*g*a[2].

2. Nirbhu*g*a abides on earth, Prat*rinn*a in heaven, the Ubhayamantare*n*a in the sky.

3. Now, if any one should chide him who recites the Nirbhu*g*a, let him answer : ' Thou art fallen from the two lower places[3].' If any one should chide him who recites the Prat*rinn*a, let him answer : 'Thou art fallen from the two higher places[4].' But he who recites the Ubhayamantare*n*a, there is no chiding him.

4. For when he turns out the Sandhi (the union of words), that is the form of Nirbhu*g*a[5]; and when he pronounces two syllables pure (without modification), that is the form of Prat*rinn*a[6]. This comes

---

[1] Cf. Rig-veda-prâtisâkhya, ed. Max Müller, p. iii, and Nachträge, p. ii.

[2] Nirbhu*g*a(n) is the recitation of the Veda without intervals, therefore the same as Sa*m*hitâ. Prat*rinn*a is the recitation of each word by itself (pada-pâ*th*a); Ubhayamantare*n*a, the between the two, is the intertwining of Sa*m*hitâ and Pada-pâ*th*a, the so-called Krama-pâ*th*a. By reciting the Sa*m*hitâ inattentively, one may use forms which belong to the Pada-text; and by reciting the Pada inattentively, one may use forms which belong to the Sa*m*hitâ-text. But in reciting the Krama both the Sa*m*hitâ and Pada forms are used together, and therefore mistakes are less likely to happen.

[3] From earth and sky. Cf. *Kh.* Up. II, 22, 3.

[4] From the sky and from heaven.

[5] Nirbhu*g*a may mean without arms, as if the arms of the words were taken away, or with two arms stretched out, the two words forming, as it were, two arms to one body.

[6] Prat*rinn*a means cut asunder, every word being separated from the others.

first [1].   By the Ubhayamantara (what is between
the two) both are fulfilled (both the sandhi and the
pada).

5. Let him who wishes for proper food say the
Nirbhu*g*a; let him who wishes for Svarga, say the
Prat*rinn*a; let him who wishes for both say the
Ubhayamantare*n*a.

6. Now if another man (an enemy) should chide
him who says the Nirbhu*g*a, let him say to him :
' Thou hast offended the earth, the deity; the earth,
the deity, will strike thee.'

If another man should chide him who says the
Prat*rinn*a, let him say to him : ' Thou hast offended
heaven, the deity; heaven, the deity, will strike
thee.'

If another man should chide him who says the
Ubhayamantare*n*a, let him say to him : ' Thou hast
offended the sky, the deity; the sky, the deity, will
strike thee.'

7. And whatever the reciter shall say to one who
speaks to him or does not speak to him, depend
upon it, it will come to pass.

8. But to a Brâhma*n*a let him not say anything
except what is auspicious.

9. Only he may curse a Brâhma*n*a in excessive
wealth [2].

10. Nay, not even in excessive wealth should he
curse a Brâhma*n*a, but he should say, 'I bow before
Brâhma*n*as,'—thus says *S*ûravîra Mâ*nd*ûkeya.

---

[1] The words were first each separate, before they were united
according to the laws of Sandhi.

[2] He may curse him, if he is exceeding rich ; or he may wish
him the curse of excessive wealth; or he may curse him, if something great depends on it.

FOURTH KHA*N*DA.

1. Next follow the imprecations [1].

2. Let him know that breath [2] is the beam (on which the whole house of the body rests).

3. If any one (a Brâhma*n*a or another man) should chide him, who by meditation has become that breath as beam [3], then, if he thinks himself strong, he says : 'I grasped the breath, the beam, well; thou dost not prevail against me who have grasped the breath as the beam.' Let him say to him : 'Breath, the beam, will forsake thee.'

4. But if he thinks himself not strong, let him say to him : 'Thou couldst not grasp him who wishes to grasp the breath as the beam. Breath, the beam, will forsake thee.'

5. And whatever the reciter shall say to one who speaks to him or does not speak to him, depend upon it, it will come to pass. But to a Brâhma*n*a let him not say anything except what is auspicious. Only he may curse a Brâhma*n*a in excessive wealth. Nay, not even in excessive wealth should he curse a Brâhma*n*a, but he should say, 'I bow before Brâhma*n*as,'—thus says *S*ûravîra Mâ*n*dûkeya.

---

[1] The commentator explains anuvyâhâra, not as imprecations, but as referring to those who teach or use the imprecations, such imprecations being necessary to guard against the loss of the benefits accruing from the meditation and worship here described ; such teachers say what follows.

[2] Breath, the union of mind and speech, as explained before. This is the opinion of Sthavira *S*âkalya, cf. III, 2, 1, 1.

[3] If he should tell him that he did not meditate on breath properly.

FIFTH KHAN̄DA.

1. Now those who repeat the Nirbhuga say:

2. 'The former half[1] is the first syllable, the latter half the second syllable, and the space between the first and second halves is the Sam̐hitâ (union).'

3. He who thus knows this Sam̐hitâ (union), becomes united with offspring, cattle, fame, glory of countenance, and the world of Svarga. He lives his full age.

4. Now Hrasva Mân̄dûkeya says : 'We reciters of Nirbhuga say, "Yes, the former half is the first syllable, and the latter half the second syllable, but the Sam̐hitâ is the space between the first and second halves in so far as by it one turns out the union (sandhi), and knows what is the accent and what is not[2], and distinguishes what is the mora and what is not."'

5. He who thus knows this Sam̐hitâ (union), becomes united with offspring, cattle, fame, glory of countenance, and the world of Svarga. He lives his full age.

6. Now his middle son, the child of his mother Prâtîbodhî[3], says : 'One pronounces these two syllables letter by letter, without entirely separating

---

[1] As spoken of before, III, 1, 1, 1.

[2] In agnim île, île by itself has no accent, but as joined by sandhi with agnim, its first syllable becomes svarita, its second prakita. In tava it, the vowel i is a short mora or mâtrâ; but if joined with va, it vanishes, and becomes long e, tavet. Comm.

[3] Prâtîbodhîputra, the son of Prâtîbodhî, she being probably one out of several wives of Hrasva. Another instance of this metronymic nomenclature occurred in Krishn̄a Devakîputra, Kh. Up. III, 7, 6. The Kashmir MS. reads Prâkîbodhî, but Pratibodha is a recognised name in Gan̄a Vidâdi, and the right reading is probably Prâtibodhî. The same MS. leaves out putra âha.

them, and without entirely uniting them[1]. Then
that mora between the first and second halves, which
indicates the union, that is the Sâman (evenness,
sliding). I therefore hold Sâman only to be the
Sa*m*hitâ (union).

7. This has also been declared by a *Ri*shi (Rv.
II, 23, 16):—

8. 'O B*ri*haspati, they know nothing higher than
Sâman.'

9. He who thus knows this Sa*m*hitâ (union), becomes united with offspring, cattle, fame, glory of
countenance, and the world of Svarga. He lives
his full age.

Sixth Khanda.

1. Târukshya[2] said: 'The Sa*m*hitâ (union) is formed
by means of the B*ri*hat and Rathantara[3] Sâmans.'

2. Verily, the Rathantara Sâman is speech, the
B*ri*hat Sâman is breath. By both, by speech and
breath, the Sa*m*hitâ is formed[4].

3. For this Upanishad (for acquiring from his
teacher the knowledge of this Sa*m*hitâ of speech
and breath) Târukshya guards (his teacher's) cows
a whole year.

4. For it alone Târukshya guards the cows a
whole year.

---

[1] So that the ê in tavet should neither be one letter e, nor two
letters a + i, but something between the two, enabling us to hear
a + i in the pronunciation of ê.

[2] The Kashmir MS. reads Târkshya, a name used before as the
title of a hymn (Ait. Âr. I, 5, 2, 8). Here Târukshya seems prefer-
able, see Pâ*n*. IV, 1, 105.

[3] See Ait. Âr. I, 4, 2, 1–4.

[4] These two, the B*ri*hat and Rathantara, are required for the
Pri*sh*t*h*astotra in the Agnish*t*oma, and they are to remind the worshipper that speech and breath are required for all actions.

5. This has also been declared by a *Ri*shi (Rv. X, 181, 1; and Rv. X, 181, 2):—

6. 'Vasish*th*a carried hither the Rathantara; 'Bharadvâ*g*a brought hither the B*ri*hat of Agni.'

7. He who thus knows this Sa*m*hitâ (union), becomes united with offspring, cattle, fame, glory of countenance, and the world of Svarga. He lives his full age.

8. Kau*nth*aravya said: 'Speech is united with breath, breath with the blowing air, the blowing air with the Vi*s*vedevas, the Vi*s*vedevas with the heavenly world, the heavenly world with Brahman. That Sa*m*hitâ is called the gradual Sa*m*hitâ.'

9. He who knows this gradual Sa*m*hitâ (union), becomes united with offspring, cattle, fame, glory of countenance, and the world of Svarga, in exactly the same manner as this Sa*m*hitâ, i.e. gradually.

10. If that worshipper, whether for his own sake or for that of another, recites (the Sa*m*hitâ), let him know when he is going to recite, that this Sa*m*hitâ went up to heaven, and that it will be even so with those who by knowing it become Devas. May it always be so!

11. He who thus knows this Sa*m*hitâ (union), becomes united with offspring, cattle, fame, glory of countenance, and the world of Svarga. He lives his full age.

12. Pañ*k*âla*k*a*nd*a said: 'The Sa*m*hitâ (union, composition) is speech.'

13. Verily, by speech the Vedas, by speech the metres are composed. Friends unite through speech, all beings unite through speech; therefore speech is everything here [1].

---

[1] Everything can be obtained by speech in this life and in the next. Comm.

14. With regard to this (view of speech being more than breath), it should be borne in mind that when we thus repeat (the Veda) or speak, breath is (absorbed) in speech; speech swallows breath. And when we are silent or sleep, speech is (absorbed) in breath; breath swallows speech. The two swallow each other. Verily, speech is the mother, breath the son.

15. This has been declared also by a *Ri*shi (Rv. X, 114, 4) :—

16. ' There is one bird; (as wind) he has entered the sky; (as breath or living soul) he saw this whole world. With my ripe mind I saw him close to me (in the heart) ; the mother (licks or) absorbs him (breath), and he absorbs the mother (speech).'

17. He who thus knows this Sa*m*hitâ (union), becomes united with offspring, cattle, fame, glory of countenance, and the world of Svarga. He lives his full age.

18. Next follows the Pra*g*âpati-Sa*m*hitâ.

19. The former half is the wife, the latter half the man ; the result of their union the son ; the act of their union the begetting ; that Sa*m*hitâ is Aditi (indestructible).

20. For Aditi (indestructible) is all this whatever there is, father, mother, son, and begetting.

21. This has also been declared by a *Ri*shi (Rv. I, 189, 10) :—

22. ' Aditi is mother, is father, is son.'

23. He who thus knows this Sa*m*hitâ (union), becomes united with offspring, cattle, fame, glory of countenance, and the world of Svarga. He lives his full age.

SECOND ADHYÂYA[1].

First Kha*nd*a.

1. Sthavira *S*âkalya said that breath is the beam[2], and as the other beams rest on the house-beam, thus the eye, the ear, the mind, the speech, the senses, the body, the whole self rests on this[3] breath.

2. Of that self the breathing is like the sibilants, the bones like the mutes, the marrow like the vowels, and the fourth part, flesh, blood, and the rest, like the semivowels[4],—so said Hrasva Mâ*nd*û-keya.

3. To us it was said to be a triad only[5].

4. Of that triad, viz. bones, marrow, and joints, there are 360 (parts) on this side (the right), and 360 on that side (the left). They make 720 together, and 720[6] are the days and nights of the year. Thus that self which consists of sight, hearing, metre, mind, and speech is like unto the days.

5. He who thus knows this self, which consists of sight, hearing, metre, mind, and speech, as like unto the days, obtains union, likeness, or nearness with the days, has sons and cattle, and lives his full age.

---

[1] In the first adhyâya meditations suggested by sa*m*hitâ, pada, and krama have been discussed. Now follow meditations suggested by certain classes of letters.

[2] Ait. Âr. III, 1, 4.

[3] The Kashmir MS. reads etasmin prâ*n*e. The self here is meant for the body, and yet it seems to be different from *s*arîra.

[4] The Kashmir MS. writes antastha without visarga, while it is otherwise most careful in writing all sibilants.

[5] *S*âkalya, as we saw, told his disciples that there were three classes only, not four. Comm. The Kashmir MS. reads traya*m* tv eva na ityetat proktam.

[6] The Kashmir MS. reads sapta vi*m*sati*s* *k*a *s*atâni.

Second Kha*n*da.

1. Next comes Kau*nth*aravya :

2. There are 360 syllables (vowels), 360 sibilants (consonants), 360 groups.

3. What we called syllables are the days, what we called sibilants are the nights, what we called groups are the junctions of days and nights. So far with regard to the gods (the days).

4. Now with regard to the body. The syllables which we explained mythologically, are physiologically the bones; the sibilants which we explained mythologically, are physiologically the marrow.

5. Marrow is the real breath (life), for marrow is seed, and without breath (life) seed is not sown. Or when it is sown without breath (life), it will decay, it will not grow.

6. The groups which we explained mythologically, are physiologically the joints.

7. Of that triad, viz. bones, marrow, and joints, there are 540 (parts) on this side (the right), and 540 on that side (the left). They make 1080 together, and 1080 are the rays of the sun. They make the Br*i*hatî verses and the day (of the Mahâvrata)[1].

8. Thus that self which consists of sight, hearing, metre, mind, and speech is like unto the syllables.

9. He who knows this self which consists of sight, hearing, metre, mind, and speech, as like unto syllables, obtains union, likeness, or nearness with the syllables, has sons and cattle, and lives his full age.

---

[1] There are in the Mahâvrata eighty tristichs of Br*i*hatîs, and as each Br*i*hatî is decreed to consist of thirty-six syllables, ten would give 360 syllables, and three times ten, 1080. Comm.

THIRD KHA*N*DA.

1. Bâdhva[1] says, there are four persons (to be meditated on and worshipped).

2. The person of the body, the person of the metres, the person of the Veda, and the Great person.

3. What we call the person of the body is this corporeal self. Its essence is the incorporeal conscious self.

4. What we call the person of the metres is this collection of letters (the Veda). Its essence is the vowel a.

5. What we call the person of the Veda is (the mind) by which we know the Vedas, the *Rig*-veda, Ya*g*ur-veda, and Sâma-veda. Its essence is Brahman[2] (m.)

6. Therefore let one chose a Brahman-priest who is full of Brahman (the Veda), and is able to see any flaw in the sacrifice.

7. What we call the Great person is the year, which causes some beings to fall together, and causes others to grow up. Its essence is yonder sun.

8. One should know that the incorporeal conscious self and yonder sun are both one and the same. Therefore the sun appears to every man singly (and differently).

9. This has also been declared by a *Ri*shi (Rv. I, 115, 1) :—

10. ' The bright face of the gods arose, the eye of Mitra, Varu*n*a, and Agni; it filled heaven and earth

---

[1] Instead of Bâdhya, the commentary and the Kashmir MS. read Bâdhva.

[2] Hira*n*yagarbha, with whom he who knows the Veda becomes identified. Comm.

and the sky,—the sun is the self of all that rests and moves.'

11. 'This I think to be the regular Sa*m*hitâ as conceived by me,' thus said Bâdhva.

12. For the Bahv*rik*as consider him (the self) in the great hymn (mahad uktha), the Adhvaryus in the sacrificial fire, the *Kh*andogas in the Mahâvrata ceremony. Him they see in this earth, in heaven, in the air, in the ether, in the water, in herbs, in trees, in the moon, in the stars, in all beings. Him alone they call Brahman.

13. That self which consists of sight, hearing, metre, mind, and speech is like unto the year.

14. He who recites to another that self which consists of sight, hearing, metre, mind, and speech, and is like unto the year,

FOURTH KHA*ND*A.

1. To him the Vedas yield no more milk, he has no luck in what he has learnt (from his Guru); he does not know the path of virtue.

2. This has also been declared by a *Ri*shi (Rv. X, 71, 6) :—

3. 'He who has forsaken the friend (the Veda), that knows his friends, in his speech there is no luck. Though he hears, he hears in vain, for he does not know the path of virtue.'

4. Here it is clearly said that he has no luck in what he has learnt, and that he does not know the path of virtue.

5. Therefore let no one who knows this, lay the sacrificial fire (belonging to the Mahâvrata) for another, let him not sing the Sâmans of the Mahâvrata

for another, let him not recite the *S*astras of that
day for another.

6. However, let him willingly do this for a father
or for an Â*k*ârya; for that is done really for
himself.

7. We have said that the incorporeal conscious
self and the sun are one [1]. When these two become
separated [2], the sun is seen as if it were the moon [3];
no rays spring from it; the sky is red like madder;
the patient cannot retain the wind, his head smells
bad like a raven's nest:—let him know then that his
self (in the body) is gone, and that he will not live
very long [4].

8. Then whatever he thinks he has to do,. let
him do it, and let him recite the following hymns:
Yad anti ya*k k*a dûrake (Rv. IX, 67, 21–27); Âd it
pratnasya retasa*h* (Rv. VIII, 6, 30); Yatra brahmâ
pavamâna (Rv. IX, 113, 6–11); Ud vaya*m* tamasas
pari (Rv. I, 50, 10).

9. Next, when the sun is seen pierced, and seems
like the nave of a cart-wheel, when he sees his own
shadow pierced, let him know then that it is so (as
stated before, i. e. that he is going to die soon).

10. Next, when he sees himself in a mirror or in
the water with a crooked head, or without a head [5], or
when his pupils are seen inverted [6] or not straight,
let him know then that it is so.

---

[1] Ait. Âr. III, 2, 3, 8.

[2] This separation of the self of the sun and the conscious self
within us is taken as a sign of approaching death, and therefore
a number of premonitory symptoms are considered in this place.

[3] ἥλιος μηνοειδής, Xen. Hist. gr. 4, 3, 10.

[4] The Kashmir MS. reads *g*îvayishyati.

[5] The Kashmir MS. reads *g*ihma*s*irasa*m* vâ*s*arîram âtmânam.

[6] A white pupil in a black eye-ball. Comm.

11. Next, let him cover his eyes and watch, then threads are seen as if falling together[1]. But if he does not see them, let him know then that it is so.

12. Next, let him cover his ears and listen, and there will be a sound as if of a burning fire or of a carriage[2]. But if he does not hear it, let him know then that it is so.

13. Next, when fire looks blue like the neck of a peacock[3], or when he sees lightning in a cloudless sky, or no lightning in a clouded sky, or when he sees as it were bright rays in a dark cloud, let him know then that it is so.

14. Next, when he sees the ground as if it were burning, let him know that it is so.

15. These are the visible signs (from 7–14).

16. Next come the dreams[4].

17. If he sees a black man with black teeth, and that man kills him; or a boar kills him; a monkey jumps on[5] him; the wind carries him along quickly; having swallowed gold he spits it out[6]; he eats honey; he chews stalks; he carries a red lotus; he drives with asses and boars; wearing a wreath of red flowers (naladas) he drives a black cow with a black calf, facing the south[7],

18. If a man sees any one of these (dreams), let

---

[1] The Kashmir MS. reads ba/irakâṇi sampatantîva.

[2] See *Kh*. Up. III, 13, 8. The Kashmir MS. and the commentary give the words rathasyevopabdis, which are left out in the printed text.

[3] The Kashmir MS. reads mayûragrîvâ ameghe.

[4] The Kashmir MS. reads svapnaḥ.

[5] The Kashmir MS. reads âskandati.

[6] The Kashmir MS. reads avagirati.

[7] The commentator separates the last dream, so as to bring their number to ten.

him fast, and cook a pot of milk, sacrifice it, accompanying each oblation with a verse of the Râtri hymn (Rv. X, 127), and then, after having fed the Brâhmanas, with other food (prepared at his house) eat himself the (rest of the) oblation.

19. Let him know that the person within all beings, not heard here [1], not reached, not thought, not subdued, not seen, not understood, not classed, but hearing, thinking, seeing, classing, sounding, understanding, knowing, is his Self.

FIFTH KHANDA [2].

1. Now next the Upanishad of the whole speech.

True all these are Upanishads of the whole speech, but this they call so (chiefly).

2. The mute consonants represent the earth, the sibilants the sky, the vowels heaven.

The mute consonants represent Agni (fire), the sibilants air, the vowels the sun.

The mute consonants represent the Rig-veda, the sibilants the Yagur-veda, the vowels the Sâma-veda.

The mute consonants represent the eye, the sibilants the ear, the vowels the mind.

The mute consonants represent the up-breathing, the sibilants the down-breathing, the vowels the back-breathing.

3. Next comes this divine lute (the human body, made by the gods). The lute made by man is an imitation of it.

4. As there is a head of this, so there is a head of that (lute, made by man). As there is a stomach

---

[1] The Kashmir MS. reads sa yatas sruto.

[2] After having inserted the preceding chapter on omina and the concluding paragraph on the highest knowledge, he now returns to the meditation on the letters.

of this, so there is the cavity[1] (in the board) of that. As there is a tongue of this, so there is a tongue[2] in that. As there are fingers of this, so there are strings of that[3]. As there are vowels of this, so there are tones of that. As there are consonants of this, so there are touches of that. As this is endowed with sound and firmly strung, so that is endowed with sound and firmly strung. As this is covered with a hairy skin, so that is covered with a hairy skin.

5. Verily, in former times they covered a lute with a hairy skin.

6. He who knows this lute made by the Devas (and meditates on it), is willingly listened to, his glory fills the earth, and wherever they speak Âryan languages, there they know him.

7. Next follows the verse, called vâgrasa, the essence of speech. When a man reciting or speaking in an assembly does not please, let him say this verse:

8. 'May the queen of all speech, who is covered, as it were, by the lips, surrounded by teeth, as if by spears, who is a thunderbolt, help me to speak well.' This is the vâgrasa, the essence of speech.

Sixth Khaṇḍa.

1. Next Krishṇa-Hârita[4] confided this Brâhmaṇa[5] concerning speech to him (his pupil):

---

[1] The Kashmir MS. reads udara evam, &c.

[2] Vâdanam, what makes the instrument speak, hastena. Comm.

[3] Here the order is inverted in the text.

[4] One of the sons of Harita, who was dark. Comm.

[5] Brâhmaṇa, in the sense of Upanishad, this secret doctrine or explanation. It forms an appendix, like the svishṭakrit at the end of a sacrifice. 'Iva,' which the commentator explains as restrictive or useless, may mean, something like a Brâhmaṇa.

2. Pra*g*âpati, the year, after having sent forth all creatures, burst. He put himself together again by means of *kh*andas (Vedas). Because he put himself together again by means of *kh*andas, therefore (the text of the Veda) is called Sa*m*hitâ (put together).

3. Of that Sa*m*hitâ the letter *n* is the strength, the letter sh the breath and self (âtman).

4. He who knows the *Ri*k verses and the letters *n* and sh for every Sa*m*hitâ, he knows the Sa*m*hitâ with strength and breath. Let him know that this is the life of the Sa*m*hitâ.

5. If the pupil asks, ' Shall I say it with the letter *n* or without it ? ' let the teacher say, 'With the letter *n*.' And if he asks, ' Shall I say it with the letter sh or without it ?' let the teacher say, ' With the letter sh [1].'

6. Hrasva Mâ*nd*ûkeya said : ' If we here recite the verses according to the Sa*m*hitâ (attending to the necessary changes of n and s into *n* and sh [2]), and if we say the adhyâya of Mâ*nd*ûkeya (Ait. Âr. III, 1), then the letters *n* and sh (strength and breath) have by this been obtained for us.'

7. Sthavira *S*âkalya said: ' If we recite the verses according to the Sa*m*hitâ, and if we say the adhyâya of Mâ*nd*ûkeya, then the letters *n* and sh have by this been obtained for us.'

8. Here the *Ri*shis, the Kâvasheyas [3], knowing

---

[1] The letters *n* and sh refer most likely to the rules of *n*atva and shatva, i. e. the changing of n and s into *n* and sh.

[2] If we know whenever n and s should be changed to *n* and sh in the Sa*m*hitâ.

[3] The Kâvasheyas said that, after they had arrived at the highest knowledge of Brahman (through the various forms of meditation and worship that lead to it and that have been described in the Upanishad) no further meditation and no further sacrifice could be

this, said : 'Why should we repeat (the Veda),
why should we sacrifice ? We offer as a sacrifice
breath in speech, or speech in breath. What is
the beginning (of one), that is the end (of the
other).'

9. Let no one tell these Samhitâs (Ait. Âr. III, 1–
III, 2) to one who is not a resident pupil, who has
not been with his teacher at least one year, and who
is not himself to become an instructor[1]. Thus say
the teachers, yea, thus say the teachers.

---

required. Instead of the morning and evening stoma they offer
breath in speech, whenever they speak, or speech in breath, when
they are silent or asleep. When speech begins, breathing ceases;
when breathing begins, speech ceases.

[1] The strict prohibition uttered at the end of the third Ârañyaka,
not to divulge a knowledge of the Samhitâ-upanishad (Ait. Âr.
III, 1–2), as here explained, is peculiar. It would have seemed
self-evident that, like the rest of the sruti or sacred literature, the
Ârañyaka too, and every portion of it, could have been learnt from
the mouth of a teacher only, and according to rule (niyamena), i. e.
by a pupil performing all the duties of a student (brahmakârin[2]),
so that no one except a regular pupil (antevâsin) could possibly
gain access to it. Nor can there be any doubt that we ought
to take the words asamvatsaravâsin and apravaktri as limitations,
and to translate, 'Let no one tell these Samhitâs to any pupil who
has not at least been a year with his master, and who does not
mean to become a teacher in turn.'

That this is the right view is confirmed by similar injunctions
given at the end of the fifth Ârañyaka. Here we have first some·
rules as to who is qualified to recite the Mahâvrata. No one is
permitted to do so, who has not passed through the Dîkshâ, the
initiation for the Agnishtoma. If the Mahâvrata is performed as a
Sattra, the sacrificer is a Hotri priest, and he naturally has passed
through that ceremony. But if the Mahâvrata is performed as an
Ekâha or Ahîna ceremony, anybody might be the sacrificer, and
therefore it was necessary to say that no one who is adîkshita, uninitiated, should recite it for another person; nor should he do so,

---

[2] Âpastamba-sûtras, translated by Bühler, p. 18.

when the Mahâvrata is performed without (or with) an altar, or if it does not last one year.   In saying, however, that one should not recite the Mahâvrata for another person, parents and teachers are not to be understood as included, because what is done for them, is done for ourselves.

After these restrictions as to the recitation of the Mahâvrata, follow other restrictions as to the teaching of it, and here we read, as at the end of the Upanishad :

4. 'Let no one teach this day, the Mahâvrata, to one who is not a regular pupil (antevâsin), and has been so for one year, certainly not to one who has not been so for one year; nor to one who is not a brahma*k*ârin and does not study the same Veda[1], certainly not to one who does not study the same Veda ; nor to one who does not come to him.

5. 'Let the teaching not be more than saying it once or twice, twice only.

6. 'One man should tell it to one man, so says *G*âtukar*n*ya.

7. 'Not to a child, nor to a man in his third stage of life.

8. 'The teacher and pupil should not stand, nor walk, nor lie down, nor sit on a couch; but they should both sit on the ground.

9. 'The pupil should not lean backward while learning, nor lean forward.   He should not be covered with too much clothing, nor assume the postures of a devotee, but without using any of the apparel of a devotee, simply elevate his knees.   Nor should he learn, when he has eaten flesh, when he has seen blood, or a corpse, or when he has done an unlawful thing[2]; when he has anointed his eyes, oiled or rubbed his body, when he has been shaved or bathed, put colour on, or ornamented himself with flower-wreaths, when he has been writing or effacing his writing[3].

10. 'Nor should he finish the reading in one day, so says *G*âtu-kar*n*ya, while according to Gâlava, he should finish it in one day. Âgnive*s*yâyana holds that he should finish all before the T*ri*kâs*î*tis[4], and then rest in another place finishing it.

11. 'And in the place where he reads this, he should not read

---

[1] See Gautama-sûtras XIV, 21, and Bühler's note.

[2] Nâvratyam âkramya is explained by the commentator by u*kkh*ish*t*âdyâkrama*n*a.

[3] This, if rightly translated, would seem to be the earliest mention of actual writing in Sanskrit literature.

[4] See Ait. Âr. I, 4, 3, 1–4.

anything else, though he may read this (the Mahâvrata) where he has read something else.

12. 'No one should bathe and become a snâtaka[1] who does not read this. Even if he has read many other things, he should not become a snâtaka if he has not read this.

13. 'Nor should he forget it, and even if he should forget anything else, he should not forget this.

14. 'No, he should never forget this.

15. 'If he does not forget this, it will be enough for himself (or for acquiring a knowledge of the Self).

16. ' It is enough, let him know this to be true.

17. 'Let him who knows this not communicate, nor dine, nor amuse himself with any one who does not know it.'

Then follow some more rules as to the reading of the Veda in general:

18. 'When the old water that stood round the roots of trees is dried up (after about the month of Pausha, January to February[2]) he should not read; nor (at any time) in the morning or in the afternoon, when the shadows meet (he should begin at sunrise so soon as the shadows divide, and end in the evening before they fall together). Nor should he read[3] when a cloud has risen; and when there is an unseasonable rain (after the months of *S*râva*n*a and Bhâdrapada, August and September[4]) he should stop his Vedic reading for three nights. Nor should he at that time tell stories, not even during the night, nor should he glory in his knowledge.

19. ' This (the Veda thus learnt and studied) is the name of that Great Being; and he who thus knows the name of that Great Being, he becomes Brahman, yea, he becomes Brahman.'

---

[1] Âpastamba-sûtras, translated by Bühler, p. 92 (I, 2, 30, 4).

[2] Âpastamba-sûtras, translated by Bühler, p. 33 (I, 3, 9, 2).

[3] Âpastamba-sûtras, translated by Bühler, p. 44 (I, 3, 11, 31).

[4] Âpastamba-sûtras, translated by Bühler, p. 33 (I, 3, 9, 1).

KAUSHÎTAKI-BRÂHMA*N*A-
UPANISHAD.

KAUSHÎTAKI-UPANISHAD.

FIRST ADHYÂYA.

1. *K*ITRA Gângyâyani[1], forsooth, wishing to perform a sacrifice, chose Âru*n*i (Uddâlaka[2], to be his chief priest). But Âru*n*i sent his son, *S*vetaketu, and said: 'Perform the sacrifice for him.' When *S*vetaketu[3] had arrived, *K*itra asked him: 'Son of Gautama[4], is there a hidden place in the world where you are able to place me, or is it the other way, and are you going to place me in the world to which it (that other way) leads[5]?'

---

[1] It is difficult to determine whether *K*itra's name was Gângyâyani or Gârgyâya*n*i. Professor Weber adopted first Gârgyâya*n*i (Indische Studien I, p. 395), afterwards Gângyâyani (ibid. II, 395). Professor Cowell adopts Gângyâyani, but he tells us that the Telugu MS. reads Gârgyâya*n*i throughout, and the other MSS. B, C do so occasionally. The commentator explains Gângyâyani as the descendant (yuvâpatyam) of Gângya. I confess a preference for Gârgyâya*n*i, because both Gangâ and Gângya are names of rare occurrence in ancient Vedic literature, but I admit that for that very reason the transition of Gângyâyani into Gârgyâya*n*i is perhaps more intelligible than that of Gârgyâya*n*i into Gângyâyani.

[2] Cf. *Kh*. Up. V, 11, 2; B*ri*h. Âr. VI, 2, 1.

[3] Cf. *Kh*. Up. V, 3; VI, 1.   [4] B*ri*h. Âr. VI, 2, 4.

[5] The question put by *K*itra to *S*vetaketu is very obscure, and was probably from the first intended to be obscure in its very wording. What *K*itra wished to ask we can gather from other passages in the Upanishads, where we see another royal sage, Pravâha*n*a Gaivali (*Kh*. Up. V, 3; B*ri*h. Âr. VI, 2), enlightening *S*vetaketu on the future life. That future life is reached by two roads;

He answered and said: 'I do not know this. But, let me ask the master.' Having approached his father, he asked : 'Thus has *K*itra asked me; how shall I answer ?'

one, the Devapatha, leading to the world of Brahman (the conditioned), beyond which there lies one other stage only, represented by knowledge of and identity with the unconditioned Brahman ; the other leading to the world of the fathers, and from thence, after the reward of good works has been consumed, back to a new round of mundane existence.   There is a third road for creatures which live and die, worms, insects, and creeping things, but they are of little consequence.   Now it is quite clear that the knowledge which king *K*itra possesses, and which *S*vetaketu does not possess, is that of the two roads after death, sometimes called the right and the left, or the southern and northern roads.   These roads are fully described in the *Kh*ândogya-upanishad and in the Br*i*had-âra*n*yaka, with certain variations, yet on the whole with the same purpose.   The northern or left road, called also the path of the Devas, passes on from light and day to the bright half of the moon ; the southern or right road, called also the path of the fathers, passes on from smoke and night to the dark half of the moon.   Both roads therefore meet in the moon, but diverge afterwards.   While the northern road passes by the six months when the sun moves towards the north, through the sun, (moon,) and the lightning to the world of Brahman, the southern passes by the six months when the sun moves towards the south, to the world of the fathers, the ether, and the moon.   The great difference, however, between the two roads is, that while those who travel on the former do not return again to a new life on earth, but reach in the end a true knowledge of the unconditioned Brahman, those who pass on to the world of the fathers and the moon return to earth to be born again and again.

The question therefore which *K*itra addresses to *S*vetaketu can refer to these two roads only, and though the text is very corrupt, and was so evidently even at the time when the commentary was written, we must try to restore it in accordance with the teaching imparted by *K*itra in what follows.   I propose to read: Gautamasya putra, asti sa*mv*r*i*ta*m* loke yasmin mâ dhâsyasy anyatamo vâdhvâ tasya (or yasya) mâ loke dhâsyasi, 'Is there a hidden place in the world where you (by your sacrificing and teaching) are able to

Âru*n*i said : ' I also do not know this. Only after having learnt the proper portion of the Veda in *K*itra's own dwelling, shall we obtain what others give us (knowledge). Come, we will both go.'

Having said this he took fuel in his hand (like a pupil), and approached *K*itra Gângyâyani, saying : 'May I come near to you?' He replied: 'You are worthy of Brahman[1], O Gautama, because you were not led away by pride. Come hither, I shall make you know clearly.'

2. And *K*itra said: All who depart from this world (or this body) go to the moon[2]. In the former, (the bright) half, the moon delights in their spirits; in the other, (the dark) half, the moon sends them on

---

place me, or is it the other way, and will you place me in the world to which it leads?' Even thus the text is by no means satisfactory, but it is better than anyam aho vâdhvâ, adopted by the commentator and explained by him : Is there a hidden place in that world in which you will place me as another, i. e. as different from the whole world or identical with the whole world, and, if as different, then having bound me (vâdhvâ=baddhvâ) and made me a different person? We may read anyataro for anyatamo vâdhvâ. The commentator sums up the question as referring to a hidden or not hidden place, where *K*itra should be placed as another person or not another person, as bound or not bound; or, as Professor Cowell renders it, ' O son of Gautama, is there any secret place in the world where thou canst set me unconnected, having fixed me there (as wood united with glue); or is there some other place where thou canst set me?' The speculations on the fate of the soul after death seem to have been peculiar to the royal families of India, while the Brahmans dwelt more on what may be called the shorter cut, a knowledge of Brahman as the true Self. To know, with them, was to be, and, after the dissolution of the body, they looked forward to immediate emancipation, without any further wanderings.

[1] Worthy to know Brahman, or, as the commentator, who reads brahmârgha, thinks, to be honoured like Brahman.

[2] Both roads lead to the moon, and diverge afterwards.

to be born again [1]. Verily, the moon is the door of
the Svarga world (the heavenly world). Now, if a
man objects to the moon (if one is not satisfied with
life there) the moon sets him free [2]. But if a man
does not object, then the moon sends him down as
rain upon this earth. And according to his deeds
and according to his knowledge he is born again
here as a worm, or as an insect, or as a fish, or as a
bird, or as a lion, or as a boar, or as a serpent [3], or
as a tiger, or as a man, or as something else in different places [4]. When he has thus returned to the
earth, some one (a sage) asks : 'Who art thou ?'
And he should answer : ' From the wise moon, who
orders the seasons [5], when it is born consisting of
fifteen parts, from the moon who is the home of our
ancestors, the seed was brought. This seed, even
me, they (the gods mentioned in the Pañkâgnividyâ [6])
gathered up in an active man, and through an active

---

[1] I should like to read aparapakshe praganayati, instead of
aparapakshena, or aparapakshe na. The negative is out of the
question, for praganayati, he sends into a new life, is exactly what
the moon does to those who do not proceed on the Devapatha to
the Brahmaloka. Therefore if the reading aparapakshena must be
retained, it should be rendered by 'the moon with the dark half
sends them into a new life.'

[2] This is supposed to be the hidden place, or rather the way to
it, when the departed leave the moon, and pass on to lightning
and to the world of Brahman. This is in fact the Devayâna, as
opposed to the Pitriyâna, described in the Khândogya-upanishad.

[3] Parasvâ, dandasûkaviseshah. There is no authority for translating it by dog; cf. Indische Studien I, 396.

[4] This might even include naraka or hell.

[5] If ritavah is here the genitive of ritu, its meaning would be
the ordainer of the seasons; cf. Hibbert Lectures, p. 247. Vika-
kshana is applied to the moon again, II, 9, and the throne of
Brahman also is called vikakshanâ, I, 3.

[6] Kh. Up. V, 4–8.

man they brought me to a mother. Then I, growing up to be born, a being living by months, whether twelve or thirteen, was together with my father, who also lived by (years of) twelve or thirteen months, that I might either know it (the true Brahman) or not know it. Therefore, O ye seasons [1], grant that I may attain immortality (knowledge of Brahman). By this my true saying, by this my toil (beginning with the dwelling in the moon and ending with my birth on earth) I am (like) a season, and the child of the seasons.' 'Who art thou?' the sage asks again. 'I am thou,' he replies. Then he sets him free [2] (to proceed onward).

3. He (at the time of death), having reached the path of the gods, comes to the world of Agni (fire), to the world of Vâyu (air), to the world of Varuna, to the world of Indra, to the world of Pragâpati (Virâg), to the world of Brahman (Hiranyagarbha). In that world there is the lake Âra [3], the moments called Yeshtiha [4], the river Vigarâ (age-less), the tree Ilya [5], the city Sâlagya, the palace Aparâgita (unconquerable), the door-keepers Indra

---

[1] The commentator takes ritavah as an accusative. I take it as a vocative, and as used in a sense analogous to the Zend ratu, an epithet of Ahura. Darmesteter, Ormazd, p. 12, n. 3.

[2] If a person fears heaven (svarga) as much as hell, because neither gives final liberation, then he is fit to proceed to a knowledge of Brahman. It would seem that after this, this person is in the same position as the other who, objecting to remain in the moon, was set free at once.

[3] Consisting of ari's, enemies, such as love, anger, &c. In the Kh. Up. VIII, 5, 3, it is called Ara.

[4] Explained to mean, killing the sacrifice, which consists in a desire for Brahman.

[5] The same as the asvatthah somasavanah in Kh. Up. VIII, 5, 3.

and Pra*g*âpati, the hall of Brahman, called Vibhu [1]
(built by vibhu, egoism), the throne Vi*k*akshanâ
(buddhi, perception), the couch Amitau*g*as (endless
splendour), and the beloved Mânasî (mind) and her
image *K*âkshushî (eye), who, as if taking flowers, are
weaving the worlds, and the Apsaras, the Ambâs
(*s*ruti, sacred scriptures), and Ambâyavîs (buddhi,
understanding), and the rivers Ambayâs (leading
to the knowledge of Brahman). To this world he
who knows this (who knows the Parya*n*ka-vidyâ)
approaches. Brahman says to him: ' Run towards
him (servants) with such worship as is due to myself.
He has reached the river Vi*g*arâ (age-less), he will
never age.'

4. Then five hundred Apsaras go towards him, one
hundred with garlands in their hands, one hundred
with ointments in their hands, one hundred with perfumes in their hands, one hundred with garments in
their hands, one hundred with fruit [2] in their hands.
They adorn him with an adornment worthy of Brahman, and when thus adorned with the adornment of
Brahman, the knower of Brahman moves towards
Brahman (neut.)[3] He comes to the lake Âra, and he
crosses it by the mind, while those who come to it
without knowing the truth [4], are drowned. He comes
to the moments called Yesh*t*iha, they flee from him.

---

[1] Vibhunâmakam pramita*m* sabhâsthalam.

[2] Some MSS. read pha*n*ahastâ*h*, and the commentator explains
pha*n*a by âbhara*n*a.

[3] Though brahman is used here as a neuter, it refers to the
conditioned Brahman.

[4] Samprativid is here explained as brahmavidyâ*s*ûnya, ignorant,
while in other places (Ait. Âr. II, 3, 1) it stands for samyagabhi*gñ*a.
If the latter is the true meaning, we might read here tam itvâsam-
prativido.

He comes to the river Vi*g*arâ, and crosses it by the mind alone, and there shakes off his good and evil deeds. His beloved relatives obtain the good, his unbeloved relatives the evil he has done. And as a man, driving in a chariot, might look at the two wheels (without being touched by them), thus he will look at day and night, thus at good and evil deeds, and at all pairs (at all correlative things, such as light and darkness, heat and cold, &c.) Being freed from good and freed from evil he, the knower of Brahman (neut.), moves towards Brahman.

5. He approaches the tree Ilya, and the odour of Brahman reaches him. He approaches the city Sâla*g*ya, and the flavour of Brahman reaches him. He approaches the palace Aparâ*g*ita, and the splendour of Brahman reaches him. He approaches the door-keepers Indra and Pra*g*âpati, and they run away from him. He approaches the hall Vibhu, and the glory of Brahman reaches him (he thinks, I am Brahman). He approaches the throne Vi*k*aksha*n*â. The Sâman verses, B*ri*had and Rathantara, are the eastern feet of that throne[1]; the Sâman verses, *S*yaita and Naudhasa, its western feet; the Sâman verses, Vairûpa and Vairâ*g*a, its sides lengthways (south and north); the Sâman verses, *S*âkvara and Raivata, its sides crossways (east and west). That throne is Pra*g*ñâ, knowledge, for by knowledge (self-knowledge) he sees clearly. He approaches the couch Amitau*g*as. That is Prâ*n*a (speech). The past and the future are its eastern feet; prosperity and earth its western feet; the Sâman verses, B*ri*had and Rathantara, are the two sides lengthways of the couch (south and north);

---

[1] Cf. Atharva-veda XV; Aufrecht, in Indische Studien I, p. 122.

the Sâman verses, Bhadra and Yag̃ñâyag̃ñîya, are its cross-sides at the head and feet (east and west); the *Rik* and Sâman are the long sheets[1] (east and west); the Yag̃us the cross-sheets (south and north); the moon-beam the cushion; the Udgîtha the (white) coverlet; prosperity the pillow[2]. On this couch sits Brahman, and he who knows this (who knows himself one with Brahman sitting on the couch) mounts it first with one foot only. Then Brahman says to him: 'Who art thou?' and he shall answer:

6. 'I am (like) a season, and the child of the seasons, sprung from the womb of endless space, from the light (from the luminous Brahman). The light, the origin of the year, which is the past, which is the present, which is all living things, and all elements, is the Self[3]. Thou art the Self. What thou art, that am I.'

Brahman says to him: 'Who am I?' He shall answer: 'That which is, the true' (Sat-tyam).

Brahman asks: 'What is the true?' He says to him: 'What is different from the gods and from the senses (prâ*n*a) that is Sat, but the gods and the

---

[1] Sheets or coverings seem more applicable here than mere threads forming the woof and warp; cf. Aufrecht, Indische Studien I, p. 131.

[2] I read udgîtha upa*s*rî*h*, *s*rîr upabarha*n*am. The Atharva text has udgîtho 'pa*s*raya*h*.

[3] This passage is corrupt, and the various readings and various interpretations of the commentators do not help us much. One view, which I have followed, as far as possible, is that it had to be explained how the same being could be the child of the seasons, or living from year to year, and, at the same time, born of the light. The answer is, Because light is the seed or cause of the year, and the year the cause of everything else. I take no responsibility for this view, and I see no way of discovering the original reading and the original meaning of these sentences.

senses are Tyam. Therefore by that name Sattya (true) is called all this whatever there is. All this thou art.'

7. This is also declared by a verse: 'This great *Ri*shi, whose belly is the Ya*g*us, the head the Sâman, the form the *Rik*, is to be known as being imperishable, as being Brahman.'

Brahman says to him: 'How dost thou obtain my male names?' He should answer: 'By breath (prâ*na*h).'

Brahman asks: 'How my female names?' He should answer: 'By speech (vâ*k*).'

Brahman asks: 'How my neuter names?' He should answer: 'By mind (manas).'

'How smells?' 'By the nose.' 'How forms?' 'By the eye.' 'How sounds?' 'By the ear.' 'How flavours of food?' 'By the tongue.' 'How actions?' 'By the hands.' 'How pleasures and pain?' 'By the body.' 'How joy, delight, and offspring?' 'By the organ.' 'How journeyings?' 'By the feet.' 'How thoughts, and what is to be known and desired?' 'By knowledge (pra*g*ñâ) alone.'

Brahman says to him: 'Water indeed is this my world[1], the whole Brahman world, and it is thine.'

Whatever victory, whatever might belongs to Brahman, that victory and that might he obtains who knows this, yea, who knows this[2].

---

[1] It sprang from water and the other elements. Comm. Professor Weber proposes to translate âpa*h* by Erlangungen, acquisitions, with reference to apnoshi, 'how dost thou acquire my names?' in what precedes.

[2] Who knows the conditioned and mythological form of Brahman as here described, sitting on the couch.

SECOND ADHYÂYA.

1. Prâna (breath)[1] is Brahman, thus says Kaushîtaki. Of this prâna, which is Brahman, the mind (manas) is the messenger, speech the housekeeper, the eye the guard, the ear the informant. He who knows mind as the messenger of prâna, which is Brahman, becomes possessed of the messenger. He who knows speech as the housekeeper, becomes possessed of the housekeeper. He who knows the eye as the guard, becomes possessed of the guard. He who knows the ear as the informant, becomes possessed of the informant.

Now to that prâna, which is Brahman, all these deities (mind, speech, eye, ear) bring an offering, though he asks not for it, and thus to him who knows this all creatures bring an offering, though he asks not for it. For him who knows this, there is this Upanishad (secret vow), ' Beg not!' As a man who has begged through a village and got nothing sits down and says, ' I shall never eat anything given by those people,' and as then those who formerly refused him press him (to accept their alms), thus is the rule for him who begs not, but the charitable will press him and say, ' Let us give to thee.'

2. Prâna (breath) is Brahman, thus says Paingya. And in that prâna, which is Brahman, the eye

---

[1] In the first chapter it was said, ' He approaches the couch Amitaugas, that is prâna, breath, spirit, life. Therefore having explained in the first adhyâya the knowledge of the couch (of Brahman), the next subject to be explained is the knowledge of prâna, the living spirit, taken for a time as Brahman, or the last cause of everything.'

stands firm behind speech, the ear stands firm behind the eye, the mind stands firm behind the ear, and the spirit stands firm behind the mind[1]. To that prâ*n*a, which is Brahman, all these deities bring an offering, though he asks not for it, and thus to him who knows this, all creatures bring an offering, though he asks not for it. For him who knows this, there is this Upanishad (secret vow), 'Beg not!' As a man who has begged through a village and got nothing sits down and says, 'I shall never eat anything given by those people,' and as then those who formerly refused him press him (to accept their alms), thus is the rule for him who begs not, but the charitable will press him and say, 'Let us give to thee.'

3. Now follows the attainment of the highest treasure (scil. prâ*n*a, spirit[2]). If a man meditates on that highest treasure, let him on a full moon or a new moon, or in the bright fortnight, under an auspicious Nakshatra, at one of these proper times, bending his right knee, offer oblations of ghee with a ladle (sruva), after having placed the fire, swept the ground[3], strewn the sacred grass, and sprinkled water. Let him say: 'The deity called Speech is

---

[1] I translate vâkparastât, *k*akshu*h*parastât, mana*h*parastât as compounds, and read *s*rotraparastât. The commentator requires this. He says that speech is uncertain, and has to be checked by the eye. The eye is uncertain, taking mother of pearl for silver, and must be checked by the ear. The ear is uncertain, and must be checked by the mind, for unless the mind is attentive, the ear hears not. The mind, lastly, depends on the spirit, for without spirit there is no mind. The commentator is right in reading rundhe or runddhe instead of rundhâte.

[2] The vital spirits are called the highest treasure, because a man surrenders everything to preserve his vital spirits or his life.

[3] Cf. Br*i*h. Âr. VI, 3, 1.

the attainer, may it attain this for me from him (who possesses and can bestow what I wish for). Svâhâ to it!'

'The deity called prâ*n*a (breath) is the attainer, may it attain this for me from him. Svâhâ to it!'

'The deity called the eye is the attainer, may it attain this for me from him. Svâhâ to it!'

'The deity called the ear is the attainer, may it attain this for me from him. Svâhâ to it!'

'The deity called mind (manas) is the attainer of it, may it attain this for me from him. Svâhâ to it.'

'The deity called pra*gñ*â (knowledge) is the attainer of it, may it attain this for me from him. Svâhâ to it!'

Then having inhaled the smell of the smoke, and having rubbed his limbs with the ointment of ghee, walking on in silence, let him declare his wish, or let him send a messenger. He will surely obtain his wish.

4. Now follows the Daiva Smara, the desire to be accomplished by the gods. If a man desires to become dear [1] to any man or woman, or to any men or women, then at one of the (fore-mentioned) proper times he offers, in exactly the same manner (as before), oblations of ghee, saying : 'I offer thy speech in myself, I (this one here [2]), Svâhâ.' 'I offer thy ear in myself, I (this one here), Svâhâ.' 'I offer thy

---

[1] As dear as prâ*n*a or life.

[2] The commentator explains these mysterious utterances by : 'I offer, I throw, in the fire, which is lit by the fuel of thy indifference or dislike, in myself, being the object of thy love, speech, the organ of speech, of thee, who art going to love me. This one, i. e. I myself, or my love, may prosper. Svâhâ, my speech, may grant approval to the oblation of me, the lover.'

mind in myself, I (this one here), Svâhâ.' ' I offer thy pragñâ (knowledge) in myself, I (this one here), Svâhâ.' Then having inhaled the smell of the smoke, and having rubbed his limbs with the ointment of ghee, walking on in silence, let him try to come in contact or let him stand speaking in the wind, (so that the wind may carry his words to the person by whom he desires to be loved). Surely he becomes dear, and they think of him.

5. Now follows the restraint (saṃyamana) instituted by Pratardana (the son of Divodâsa): they call it the inner Agni-hotra. So long as a man speaks, he cannot breathe, he offers all the while his prâṇa (breath) in his speech. And so long as a man breathes, he cannot speak, he offers all the while his speech in his breath. These two endless and immortal oblations he offers always, whether waking or sleeping. Whatever other oblations there are (those, e. g. of the ordinary Agnihotra, consisting of milk and other things), they have an end, for they consist of works (which, like all works, have an end). The ancients, knowing this (the best Agnihotra), did not offer the (ordinary) Agnihotra.

6. Uktha [1] is Brahman, thus said Sushkabhriṅgâra. Let him meditate on it (the uktha) as the same with the Rik, and all beings will praise him as the best. Let him meditate on it as the same with the Yagus, and all beings will join before him

---

[1] Uktha, a Vedic hymn, has been identified with prâṇa, breath, in the Kâṇva and other Sâkhâs (Brih. Âr. V, 13, 1; Ait. Âr. II, 1, 2). Here uktha, i. e. the prâṇa of the uktha, is further identified with Brahman. As uktha (the hymn) is prâṇa, and as the sacrifice is performed with hymns, the sacrifice, too, is uktha, and therefore prâṇa, and therefore Brahman. Comm.

as the best. Let him meditate on it as the same
with the Sâman, and all beings will bow before
him as the best[1]. Let him meditate on it as the
same with might, let him meditate on it as the same
with glory, let him meditate on it as the same with
splendour. For as the bow is among weapons the
mightiest, the most glorious, the most splendid, thus
is he who knows this among all beings the mightiest,
the most glorious, the most splendid. The Adhvaryu
conceives the fire of the altar, which is used for the
sacrifice, to be himself. In it he (the Adhvaryu)
weaves the Ya*g*us portion of the sacrifice. And in
the Ya*g*us portion the Hot*ri* weaves the *Rik* portion
of the sacrifice. And in the *Rik* portion the Udgât*ri* weaves the Sâman portion of the sacrifice.
He (the Adhvaryu or prâ*n*a) is the self of the
threefold knowledge; he indeed is the self of it
(of prâ*n*a). He who knows this is the self of it
(becomes prâ*n*a[2]).

---

[1] The verbs ar*k*, yu*g*, and sannam are not used idiomatically,
but with reference to the words *rik*, ya*g*us, and sâman.

[2] The commentator explains this somewhat differently. He
takes it to be the object of the last paragraph to show that the
Prâ*n*a-vidyâ can ultimately produce final liberation, and not only
temporal rewards. The Adhvaryu priest, he says, takes what is
called uktha, and has been identified with *Rik*, Ya*g*us, and Sâman
hymns, all contained in the mouth, as being outwardly the sacrificial fire of the altar, because that fire cannot be lighted without
such hymns. Thus the self of the Adhvaryu priest becomes identified, not only with the uktha, the hymns, but also with the sacrificial
fire, and he meditates on himself as fire, as hymn (uktha), and as
breath (prâ*n*a). I read sa esha sarvasyai trayyai vidyâyâ âtmâ,
esha u evâsyâtmâ. Etadâtmâ bhavati ya eva*m* veda. But if we
read asyâtmâ, we cannot with the commentator explain it by asyâ
uktâyâs trayyâ âtmâ, but must refer asya to prâ*n*a, breath, life,
which is here to be identified with Brahman.

7. Next follow the three kinds of meditation of the all-conquering (sarva*g*it) Kaushîtaki. The all-conquering Kaushîtaki adores the sun when rising, having put on the sacrificial cord[1], having brought water, and having thrice sprinkled the water-cup, saying : 'Thou art the deliverer, deliver me from sin.' In the same manner he adores the sun when in the zenith, saying : 'Thou art the highest deliverer, deliver me highly from sin.' In the same manner he adores the sun when setting, saying : 'Thou art the full deliverer, deliver me fully from sin.' Thus he fully removes whatever sin he committed by day and by night. And in the same manner he who knows this, likewise adores the sun, and fully removes whatever sin he committed by day and by night.

8. Then (secondly) let him worship every month (in the year) at the time of the new moon, the moon as it is seen in the west in the same manner (as before described with regard to the sun), or let him send forth his speech toward the moon with two green blades of grass, saying : 'O thou who art mistress of immortal joy, through that gentle heart of mine which abides in the moon, may I never weep for misfortune concerning my children.'

The children of him (who thus adores the moon) do not indeed die before him. Thus it is with a man to whom a son is already born.

Now for one to whom no son is born as yet. He mutters the three *Rik* verses. 'Increase, O Soma! may vigour come to thee' (Rv. I, 91, 16 ; IX, 31, 4).

---

[1] This is one of the earliest, if not the earliest mention of the ya*g*ñopavîta, the sacred cord as worn over the left shoulder for sacrificial purposes ; cf. Taitt. Brâhm. III, 10, 19, 12.

'May milk, may food go to thee' (Rv. I, 91, 18);
'That ray which the Âdityas gladden.'

Having muttered these three *Rik* verses, he says :
'Do not increase by our breath (prâ*n*a), by our offspring, by our cattle; he who hates us and whom we
hate, increase by his breath, by his offspring, by his
cattle. Thus I turn the turn of the god, I return
the turn of Âditya[1].' After these words, having
raised the right arm (toward Soma), he lets it go
again[2].

---

[1] This refers to movements of the arm, following the moon and
the sun.

[2] It is extremely difficult to translate the Vedic verses which are
quoted in the Upanishads. They are sometimes slightly changed
on purpose (see § 11), frequently turned from their original purport
by the authors of the Upanishads themselves, and then again sub-
jected to the most fanciful interpretations by the various commentators on the Upanishads. In our paragraph (§ 8) the text followed
by the commentator differs from the printed text. The commentator seems to have read : Yat te susîma*m* hr*i*dayam adhi *k*andra-
masi *sri*tam, tenâm*ri*tatvasye*s*âne mâham pautram agha*m* rudam.
I have translated according to the commentator, at least up to
a certain point, for, as Professor Cowell remarks, there is an under-
current in the commentator's explanation, implying a comparison
between the husband as the sun or fire, and the wife as the moon,
which it would be difficult to render in an English translation.
The same or a very similar verse occurs in § 10, while other modifications of it may be seen in Â*s*val. G*ri*hya-sûtras I, 13, 7, and elsewhere. The translation of the verses in full, of three of which the
Upanishad gives the beginnings only, would be according to the
commentator : '(O goddess of the moon) who hast obtained immortal joy through that which is a beautiful (portion of the sun)
placed in the moon, and filling thy heart (with pleasure), may
I never weep for misfortune concerning my children.'
Rv. I, 91, 16; IX, 31, 4. 'O goddess of the moon, increase !
may the vigour from everywhere (from every limb of the fire or the
sun) go to thee ! Help us in the attainment of food.' Rv. I, 91,
18. 'O goddess of the moon, may the streams of thy milk go
well to our sons, those streams of milk which are invigorating, and

9. Then (thirdly) let him worship on the day of the full moon the moon as it is seen in the east in the same manner, saying: 'Thou art Soma, the king, the wise, the five-mouthed, the lord of creatures. The Brâhma*n*a is one of thy mouths; with that mouth thou eatest the kings (Kshatriyas); make me an eater of food by that mouth! The king is one of thy mouths; with that mouth thou eatest the people (Vai*s*yas); make me an eater of food by that mouth! The hawk is one of thy mouths; with that mouth thou eatest the birds; make me an eater of food by that mouth! Fire is one of thy mouths; with that mouth thou eatest this world; make me an eater of food by that mouth! In thee there is the fifth mouth; with that mouth thou eatest all beings; make me an eater of food by that mouth! Do not decrease by our life, by our offspring, by our cattle; he who hates us and whom we hate, decrease by his life, by his offspring, by his cattle. Thus I turn the turn of the god, I return the turn of Âditya.' After these words, having raised the right arm, he lets it go again.

10. Next (having addressed these prayers to Soma) when being with his wife, let him stroke her

---

help to conquer the enemy. O Soma-goddess, increasing for immortal happiness (for the birth of a son), do thou place the highest glory (the streams of thy milk) in the sky.' 'That ray (sushum*n*â) which (as a woman) the Âdityas gladden, that Soma which as imperishable the imperishable Âdityas drink, may the guardian of the world (Pra*g*âpati), B*ri*haspati, and king Varu*n*a gladden us by it.'

The translations are made by the commentator regardless of grammar and sense: yet they command a certain authority, and must be taken into account as throwing light on the latest development of Indian mysticism.

heart, saying: 'O fair one, who hast obtained
immortal joy by that which has entered thy heart
through Pra*g*âpati, mayest thou never fall into sorrow about thy children [1].' Her children then do not
die before her.

11. Next, if a man has been absent and returns
home, let him smell (kiss) his son's head, saying:
'Thou springest from every limb, thou art born from
the heart, thou, my son, art my self indeed, live thou
a hundred harvests.' He gives him his name,
saying: 'Be thou a stone, be thou an axe, be thou
solid [2] gold; thou, my son, art light indeed, live thou
a hundred harvests.' He pronounces his name.
Then he embraces him, saying: 'As Pra*g*âpati (the
lord of creatures) embraced his creatures for their
welfare, thus I embrace thee,' (pronouncing his name.)
Then he mutters into his right ear, saying: 'O thou,
quick Maghavan, give to him' (Rv. III, 36, 10 [3]).
'O Indra, bestow the best wishes' (Rv. II, 21, 6),
thus he whispers into his left ear. Let him then
thrice smell (kiss) his head, saying: 'Do not cut off
(the line of our race), do not suffer. Live a hundred harvests of life; I kiss thy head, O son, with
thy name.' He then thrice makes a lowing sound
over his head, saying: 'I low over thee with the
lowing sound of cows.'

12. Next follows the Daiva Parimara [4], the dying
around of the gods (the absorption of the two

---

[1] Cf. Âsvalâyana G*r*ihya-sûtras I, 13, 7.

[2] Widely scattered, everywhere desired. Comm. Professor
Cowell proposes unscattered, hoarded, or unconcealed.

[3] The original has asme, to us, not asmai, to him.

[4] Cf. Taitt. Up. III, 10, 4; Ait. Brâhm. V, 28; Colebrooke,
Miscellaneous Essays (1873), II, p. 39.

classes of gods, mentioned before, into prâ*n*a or Brahman). This Brahman shines forth indeed when the fire burns, and it dies when it burns not. Its splendour goes to the sun alone, the life (prâ*n*a, the moving principle) to the air.

This Brahman shines forth indeed when the sun is seen, and it dies when it is not seen. Its splendour goes to the moon alone, the life (prâ*n*a) to the air.

This Brahman shines forth indeed when the moon is seen, and it dies when it is not seen. Its splendour goes to the lightning alone, its life (prâ*n*a) to the air.

This Brahman shines forth indeed when the lightning flashes, and it dies when it flashes not. Its splendour goes to the air, and the life (prâ*n*a) to the air.

Thus all these deities (i. e. fire, sun, moon, lightning), having entered the air, though dead, do not vanish; and out of the very air they rise again. So much with reference to the deities (mythological). Now then with reference to the body (physiological).

13. This Brahman shines forth indeed when one speaks with speech, and it dies when one does not speak. His splendour goes to the eye alone, the life (prâ*n*a) to breath (prâ*n*a).

This Brahman shines forth indeed when one sees with the eye, and it dies when one does not see. Its splendour goes to the ear alone, the life (prâ*n*a) to breath (prâ*n*a).

This Brahman shines forth indeed when one hears with the ear, and it dies when one does not hear. Its splendour goes to the mind alone, the life (prâ*n*a) to breath (prâ*n*a).

This Brahman shines forth indeed when one
thinks with the mind, and it dies when one does
not think. Its splendour goes to the breath (prâ*n*a)
alone, and the life (prâ*n*a) to breath (prâ*n*a).

Thus all these deities (the senses, &c.), having
entered breath or life (prâ*n*a) alone, though dead, do
not vanish ; and out of very breath (prâ*n*a) they rise
again. And if two mountains, the southern and
northern, were to move forward trying to crush him
who knows this, they would not crush him. But
those who hate him and those whom he hates, they
die around him.

14. Next follows the Ni*hs*reyasâdâna[1] (the accept-
ing of the pre-eminence of prâ*n*a (breath or life)
by the other gods). The deities (speech, eye, ear,
mind), contending with each for who was the best,
went out of this body, and the body lay without
breathing, withered, like a log of wood. Then
speech went into it, but speaking by speech, it lay
still. Then the eye went into it, but speaking by
speech, and seeing by the eye, it lay still. Then the
ear went into it, but speaking by speech, seeing by
the eye, hearing by the ear, it lay still. Then mind
went into it, but speaking by speech, seeing by the
eye, hearing by the ear, thinking by the mind, it lay
still. Then breath (prâ*n*a, life) went into it, and thence
it rose at once. All these deities, having recognised
the pre-eminence in prâ*n*a, and having comprehended
prâ*n*a alone as the conscious self (pra*gñ*âtman)[2], went
out of this body with all these (five different kinds of

---

[1] For other versions of this story see *Kh.* Up. V, 1, note 2 ; Ait.
Âr. II, 1, 4, 9 ; B*ri*h. Âr. VI, 1, 1–14 ; and Kaush. Up. III, 3.
[2] Cf. *Kh.* Up. VII, 15, note.

prâ*n*a), and resting in the air (knowing that prâ*n*a had entered the air), and merged in the ether (âkâ*s*a), they went to heaven. And in the same manner he who knows this, having recognised the pre-eminence in prâ*n*a, and having comprehended prâ*n*a alone as the conscious self (pra*g*ñâtman), goes out of this body with all these (does no longer believe in this body), and resting in the air, and merged in the ether, he goes to heaven, he goes to where those gods (speech, &c.) are. And having reached this he, who knows this, becomes immortal with that immortality which those gods enjoy.

15. Next follows the father's tradition to the son, and thus they explain it[1]. The father, when going to depart, calls his son, after having strewn the house with fresh grass, and having laid the sacrificial fire, and having placed near it a pot of water with a jug (full of rice), himself covered with a new cloth, and dressed in white. He places himself above his son, touching his organs with his own organs, or he may deliver the tradition to him while he sits before him. Then he delivers it to him. The father says: 'Let me place my speech in thee.' The son says: 'I take thy speech in me.' The father says: 'Let me place my scent (prâ*n*a) in thee.' The son says: 'I take thy scent in me.' The father says: 'Let me place my eye in thee.' The son says: 'I take thy eye in me.' The father says: 'Let me place my ear in thee.' The son says: 'I take thy ear in me.' The father says: 'Let me place my tastes of food in thee.' The son says: 'I take thy tastes of food in me.' The father says: 'Let me place my actions

---

[1] Cf. B*ri*had-âra*n*yaka I, 5, 17.

in thee.' The son says: 'I take thy actions in me.'
The father says : 'Let me place my pleasure and
pain in thee.' The son says: 'I take thy pleasure
and pain in me.' The father says : 'Let me place
happiness, joy, and offspring in thee.' The son says:
'I take thy happiness, joy, and offspring in me.' The
father says : 'Let me place my walking in thee.'
The son says : 'I take thy walking in me [1].' The
father says : 'Let me place my mind in thee.' The
son says: 'I take thy mind in me.' The father says:
'Let me place my knowledge (pragñâ) in thee.' The
son says : 'I take thy knowledge in me.' But if the
father is very ill, he may say shortly: 'Let me place
my spirits (prânas) in thee,' and the son : 'I take
thy spirits in me.'

Then the son walks round his father keeping his
right side towards him, and goes away. The father
calls after him: ' May fame, glory of countenance, and
honour always follow thee.' Then the other looks
back over his left shoulder, covering himself with his
hand or the hem of his garment, saying : 'Obtain
the heavenly worlds (svarga) and all desires.'

If the father recovers, let him be under the
authority of his son, or let him wander about (as
an ascetic). But if he departs, then let them
despatch him, as he ought to be despatched, yea,
as he ought to be despatched [2].

---

[1] Another sâkhâ adds here dhiyah, the thoughts (active), vignâta-
vyam, their object, and kâmâh, desires.

[2] I have taken samâpayati in the sense of performing the last
duties towards a dead person, though I confess I know of no
parallel passage in which samâpayati occurs in that sense. Professor Cowell translates: 'If he dies, then let them cause the son
duly to receive the tradition, as the tradition is to be given.' The
text itself varies, for the reading presupposed by the commentator
is enam (putram) samâpayati, instead of enam samâpayeyuh.

THIRD ADHYÂYA[1].

1. Pratardana, forsooth, the son of Divodâsa (king of Kâsî), came by means of fighting and strength to the beloved abode of Indra. Indra said to him : ' Pratardana, let me give you a boon to choose.' And Pratardana answered : 'Do you yourself choose that boon for me which you deem most beneficial for a man.' Indra said to him : ' No one who chooses, chooses for another ; choose thyself.' Then Pratardana replied : 'Then that boon to choose is no boon for me.'

Then, however, Indra did not swerve from the truth, for Indra is truth. Indra said to him : ' Know me only ; that is what I deem most beneficial for man, that he should know me. I slew the three-headed son of Tvash*tri* ; I delivered the Arunmukhas, the devotees, to the wolves (sâlâv*ri*ka) ; breaking many treaties, I killed the people of Prahlâda in heaven, the people of Puloma in the sky, the people of Kâla-kañ*g*a on earth[2]. And not one hair of me was harmed there. And he who knows me thus, by no deed of his is his life harmed, not by the murder of

---

[1] The object now is to explain the true Brahma-vidyâ, while the first and second chapters are only introductory, treating of the worship of the couch (paryankopâsanâ) and of the worship of prâ*n*a.

[2] This refers to heroic deeds performed by Indra, as represented in the hymns of the Rig-veda. See Rig-veda V, 34, 4, and Sâya*n*a's commentary ; Ait. Brâhm. VII, 28. Weber, Indische Studien I, 410–418, has tried to discover an original physical meaning in the heroic deeds ascribed to Indra. A curious remark is made by the commentator, who says that the skulls of the Arunmukhas were turned into the thorns of the desert (karîra) which remain to this day,—a very common phase in popular tradition.

'his mother, not by the murder of his father, not by theft, not by the killing of a Brahman. If he is going to commit a sin, the bloom[1] does not depart from his face.'

2. Indra said : ' I am prâ*n*a, meditate on me as the conscious self (pra*g*ñâtman), as life, as immortality. Life is prâ*n*a, prâ*n*a is life. Immortality is prâ*n*a, prâ*n*a is immortality. As long as prâ*n*a dwells in this body, so long surely there is life. By prâ*n*a he obtains immortality in the other world, by knowledge true conception. He who meditates on me as life and immortality, gains his full life in this world, and obtains in the Svarga world immortality and indestructibility.'

(Pratardana said) : ' Some maintain here, that the prâ*n*as become one, for (otherwise) no one could at the same time make known a name by speech, see a form with the eye, hear a sound with the ear, think a thought with the mind. After having become one, the prâ*n*as perceive all these together, one by one. While speech speaks, all prâ*n*as speak after it. While the eye sees, all prâ*n*as see after it. While the ear hears, all prâ*n*as hear after it. While the mind thinks, all prâ*n*as think after it. While the prâ*n*a breathes, all prâ*n*as breathe after it.'

' Thus it is indeed,' said Indra, ' but nevertheless there is a pre-eminence among the prâ*n*as[2].

3. Man lives deprived of speech, for we see dumb people. Man lives deprived of sight, for we see

---

[1] Professor Cowell compares Taittirîya-Sa*m*hitâ III, 1, 1, nâsya nîta*m* na haro vyeti.

[2] Prâ*n*âs, in the plural, is supposed to stand for the five senses as modifications of breath. It would be better if we could read prâ*n*asya ni*h*sreyasam. See before, II, 14.

blind people. Man lives deprived of hearing, for
we see deaf people. Man lives deprived of mind,
for we see infants. Man lives deprived of his arms,
deprived of his legs, for we see it thus. But prâ*n*a
alone is the conscious self (prag̃ñâtman), and having
laid hold of this body, it makes it rise up. Therefore it is said, Let man worship it alone as uktha[1].
What is prâ*n*a, that is prag̃ñâ (self-consciousness);
what is prag̃ñâ (self-consciousness), that is prâ*n*a, for
together they (prag̃ñâ and prâ*n*a) live in this body,
and together they go out of it. Of that, this is the
evidence, this is the understanding. When a man,
being thus asleep, sees no dream whatever, he becomes one with that prâ*n*a alone[2]. Then speech
goes to him (when he is absorbed in prâ*n*a) with
all names, the eye with all forms, the ear with all
sounds, the mind with all thoughts. And when
he awakes, then, as from a burning fire sparks
proceed in all directions, thus from that self the
prâ*n*as (speech, &c.) proceed, each towards its place;
from the prâ*n*as the gods (Agni, &c.), from the gods
the worlds.

Of this, this is the proof, this is the understanding.
When a man is thus sick, going to die, falling into
weakness and faintness, they say: 'His thought has
departed, he hears not, he sees not, he speaks not,
he thinks not.' Then he becomes one with that
prâ*n*a alone. Then speech goes to him (who is
absorbed in prâ*n*a) with all names, the eye with all

---

[1] Uktha, hymn, is artificially derived from ut-thâpayati, to raise
up, and hence uktha, hymn, is to be meditated on as prâ*n*a, breath,
which likewise raises up the body. See Ait. Âr. II, 1, 15.

[2] He is absorbed in prâ*n*a. Or should it be prâ*n*a*h* as
nominative?

forms, the ear with all sounds, the mind with all thoughts. And when he departs from this body, he departs together with all these [1].

4. Speech gives up to him (who is absorbed in prâ*n*a) all names, so that by speech he obtains all names. The nose gives up to him all odours, so that by scent he obtains all odours. The eye gives up to him all forms, so that by the eye he obtains all forms. The ear gives up to him all sounds, so that by the ear he obtains all sounds. The mind gives up to him all thoughts, so that by the mind he obtains all thoughts. This is the complete absorption in prâ*n*a. And what is prâ*n*a is pra*g*ñâ (self-consciousness), what is pra*g*ñâ (self-consciousness) is prâ*n*a. For together do these two live in the body, and together do they depart.

Now we shall explain how all things become one in that pra*g*ñâ (self-consciousness).

5. Speech is one portion taken out [2] of pra*g*ñâ (self-conscious knowledge), the word is its object, placed outside. The nose is one portion taken out of it, the odour is its object, placed outside. The eye is one portion taken out of it, the form is its object, placed outside. The ear is one portion taken out of it, the sound is its object, placed outside. The tongue is one portion taken out of it, the taste of food is its object, placed outside. The two hands

---

[1] According to another reading we might translate, 'Speech takes away all names from that body; and prâ*n*a, in which speech is absorbed, thus obtains all names.'

[2] I read udû*lh*am or udû*dh*am, instead of adû*dh*am, explained by the commentator as adûduhat. Professor Cowell translates, 'Speech verily milked one portion thereof,' which may have been the original purport of the writer.

are one portion taken out of it, their action is their object, placed outside. The body is one portion taken out of it, its pleasure and pain are its object, placed outside. The organ is one portion taken out of it, happiness, joy, and offspring are its object, placed outside. The two feet are one portion taken out of it, movements are their object, placed outside. Mind is one portion taken out of it, thoughts and desires are its object, placed outside.

6. Having by pragñâ (self-conscious knowledge) taken possession of speech, he obtains by speech all words. Having by pragñâ taken possession of the nose, he obtains all odours. Having by pragñâ taken possession of the eye, he obtains all forms. Having by pragñâ taken possession of the ear, he obtains all sounds. Having by pragñâ taken possession of the tongue, he obtains all tastes of food. Having by pragñâ taken possession of the two hands, he obtains all actions. Having by pragñâ taken possession of the body, he obtains pleasure and pain. Having by pragñâ taken possession of the organ, he obtains happiness, joy, and offspring. Having by pragñâ taken possession of the two feet, he obtains all movements. Having by pragñâ taken possession of mind, he obtains all thoughts.

7. For without pragñâ (self-consciousness) speech does not make known (to the self) any word[1]. 'My

---

[1] Professor Cowell has translated a passage from the commentary which is interesting as showing that its author and the author of the Upanishad too had a clear conception of the correlative nature of knowledge. 'The organ of sense,' he says, 'cannot exist without pragñâ (self-consciousness), nor the objects of sense be obtained without the organ, therefore—on the principle, that when one thing cannot exist without another, that thing is said to be identical with the other—as the cloth, for instance, being

mind was absent,' he says, 'I did not perceive that word.' Without pragñâ the nose does not make known any odour. 'My mind was absent,' he says, 'I did not perceive that odour.' Without pragñâ the eye does not make known any form. 'My mind was absent,' he says, 'I did not perceive that form.' Without pragñâ the ear does not make known any sound. 'My mind was absent,' he says, 'I did not perceive that sound.' Without pragñâ the tongue does not make known any taste. 'My mind was absent,' he says, 'I did not perceive that taste.' Without pragñâ the two hands do not make known any act. 'Our mind was absent,' they say, 'we did not perceive any act.' Without pragñâ the body does not make known pleasure or pain. 'My mind was absent,' he says, 'I did not perceive that pleasure or pain.' Without pragñâ the organ does not make known happiness, joy, or offspring. 'My mind was absent,' he says, 'I did not perceive that happiness, joy, or offspring.' Without pragñâ the two feet do not make known any movement. 'Our mind was absent,' they say, 'we did not perceive that movement.' Without pragñâ no thought succeeds, nothing can be known that is to be known.

8. Let no man try to find out what speech is, let him know the speaker. Let no man try to find out what odour is, let him know him who smells. Let no man try to find out what form is, let him know the seer. Let no man try to find out what sound is, let

---

never perceived without the threads, is identical with them, or the (false perception of) silver being never found without the mother of pearl is identical with it, so the objects of sense being never found without the organs are identical with them, and the organs being never found without pragñâ (self-consciousness) are identical with it.

him know the hearer. Let no man try to find out
the tastes of food, let him know the knower of
tastes. Let no man try to find out what action is,
let him know the agent. Let no man try to find
out what pleasure and pain are, let him know the
knower of pleasure and pain. Let no man try to
find out what happiness, joy, and offspring are, let
him know the knower of happiness, joy, and offspring.
Let no man try to find out what movement is, let him
know the mover. Let no man try to find out what
mind is, let him know the thinker. These ten objects
(what is spoken, smelled, seen, &c.) have reference to pra*g*ñâ (self-consciousness), the ten subjects
(speech, the senses, mind) have reference to objects.
If there were no objects, there would be no subjects;
and if there were no subjects, there would be no
objects. For on either side alone nothing could be
achieved. But that (the self of pra*g*ñâ, consciousness, and prâ*n*a, life) is not many, (but one.) For as
in a car the circumference of a wheel is placed on
the spokes, and the spokes on the nave, thus are
these objects (circumference) placed on the subjects
(spokes), and the subjects on the prâ*n*a. And that
prâ*n*a (breath, the living and breathing power) indeed is the self of pra*g*ñâ (the self-conscious self),
blessed, imperishable, immortal. He does not increase by a good action, nor decrease by a bad
action. For he (the self of prâ*n*a and pra*g*ñâ) makes
him, whom he wishes to lead up from these worlds,
do a good deed; and the same makes him, whom
he wishes to lead down from these worlds, do a bad
deed [1]. And he is the guardian of the world, he is

---

[1] The other text says, 'whom he wishes to draw after him; and
whom he wishes to draw away from these worlds.' Râmatîrtha, in

the king of the world, he is the lord of the universe,—
and he is my (Indra's) self, thus let it be known,
yea, thus let it be known!

FOURTH ADHYÂYA [1].

1. There was formerly Gârgya Bâlâki [2], famous as
a man of great reading; for it was said of him that
he lived among the Usînaras, among the Satvat-
Matsyas, the Kuru-Pañkâlas, the Kâsî-Videhas [3].
Having gone to Agâtasatru, (the king) of Kâsî, he
said to him : ' Shall I tell you Brahman ? ' Agâtasatru said to him : ' We give a thousand (cows) for
that speech (of yours), for verily all people run away,
saying, " Ganaka (the king of Mithilâ) is our father
(patron)." '

2.[4] BRIHAD-ÂRANYAKA-UPANISHAD.	KAUSHÎTAKI-BRÂHMANA-UPANISHAD.
i. Âditye purushah.	i. Id.
atishthâh sarveshâm	brihat pândaravâsâ

his commentary on the Mait. Up. 3, 2, quotes the text as translated
above.

[1] Prâna, breath or life, has been explained in the preceding
chapter. But this prâna is not yet the highest point that has to
be reached. Prâna, life, even as united with pragñâ, consciousness,
is only a covering of something else, viz. the Self, and this Highest
Self has now to be explained.

[2] The same story is told in the Brihad-âranyaka II, 1 seq., but
with important variations.

[3] I take iti to depend on samspashta, and read satvanmatsyeshu,
though the commentary seems to have read so 'vasan, or sa vasan,
for savasan.   See Introduction, p. lxxvii.

[4] The second paragraph forms a kind of table of contents for
the discussion which is to follow. I have given instead a fuller
table of contents, taken from the Brihad-âranyaka II, as compared
with the Kaushîtaki-upanishad in its two texts. The variations of
text A are given in small letters. In text B, the table of contents
is given at the end of the discussion, in § 18.

bhûtânâm mûrdhâ râgâ.	(*pânduravâsâ*) atish-thâh sarveshâm bhûtânâm mûrdhâ.
ii. *K*andre purusha*h*. br*i*hat pâ*nd*aravâsâ*h* somo râ*g*â. (Nâ-syânna*m* kshîyate, is the reward.)	ii. *K*andramasi. somo râ*g*â, annasyâ-tmâ. Only annasyâtmâ.
iii. Vidyuti purusha*h*. te*g*asvî. ·	iii. Id. te*g*asy âtmâ. satya-syâtmâ.
	iii^b. stanayitnau puru-sha*h*. *s*abdasyâtmâ.
iv. Âkâ*s*e purusha*h*. pûr*n*am apravarti.	iv. Id. (5) pûr*n*am apravarti brahma. apravritti.
v. Vâyau purusha*h*. indro vaiku*nth*o 'pa-râ*g*itâ senâ.	v. Id. (4) Id.
vi. Agnau purusha*h*. vishâsahi*h*.	vi. Id. Id.
vii. Apsu purusha*h*. pratirûpa*h*.	vii. Id. nâmnasyâtmâ. tegasa âtmâ.
viii. Âdar*s*e purusha*h*. ro*k*ish*n*u*h*.	viii. Id. pratirûpa*h*.
	viii^b. prati*s*rutkâyâm pu-rusha*h*. (9) dvitîyo 'napaga*h*. a-suh.
ix. Yantam pa*sk*â*k kh*ab-da*h*. asu*h*.	ix. Ya*h* *s*abda*h* purus-ham anveti. (10)*s*abde. Id. mrityuh.

x. Dikshu purusha*h*.
dvitîyo 'napaga*h*.

xi. *Kh*âyâmaya*h* puru-
sha*h*.
m*ri*tyu*h*.

xii. Âtmani purusha*h*.
âtmanvî.

x. Deest.

x. *Kh*âyâpurusha*h*. (8ᵇ)
khâyâyâm.
Id. dvitîyo 'napagah.

xi. Sârîra*h*   purusha*h*.
(12) sarîre purushah.
pra*g*âpati*h*.

xii. Ya*h* prâ*g*ña âtmâ,
yenaitat   supta*h*
svapnayâ *k*arati.
Yamo râ*g*â. (11) puru-
sha*h*   svapnayâ   karati
yamo râgâ.

xiii. Dakshi*n*e 'kshan purusha*h*.
nâmna (vâka) âtmâ,
agner âtmâ, *g*yoti-
sha âtmâ.

xiv. Savye 'kshan puru-
sha*h*.
satyasyâtmâ,vidyuta
âtmâ, te*g*asa âtmâ.

3. Bâlâki said: ' The person that is in the sun,
on him I meditate (as Brahman).'

A*g*âta*s*atru said to him : ' No, no! do not challenge me (to a disputation) on this ¹. I meditate on
him who is called great, clad in white raiment ², the
supreme, the head of all beings. Whoso meditates

¹ The king means to say that he knows this already, and that he
can mention not only the predicates of the person in the sun thus
meditated on as Brahman, but also the rewards of such meditation.

² This is properly a predicate of the moon, and used as such in
the B*ri*had-âra*n*yaka-upanishad, in the second paragraph of the
dialogue.

on him thus, becomes supreme, and the head of all beings.'

4. Bâlâki said: 'The person that is in the moon, on him I meditate.'

Agâtasatru said to him: 'Do not challenge me on this. I meditate on him as Soma, the king, the self, (source) of all food. Whoso meditates on him thus, becomes the self, (source) of all food.'

5. Bâlâki said: 'The person that is in the lightning, on him I meditate.'

Agâtasatru said to him · 'Do not challenge me on this. I meditate on him as the self in light. Whoso meditates on him thus, becomes the self in light.'

6. Bâlâki said: 'The person that is in the thunder, on him I meditate.'

Agâtasatru said to him: 'Do not challenge me on this. I meditate on him as the self of sound [1]. Whoso meditates on him thus, becomes the self of sound.'

7. Bâlâki said: 'The person that is in the ether, on him I meditate.'

Agâtasatru said to him: 'Do not challenge me on this. I meditate on him as the full, quiescent Brahman. Whoso meditates on him thus, is filled with offspring and cattle. Neither he himself nor his offspring dies before the time.'

8. Bâlâki said: 'The person that is in the air, on him I meditate.'

Agâtasatru said to him: 'Do not challenge me on this. I meditate on him as Indra Vaikuntha, as the unconquerable army. Whoso meditates on him thus, becomes victorious, unconquerable, conquering his enemies.'

---

[1] This is not mentioned in the Brihad-âranyaka.

9. Bâlâki said: 'The person that is in the fire, on him I meditate.'

Agâtasatru said to him: 'Do not challenge me on this. I meditate on him as powerful. Whoso meditates on him thus, becomes powerful among others[1].'

10. Bâlâki said: 'The person that is in the water, on him I meditate.'

Agâtasatru said to him: 'Do not challenge me on this. I meditate on him as the self of the name. Whoso meditates on him thus, becomes the self of the name.' So far with regard to deities (mythological); now with regard to the body (physiological).

11. Bâlâki said: 'The person that is in the mirror, on him I meditate.'

Agâtasatru said to him: 'Do not challenge me on this. I meditate on him as the likeness. Whoso meditates on him thus, to him a son is born in his family who is his likeness, not one who is not his likeness.'

12. Bâlâki said: 'The person that is in the echo, on him I meditate.'

Agâtasatru said to him: 'Do not challenge me on this. I meditate on him as the second, who never goes away. Whoso meditates on him thus, he gets a second from his second (his wife), he becomes doubled[2].'

13. Bâlâki said: 'The sound that follows a man, on that I meditate.

Agâtasatru said to him: 'Do not challenge me on

---

[1] Instead of anyeshu, the second text, as printed by Professor Cowell, has anv esha.

[2] This paragraph does not occur in the Brihad-âranyaka.

this. I meditate on him as life. Whoso meditates on him thus, neither he himself nor his offspring will faint before the time.'

14. Bâlâki said: 'The person that is in the shadow, on him I meditate.'

A*g*âta*s*atru said to him: 'Do not challenge me on this. I meditate on him as death. Whoso meditates on him thus, neither he himself nor his offspring will die before the time.'

15. Bâlâki said: 'The person that is embodied, on him I meditate.'

A*g*âta*s*atru said to him: 'Do not challenge me on this. I meditate on him as Lord of creatures. Whoso meditates on him thus, is multiplied in offspring and cattle.'

16. Bâlâki said: 'The Self which is conscious (prâ*g*ña), and by whom he who sleeps here, walks about in sleep, on him I meditate.'

A*g*âta*s*atru said to him: 'Do not challenge me on this. I meditate on him as Yama the king. Whoso meditates on him thus, everything is subdued for his excellencies.'

17. Bâlâki said: 'The person that is in the right eye, on him I meditate.'

A*g*âta*s*atru said to him: 'Do not challenge me on this. I meditate on him as the self of the name, as the self of fire, as the self of splendour. Whoso meditates on him thus, he becomes the self of these.'

18. Bâlâki said: 'The person that is in the left eye, on him I meditate.'

A*g*âta*s*atru said to him: 'Do not challenge me on this. I meditate on him as the self of the true, as the self of lightning, as the self of light. Whoso meditates on him thus, he becomes the self of these.'

19. After this Bâlâki became silent. A*g*âta*s*atru said to him: 'Thus far only (do you know), O Bâlâki?' 'Thus far only,' replied Bâlâki.

Then A*g*âta*s*atru said to him: 'Vainly did you challenge me, saying: 'Shall I tell you Brahman? O Bâlâki, he who is the maker of those persons (whom you mentioned), he of whom all this is the work, he alone is to be known.'

Thereupon Bâlâki came, carrying fuel in his hand, saying: 'May I come to you as a pupil?' A*g*âta*s*atru said to him: 'I deem it improper that a Kshatriya should initiate a Brâhma*n*a. Come, I shall make you know clearly.' Then taking him by the hand, he went forth. And the two together came to a person who was asleep. And A*g*âta*s*atru called him, saying: 'Thou great one, clad in white raiment, Soma, King[1].' But he remained lying. Then he pushed him with a stick, and he rose at once. Then said A*g*âta*s*atru to him: 'Bâlâki, where did this person here sleep? Where was he? Whence came he thus back?' Bâlâki did not know.

20. And A*g*âta*s*atru said to him: 'Where this person here slept, where he was, whence he thus came back, is this: The arteries of the heart called Hita extend from the heart of the person towards the surrounding body. Small as a hair divided a thousand times, they stand full of a thin fluid of various colours, white, black, yellow, red. In these the person is when sleeping he sees no dream.

---

[1] See § 3 init.

Then he becomes one with that prâna alone. Then speech goes to him with all names, the eye with all forms, the ear with all sounds, the mind with all thoughts. And when he awakes, then, as from a burning fire, sparks proceed in all directions, thus from that self the prânas (speech, &c.) proceed, each towards its place, from the prânas the gods, from the gods the worlds. And as a razor might be fitted in a razor-case, or as fire in the fire-place (the arani on the altar), even thus this conscious self enters the self of the body (considers the body as himself) to the very hairs and nails. And the other selfs (such as speech, &c.) follow that self, as his people follow the master of the house. And as the master feeds with his people, nay, as his people feed on the master, thus does this conscious self feed with the other selfs, as a master with his people, and the other selfs follow him, as his people follow the master. So long as Indra did not understand that self, the Asuras conquered him. When he understood it, he conquered the Asuras and obtained the pre-eminence among all gods, sovereignty, supremacy. And thus also he who knows this obtains pre-eminence among all beings, sovereignty, supremacy,—yea, he who knows this.

VÂ*G*ASANEYI-SA*M*HITÂ-UPANISHAD,

SOMETIMES CALLED

ÎSÂVÂSYA OR ÎSÂ-UPANISHAD.

VÂGASANEYI-SAMHITÂ-UPANISHAD.

1. ALL this, whatsoever moves on earth, is to be hidden in the Lord (the Self). When thou hast surrendered all this, then thou mayest enjoy. Do not covet the wealth of any man!

2. Though a man may wish to live a hundred years, performing works, it will be thus with him; but not in any other way: work will thus not cling to a man.

3. There are the worlds of the Asuras [1] covered with blind darkness. Those who have destroyed their self (who perform works, without having arrived at a knowledge of the true Self), go after death to those worlds.

4. That one (the Self), though never stirring, is swifter than thought. The Devas (senses) never reached it, it walked [2] before them. Though standing still, it overtakes the others who are running. Mâtariṣvan (the wind, the moving spirit) bestows powers [3] on it.

---

[1] Asuryà,Vâg. Samhitâ; asûryâ, Upan. Asuryà in the Upanishads in the sense of belonging to the Asuras, i.e. gods, is exceptional. I should prefer asûryá, sunless, as we find asûryé támasi in the Rig-veda, V, 32, 6.

[2] Pûrvam arṣat, Vâg. Samh.; pûrvam arshat, Upan. Mahîdhara suggests also arṣat as a contraction of a-riṣat, not perishing.

[3] Apas is explained by karmâni, acts, in which case it would be meant for ápas, opus. But the Vâg. Samhitâ accentuates apás, i.e.

5. It stirs and it stirs not; it is far, and likewise near[1]. It is inside of all this, and it is outside of all this.

6. And he who beholds all beings in the Self, and the Self in all beings, he never turns away from it[2].

7. When to a man who understands, the Self has become all things, what sorrow, what trouble can there be to him who once beheld that unity?

8. He[3] (the Self) encircled all, bright, incorporeal, scatheless, without muscles, pure, untouched by evil; a seer, wise, omnipresent, self-existent, he disposed all things rightly for eternal years.

9. All who worship what is not real knowledge (good works), enter into blind darkness : those who delight in real knowledge, enter, as it were, into greater darkness.

10. One thing, they say, is obtained from real knowledge; another, they say, from what is not knowledge. Thus we have heard from the wise who taught us this[4].

11. He who knows at the same time both knowledge and not-knowledge, overcomes death through not-knowledge, and obtains immortality through knowledge.

12. All who worship what is not the true cause,

---

aquas, and Ânandagiri explains that water stands for acts, because most sacrificial acts are performed with water.

[1] Tad v antike, Vâg. Samh.; tadvad antike, Upan.

[2] Vikikitsati, Vâg. Samh.; vigugupsate, Upan.

[3] Sankara takes the subject to be the Self, and explains the neuter adjectives as masculines. Mahîdhara takes the subject to be the man who has acquired a knowledge of the Self, and who reaches the bright, incorporeal Brahman, &c. Mahîdhara, however, likewise allows the former explanation.

[4] Cf. Talavak. Up. I, 4; vidyâyâh, avidyâyâh, Vâg. Samh.; vidyayâ, avidyayâ, Upan.

enter into blind darkness : those who delight in the true cause, enter, as it were, into greater darkness.

13. One thing, they say, is obtained from (knowledge of) the cause; another, they say, from (knowledge of) what is not the cause. Thus we have heard from the wise who taught us this.

14. He who knows at the same time both the cause and the destruction (the perishable body), overcomes death by destruction (the perishable body), and obtains immortality through (knowledge of) the true cause.

15. The door of the True is covered with a golden disk[1]. Open that, O Pûshan, that we may see the nature of the True[2].

16. O Pûshan, only seer, Yama (judge), Sûrya (sun), son of Pragâpati, spread thy rays and gather them! The light which is thy fairest form, I see it. I am what He is (viz. the person in the sun)[3].

17. Breath[4] to air, and to the immortal! Then this my body ends in ashes. Om! Mind, remember! Remember thy deeds! Mind, remember! Remember thy deeds[5]!

18. Agni, lead us on to wealth (beatitude) by a good path, thou, O God, who knowest all things!

---

[1] Mahîdhara on verse 17: 'The face of the true (purusha in the sun) is covered by a golden disk.'

[2] Cf. Maitr. Up. VI, 35.

[3] Asau purushah should probably be omitted.

[4] These lines are supposed to be uttered by a man in the hour of death.

[5] The Vâgasaneyi-samhitâ reads: Om, krato smara, klibe smara, kritam smara. Uvata holds that Agni, fire, who has been worshipped in youth and manhood, is here invoked in the form of mind, or that kratu is meant for sacrifice. 'Agni, remember me! Think of the world! Remember my deeds!'

Keep far from us crooked evil, and we shall offer
thee the fullest praise! (Rv. I, 189, 1.)

This Upanishad, though apparently simple and intelligible, is in
reality one of the most difficult to understand properly. Coming
at the end of the Vâgasaneyi-samhitâ, in which the sacrifices and
the hymns to be used by the officiating priests have been described,
it begins by declaring that all has to be surrendered to the Lord.
The name îs, lord, is peculiar, as having a far more personal colour-
ing than Âtman, Self, or Brahman, the usual names given by the
Upanishads to what is the object of the highest knowledge.

Next follows a permission to continue the performance of sacrifices, provided that all desires have been surrendered. And here
occurs our first difficulty, which has perplexed ancient as well as
modern commentators.

I shall try, first of all, to justify my own translation. I hold that
the Upanishad wishes to teach the uselessness by themselves of all
good works, whether we call them sacrificial, legal, or moral, and
yet, at the same time, to recognise, if not the necessity, at least the
harmlessness of good works, provided they are performed without
any selfish motives, without any desire of reward, but simply as a
preparation for higher knowledge, as a means, in fact, of subduing
all passions, and producing that serenity of mind without which
man is incapable of receiving the highest knowledge. From that
point of view the Upanishad may well say, Let a man wish to live
here his appointed time, let him even perform all works. If only
he knows that all must be surrendered to the Lord, then the work
done by him will not cling to him. It will not work on and produce
effect after effect, nor will it involve him in a succession of new
births in which to enjoy the reward of his works, but it will leave him
free to enjoy the blessings of the highest knowledge. It will have
served as a preparation for that higher knowledge which the Upanishad imparts, and which secures freedom from further births.

The expression 'na karma lipyate nare' seems to me to admit
of this one explanation only, viz. that work done does not cling to
man, provided he has acquired the highest knowledge. Similar
expressions occur again and again. Lip was, no doubt, used
originally of evil deeds which became, as it were, engrained in man;
but afterwards of all work, even of good work, if done with a
desire of reward. The doctrine of the Upanishads is throughout
that orthodoxy and sacrifice can procure a limited beatitude only,

and that they are a hindrance to real salvation, which can be obtained by knowledge alone. In our passage therefore we can recognise one meaning only, viz. that work does not cling to man or stain him, if only he knows, i. e. if he has been enlightened by the Upanishad.

Sankara, in his commentary on the Vedânta-sûtras III, 4, 7; 13; 14, takes the same view of this passage. The opponent of Bâdarâya*n*a, in this case, *G*aimini himself, maintains that karma, work, is indispensable to knowledge, and among other arguments, he says, III, 4, 7, that it is so 'Niyamât,' 'Because it is so laid down by the law.' The passage here referred to is, according to Sankara, our very verse, which, he thinks, should be translated as follows: 'Let a man wish to live a hundred years here (in this body) performing works; thus will an evil deed not cling to thee, while thou art a man; there is no other way but this by which to escape the influence of works.' In answer to this, Bâdarâya*n*a says, first of all, III, 4, 13, that this rule may refer to all men in general, and not to one who knows; or, III, 4, 14, if it refers to a man who knows, that then the permission to perform works is only intended to exalt the value of knowledge, the meaning being that even to a man who performs sacrifices all his life, work does not cling, if only he knows;—such being the power of knowledge.

The same Sankara, however, who here sees quite clearly that this verse refers to a man who knows, explains it in the Upanishad as referring to a man who does not know (itarasyânâtma*g*ñatayât-magraha*n*â*s*aktasya). It would then mean: 'Let such a one, while performing works here on earth, wish to live a hundred years. In this manner there is no other way for him but this (the performance of sacrifices), so that an evil deed should not be engrained, or so that he should not be stained by such a deed.' The first and second verses of the Upanishad would thus represent the two paths of life, that of knowledge and that of works, and the following verses would explain the rewards assigned to each.

Mahîdhara, in his commentary on the Vâ*g*asaneyi-sa*m*hitâ, steers at first a middle course. He would translate: 'Let one who performs the Agnihotra and other sacrifices, without any desire of reward, wish to live here a hundred years. If thou do so, there will be salvation for thee, not otherwise. There are many roads that lead to heaven, but one only leading to salvation, namely, perform-ance of good works, without any desire of reward, which produces a pure heart. Work thus done, merely as a preparation for salvation, does not cling to man, i. e. it produces a pure heart, but does not entail any further consequences.' So far he agrees with Uva*t*a's explanation[1]. He allows, however, another explanation also, so that the second line would convey the meaning: ' If a man lives thus (performing good works), then there is no other way by which an evil deed should not be engrained; i. e. in order to escape the power of sin, he must all his life perform sacred acts.'

Next follows a description of the lot of those who, immersed in works, have not arrived at the highest knowledge, and have not recovered their true self in the Highest Self, or Brahman. That Brahman, though the name is not used here, is then described, and salvation is promised to the man who beholds all things in the Self and the Self in all things.

The verses 9–14 are again full of difficulty, not so much in themselves as in their relation to the general system of thought which prevails in the Upanishads, and forms the foundation of the Vedânta philosophy. The commentators vary considerably in their interpretations. *S*ankara explains avidyâ, not-knowledge, by good works, particularly sacrifice, performed with a hope of reward ; vidyâ, or knowledge, by a knowledge of the gods, but not, as yet, of the highest Brahman. The former is generally supposed to lead the sacrificer to the pit*ri*loka, the world of the fathers, from whence he returns to a series of new births ; the latter to the devaloka, the world of the gods, from whence he may either proceed to Brahman, or enter upon a new round of existences. The question then arises, how in our passage the former could be said to lead to blind darkness, the latter to still greater darkness. But for that statement, I have no doubt that all the commentators would, as usual, have taken vidyâ for the knowledge of the Highest Brahman, and avidyâ for orthodox belief in the gods and good works, the former securing immortality in the sense of freedom from new births, while the reward of the latter is blessedness in heaven for a limited period, but without freedom from new births.

This antithesis between vidyâ and avidyâ seems to me so firmly established that I cannot bring myself to surrender it here. Though this Upanishad has its own very peculiar character, yet its object is, after all, to impart a knowledge of the Highest Self, and not to inculcate merely a difference between faith in the ordinary gods and good works. It was distinctly said before (ver. 3), that those who have destroyed their self, i. e. who perform works only,

---

[1] Uva*t*a explains *g*i*g*îshivishe*h* for *g*i*g*îvishet as a purusha-vyataya*h*.

and have not arrived at a knowledge of the true Self, go to the
worlds of the Asuras, which are covered with blind darkness. If
then the same blind darkness is said in verse 9 to be the lot of those
who worship not-knowledge, this can only mean those who have
not discovered the true Self, but are satisfied with the performance
of good works. And if those who perform good works are opposed
to others who delight in true knowledge, that knowledge can be
the knowledge of the true Self only.

The difficulty therefore which has perplexed Sankara is this,
how, while the orthodox believer is said to enter into blind darkness, the true disciple, who has acquired a knowledge of the true
Self, could be said to enter into still greater darkness. While
Sankara in this case seems hardly to have caught the drift of the
Upanishad, Uvata and Mahîdhara propose an explanation which is
far more satisfactory. They perceive that the chief stress must be
laid on the words ubhayam saha, ' both together,' in verses 11 and
14. The doctrine of certain Vedânta philosophers was that works,
though they cannot by themselves lead to salvation, are useful as a
preparation for the highest knowledge, and that those who imagine
that they can attain the highest knowledge without such previous
preparation, are utterly mistaken. From this point of view therefore the author of the Upanishad might well say that those who
give themselves to what is not knowledge, i. e. to sacrificial and
other good works, enter into darkness, but that those who delight
altogether in knowledge, despising the previous discipline of works,
deceive themselves and enter into still greater darkness.

Then follows the next verse, simply stating that, according to
the teaching of wise people, the reward of knowledge is one thing,
the reward of ignorance, i. e. trust in sacrifice, another. Here
Mahîdhara is right again by assigning the pitriloka, the world of
the fathers, as the reward of the ignorant; the devaloka, the
world of the gods, as the reward of the enlightened, provided that
from the world of the gods they pass on to the knowledge of the
Highest Self or Brahman.

The third verse contains the strongest confirmation of Mahîdhara's view. Here it is laid down distinctly that he only who
knows both together, both what is called ignorance and what is
called knowledge, can be saved, because by good works he overcomes death, here explained by natural works, and by knowledge
he obtains the Immortal, here explained by oneness with the gods,
the last step that leads on to oneness with Brahman.

Uvata, who takes the same view of these verses, explains at once, and even more boldly than Mahîdhara[1], vidyâ, or knowledge, by brahmavignâna, knowledge of Brahman, which by itself, and if not preceded by works, leads to even greater darkness than what is called ignorance, i. e. sacrifice and orthodoxy without knowledge.

The three corresponding verses, treating of sambhûti and asambhûti instead of vidyâ and avidyâ, stand first in the Vâgasaneyi-samhitâ. They must necessarily be explained in accordance with our explanation of the former verses, i. e. sambhûti must correspond to vidyâ, it must be meant for the true cause, i. e. for Brahman, while asambhûti must correspond with avidyâ, as a name of what is not real, but phenomenal only and perishable.

Mahîdhara thinks that these verses refer to the Bauddhas, which can hardly be admitted, unless we take Buddhist in a very general sense. Uva/a puts the Lokâyatas in their place[2]. It is curious also to observe that Mahîdhara, following Uva/a, explains asambhûti at first by the denial of the resurrection of the body, while he takes sambhûti rightly for Brahman. I have chiefly followed Uva/a's commentary, except in his first explanation of asambhûti, resurrection[3]. In what follows Uva/a explains sambhûti rightly by the only cause of the origin of the whole world, i. e. Brahman[4], while he takes vinâsa, destruction, as a name of the perishable body[5].

Sankara sees much more in these three verses than Uva/a. He takes asambhûti as a name of Prakriti, the undeveloped cause, sambhûti as a name of the phenomenal Brahman or Hiranyagarbha. From a worship of the latter a man obtains supernatural powers, from devotion to the former, absorption in Prakriti.

Mahîdhara also takes a similar view, and he allows, like Sankara, another reading, viz. sambhûtim avinâsam ka, and avinâsena mrityum tîrtvâ. In this case the sense would be: ' He who knows the worship both of the developed and the undeveloped, overcomes

---

[1] Mahîdhara decides in the end that vidyâ and amritam must here be taken in a limited or relative sense, tasmâd vidyopâsanâ-mritam kâpekshikam iti dik, and so agrees on the whole with Sankara, pp. 25–27.

[2] Shad anush/ubhah, lokâyatikâh prastûyante yeshâm etad darsanam.

[3] Mritasya satah punah sambhavo nâsti, atah sarîragrahanâd asmâkam muktir eva.

[4] Samastasya gagatah sambhavaikahetu brahma.

[5] Vinâsam vinâsi ka vapuh sarîram.

death, i. e. such evil as sin, passion, &c., through worship of the undeveloped, while he obtains through worship of the developed, i. e. of Hiranyagarbha, immortality, absorption in Prakriti.'

All these forced explanations to which the commentators have recourse, arise from the shifting views held by various authorities with regard to the value of works. Our Upanishad seems to me to propound the doctrine that works, though in themselves useless, or even mischievous, if performed with a view to any present or future rewards, are necessary as a preparatory discipline. This is or was for a long time the orthodox view. Each man was required to pass through the âsramas, or stages of student and householder, before he was admitted to the freedom of a Sannyâsin. As on a ladder, no step was to be skipped. Those who attempted to do so, were considered to have broken the old law, and in some respects they may indeed be looked upon as the true precursors of the Buddhists.

Nevertheless the opposite doctrine, that a man whose mind had become enlightened, might at once drop the fetters of the law, without performing all the tedious duties of student and house-holder, had strong supporters too among orthodox philosophers. Cases of such rapid conversion occur in the ancient traditions, and Bâdarâyana himself was obliged to admit the possibility of freedom and salvation without works, though maintaining the superiority of the usual course, which led on gradually from works to enlighten-ment and salvation[1]. It was from an unwillingness to assent to the decided teaching of the Îsâ-upanishad that Sankara attempted to explain vidyâ, knowledge, in a limited sense, as knowledge of the gods, and not yet knowledge of Brahman. He would not admit that knowledge without works could lead to darkness, and even to greater darkness than works without knowledge. Our Upanishad seems to have dreaded libertinism, knowledge without works, more even than ritualism, works without knowledge, and its true object was to show that orthodoxy and sacrifice, though useless in themselves, must always form the preparation for higher enlightenment.

How misleading Sankara's explanation may prove, we can see from the translation of this Upanishad by Rammohun Roy. He followed Sankara implicitly, and this is the sense which he drew from the text:—

'9. Those observers of religious rites that perform only the worship of the sacred fire, and oblations to sages, to ancestors,

---

[1] Vedânta-sûtras III, 4, 36-39.

to men, and to other creatures, without regarding the worship of
celestial gods, shall enter into the dark region : and those practisers
of religious ceremonies who habitually worship the celestial gods
only, disregarding the worship of the sacred fire, and oblations to
sages, to ancestors, to men, and to other creatures, shall enter into
a region still darker than the former.

' 10. It is said that adoration of the celestial gods produces one
consequence ; and that the performance of the worship of sacred
fire, and oblations to sages, to ancestors, to men, and to other
creatures, produce another : thus have we heard from learned men,
who have distinctly explained the subject to us.

' 11. Of those observers of ceremonies whosoever, knowing that
adoration of celestial gods, as well as the worship of the sacred
fire, and oblation to sages, to ancestors, to men, and to other
creatures, should be observed alike by the same individual, performs them both, will, by means of the latter, surmount the
obstacles presented by natural temptations, and will attain the state
of the celestial gods through the practice of the former.

' 12. Those observers of religious rites who worship Prak*r*ti
alone (Prak*r*ti or nature, who, though insensible, influenced by the
Supreme Spirit, operates throughout the universe) shall enter into the
dark region : and those practisers of religious ceremonies that are
devoted to worship solely the prior operating sensitive particle,
allegorically called Brahmá, shall enter into a region much more
dark than the former.

' 13. It is said that one consequence may be attained by the
worship of Brahmá, and another by the adoration of Prak*r*ti.
Thus have we heard from learned men, who have distinctly explained the subject to us.

' 14. Of those observers of ceremonies, whatever person, knowing that the adoration of Prak*r*ti and that of Brahmá should be
together observed by the same individual, performs them both,
will by means of the latter overcome indigence, and will attain the
state of Prak*r*ti, through the practice of the former.'

A CATALOG OF SELECTED
DOVER BOOKS
IN ALL FIELDS OF INTEREST

A CATALOG OF SELECTED DOVER
BOOKS IN ALL FIELDS OF INTEREST

CONCERNING THE SPIRITUAL IN ART, Wassily Kandinsky. Pioneering work by father of abstract art. Thoughts on color theory, nature of art. Analysis of earlier masters. 12 illustrations. 80pp. of text. 5⅜ x 8½. 23411-8 Pa. $3.95

ANIMALS: 1,419 Copyright-Free Illustrations of Mammals, Birds, Fish, Insects, etc., Jim Harter (ed.). Clear wood engravings present, in extremely lifelike poses, over 1,000 species of animals. One of the most extensive pictorial sourcebooks of its kind. Captions. Index. 284pp. 9 x 12. 23766-4 Pa. $12.95

CELTIC ART: The Methods of Construction, George Bain. Simple geometric techniques for making Celtic interlacements, spirals, Kells-type initials, animals, humans, etc. Over 500 illustrations. 160pp. 9 x 12. (USO) 22923-8 Pa. $9.95

AN ATLAS OF ANATOMY FOR ARTISTS, Fritz Schider. Most thorough reference work on art anatomy in the world. Hundreds of illustrations, including selections from works by Vesalius, Leonardo, Goya, Ingres, Michelangelo, others. 593 illustrations. 192pp. 7⅛ x 10¼. 20241-0 Pa. $9.95

CELTIC HAND STROKE-BY-STROKE (Irish Half-Uncial from "The Book of Kells"): An Arthur Baker Calligraphy Manual, Arthur Baker. Complete guide to creating each letter of the alphabet in distinctive Celtic manner. Covers hand position, strokes, pens, inks, paper, more. Illustrated. 48pp. 8¼ x 11. 24336-2 Pa. $3.95

EASY ORIGAMI, John Montroll. Charming collection of 32 projects (hat, cup, pelican, piano, swan, many more) specially designed for the novice origami hobbyist. Clearly illustrated easy-to-follow instructions insure that even beginning papercrafters will achieve successful results. 48pp. 8¼ x 11. 27298-2 Pa. $3.50

THE COMPLETE BOOK OF BIRDHOUSE CONSTRUCTION FOR WOODWORKERS, Scott D. Campbell. Detailed instructions, illustrations, tables. Also data on bird habitat and instinct patterns. Bibliography. 3 tables. 63 illustrations in 15 figures. 48pp. 5¼ x 8½. 24407-5 Pa. $2.50

BLOOMINGDALE'S ILLUSTRATED 1886 CATALOG: Fashions, Dry Goods and Housewares, Bloomingdale Brothers. Famed merchants' extremely rare catalog depicting about 1,700 products: clothing, housewares, firearms, dry goods, jewelry, more. Invaluable for dating, identifying vintage items. Also, copyright-free graphics for artists, designers. Co-published with Henry Ford Museum & Greenfield Village. 160pp. 8¼ x 11. 25780-0 Pa. $10.95

HISTORIC COSTUME IN PICTURES, Braun & Schneider. Over 1,450 costumed figures in clearly detailed engravings—from dawn of civilization to end of 19th century. Captions. Many folk costumes. 256pp. 8⅜ x 11¾. 23150-X Pa. $12.95

STICKLEY CRAFTSMAN FURNITURE CATALOGS, Gustav Stickley and L. & J. G. Stickley. Beautiful, functional furniture in two authentic catalogs from 1910. 594 illustrations, including 277 photos, show settles, rockers, armchairs, reclining chairs, bookcases, desks, tables. 183pp. 6½ x 9¼. 23838-5 Pa. $9.95

AMERICAN LOCOMOTIVES IN HISTORIC PHOTOGRAPHS: 1858 to 1949, Ron Ziel (ed.). A rare collection of 126 meticulously detailed official photographs, called "builder portraits," of American locomotives that majestically chronicle the rise of steam locomotive power in America. Introduction. Detailed captions. xi + 129pp. 9 x 12. 27393-8 Pa. $12.95

AMERICA'S LIGHTHOUSES: An Illustrated History, Francis Ross Holland, Jr. Delightfully written, profusely illustrated fact-filled survey of over 200 American lighthouses since 1716. History, anecdotes, technological advances, more. 240pp. 8 x 10¾. 25576-X Pa. $12.95

TOWARDS A NEW ARCHITECTURE, Le Corbusier. Pioneering manifesto by founder of "International School." Technical and aesthetic theories, views of industry, economics, relation of form to function, "mass-production split" and much more. Profusely illustrated. 320pp. 6⅛ x 9¼. (USO) 25023-7 Pa. $9.95

HOW THE OTHER HALF LIVES, Jacob Riis. Famous journalistic record, exposing poverty and degradation of New York slums around 1900, by major social reformer. 100 striking and influential photographs. 233pp. 10 x 7⅞. 22012-5 Pa. $10.95

FRUIT KEY AND TWIG KEY TO TREES AND SHRUBS, William M. Harlow. One of the handiest and most widely used identification aids. Fruit key covers 120 deciduous and evergreen species; twig key 160 deciduous species. Easily used. Over 300 photographs. 126pp. 5⅜ x 8½. 20511-8 Pa. $3.95

COMMON BIRD SONGS, Dr. Donald J. Borror. Songs of 60 most common U.S. birds: robins, sparrows, cardinals, bluejays, finches, more—arranged in order of increasing complexity. Up to 9 variations of songs of each species. Cassette and manual 99911-4 $8.95

ORCHIDS AS HOUSE PLANTS, Rebecca Tyson Northen. Grow cattleyas and many other kinds of orchids—in a window, in a case, or under artificial light. 63 illustrations. 148pp. 5⅜ x 8½. 23261-1 Pa. $4.95

MONSTER MAZES, Dave Phillips. Masterful mazes at four levels of difficulty. Avoid deadly perils and evil creatures to find magical treasures. Solutions for all 32 exciting illustrated puzzles. 48pp. 8¼ x 11. 26005-4 Pa. $2.95

MOZART'S DON GIOVANNI (DOVER OPERA LIBRETTO SERIES), Wolfgang Amadeus Mozart. Introduced and translated by Ellen H. Bleiler. Standard Italian libretto, with complete English translation. Convenient and thoroughly portable—an ideal companion for reading along with a recording or the performance itself. Introduction. List of characters. Plot summary. 121pp. 5¼ x 8½. 24944-1 Pa. $2.95

TECHNICAL MANUAL AND DICTIONARY OF CLASSICAL BALLET, Gail Grant. Defines, explains, comments on steps, movements, poses and concepts. 15-page pictorial section. Basic book for student, viewer. 127pp. 5⅜ x 8½. 21843-0 Pa. $4.95

BRASS INSTRUMENTS: Their History and Development, Anthony Baines. Authoritative, updated survey of the evolution of trumpets, trombones, bugles, cornets, French horns, tubas and other brass wind instruments. Over 140 illustrations and 48 music examples. Corrected and updated by author. New preface. Bibliography. 320pp. 5⅜ x 8½. 27574-4 Pa. $9.95

HOLLYWOOD GLAMOR PORTRAITS, John Kobal (ed.). 145 photos from 1926-49. Harlow, Gable, Bogart, Bacall; 94 stars in all. Full background on photographers, technical aspects. 160pp. 8⅜ x 11¼. 23352-9 Pa. $12.95

MAX AND MORITZ, Wilhelm Busch. Great humor classic in both German and English. Also 10 other works: "Cat and Mouse," "Plisch and Plumm," etc. 216pp. 5⅜ x 8½. 20181-3 Pa. $6.95

THE RAVEN AND OTHER FAVORITE POEMS, Edgar Allan Poe. Over 40 of the author's most memorable poems: "The Bells," "Ulalume," "Israfel," "To Helen," "The Conqueror Worm," "Eldorado," "Annabel Lee," many more. Alphabetic lists of titles and first lines. 64pp. 5$\frac{3}{16}$ x 8¼. 26685-0 Pa. $1.00

PERSONAL MEMOIRS OF U. S. GRANT, Ulysses Simpson Grant. Intelligent, deeply moving firsthand account of Civil War campaigns, considered by many the finest military memoirs ever written. Includes letters, historic photographs, maps and more. 528pp. 6⅛ x 9¼. 28587-1 Pa. $11.95

AMULETS AND SUPERSTITIONS, E. A. Wallis Budge. Comprehensive discourse on origin, powers of amulets in many ancient cultures: Arab, Persian Babylonian, Assyrian, Egyptian, Gnostic, Hebrew, Phoenician, Syriac, etc. Covers cross, swastika, crucifix, seals, rings, stones, etc. 584pp. 5⅜ x 8½. 23573-4 Pa. $12.95

RUSSIAN STORIES/PYCCKNE PACCKA3bl: A Dual-Language Book, edited by Gleb Struve. Twelve tales by such masters as Chekhov, Tolstoy, Dostoevsky, Pushkin, others. Excellent word-for-word English translations on facing pages, plus teaching and study aids, Russian/English vocabulary, biographical/critical introductions, more. 416pp. 5⅜ x 8½. 26244-8 Pa. $8.95

PHILADELPHIA THEN AND NOW: 60 Sites Photographed in the Past and Present, Kenneth Finkel and Susan Oyama. Rare photographs of City Hall, Logan Square, Independence Hall, Betsy Ross House, other landmarks juxtaposed with contemporary views. Captures changing face of historic city. Introduction. Captions. 128pp. 8¼ x 11. 25790-8 Pa. $9.95

AIA ARCHITECTURAL GUIDE TO NASSAU AND SUFFOLK COUNTIES, LONG ISLAND, The American Institute of Architects, Long Island Chapter, and the Society for the Preservation of Long Island Antiquities. Comprehensive, well-researched and generously illustrated volume brings to life over three centuries of Long Island's great architectural heritage. More than 240 photographs with authoritative, extensively detailed captions. 176pp. 8¼ x 11. 26946-9 Pa. $14.95

NORTH AMERICAN INDIAN LIFE: Customs and Traditions of 23 Tribes, Elsie Clews Parsons (ed.). 27 fictionalized essays by noted anthropologists examine religion, customs, government, additional facets of life among the Winnebago, Crow, Zuni, Eskimo, other tribes. 480pp. 6⅛ x 9¼. 27377-6 Pa. $10.95

FRANK LLOYD WRIGHT'S HOLLYHOCK HOUSE, Donald Hoffmann. Lavishly illustrated, carefully documented study of one of Wright's most controversial residential designs. Over 120 photographs, floor plans, elevations, etc. Detailed perceptive text by noted Wright scholar. Index. 128pp. 9¼ x 10¾. 27133-1 Pa. $11.95

THE MALE AND FEMALE FIGURE IN MOTION: 60 Classic Photographic Sequences, Eadweard Muybridge. 60 true-action photographs of men and women walking, running, climbing, bending, turning, etc., reproduced from rare 19th-century masterpiece. vi + 121pp. 9 x 12.   24745-7 Pa. $10.95

1001 QUESTIONS ANSWERED ABOUT THE SEASHORE, N. J. Berrill and Jacquelyn Berrill. Queries answered about dolphins, sea snails, sponges, starfish, fishes, shore birds, many others. Covers appearance, breeding, growth, feeding, much more. 305pp. 5¼ x 8¼.   23366-9 Pa. $8.95

GUIDE TO OWL WATCHING IN NORTH AMERICA, Donald S. Heintzelman. Superb guide offers complete data and descriptions of 19 species: barn owl, screech owl, snowy owl, many more. Expert coverage of owl-watching equipment, conservation, migrations and invasions, etc. Guide to observing sites. 84 illustrations. xiii + 193pp. 5⅜ x 8½.   27344-X Pa. $8.95

MEDICINAL AND OTHER USES OF NORTH AMERICAN PLANTS: A Historical Survey with Special Reference to the Eastern Indian Tribes, Charlotte Erichsen-Brown. Chronological historical citations document 500 years of usage of plants, trees, shrubs native to eastern Canada, northeastern U.S. Also complete identifying information. 343 illustrations. 544pp. 6½ x 9¼.   25951-X Pa. $12.95

STORYBOOK MAZES, Dave Phillips. 23 stories and mazes on two-page spreads: Wizard of Oz, Treasure Island, Robin Hood, etc. Solutions. 64pp. 8¼ x 11. 23628-5 Pa. $2.95

NEGRO FOLK MUSIC, U.S.A., Harold Courlander. Noted folklorist's scholarly yet readable analysis of rich and varied musical tradition. Includes authentic versions of over 40 folk songs. Valuable bibliography and discography. xi + 324pp. 5⅜ x 8½. 27350-4 Pa. $9.95

MOVIE-STAR PORTRAITS OF THE FORTIES, John Kobal (ed.). 163 glamor, studio photos of 106 stars of the 1940s: Rita Hayworth, Ava Gardner, Marlon Brando, Clark Gable, many more. 176pp. 8⅜ x 11¼.   23546-7 Pa. $12.95

BENCHLEY LOST AND FOUND, Robert Benchley. Finest humor from early 30s, about pet peeves, child psychologists, post office and others. Mostly unavailable elsewhere. 73 illustrations by Peter Arno and others. 183pp. 5⅜ x 8½. 22410-4 Pa. $6.95

YEKL and THE IMPORTED BRIDEGROOM AND OTHER STORIES OF YIDDISH NEW YORK, Abraham Cahan. Film Hester Street based on Yekl (1896). Novel, other stories among first about Jewish immigrants on N.Y.'s East Side. 240pp. 5⅜ x 8½.   22427-9 Pa. $6.95

SELECTED POEMS, Walt Whitman. Generous sampling from *Leaves of Grass.* Twenty-four poems include "I Hear America Singing," "Song of the Open Road," "I Sing the Body Electric," "When Lilacs Last in the Dooryard Bloom'd," "O Captain! My Captain!"—all reprinted from an authoritative edition. Lists of titles and first lines. 128pp. 5³⁄₁₆ x 8¼.   26878-0 Pa. $1.00

CATALOG OF DOVER BOOKS

THE BEST TALES OF HOFFMANN, E. T. A. Hoffmann. 10 of Hoffmann's most important stories: "Nutcracker and the King of Mice," "The Golden Flowerpot," etc. 458pp. 5⅜ x 8½. 21793-0 Pa. $9.95

FROM FETISH TO GOD IN ANCIENT EGYPT, E. A. Wallis Budge. Rich detailed survey of Egyptian conception of "God" and gods, magic, cult of animals, Osiris, more. Also, superb English translations of hymns and legends. 240 illustrations. 545pp. 5⅜ x 8½. 25803-3 Pa. $13.95

FRENCH STORIES/CONTES FRANÇAIS: A Dual-Language Book, Wallace Fowlie. Ten stories by French masters, Voltaire to Camus: "Micromegas" by Voltaire; "The Atheist's Mass" by Balzac; "Minuet" by de Maupassant; "The Guest" by Camus, six more. Excellent English translations on facing pages. Also French-English vocabulary list, exercises, more. 352pp. 5⅜ x 8½. 26443-2 Pa. $8.95

CHICAGO AT THE TURN OF THE CENTURY IN PHOTOGRAPHS: 122 Historic Views from the Collections of the Chicago Historical Society, Larry A. Viskochil. Rare large-format prints offer detailed views of City Hall, State Street, the Loop, Hull House, Union Station, many other landmarks, circa 1904-1913. Introduction. Captions. Maps. 144pp. 9⅜ x 12¼. 24656-6 Pa. $12.95

OLD BROOKLYN IN EARLY PHOTOGRAPHS, 1865-1929, William Lee Younger. Luna Park, Gravesend race track, construction of Grand Army Plaza, moving of Hotel Brighton, etc. 157 previously unpublished photographs. 165pp. 8⅞ x 11¾. 23587-4 Pa. $13.95

THE MYTHS OF THE NORTH AMERICAN INDIANS, Lewis Spence. Rich anthology of the myths and legends of the Algonquins, Iroquois, Pawnees and Sioux, prefaced by an extensive historical and ethnological commentary. 36 illustrations. 480pp. 5⅜ x 8½. 25967-6 Pa. $8.95

AN ENCYCLOPEDIA OF BATTLES: Accounts of Over 1,560 Battles from 1479 B.C. to the Present, David Eggenberger. Essential details of every major battle in recorded history from the first battle of Megiddo in 1479 B.C. to Grenada in 1984. List of Battle Maps. New Appendix covering the years 1967-1984. Index. 99 illustrations. 544pp. 6½ x 9¼. 24913-1 Pa. $14.95

SAILING ALONE AROUND THE WORLD, Captain Joshua Slocum. First man to sail around the world, alone, in small boat. One of great feats of seamanship told in delightful manner. 67 illustrations. 294pp. 5⅜ x 8½. 20326-3 Pa. $5.95

ANARCHISM AND OTHER ESSAYS, Emma Goldman. Powerful, penetrating, prophetic essays on direct action, role of minorities, prison reform, puritan hypocrisy, violence, etc. 271pp. 5⅜ x 8½. 22484-8 Pa. $6.95

MYTHS OF THE HINDUS AND BUDDHISTS, Ananda K. Coomaraswamy and Sister Nivedita. Great stories of the epics; deeds of Krishna, Shiva, taken from puranas, Vedas, folk tales; etc. 32 illustrations. 400pp. 5⅜ x 8½. 21759-0 Pa. $10.95

BEYOND PSYCHOLOGY, Otto Rank. Fear of death, desire of immortality, nature of sexuality, social organization, creativity, according to Rankian system. 291pp. 5⅜ x 8½. 20485-5 Pa. $8.95

A THEOLOGICO-POLITICAL TREATISE, Benedict Spinoza. Also contains unfinished Political Treatise. Great classic on religious liberty, theory of government on common consent. R. Elwes translation. Total of 421pp. 5⅜ x 8½. 20249-6 Pa. $9.95

CATALOG OF DOVER BOOKS

MY BONDAGE AND MY FREEDOM, Frederick Douglass. Born a slave, Douglass became outspoken force in antislavery movement. The best of Douglass' autobiographies. Graphic description of slave life. 464pp. 5⅜ x 8½. 22457-0 Pa. $8.95

FOLLOWING THE EQUATOR: A Journey Around the World, Mark Twain. Fascinating humorous account of 1897 voyage to Hawaii, Australia, India, New Zealand, etc. Ironic, bemused reports on peoples, customs, climate, flora and fauna, politics, much more. 197 illustrations. 720pp. 5⅜ x 8½. 26113-1 Pa. $15.95

THE PEOPLE CALLED SHAKERS, Edward D. Andrews. Definitive study of Shakers: origins, beliefs, practices, dances, social organization, furniture and crafts, etc. 33 illustrations. 351pp. 5⅜ x 8½. 21081-2 Pa. $8.95

THE MYTHS OF GREECE AND ROME, H. A. Guerber. A classic of mythology, generously illustrated, long prized for its simple, graphic, accurate retelling of the principal myths of Greece and Rome, and for its commentary on their origins and significance. With 64 illustrations by Michelangelo, Raphael, Titian, Rubens, Canova, Bernini and others. 480pp. 5⅜ x 8½. 27584-1 Pa. $9.95

PSYCHOLOGY OF MUSIC, Carl E. Seashore. Classic work discusses music as a medium from psychological viewpoint. Clear treatment of physical acoustics, auditory apparatus, sound perception, development of musical skills, nature of musical feeling, host of other topics. 88 figures. 408pp. 5⅜ x 8½. 21851-1 Pa. $10.95

THE PHILOSOPHY OF HISTORY, Georg W. Hegel. Great classic of Western thought develops concept that history is not chance but rational process, the evolution of freedom. 457pp. 5⅜ x 8½. 20112-0 Pa. $9.95

THE BOOK OF TEA, Kakuzo Okakura. Minor classic of the Orient: entertaining, charming explanation, interpretation of traditional Japanese culture in terms of tea ceremony. 94pp. 5⅜ x 8½. 20070-1 Pa. $3.95

LIFE IN ANCIENT EGYPT, Adolf Erman. Fullest, most thorough, detailed older account with much not in more recent books, domestic life, religion, magic, medicine, commerce, much more. Many illustrations reproduce tomb paintings, carvings, hieroglyphs, etc. 597pp. 5⅜ x 8½. 22632-8 Pa. $11.95

SUNDIALS, Their Theory and Construction, Albert Waugh. Far and away the best, most thorough coverage of ideas, mathematics concerned, types, construction, adjusting anywhere. Simple, nontechnical treatment allows even children to build several of these dials. Over 100 illustrations. 230pp. 5⅜ x 8½. 22947-5 Pa. $7.95

DYNAMICS OF FLUIDS IN POROUS MEDIA, Jacob Bear. For advanced students of ground water hydrology, soil mechanics and physics, drainage and irrigation engineering, and more. 335 illustrations. Exercises, with answers. 784pp. 6⅛ x 9¼. 65675-6 Pa. $19.95

SONGS OF EXPERIENCE: Facsimile Reproduction with 26 Plates in Full Color, William Blake. 26 full-color plates from a rare 1826 edition. Includes "TheTyger," "London," "Holy Thursday," and other poems. Printed text of poems. 48pp. 5¼ x 7. 24636-1 Pa. $4.95

OLD-TIME VIGNETTES IN FULL COLOR, Carol Belanger Grafton (ed.). Over 390 charming, often sentimental illustrations, selected from archives of Victorian graphics—pretty women posing, children playing, food, flowers, kittens and puppies, smiling cherubs, birds and butterflies, much more. All copyright-free. 48pp. 9¼ x 12¼. 27269-9 Pa. $7.95

PERSPECTIVE FOR ARTISTS, Rex Vicat Cole. Depth, perspective of sky and sea, shadows, much more, not usually covered. 391 diagrams, 81 reproductions of drawings and paintings. 279pp. 5⅜ x 8½. 22487-2 Pa. $7.95

DRAWING THE LIVING FIGURE, Joseph Sheppard. Innovative approach to artistic anatomy focuses on specifics of surface anatomy, rather than muscles and bones. Over 170 drawings of live models in front, back and side views, and in widely varying poses. Accompanying diagrams. 177 illustrations. Introduction. Index. 144pp. 8⅜ x11¼. 26723-7 Pa. $8.95

GOTHIC AND OLD ENGLISH ALPHABETS: 100 Complete Fonts, Dan X. Solo. Add power, elegance to posters, signs, other graphics with 100 stunning copyright-free alphabets: Blackstone, Dolbey, Germania, 97 more–including many lower-case, numerals, punctuation marks. 104pp. 8⅛ x 11. 24695-7 Pa. $8.95

HOW TO DO BEADWORK, Mary White. Fundamental book on craft from simple projects to five-bead chains and woven works. 106 illustrations. 142pp. 5⅜ x 8. 20697-1 Pa. $4.95

THE BOOK OF WOOD CARVING, Charles Marshall Sayers. Finest book for beginners discusses fundamentals and offers 34 designs. "Absolutely first rate . . . well thought out and well executed."–E. J. Tangerman. 118pp. 7¾ x 10⅝. 23654-4 Pa. $6.95

ILLUSTRATED CATALOG OF CIVIL WAR MILITARY GOODS: Union Army Weapons, Insignia, Uniform Accessories, and Other Equipment, Schuyler, Hartley, and Graham. Rare, profusely illustrated 1846 catalog includes Union Army uniform and dress regulations, arms and ammunition, coats, insignia, flags, swords, rifles, etc. 226 illustrations. 160pp. 9 x 12. 24939-5 Pa. $10.95

WOMEN'S FASHIONS OF THE EARLY 1900s: An Unabridged Republication of "New York Fashions, 1909," National Cloak & Suit Co. Rare catalog of mail-order fashions documents women's and children's clothing styles shortly after the turn of the century. Captions offer full descriptions, prices. Invaluable resource for fashion, costume historians. Approximately 725 illustrations. 128pp. 8⅜ x 11¼. 27276-1 Pa. $11.95

THE 1912 AND 1915 GUSTAV STICKLEY FURNITURE CATALOGS, Gustav Stickley. With over 200 detailed illustrations and descriptions, these two catalogs are essential reading and reference materials and identification guides for Stickley furniture. Captions cite materials, dimensions and prices. 112pp. 6½ x 9¼. 26676-1 Pa. $9.95

EARLY AMERICAN LOCOMOTIVES, John H. White, Jr. Finest locomotive engravings from early 19th century: historical (1804–74), main-line (after 1870), special, foreign, etc. 147 plates. 142pp. 11⅜ x 8¼. 22772-3 Pa. $10.95

THE TALL SHIPS OF TODAY IN PHOTOGRAPHS, Frank O. Braynard. Lavishly illustrated tribute to nearly 100 majestic contemporary sailing vessels: Amerigo Vespucci, Clearwater, Constitution, Eagle, Mayflower, Sea Cloud, Victory, many more. Authoritative captions provide statistics, background on each ship. 190 black-and-white photographs and illustrations. Introduction. 128pp. 8⅞ x 11¾. 27163-3 Pa. $13.95

EARLY NINETEENTH-CENTURY CRAFTS AND TRADES, Peter Stockham (ed.). Extremely rare 1807 volume describes to youngsters the crafts and trades of the day: brickmaker, weaver, dressmaker, bookbinder, ropemaker, saddler, many more. Quaint prose, charming illustrations for each craft. 20 black-and-white line illustrations. 192pp. 4⅝ x 6. 27293-1 Pa. $4.95

VICTORIAN FASHIONS AND COSTUMES FROM HARPER'S BAZAR, 1867–1898, Stella Blum (ed.). Day costumes, evening wear, sports clothes, shoes, hats, other accessories in over 1,000 detailed engravings. 320pp. 9⅜ x 12¼. 22990-4 Pa. $14.95

GUSTAV STICKLEY, THE CRAFTSMAN, Mary Ann Smith. Superb study surveys broad scope of Stickley's achievement, especially in architecture. Design philosophy, rise and fall of the Craftsman empire, descriptions and floor plans for many Craftsman houses, more. 86 black-and-white halftones. 31 line illustrations. Introduction 208pp. 6½ x 9¼. 27210-9 Pa. $9.95

THE LONG ISLAND RAIL ROAD IN EARLY PHOTOGRAPHS, Ron Ziel. Over 220 rare photos, informative text document origin (1844) and development of rail service on Long Island. Vintage views of early trains, locomotives, stations, passengers, crews, much more. Captions. 8⅞ x 11¾. 26301-0 Pa. $13.95

THE BOOK OF OLD SHIPS: From Egyptian Galleys to Clipper Ships, Henry B. Culver. Superb, authoritative history of sailing vessels, with 80 magnificent line illustrations. Galley, bark, caravel, longship, whaler, many more. Detailed, informative text on each vessel by noted naval historian. Introduction. 256pp. 5⅜ x 8½. 27332-6 Pa. $7.95

TEN BOOKS ON ARCHITECTURE, Vitruvius. The most important book ever written on architecture. Early Roman aesthetics, technology, classical orders, site selection, all other aspects. Morgan translation. 331pp. 5⅜ x 8½. 20645-9 Pa. $8.95

THE IIUMAN FIGURE IN MOTION, Eadweard Muybridge. More than 4,500 stopped-action photos, in action series, showing undraped men, women, children jumping, lying down, throwing, sitting, wrestling, carrying, etc. 390pp. 7⅞ x 10⅝. 20204-6 Clothbd. $25.95

TREES OF THE EASTERN AND CENTRAL UNITED STATES AND CANADA, William M. Harlow. Best one-volume guide to 140 trees. Full descriptions, woodlore, range, etc. Over 600 illustrations. Handy size. 288pp. 4½ x 6⅜. 20395-6 Pa. $6.95

SONGS OF WESTERN BIRDS, Dr. Donald J. Borror. Complete song and call repertoire of 60 western species, including flycatchers, juncoes, cactus wrens, many more—includes fully illustrated booklet. Cassette and manual 99913-0 $8.95

GROWING AND USING HERBS AND SPICES, Milo Miloradovich. Versatile handbook provides all the information needed for cultivation and use of all the herbs and spices available in North America. 4 illustrations. Index. Glossary. 236pp. 5⅜ x 8½. 25058-X Pa. $6.95

BIG BOOK OF MAZES AND LABYRINTHS, Walter Shepherd. 50 mazes and labyrinths in all—classical, solid, ripple, and more—in one great volume. Perfect inexpensive puzzler for clever youngsters. Full solutions. 112pp. 8⅛ x 11. 22951-3 Pa. $4.95

PIANO TUNING, J. Cree Fischer. Clearest, best book for beginner, amateur. Simple repairs, raising dropped notes, tuning by easy method of flattened fifths. No previous skills needed. 4 illustrations. 201pp. 5⅜ x 8½. 23267-0 Pa. $6.95

A SOURCE BOOK IN THEATRICAL HISTORY, A. M. Nagler. Contemporary observers on acting, directing, make-up, costuming, stage props, machinery, scene design, from Ancient Greece to Chekhov. 611pp. 5⅜ x 8½. 20515-0 Pa. $12.95

THE COMPLETE NONSENSE OF EDWARD LEAR, Edward Lear. All nonsense limericks, zany alphabets, Owl and Pussycat, songs, nonsense botany, etc., illustrated by Lear. Total of 320pp. 5⅜ x 8½. (USO) 20167-8 Pa. $6.95

VICTORIAN PARLOUR POETRY: An Annotated Anthology, Michael R. Turner. 117 gems by Longfellow, Tennyson, Browning, many lesser-known poets. "The Village Blacksmith," "Curfew Must Not Ring Tonight," "Only a Baby Small," dozens more, often difficult to find elsewhere. Index of poets, titles, first lines. xxiii + 325pp. 5⅜ x 8¼. 27044-0 Pa. $8.95

DUBLINERS, James Joyce. Fifteen stories offer vivid, tightly focused observations of the lives of Dublin's poorer classes. At least one, "The Dead," is considered a masterpiece. Reprinted complete and unabridged from standard edition. 160pp. 5³⁄₁₆ x 8¼. 26870-5 Pa. $1.00

THE HAUNTED MONASTERY and THE CHINESE MAZE MURDERS, Robert van Gulik. Two full novels by van Gulik, set in 7th-century China, continue adventures of Judge Dee and his companions. An evil Taoist monastery, seemingly supernatural events; overgrown topiary maze hides strange crimes. 27 illustrations. 328pp. 5⅜ x 8½. 23502-5 Pa. $8.95

THE BOOK OF THE SACRED MAGIC OF ABRAMELIN THE MAGE, translated by S. MacGregor Mathers. Medieval manuscript of ceremonial magic. Basic document in Aleister Crowley, Golden Dawn groups. 268pp. 5⅜ x 8½. 23211-5 Pa. $8.95

NEW RUSSIAN-ENGLISH AND ENGLISH-RUSSIAN DICTIONARY, M. A. O'Brien. This is a remarkably handy Russian dictionary, containing a surprising amount of information, including over 70,000 entries. 366pp. 4½ x 6⅛. 20208-9 Pa. $9.95

HISTORIC HOMES OF THE AMERICAN PRESIDENTS, Second, Revised Edition, Irvin Haas. A traveler's guide to American Presidential homes, most open to the public, depicting and describing homes occupied by every American President from George Washington to George Bush. With visiting hours, admission charges, travel routes. 175 photographs. Index. 160pp. 8¼ x 11. 26751-2 Pa. $11.95

NEW YORK IN THE FORTIES, Andreas Feininger. 162 brilliant photographs by the well-known photographer, formerly with *Life* magazine. Commuters, shoppers, Times Square at night, much else from city at its peak. Captions by John von Hartz. 181pp. 9¼ x 10¾. 23585-8 Pa. $12.95

INDIAN SIGN LANGUAGE, William Tomkins. Over 525 signs developed by Sioux and other tribes. Written instructions and diagrams. Also 290 pictographs. 111pp. 6⅛ x 9¼. 22029-X Pa. $3.95

ANATOMY: A Complete Guide for Artists, Joseph Sheppard. A master of figure drawing shows artists how to render human anatomy convincingly. Over 460 illustrations. 224pp. 8⅜ x 11¼. 27279-6 Pa. $10.95

MEDIEVAL CALLIGRAPHY: Its History and Technique, Marc Drogin. Spirited history, comprehensive instruction manual covers 13 styles (ca. 4th century thru 15th). Excellent photographs; directions for duplicating medieval techniques with modern tools. 224pp. 8⅜ x 11¼. 26142-5 Pa. $12.95

DRIED FLOWERS: How to Prepare Them, Sarah Whitlock and Martha Rankin. Complete instructions on how to use silica gel, meal and borax, perlite aggregate, sand and borax, glycerine and water to create attractive permanent flower arrangements. 12 illustrations. 32pp. 5⅜ x 8½. 21802-3 Pa. $1.00

EASY-TO-MAKE BIRD FEEDERS FOR WOODWORKERS, Scott D. Campbell. Detailed, simple-to-use guide for designing, constructing, caring for and using feeders. Text, illustrations for 12 classic and contemporary designs. 96pp. 5⅜ x 8½. 25847-5 Pa. $2.95

SCOTTISH WONDER TALES FROM MYTH AND LEGEND, Donald A. Mackenzie. 16 lively tales tell of giants rumbling down mountainsides, of a magic wand that turns stone pillars into warriors, of gods and goddesses, evil hags, powerful forces and more. 240pp. 5⅜ x 8½. 29677-6 Pa. $6.95

THE HISTORY OF UNDERCLOTHES, C. Willett Cunnington and Phyllis Cunnington. Fascinating, well-documented survey covering six centuries of English undergarments, enhanced with over 100 illustrations: 12th-century laced-up bodice, footed long drawers (1795), 19th-century bustles, 19th-century corsets for men, Victorian "bust improvers," much more. 272pp. 5⅝ x 8¼. 27124-2 Pa. $9.95

ARTS AND CRAFTS FURNITURE: The Complete Brooks Catalog of 1912, Brooks Manufacturing Co. Photos and detailed descriptions of more than 150 now very collectible furniture designs from the Arts and Crafts movement depict davenports, settees, buffets, desks, tables, chairs, bedsteads, dressers and more, all built of solid, quarter-sawed oak. Invaluable for students and enthusiasts of antiques, Americana and the decorative arts. 80pp. 6½ x 9¼. 27471-3 Pa. $8.95

HOW WE INVENTED THE AIRPLANE: An Illustrated History, Orville Wright. Fascinating firsthand account covers early experiments, construction of planes and motors, first flights, much more. Introduction and commentary by Fred C. Kelly. 76 photographs. 96pp. 8¼ x 11. 25662-6 Pa. $8.95

THE ARTS OF THE SAILOR: Knotting, Splicing and Ropework, Hervey Garrett Smith. Indispensable shipboard reference covers tools, basic knots and useful hitches; handsewing and canvas work, more. Over 100 illustrations. Delightful reading for sea lovers. 256pp. 5⅜ x 8½. 26440-8 Pa. $7.95

FRANK LLOYD WRIGHT'S FALLINGWATER: The House and Its History, Second, Revised Edition, Donald Hoffmann. A total revision–both in text and illustrations–of the standard document on Fallingwater, the boldest, most personal architectural statement of Wright's mature years, updated with valuable new material from the recently opened Frank Lloyd Wright Archives. "Fascinating"–*The New York Times*. 116 illustrations. 128pp. 9¼ x 10¾. 27430-6 Pa. $11.95

CATALOG OF DOVER BOOKS

PHOTOGRAPHIC SKETCHBOOK OF THE CIVIL WAR, Alexander Gardner. 100 photos taken on field during the Civil War. Famous shots of Manassas Harper's Ferry, Lincoln, Richmond, slave pens, etc. 244pp. 10⅝ x 8¼.   22731-6 Pa. $9.95

FIVE ACRES AND INDEPENDENCE, Maurice G. Kains. Great back-to-the-land classic explains basics of self-sufficient farming. The one book to get. 95 illustrations. 397pp. 5⅜ x 8½.   20974-1 Pa. $7.95

SONGS OF EASTERN BIRDS, Dr. Donald J. Borror. Songs and calls of 60 species most common to eastern U.S.: warblers, woodpeckers, flycatchers, thrushes, larks, many more in high-quality recording.   Cassette and manual 99912-2 $9.95

A MODERN HERBAL, Margaret Grieve. Much the fullest, most exact, most useful compilation of herbal material. Gigantic alphabetical encyclopedia, from aconite to zedoary, gives botanical information, medical properties, folklore, economic uses, much else. Indispensable to serious reader. 161 illustrations. 888pp. 6½ x 9¼. 2-vol. set. (USO)   Vol. I: 22798-7 Pa. $9.95
Vol. II: 22799-5 Pa. $9.95

HIDDEN TREASURE MAZE BOOK, Dave Phillips. Solve 34 challenging mazes accompanied by heroic tales of adventure. Evil dragons, people-eating plants, blood-thirsty giants, many more dangerous adversaries lurk at every twist and turn. 34 mazes, stories, solutions. 48pp. 8¼ x 11.   24566-7 Pa. $2.95

LETTERS OF W. A. MOZART, Wolfgang A. Mozart. Remarkable letters show bawdy wit, humor, imagination, musical insights, contemporary musical world; includes some letters from Leopold Mozart. 276pp. 5⅜ x 8½.   22859-2 Pa. $7.95

BASIC PRINCIPLES OF CLASSICAL BALLET, Agrippina Vaganova. Great Russian theoretician, teacher explains methods for teaching classical ballet. 118 illustrations. 175pp. 5⅜ x 8½.   22036-2 Pa. $5.95

THE JUMPING FROG, Mark Twain. Revenge edition. The original story of The Celebrated Jumping Frog of Calaveras County, a hapless French translation, and Twain's hilarious "retranslation" from the French. 12 illustrations. 66pp. 5⅜ x 8½.   22686-7 Pa. $3.95

BEST REMEMBERED POEMS, Martin Gardner (ed.). The 126 poems in this superb collection of 19th- and 20th-century British and American verse range from Shelley's "To a Skylark" to the impassioned "Renascence" of Edna St. Vincent Millay and to Edward Lear's whimsical "The Owl and the Pussycat." 224pp. 5⅜ x 8½.   27165-X Pa. $4.95

COMPLETE SONNETS, William Shakespeare. Over 150 exquisite poems deal with love, friendship, the tyranny of time, beauty's evanescence, death and other themes in language of remarkable power, precision and beauty. Glossary of archaic terms. 80pp. 5³⁄₁₆ x 8¼.   26686-9 Pa. $1.00

BODIES IN A BOOKSHOP, R. T. Campbell. Challenging mystery of blackmail and murder with ingenious plot and superbly drawn characters. In the best tradition of British suspense fiction. 192pp. 5⅜ x 8½.   24720-1 Pa. $6.95

CATALOG OF DOVER BOOKS

THE WIT AND HUMOR OF OSCAR WILDE, Alvin Redman (ed.). More than 1,000 ripostes, paradoxes, wisecracks: Work is the curse of the drinking classes; I can resist everything except temptation; etc. 258pp. 5⅜ x 8½. 20602-5 Pa. $5.95

SHAKESPEARE LEXICON AND QUOTATION DICTIONARY, Alexander Schmidt. Full definitions, locations, shades of meaning in every word in plays and poems. More than 50,000 exact quotations. 1,485pp. 6½ x 9¼. 2-vol. set.
Vol. 1: 22726-X Pa. $16.95
Vol. 2: 22727-8 Pa. $16.95

SELECTED POEMS, Emily Dickinson. Over 100 best-known, best-loved poems by one of America's foremost poets, reprinted from authoritative early editions. No comparable edition at this price. Index of first lines. 64pp. 5$\frac{3}{16}$ x 8¼. 26466-1 Pa. $1.00

CELEBRATED CASES OF JUDGE DEE (DEE GOONG AN), translated by Robert van Gulik. Authentic 18th-century Chinese detective novel; Dee and associates solve three interlocked cases. Led to van Gulik's own stories with same characters. Extensive introduction. 9 illustrations. 237pp. 5⅜ x 8½. 23337-5 Pa. $6.95

THE MALLEUS MALEFICARUM OF KRAMER AND SPRENGER, translated by Montague Summers. Full text of most important witchhunter's "bible," used by both Catholics and Protestants. 278pp. 6⅝ x 10. 22802-9 Pa. $12.95

SPANISH STORIES/CUENTOS ESPAÑOLES: A Dual-Language Book, Angel Flores (ed.). Unique format offers 13 great stories in Spanish by Cervantes, Borges, others. Faithful English translations on facing pages. 352pp. 5⅜ x 8½. 25399-6 Pa. $8.95

THE CHICAGO WORLD'S FAIR OF 1893: A Photographic Record, Stanley Appelbaum (ed.). 128 rare photos show 200 buildings, Beaux-Arts architecture, Midway, original Ferris Wheel, Edison's kinetoscope, more. Architectural emphasis; full text. 116pp. 8¼ x 11. 23990-X Pa. $9.95

OLD QUEENS, N.Y., IN EARLY PHOTOGRAPHS, Vincent F. Seyfried and William Asadorian. Over 160 rare photographs of Maspeth, Jamaica, Jackson Heights, and other areas. Vintage views of DeWitt Clinton mansion, 1939 World's Fair and more. Captions. 192pp. 8⅞ x 11. 26358-4 Pa. $12.95

CAPTURED BY THE INDIANS: 15 Firsthand Accounts, 1750-1870, Frederick Drimmer. Astounding true historical accounts of grisly torture, bloody conflicts, relentless pursuits, miraculous escapes and more, by people who lived to tell the tale. 384pp. 5⅜ x 8½. 24901-8 Pa. $8.95

THE WORLD'S GREAT SPEECHES, Lewis Copeland and Lawrence W. Lamm (eds.). Vast collection of 278 speeches of Greeks to 1970. Powerful and effective models; unique look at history. 842pp. 5⅜ x 8½. 20468-5 Pa. $14.95

THE BOOK OF THE SWORD, Sir Richard F. Burton. Great Victorian scholar/adventurer's eloquent, erudite history of the "queen of weapons"–from prehistory to early Roman Empire. Evolution and development of early swords, variations (sabre, broadsword, cutlass, scimitar, etc.), much more. 336pp. 6⅛ x 9¼. 25434-8 Pa. $9.95

AUTOBIOGRAPHY: The Story of My Experiments with Truth, Mohandas K. Gandhi. Boyhood, legal studies, purification, the growth of the Satyagraha (nonviolent protest) movement. Critical, inspiring work of the man responsible for the freedom of India. 480pp. 5⅜ x 8½. (USO) 24593-4 Pa. $8.95

CELTIC MYTHS AND LEGENDS, T. W. Rolleston. Masterful retelling of Irish and Welsh stories and tales. Cuchulain, King Arthur, Deirdre, the Grail, many more. First paperback edition. 58 full-page illustrations. 512pp. 5⅜ x 8½. 26507-2 Pa. $9.95

THE PRINCIPLES OF PSYCHOLOGY, William James. Famous long course complete, unabridged. Stream of thought, time perception, memory, experimental methods; great work decades ahead of its time. 94 figures. 1,391pp. 5⅜ x 8½. 2-vol. set.
Vol. I: 20381-6 Pa. $12.95
Vol. II: 20382-4 Pa. $12.95

THE WORLD AS WILL AND REPRESENTATION, Arthur Schopenhauer. Definitive English translation of Schopenhauer's life work, correcting more than 1,000 errors, omissions in earlier translations. Translated by E. F. J. Payne. Total of 1,269pp. 5⅜ x 8½. 2-vol. set. Vol. 1: 21761-2 Pa. $11.95
Vol. 2: 21762-0 Pa. $12.95

MAGIC AND MYSTERY IN TIBET, Madame Alexandra David-Neel. Experiences among lamas, magicians, sages, sorcerers, Bonpa wizards. A true psychic discovery. 32 illustrations. 321pp. 5⅜ x 8½. (USO) 22682-4 Pa. $8.95

THE EGYPTIAN BOOK OF THE DEAD, E. A. Wallis Budge. Complete reproduction of Ani's papyrus, finest ever found. Full hieroglyphic text, interlinear transliteration, word-for-word translation, smooth translation. 533pp. 6½ x 9¼.
21866-X Pa. $10.95

MATHEMATICS FOR THE NONMATHEMATICIAN, Morris Kline. Detailed, college-level treatment of mathematics in cultural and historical context, with numerous exercises. Recommended Reading Lists. Tables. Numerous figures. 641pp. 5⅜ x 8½.
24823-2 Pa. $11.95

THEORY OF WING SECTIONS: Including a Summary of Airfoil Data, Ira H. Abbott and A. E. von Doenhoff. Concise compilation of subsonic aerodynamic characteristics of NACA wing sections, plus description of theory. 350pp. of tables. 693pp. 5⅜ x 8½. 60586-8 Pa. $14.95

THE RIME OF THE ANCIENT MARINER, Gustave Doré, S. T. Coleridge. Doré's finest work; 34 plates capture moods, subtleties of poem. Flawless full-size reproductions printed on facing pages with authoritative text of poem. "Beautiful. Simply beautiful."–*Publisher's Weekly*. 77pp. 9¼ x 12. 22305-1 Pa. $6.95

NORTH AMERICAN INDIAN DESIGNS FOR ARTISTS AND CRAFTSPEOPLE, Eva Wilson. Over 360 authentic copyright-free designs adapted from Navajo blankets, Hopi pottery, Sioux buffalo hides, more. Geometrics, symbolic figures, plant and animal motifs, etc. 128pp. 8⅜ x 11. (EUK) 25341-4 Pa. $8.95

SCULPTURE: Principles and Practice, Louis Slobodkin. Step-by-step approach to clay, plaster, metals, stone; classical and modern. 253 drawings, photos. 255pp. 8⅛ x 11.
22960-2 Pa. $11.95

THE INFLUENCE OF SEA POWER UPON HISTORY, 1660–1783, A. T. Mahan. Influential classic of naval history and tactics still used as text in war colleges. First paperback edition. 4 maps. 24 battle plans. 640pp. 5⅜ x 8½.   25509-3 Pa. $12.95

THE STORY OF THE TITANIC AS TOLD BY ITS SURVIVORS, Jack Winocour (ed.). What it was really like. Panic, despair, shocking inefficiency, and a little heroism. More thrilling than any fictional account. 26 illustrations. 320pp. 5⅜ x 8½.
20610-6 Pa. $8.95

FAIRY AND FOLK TALES OF THE IRISH PEASANTRY, William Butler Yeats (ed.). Treasury of 64 tales from the twilight world of Celtic myth and legend: "The Soul Cages," "The Kildare Pooka," "King O'Toole and his Goose," many more. Introduction and Notes by W. B. Yeats. 352pp. 5⅜ x 8½.   26941-8 Pa. $8.95

BUDDHIST MAHAYANA TEXTS, E. B. Cowell and Others (eds.). Superb, accurate translations of basic documents in Mahayana Buddhism, highly important in history of religions. The Buddha-karita of Asvaghosha, Larger Sukhavativyuha, more. 448pp. 5⅜ x 8½.   25552-2 Pa. $12.95

ONE TWO THREE . . . INFINITY: Facts and Speculations of Science, George Gamow. Great physicist's fascinating, readable overview of contemporary science: number theory, relativity, fourth dimension, entropy, genes, atomic structure, much more. 128 illustrations. Index. 352pp. 5⅜ x 8½.   25664-2 Pa. $8.95

ENGINEERING IN HISTORY, Richard Shelton Kirby, et al. Broad, nontechnical survey of history's major technological advances: birth of Greek science, industrial revolution, electricity and applied science, 20th-century automation, much more. 181 illustrations. ". . . excellent . . ."–*Isis.* Bibliography. vii + 530pp. 5⅜ x 8¼.
26412-2 Pa. $14.95

DALÍ ON MODERN ART: The Cuckolds of Antiquated Modern Art, Salvador Dalí. Influential painter skewers modern art and its practitioners. Outrageous evaluations of Picasso, Cézanne, Turner, more. 15 renderings of paintings discussed. 44 calligraphic decorations by Dalí. 96pp. 5⅜ x 8½. (USO)   29220-7 Pa. $4.95

ANTIQUE PLAYING CARDS: A Pictorial History, Henry René D'Allemagne. Over 900 elaborate, decorative images from rare playing cards (14th–20th centuries): Bacchus, death, dancing dogs, hunting scenes, royal coats of arms, players cheating, much more. 96pp. 9¼ x 12¼.   29265-7 Pa. $11.95

MAKING FURNITURE MASTERPIECES: 30 Projects with Measured Drawings, Franklin H. Gottshall. Step-by-step instructions, illustrations for constructing handsome, useful pieces, among them a Sheraton desk, Chippendale chair, Spanish desk, Queen Anne table and a William and Mary dressing mirror. 224pp. 8⅛ x 11¼.
29338-6 Pa. $13.95

THE FOSSIL BOOK: A Record of Prehistoric Life, Patricia V. Rich et al. Profusely illustrated definitive guide covers everything from single-celled organisms and dinosaurs to birds and mammals and the interplay between climate and man. Over 1,500 illustrations. 760pp. 7½ x 10⅛.   29371-8 Pa. $29.95

Prices subject to change without notice.

Available at your book dealer or write for free catalog to Dept. GI, Dover Publications, Inc., 31 East 2nd St., Mineola, N.Y. 11501. Dover publishes more than 500 books each year on science, elementary and advanced mathematics, biology, music, art, literary history, social sciences and other areas.